UNLIKELY WARRIORS

UNLIKELY WARRIORS

THE ARMY SECURITY AGENCY'S SECRET WAR IN VIETNAM 1961-1973

LONNIE M. LONG
GARY B. BLACKBURN

iUniverse, Inc.
Bloomington

Unlikely Warriors
The Army Security Agency's Secret War in Vietnam 1961-1973

iUniverse books may be ordered through booksellers or by contacting:

iUniverse
1663 Liberty Drive
Bloomington, IN 47403
www.iuniverse.com
1-800-Authors (1-800-288-4677)

Cover photo, "Mother Hen," by Bruce Boydstun, 144th Aviation Company (RR), ASA, Nha Trang
Cover created by Don Reber, 146th Aviation Company (RR), ASA, Saigon

ISBN: 978-1-4759-9057-7 (sc)
ISBN: 978-1-4759-9058-4 (hc)
ISBN: 978-1-4759-9059-1 (e)

Library of Congress Control Number: 2013908553

Printed in the United States of America.

iUniverse rev. date: 05/13/2013

"THEY SERVED IN SILENCE"
—National Cryptologic Memorial

CONTENTS

DEDICATION

This book is dedicated to
our buddy and hero
Johnny Link

Sgt. John Francis Link

Our story

On December 26, 1965, Gary Blackburn moved from Iowa to North Carolina and two friends rode with him, helping to drive and pay for gas. Both were active-duty U.S. Army soldiers: Reed Vass from Eldon was in an ordnance unit at Aberdeen Proving Ground, Maryland, and Johnny Link, a redheaded Irishman from Ottumwa, brash, charming and "full of himself," was headed for Special Forces training at Ft. Bragg.

The three young men drove straight through to Carolina; there were few interstates in those days, and they took turns driving. Sometime during the night, Gary was sleeping in the backseat and was awakened when the car stopped on the side of a deserted highway in rural Kentucky. He remembers flashing blue lights and the cold stillness. John had been driving and was digging for his wallet as he rolled down the window. There is no way of knowing how fast Johnny was going or what he said to the Kentucky state trooper, but as usual, he managed to charm his way out of a ticket and the three were soon back on the road. They arrived in Greensboro early the next morning, dropped Reed off at the Greyhound station, and then drove the 85 miles to Special Forces Headquarters at Ft. Bragg where John would undergo his training.

Lonnie Long and Gary had an apartment in Guilford College, near Greensboro. Gary had been out of the Air Force for a year, and Lonnie was just out of the Army, having finished an extended tour in Vietnam. John showed up at the door nearly every weekend; their place was his safe-haven. The small apartment had one bedroom with twin beds and a couch, and sometimes John would bring two or three buddies with him. His Green Beret training took almost a year, and on many a Sunday morning there were male bodies sprawled all over the place. John was all personality, and no one could resist the boyish grin that flashed across his freckled face. Besides, Lonnie and Gary had served their military time, and these young soldiers were all headed for Vietnam. At least one would not return alive, but he would return a hero.

John's Story

In 1979, Vietnam veteran and author Jim Morris published a book entitled *War Story*. Chapter 32 chronicles a 1968 mission during which Major Morris accompanied the elite Special Forces Detachment B-52. Morris, a former Green Beret working as an Army public information officer, told of encountering "a big redheaded trooper" in the middle of a firefight east of Hue. The following account draws from that chapter.

"He looked to be about twenty-three or twenty-four." Maj. Morris writes. "Following him was a slender clean cut looking kid with black hair."

The redhead said they needed help hauling some fifteen wounded men out of a bomb crater, so Morris followed the two young soldiers back through the trees. The redhead led the way, calling for others to help as they went, but the fighting had been heavy, and no one volunteered. Morris and the two soldiers came to an embankment that overlooked an expanse of flat land. From there he could see a large bomb crater filled with wounded Green Berets and Marine helicopter pilots. They were pinned down by enemy fire from three directions.

"There was scarcely a blade of grass between us and the crater," he recalls. The redhead scrambled down the five-foot bank and broke through the trees with the kid right behind him.

"The two young men started running toward the crater with rounds kicking up dirt at their heels," Morris says. "I didn't see them get hit, but if they weren't, it was a miracle." He knew they were not going to make it back alive unless they had covering fire; there was an NVA machine gun firing at them from the tree line across the field.

Morris and another soldier opened fire on the machine gun as the redhead and his buddy began to move the "herd of camouflaged troopers" across the open field. The first group of men made it across, up the bank and into the cover of the trees, quickly followed by the rest. Finally, there were only two left, and both were wounded.

"Let's go!" Morris yelled.

"Sir, I'm too weak to make it. You've got to pull me up." It was the dark-haired kid and behind him was the redhead. They were struggling to climb up the bank. Morris knew that if he quit firing the machine gun would open up again, but he had to help.

"I'll try and push him," the redhead said. Morris put down his weapon and reached down to grab the youngster's outstretched arm. As the two labored to lift the kid up the steep incline, machine gun rounds began to hit all around them. The redhead leaned in to shield the younger man with his body and Morris was hit in the arm. Bleeding profusely, he could no longer assist the two young soldiers.

"I couldn't have helped them if I'd stayed," he says, "and I'd have died. But I still felt rotten...Beret or no beret, we were just guys. There are no supermen and damned few heroes; almost no live ones."

Later that night, as the team medic struggled to save Morris' arm in a field hospital, he told the major the redhead was named John Link. The "kid" they were trying to save was named Merriman.

"Did you get them up?" Morris asked anxiously.

The medic nodded. "Yeah, Link's got three slugs in the back. He's unconscious. Merriman's got three in the legs."

Morris asked if they would make it.

"Merriman will," the medic said. "We're not so sure about Link."

The next morning, the unit withdrew, carrying their wounded and dead in ponchos slung from bamboo poles. Morris asked the medic how Link and Merriman were.

He replied, "John Link died this morning, just as we left out. Merriman's going to make it okay."

"I felt depressed," Morris says, "not guilty, just bad. No, that's bullshit. I felt guilty."

When they reached the landing zone, Morris recalls the two troopers carrying John Link's body reverently lowering it to the ground about eight feet from him.

A grim-faced Green Beret knelt beside Link's body and patted the pole it was slung from. "Well, John, old buddy," he said, "Goddamn!" He got up and walked off, head bowed.

Merriman was lying on the ground smoking a cigarette a few feet from Link.

Morris got to his feet and walked over. "Hey listen. I feel rotten about leaving you guys like that."

Merriman shook his head and responded, "Forget it, sir. You had to. I saw what happened."

"That made me feel a little better," Morris said, "but not much."

"How long before you got out?" he asked the kid.

With a slight frown, Merriman told him, "Fifteen minutes."

"My God, that long?"

Merriman nodded. "Yes sir, but we had already taken the rounds while you were there. We just lay quiet and he didn't fire anymore."

"The President of the United States takes pride in presenting the Distinguished Service Cross [second only to the Medal of Honor] to John Francis Link, Sergeant, U.S. Army, for extraordinary heroism in connection with military operations involving conflict with an armed hostile force in the Republic of Vietnam, while serving with Detachment B-52, 5th Special Forces Group (Airborne), 1st Special Forces.

Specialist Four Link distinguished himself by exceptionally valorous actions on 29 March 1968 as Special Forces advisor to a Vietnamese platoon conducting a combat operation in enemy territory. The unit had just completed a helicopter assault into an exposed landing zone when it was subjected to automatic weapons, rocket, grenade, and mortar fire from an enemy force occupying positions on three sides of the landing zone.

Braving a withering hail of hostile fire, Specialist Link raced across the open clearing and removed equipment from two helicopters which had been shot down by the savage fusillade. He placed fierce fire on the enemy and assisted three wounded comrades to the relative safety of a rise of ground at the edge of the landing zone. Continuing to expose himself to the barrage, Specialist Link fearlessly left his unit's hasty defensive perimeter numerous times throughout the raging battle to treat casualties and pull them to cover. He was thrown to the ground and wounded by rocket and mortar fire, but got up and courageously resumed his lifesaving efforts. While shielding the body of a fallen soldier from the ravaging enemy fire, Specialist Link was mortally wounded.

Specialist Four Link's extraordinary heroism and devotion to duty, at the cost of his life, were in keeping with the highest traditions of the military service and reflect great credit upon himself, his unit, and the United States Army."

Headquarters, U.S. Army, Vietnam, General Orders No. 1840 (20 April 1968)

By 1968, Gary was working for Eastern Air Lines and still living in Guilford College; Lonnie was married, working for National Airlines, and living in Miami, Florida. They both flew to Iowa for John's Funeral Mass at St. Patrick's Catholic Church in Ottumwa on Wednesday, April 17, 1968.

AN INTRODUCTION

The young soldier walked out of the back gate of Davis Station. The gate was located near the end of the runway, and led to the flight line by the Huey pad at Tan Son Nhut airbase near Saigon. It was 5:15 a.m., early in 1965. The soldier was one of less than a thousand members of a shadowy group recruited and trained by the Army Security Agency, the National Security Agency's ground force in Vietnam. He carried the military occupational specialty (M.O.S.) of 058, manual-Morse intercept operator. Until 1965, even an ASA soldier's M.O.S. was classified, and he was listed under a fictional M.O.S. of General Duties. The ASA units carried the camouflaged and euphemistic title "radio research units," and their mission was so highly classified that only the top-most echelons of the U.S. command in Vietnam had any inkling of what their mission was, assuming they had the need to know.

Back gate of Davis Station–1965 (Photo: © L. Long)

As the young man walked, he was more focused than usual at that early hour. During the previous day's flight, a small caliber round had come through the bottom of the De Havilland Beaver as he and the Major piloting the plane were flying a mission near the Cambodian border. They had flown over the same area near a U.S. Special Forces outpost for three consecutive days, and each day, using their specially-equipped aircraft for locating low-level transmitters, they had plotted a Viet Cong unit moving ever closer to the camp. Taking ground fire was not unusual, especially when flying low over the same area for several consecutive days. The VC round had penetrated the belly of the plane and exploded a cushion lying on the floor of the plane near the Thompson sub-machine gun, but what made this occurrence different was the fact that the round had exited the plane just above the soldier's head. Had he not been leaning forward while working the target signal, the round could have taken off the back of his flight helmet, or worse, and if that were not enough, something very unusual had taken place upon his return.

Spc.4 Ken Kennedy and RU-6 Beaver (Photo: © L. Long)

After plotting the latest triangulation of the enemy unit transmitter, a Sergeant had escorted the Spc.4 to a nearby building. The Major he had flown with was waiting there, along with several civilians and an Air Force officer, and laid out on a table was a map of the area near the Parrot's Beak and the Special Forces camp. Their questions were straight-forward: How sure was he of the call signs he had copied? Did the transmissions sound the same, and could he identify the "fist" (the unique characteristics of the operator sending the message) of the VC sender? How confident were he and the Major of the locations they had marked on the map in order to get their triangulation of the signal? He had been dismissed after his debriefing.

Unable to discuss the unusual meeting with anyone, the young man had gone back to his bunk, changed clothes, hopped in the "dong" wagon for a ride to the main gate, and caught a yellow and blue Renault cab to downtown Saigon. The concerns of the day began to fade after several "Ba-mui-ba" beers (rumored to have a formaldehyde base).

Today looked to be a better day. He had always liked morning flights. The plane had not been sitting in the sun all day; the morning temperature was actually cool for Vietnam, around 80 degrees, and the flights were usually smoother before the afternoon build-up of storms. His thoughts turned to home and the circumstances that had brought him to this point.

After graduating from a small high school in North Carolina, the young man had gone on to Wake Forest. College, however, was a different world and required a commitment that he was not ready to make. After a year of less than stellar academic performance, he had decided to enlist in the Army. His father had fought at the Battle of the Bulge, earning a Bronze Star and a Purple Heart, and like most young men his age, he had grown up watching World War II movies. The Army looked more exciting than the alternatives he now faced.

When he walked into the recruiting office, he had told the recruiter he was ready to enlist and wanted to go overseas. The recruiter indicated that he could guarantee an overseas assignment, but that would mean he could not guarantee his career field. He could be assigned to any job: infantry, truck driver or, God forbid, cook.

Upon learning that the young man had a year of college, the recruiter immediately started talking about the Army Security Agency. He could not reveal anything about the "secret mission" of the organization, but indicated that the vast majority of young men selected for it were sent overseas. If the recruit could qualify on a battery of tests, he would become part of an elite unit. He signed the forms and boarded a bus that night for Ft. Jackson, South Carolina.

Basic Training had been a real eye-opener. It quickly dawned on each new recruit that the Army now owned him for the next three years, but after the traditional G.I. haircut and the issue of ill-fitting uniforms, he had settled into his new Army life. His barracks was located on "tank hill" across from the beer hall and every night, a new hit-record, "Sherry" by Frankie Valli and the Four Seasons, had been played on the jukebox a minimum of fifty times. He still smelled beer when he heard that song.

He did have one fond memory of his time at Ft. Jackson. He had obtained a weekend pass and boarded a Trailways bus to Newberry, South Carolina. His grandmother had driven down from High Point (North Carolina) to meet him, and they had spent the weekend with his great-grandmother who was then in her late eighties. That was the last time he saw his great-grandmother.

Soon after, reality set in. During his semi-final week of basic, while on bivouac, the Cuban Missile Crisis shook the country and reminded the young soldier that he was in the Army and was being prepared for war. Troops with tanks and artillery were moving through Ft. Jackson on their way to Miami. Two nights later (one week short of graduation), the young recruit and thirteen others were awakened in the middle of the night and told to pack their duffle bags.

They were the chosen few who had qualified for the Army Security Agency. It was interesting because, with few exceptions, they were the same group that had been called out, shown a movie, and asked to consider extending their time in the Army so they could attend Officer Candidate School. They had all declined. Now the men were given their personnel files and new orders, and they were trucked to the train station in Columbia to board a train bound for Boston. Their next duty assignment would be the ASA School at Ft. Devens, Massachusetts. They would never graduate from basic training. Their time in the regular Army was over before it had really begun.

The trip to New England had been memorable. The men arrived in Washington, D.C., in the early morning hours and had made friends with the conductor on the train. As attractive young ladies began to board, most of whom were on their way to the Saturday Ivy League football games, he directed them to the car with the young soldiers. One of the guys actually had a guitar and the new-found friends sang songs and talked all the way up the East Coast.

At Tan Son Nhut, the soldier was jolted back to reality. He had arrived at a converted hangar, and the MPs inside the door asked him to show his security badge. He walked a short way down the hall and entered the third room on the right. There were large maps of all the target areas the airborne radio-direction-finders (ARDF) were working. They were mounted on plywood and covered in plastic to allow the operators to plot their fixes with a grease pencil. After receiving a short briefing, he picked up his weapon and flight helmet and headed out the door and around the corner to the flight line. A few minutes later the Major arrived for the preflight check. He always liked to fly with the Major, who was also the commanding officer of the small but growing aviation section of the 3rd Radio Research Unit.

Maj. Stanley Frick (Photo: © L. Long)

It was rumored the Major had started his military career as a forward artillery observer during the Korean War. It was said his claim to fame was that while serving at the front lines, he had observed a group which included both Chinese and Russian general staff. He had called in artillery, and with the first round eliminated some very high-ranking enemy officers.

The intercept operator climbed into the back of the plane directly behind the pilot, and adjusted the straps on his parachute, which also served as his back seat-cushion. After completing the preflight, the Major climbed into the cockpit and yelled "clear" to no one in particular. The radial engine began to sputter, then came roaring to life. As they started to taxi, the sun was beginning to rise over the South China Sea, and the sky to the east was turning a beautiful pink, highlighting the building clouds. The soldier's thoughts once again turned to how he had arrived at this point in time, in the middle of what was fast becoming a major war. His unit had already lost three soldiers. One had died in combat, and two others had been blown up by a guerilla bomb planted under the bleachers at a unit softball game.

The training at Ft. Devens had lasted for six months, which meant surviving a brutally cold Massachusetts winter. There was also some culture shock for a Southern boy. He remembered his first briefing where it was explained that a milk shake was called a " frap" and that Coke was called a "pop." The ASA School was a complex of beautiful, multi-storied brick buildings that looked like a university. The barracks, however, were a collection of World War II-era two-story wooden structures that, it was rumored, had been condemned. The barracks were heated by coal-fired furnaces, and when they failed, which was frequently, the water-filled "butt cans" on the columns inside the barracks would freeze solid.

He had been told during basic that he had missed being assigned to the Defense Language Institute in Monterey, California by one point, and therefore would be going to Manual Morse Intercept School. He would become what the guys at ASA called a "ditty bopper." The first day of classes, everyone had been seated at a long table and given a headset. When the class began, they listened to a tape-recording and heard: "dit dah, Alpha; dit dah, Alpha."

The Army Security Agency School at Ft. Devens (Photo: © L. Long)

Although slow at first, the young man began to get a feel for the new task at hand, and eventually, he was given a special green badge that read: "AOG." That meant "Ahead of the Game" and provided him with additional time off for working out at the gym or getting a haircut. As the classes progressed, the soldiers had been introduced to special manual Morse codes such as "QRU IMI K." When sent in code, it means "do you have anything (traffic) for me?" The men also learned to copy what they heard on old, specially-equipped typewriters. The typewriters had sprockets that held accordioned six-ply paper with carbon paper between each sheet. He had to beat the hell out of the keys to print all six sheets.

During his stay at Ft. Devens, the young trainee had called his father to say "hello" to the family. His dad was a plant engineer who had attended North Carolina State on the G.I. Bill after the war. He had moved the family back to North Carolina from a small town in N.E. Georgia after receiving a promotion a few years before. His father told him that he had received several phone calls over the past few days from prominent businessmen in the small Georgia town. There had been two FBI agents asking questions about his son, and the men wanted to know if the boy was in trouble or if there was a problem. He and his dad had a good laugh. It was all part of the background investigation that would provide the soldier with the top-secret-cryptographic security clearance required to work for the ASA.

Winter–1963 (Photo: © L. Long)

A week before graduation that April, each trainee had been asked to fill out a "dream sheet" listing his first three choices of where he would like to serve overseas. A few days later the assignments were posted, and no one got his first or even his third choice. The top half of the class was going to Korea, the lower half to Taiwan.

The soldier smiled at the memory, and then was startled by a loud roar of engines. His aircraft had taxied to third in line for takeoff just as two F-100 Super Saber jet fighters roared down the runway and into the air. The Huns climbed quickly and were gone. A few minutes later the U-6A taxied into position for takeoff. The small plane began to move forward; the Major added power; the 450hp radial engine roared, and slowly the tail came off the ground. When the plane was clear of the airport traffic, the Major and operator went through a brief communications check; then the young man relaxed and returned to his thoughts. It would take fifteen-to-twenty minutes for them to arrive over the target area.

Taiwan! His 15-month tour there had been a dream. He had been assigned to the ASA 76th Special Operations Unit located on a joint service base, Shu Lin Kou Air Station. Lin-Kou was a very small U.S. Air Force outpost at the end of a steep and winding mountain road twenty kilometers north of Taipei, the capital of Nationalist China. It was manned by U.S. Air Force Security Service (USAFSS), Naval Security Group (NSG), and ASA personnel. Since the mess hall was an Air Force facility, it served incredible meals that included steak, pizza, and even ice cream. Each barracks had a houseboy that not only polished each soldier's boots and brass, but also cleaned his rifle for inspection. The small base even had a pool, an enlisted men's club, a library, and a theater. Boy, if those dog-face sergeants in basic could see him now.

Lonnie at Shu Lin Kou–1963 (Photo: © L. Long)

All the intercept operators at Lin-Kou were assigned shift (aka trick) work, and other than showing up for duty, the men were free to come and go as they pleased. At the time of his arrival, the Air Force was understaffed, so the new

9

op was assigned to work a position on a Security Service "flight." The work was interesting, especially when approximately once a month the Nationalist Air Force flew fighters off both ends of the island into the Taiwan Straits in order to bring up the CHICOM air defense networks. The amount of intelligence the operators were able to gather in a couple of hours was amazing.

It was during his Air Force assignment that the young soldier met Gary. They shared an interest in photography and other areas and had become buddies. Gary had grown up on a farm in southern Iowa and graduated from high school in a tiny town with seven other members in his senior class. After enlisting in the Air Force, he had been selected to undergo the Security Service battery of tests and had ended up at the Institute of Far Eastern Languages at Yale University, studying Mandarin Chinese. After Yale, there had been a six-month intensive course in technical Chinese at Goodfellow A.F.B. in Texas, a six-month stint with NSA at Torii Station in Okinawa, and then on to Taiwan. The two young men would become life-long friends.

Gary goes home—December 1963 (Photo: © G. Blackburn)

When the soldier first arrived in Taiwan, one of the more experienced guys had been kind enough to take him downtown. They had a few drinks at the Army's "63 Club," and then he had been introduced to the local G.I. bar scene in Taipei. There, he had met a beautiful "Suzy Wong" bar girl who, upon learning he was a new Army arrival, proceeded to tell him how many stripes he had (he was wearing civilian clothing), what his monthly salary was to the penny (not much), and after some time was willing to share a secret with him. She knew exactly what he did at Lin-Kou. She said, "You listen mainland!" —So much for being part of a top-secret organization.

He truly enjoyed his time in Taiwan. He and Gary had traveled the island; he had learned a little Chinese, and expanded his knowledge through those he met along the way. There was Father Dalheimer, an American Jesuit priest serving a small congregation in central Taiwan; and Jack, an American who worked for the U.S. Aide to Industrial Development, along with Jack's Chinese wife and their beautiful little daughter. He had spent time with them and attended parties at their home. He had also become close friends with Alice, a waitress at the enlisted men's club on base. She had helped him with his Chinese and included him in dinners with her sister and their extended family.

He had been honored to serve with the other ASA ops on "trick 3" and had made many friends among the airmen, but the time had approached for him to make a decision. Gary had rotated back to the States at the end of 1963 and was stationed in Texas at the only Security Service base in the U.S. The young soldier had a year left on his enlistment and now faced returning to the States himself. ASA had very few active duty stations within the U.S., so it was likely that he would be assigned to some chicken-shit outfit and end up playing "regular Army" for the next year. He was not thrilled with the thought.

He was somewhat aware of what was going on in Vietnam. He had grown up watching news reels and had studied about the French-Indochina War in the 1950s, but knew little about the modern country. There was a rumor that anyone serving there would be eligible for the new G.I. Bill, so he made the decision to volunteer for Vietnam. He should have had some doubts about the wisdom of his decision when his paperwork was immediately approved. Up to that point, the Army had never approved anything for which he had applied. Later, in order to qualify for the aviation section, he had applied to extend his time in Vietnam, and that had been approved the same day it was submitted.

As if intended to shake him from his dreams of Taiwan, two Vietnamese Air Force A1-E Skyraiders flew up beside their plane. The prop-driven attack aircraft were fully loaded with armament. They dipped their wings in recognition, but as the planes with the V.N.A.F. markings flew by, the soldier realized that both pilots were obviously Americans. What a war!

During his first week in Vietnam, he had been given a tour of Whitebirch, the main operations/intercept center near Tan Son Nhut Air Base, but had been told to stand by for further orders. In a few days, he was assigned to the 3rd Radio Research Company, Det. J, in Phu Bai, thirteen kilometers south of the old imperial city of Hue. Highway 1 north of Hue was the "street" described in Bernard Fall's book: "Street Without Joy, The French Debacle in Indochina." Hue was the cultural and educational center of the country, and the Imperial Palace was a sight to behold.

Base Theater—Phu Bai (Photo: © L. Long)

Det. J was a fast-growing intercept facility located across from the airport at Phu Bai. It sat amid sand dunes just off Highway 1. There was a large permanent structure surrounded by a fence with barbed wire on top. There was a mess hall, a small enlisted men's club with a sign that said you "Must be 21 to drink" (which no one paid any attention to), and a base theater consisting of wooden benches and a large piece of plywood painted white for the screen. Each week there would be 16 mm movies of TV shows sent by some genius "REM-F" (Don't ask if you don't know.) in Japan or somewhere. Occasionally, there was a real treat when they were shown "The Ed Sullivan Show." It might be one or two years old, but it was a connection to the world. Most of the time, however, their entertainment consisted of the TV series "Combat" starring Rick Jansen as Lt. Gil Hanley and Vic Morrow as Sgt. Chip Saunders. It was a wonderful diversion, especially on the nights when it was accompanied by sound effects from the South Vietnamese artillery base just down the road with their 105 mm and 155 mm howitzers. If they fired over the compound unexpectedly, several of the men would hit the floor. It was great entertainment for lonely G.I.s in the bowels of Vietnam.

Originally designated as a mobile unit, the troops of Det. J had developed their own unofficial crest, what was called a beer-can pin. Shaped as a shield, the background was blue and red with "3rd RRU Det. J" across the top. At the bottom was a wheel with broken spokes to indicate how mobile they were, and in the middle was an outline of a French toilet with lightning shooting out of the crapper for the intelligence they gathered. Above that were the Vietnamese words "Khong Biet" or "We Don't Understand."

3rd RRU "Crapper" Crest (Photo: © L. Long)

Duty at Phu Bai was not bad, but it was the same old trick work, and much of the time travel to Hue was restricted due to VC activity in the area. He had been able to avoid most of the work parties, better known as "sand bag details," by becoming the .50 cal. machine gunner on one of the three armored personnel carriers. Occasionally, the APC crews could escape the base and run the vehicles over the sand dunes outside the camp perimeter. There really was not much to do off-duty but drink, and that got old fast.

Enlisted Men's Club–Phu Bai (Photo: © L. Long)

But, the soldier had planned a real escape. Just after arriving, he had put in his paper work to fly with the aviation section. A few months later, he had flown to Saigon for his flight physical, and just as New Year 1965 arrived, so did his orders to Saigon.

Suddenly his intercom crackled to life, and the Major told him to climb into the right seat immediately. As he maneuvered by the radios and squeezed between the seats, he understood why. They had arrived over their target area, and in the distance he could see two fast-movers (F-100s) rolling in for a bombing run. Black smoke billowed from the U.S. Special Forces camp below, and it was obvious that they had been hit hard during the night. Tactical aircraft were making bombing and strafing runs along the jungle lines surrounding the camp. He knew his previous day's target would not be up and sending. There was nothing the ASA team could do but move off to the side and watch the show.

As he and the Major watched, the young soldier could feel the war expanding. Pleiku had been hit hard, and U.S. bases were being attacked weekly. The Marines had landed at Da Nang, and there was a strong rumor the 1st Infantry Division, the Big Red One, was coming to Vietnam. He knew that tomorrow he and the major, or another crew would fly out to work the area, but it would be quiet for a while. The next contact with this V.C. target would probably have them holed up across the Cambodian border as they regrouped, repaired, and resupplied to come back. He prayed that the intelligence he and the Major had intercepted over the past few days had given the Green Berets enough advance warning to prepare for the attack that had hit them last night. Maybe he had helped save the lives of some of those men.

He had always been a student of history; was this conflict going to turn into another French-Indochina War? Was that where this was heading? How many Americans and Vietnamese would die in this struggle; how had they reached this point?

He made a decision that one day he would try to put all this into some kind of order. He wanted to try and make some sense of the death and destruction he saw below him and the impending war that he feared would not only destroy Vietnam but also tear apart his own country as well.

PROLOGUE: SETTING THE STAGE

Vietnam — It is a word, a name, a place, a symbol for many things, depending on who is saying it, and who is hearing it. For most Americans who lived through the 60s and 70s, the name brings back a flood of memories of a tumultuous period in U.S. history. For those who opposed the war, led mainly by college students, anti-establishment hippies, and the "new left," it was an exciting period that sprang from the civil rights movement, fueled by the media and increasing public support. For those who were actually fighting the war, it was a period of great sacrifice and heroism, combined with frustration, ever-increasing disillusionment and ultimately, for many, a feeling of betrayal. However, the forces that would shape the futures of many of those young warriors and civilians in what become known as the Vietnam War had been put in place not just years before, but centuries.

Most Americans had never heard of Vietnam before the late 50s or early 60s, but Vietnam has a long and proud history that goes back several thousand years. According to Vietnamese legend, the original kingdom of Viet Nam was founded around 3000 B.C. and extended from southern China to the northern boundaries of Indonesia. That dynasty, according to tradition, survived almost three millennia before being conquered by China's Han Dynasty in 111 B.C.

Freedom was finally realized in 939 A.D. when General Ngo Quyen drove out the Chinese and established the first of the "Great Dynasties." The nation was able to remain independent for most of the next thousand years, but a "tradition of resistance" had been forever instilled within the Vietnamese and would be used effectively by the communists in the 20th century.

By the 17th century, Vietnam had been bifurcated. The northern half was called Tonkin by Europeans, and the southern half was called Cochin China. They were ruled by two separate Vietnamese royal houses: the Trinhs and the Nguyens. The later Nguyen emperors saw westerners as a threat and brutally suppressed Catholicism. There were frequent uprisings against the regime, and the French used those events as an excuse to invade Vietnam. Under orders of Napoleon III, French gunships attacked the port of Da Nang in 1858, causing significant damage, and over the next twelve years, French troops expanded their control over all six provinces in the Mekong Delta forming a French colony. A few years later, French troops landed in northern Vietnam, and France assumed control over all of Vietnam after the Sino-French war ended in 1885. French Indochina was formed in October 1887 and would eventually include all of Vietnam, Cambodia, and Laos. Vietnamese resistance movements broke out in occupied areas, but they enjoyed few successes over the next twenty years. The rebel leaders eventually came to the realization that they could not defeat the French military without modernization.

During the 1920s and 30s, desperation became a factor, and more radical movements were introduced among the various rebel groups within Vietnam. The most radical of those movements were not indigenous, but originated outside the country. The Vietnamese Nationalist Party was founded in 1927, modeled after the Kuomintang in China. The group launched an armed mutiny in Tonkin in 1930, but its top leadership was captured and executed by guillotine. Three different communist parties emerged as Marxism was introduced into the region. These later merged into the Indochinese Communist Party. The group enjoyed popular support, but was nearly wiped out by the French with the execution of two of its top leaders. Then, in 1940, the Japanese invaded Indochina.

Ho Chi Minh

In 1941, a Marxist revolutionary who had lived in France since 1911 and helped found the French Communist Party (in 1924), arrived in northern Vietnam. He had coordinated the unification of the Vietnamese communist parties in 1930 and later helped to build communist movements throughout Southeast Asia. His name was Nguyen Ai Quoc, but he was now known as Ho Chi Minh, and he was there to form the Viet Minh Front. It was billed as an umbrella group to bring together all of the various organizations fighting for Vietnamese independence, but it was dominated by the Communist Party. The Viet Minh had a small armed force, and much of their early support is said to have come from the U.S. Office of Strategic Services. The O.S.S. was the forerunner of the C.I.A., and the Viet Minh assisted them by collecting intelligence on the Japanese occupying force. In return, the O.S.S. helped to arm, train, and supply the organization. Other non-communist Vietnamese groups also joined the Viet Minh with backing from the Kuomintang, the non-communist government of China.

By early 1945, with Allied Forces in firm control of the war in both Europe and Asia, the French government began taking measures that would insure resumption of their rule in Vietnam. But, much to their chagrin, the Japanese gave power to a puppet emperor, Bao Dai, who was heir to the Nguyen Dynasty, and declared Vietnam independent. Ho Chi Minh, who already had his Vietnamese independence movement in place, seized Hanoi, deposed Bao Dai, and declared the Democratic Republic of Vietnam on September 2, 1945, the day the Japanese surrendered in Tokyo.

New "modern" agencies-ASA and NSA

Before President Harry S. Truman had officially declared an end to the hostilities, the U.S. Army had made the decision to create a new agency. They were going to concentrate the entire spectrum of electronic communications exploitation under the auspices of a single entity. On September 15, 1945, the Signal Security Agency was split away from the Army Signal Corps and renamed the Army Security Agency (ASA). It would assume immediate responsibility for "all signals intelligence and security establishments, units, and personnel" of the Army. ASA inherited the mission, functions and assets of the S.S.A. and added communications intelligence (COMINT) and communications security (COMSEC) resources within its purview.

The new agency was almost completely self-sufficient within the

Army organization. ASA had its own operational mission, administered its own personnel system, ran its own schools, handled its own supplies, and conducted its own research and development. The drawdown after the end of the war affected ASA just as it did all of the military forces, and it required some realignment, but the agency's cryptologic activities continued to be indispensable to national security.

ASA's prime field assets were seven large stations left over from WWII: Asmara, Ethiopia; Clark Field, Philippines; Fairbanks, Alaska; Helemano, Hawaii; Herzo Base, Germany; Two Rock Ranch, California; and Vint Hill Farms, Virginia. It exercised command and control of its overseas operations through regional headquarters in Europe and the Pacific, and overall direction of its cryptologic and analysis effort was centralized at its headquarters, Arlington Hall Station, Virginia.

The U.S. Navy and U.S. Air Force also had their own communications intelligence and security branches: the Naval Security Group (NSG) and U.S. Air Force Security Service (USAFSS). On May 20, 1949, the Department of Defense established the Armed Forces Security Agency (AFSA) under command of the Joint Chiefs of Staff. Its sole function was to direct the communications and electronic intelligence activities of the U.S. military intelligence agencies; unfortunately, it had little power or effective coordination capabilities.

In December 1951, Walter Bedell Smith, the Director of the CIA, sent a memo to James D. Lay, Executive Secretary of the National Security Council, observing that AFSA had been ineffective and recommending a survey of COMINT activities. The proposal was approved, and the survey was completed by June 1952. Survey results indicated the need for a greater degree of direction and coordination at the national level, and a letter of authorization was written by President Truman in June 1952, creating the National Security Agency (NSA). The agency was formally established through a revision of the NSC Intelligence Directive 9 in October 1952, and officially came into existence on November 4, 1952.

The letter President Truman signed authorizing creation of the agency remained classified for more than a generation, and there was no mention of NSA in any government documents or manuals until 1957.

Major Dewey

Deliberately borrowing from the Declaration of Independence of the United States of America, Ho Chi Minh had proclaimed on September 2, 1945: "We hold the truth that all men are created equal, that they are endowed by their Creator with certain unalienable rights, among them life, liberty and the pursuit of happiness."

Some three weeks later, the first American serviceman would die in Vietnam. Major A. Peter Dewey was head of an O.S.S. team that was sent to Saigon to repatriate and evacuate American P.O.W.s who were being held there by the Japanese. He was killed by Annamese (Viet Minh) dissidents while driving in a jeep on his way from the Saigon airport to O.S.S. headquarters on the edge of Saigon. It was later reported that Maj. Dewey and his passenger had been mistaken for Frenchmen.

The French-Indochina War

The ink was barely dry on Ho's declaration when the victorious Allies turned control of Vietnam back over to the British and Chinese, and in 1946, the British, with no apparent consideration for the hopes and desires of the Vietnamese people, ceded the south back over to the French. The Viet Minh retained control only in areas of the north. Forced to negotiate with the hated French, Ho Chi Minh reached an agreement that would recognize his independent Vietnam as part of the French Union, but would allow the French to keep 25,000 troops in northern Vietnam until 1951. Neither side was happy with the agreement, but Ho accepted the terms. The French reneged, and attacked the northern port of Haiphong with a heavy naval bombardment that resulted in thousands of Vietnamese civilian casualties. The Viet Minh evacuated the city, but Vietnamese General Vo Nguyen Giap soon returned with a 30,000-man force to attack the French. The French-Indochina War had begun.

The war lasted for nine bloody years with the French using conventional warfare against General Giap's guerrilla fighters and tactics. There were numerous offensives and counter-offensives resulting in great loss of life on both sides of the conflict. The Soviet Union supplied the Vietnamese with weapons for years, but after Mao Tse Tung and his communist forces took control of mainland China in 1949, Ho Chi Minh received significantly more support from the Chinese. That support included heavy weapons, ammunition and supplies, plus a safe haven for training and treating Viet Minh wounded.

The gathering of communications intelligence in Southeast Asia began literally at the end of World War II. The first recorded intercept of a Viet Minh transmission occurred just three weeks after the Japanese signed the surrender documents aboard the *U.S.S. Missouri*, September 23, 1945. That was the day that the undeclared portion of the First Indochina war began. Fighting erupted between Viet Minh troops and 1,400 French colonial soldiers who had just been released from Japanese internment camps by the British. The recently named U.S. Army Security Agency (ASA) headquarters at Arlington Hall, Virginia, intercepted a message transmitted to Moscow from the old French colonial radio station in Hanoi. The message, sent in English and without encryption, was from Ho Chi Minh to Joseph Stalin. It announced the formation of the Provisional Government of the Viet Nam Republic, and asked for assistance for flood victims in Tonkin, the northernmost region of Vietnam.

Earlier that month, per orders from Ho, General Giap had created the Viet Minh's first cryptographic section. Using a single copy of French Captain Roger Baudoin's *Elements Cryptographic,* a small team began to teach themselves basic codes and to experiment with various cryptographic techniques. The French had always been careful not to train any Vietnamese in cryptography, even though they had used it for many years in Indochina. By early 1946, the Viet Minh had established a small network of radio stations which were transmitting with a minimum of communications security. That provided Hanoi communication with its military units through a network of outlying stations in the three regions of Vietnam. In 1946, the ASA began monitoring Viet Minh communications from an intercept site located at Las Pinas on the south side of Manila Bay in the Philippines.

The French were listening too, and by 1946, when the war became official, they had a fully-functioning radio-intercept and direction-finding operation in place in Saigon. Their operators had already identified many of the Viet Minh networks and were performing traffic analysis. They were also monitoring the communication of other countries throughout Southeast Asia, being limited only by a shortage of linguists.

As the Indochina War progressed, the Viet Minh relied more and more on conventional communications: radio, telephone and telegraph. The French were able to read and analyze most of the radio communications, providing themselves with all kinds of useful information, but placing too much reliance on that one intelligence source could also create major difficulties. If the Viet Minh changed their communication codes, or successfully observed radio silence for an extended period of time, the French were left totally in the dark until the new code was broken or regular communications were restored. The French suffered some major battle losses in the early 50s due to their somewhat myopic (or cyclopic) approach to intelligence gathering.

Radio direction finding (RDF or DF) was an area in which the French truly excelled. They initially used fixed base RDF with permanent bases in Hanoi and Saigon, and targeted communications from China, Burma, and the Viet Minh. They were able to easily and efficiently follow large movements of Viet Minh troops by tracking their radio communications. They also used mobile RDF units to assist in triangulation, which made their tracking even more accurate.

In 1948, the decision was made to outfit a French Air Force plane with RDF equipment, thus originating the first airborne radio direction finding (ARDF) effort in Vietnam. There was no Viet Minh air force, so the French were free to fly wherever they chose, so long as they stayed out of range of ground fire. The results were extraordinary and ARDF became a useful tool to track the movement of large Viet Minh forces.

One of the major reasons for French overconfidence heading into the Battle of Dien Bien Phu in early 1954 was their firm belief that they would know everything they needed to know about the opposing forces. French cryptologists had broken both the operational and logistical Viet Minh encryption codes, and the French Generals felt extremely confident in their abilities to be one or two steps ahead of General Giap and his ragtag forces. Of course, it did not turn out the way they had planned.

A humiliating end: Dien Bien Phu

French signal intelligence operatives had been increasingly successful during the war with their communications intercept effort and were proud of their abilities to analyze Viet Minh communications. They had repeatedly assured their military commanders that there was little chance of them being surprised by a strong enemy force, but early in 1954, they overestimated their intelligence gathering capabilities, and totally underestimated their opponent in almost every area. As a result, the French commanders allowed their forces to be trapped in a truly indefensible position, so remote that it could be neither relieved nor effectively resupplied during the course of a two-month siege.

By the time the battle began on March 13th, the French with 13,000 troops were surrounded by five Viet Minh divisions totaling some 70,000 men. In addition, General Giap's forces controlled all of the high ground, and instead of a massive frontal assault, he ordered his men to dig a trench completely surrounding the French fortifications. They then dug trenches and tunnels from the main trench in toward the center, bringing his troops ever nearer to their ultimate victory.

Using massive hand labor, his forces had brought in significant artillery, including twenty 105mm American howitzers that the Chinese had captured in Korea and twenty 75mm howitzers, along with one hundred 12.7mm and eighty 37mm anti-aircraft guns. And they had

200,000 artillery shells in their arsenal. All of this had been accomplished without sufficient detection by France's vaunted communications intelligence program to sound any alarms. The intelligence service had reported multiple Viet Minh units in the Dien Bien Phu area but had been unable to determine size, and French Commander Henri Navarre refused to believe that the units could be of division size. He also rejected the possibility that the Vietnamese were capable of launching a multi-divisional operation against his forces.

Once the siege began, the Chinese and Russians made sure that General Giap and his forces were well supplied. Surrounded by heavy artillery and antiaircraft positions, subjected week after week to what the Chinese call "human-wave" attacks and monsoon rains, the French forces and their fortifications were literally battered into a sea of mud. Viet Minh casualties are estimated to have been a staggering 23,000 men, but their forces would outlast the French.

Dien Bien Phu was France's greatest defeat of the modern era. Over 7,700 French soldiers died or were M.I.A., and 11,000 more were taken prisoner, many of whom were never repatriated. Ultimately, only about 3,000 survived the forced marches and prison camps. Whatever political support for the war that still remained in Paris was completely destroyed by the disaster at Dien Bien Phu.

Viet Minh troops herd thousands of French P.O.W.s (Photo: Public Domain)

The deaths of "Earthquake" and Wally

It was a little known fact among Americans in the 1950s that the U.S. was already involved in the war in Indochina. Civil Air Transport, which was a proprietary airline of the C.I.A., transported supplies and troops for the French as early as 1953. During the Battle of Dien Bien Phu, C.A.T. supplied the French Garrison by parachuting in troops and supplies using covert U.S. Air Force C-119s marked with French Air Force insignia.

Two American pilots were killed during the siege. On the afternoon of 06 May 1954, six unarmed Civil Air Transport C-119 Flying Boxcars departed Haiphong's Cat Bi airbase for Dien Bien Phu. One of the planes flown by James "Earthquake McGoon" McGovern, Jr., and his copilot Wallace "Wally" Buford was slated to drop a howitzer and desperately-needed ammunition to the beleaguered French paratroopers holding out at an encampment named "Isabelle." As they approached the drop zone, the port engine was riddled by 37 mm antiaircraft fire; a second burst damaged the horizontal stabilizer, both seriously impairing the crew's ability to maintain level flight. "I've got a direct hit," McGovern radioed.

James "Earthquake McGoon" McGovern (Photo: U.S. Army)

McGovern and Buford struggled for forty minutes to keep their aircraft aloft. They hoped to fly seventy-five miles and attempt an emergency landing at a remote landing strip near Muong Het in neighboring Laos. Just a few hundred yards short of their destination, a wing tip clipped a tree. "Looks like this is it, son," McGovern radioed, then the aircraft cart-wheeled, broke in half and burned near the Sang Ma River. McGovern, Buford, and two French crewmen died in the crash. A young French Army officer, Lt. Jean Arlaux, and a Malay paratrooper were thrown clear and survived the crash, but were taken prisoner by the Viet Minh. The paratrooper later died of his injuries.

James B. McGovern, Jr., thirty-two years old, was a World War II fighter ace who had been recruited by Gen. Claire Chennault to fly for C.A.T. He was given the nickname "Earthquake McGoon" (after the Li'l Abner comic strip character) during WWII because of his last name and because he was considered to be large for a fighter pilot. He was five-feet-ten and by war's end weighed in at over 260 lbs.

Wallace "Wally" Buford (Photo: U.S. Army)

Wallace A. Buford, twenty-eight years old, was a Korean War bomber pilot who had received two Distinguished Flying Crosses and a Purple Heart by the end of that conflict. He had gone back to college and was working on a degree in engineering when he saw an advertisement for C-119 pilots and volunteered. One year later, McGovern and Buford became the only Americans to die in combat in the first Indochina war. The French garrison surrendered the next day.

James McGovern's remains were not located until 2002, when they were discovered in an unmarked grave in northern Laos. Laboratory experts at JPAC, the U.S. military's Joint POW/MIA Accounting Command in Hawaii, positively identified him in September 2006. He was buried with full military honors at Arlington National Cemetery on May 24, 2007. The remains of Wally Buford and the other two French crewmen have not been recovered.

On February 24, 2005, the President of France posthumously awarded McGovern and Buford the Legion of Honour with the rank of Knight for their actions in supplying Dien Bien Phu in 1954. Ironically, neither McGovern nor Buford have been so memorialized in their own country. Their names do not appear on the CIA's Memorial Wall because they did not work directly for the agency. (The super-secret organization refused to even acknowledge an affiliation with C.A.T. until the 1990s.) Nor are their names found on the Vietnam Veteran's Memorial Wall, for although they could certainly be considered early U.S. fatalities in the Vietnam War and were highly-decorated American veterans, they were not active-duty members of the U.S. military.

The American-Indochina War

In many ways, the French war was a preview and should have been a forewarning for U.S. involvement in Vietnam some fifteen years later. The U.S. would take the French role, making many of the same mistakes, complicated by the same weakening support at home and the same political infighting that turned victories into defeats. Ho Chi Minh and his General Giap would play their same roles to perfection with eventual success in both wars. They were fighting on their home field, and they had nothing but time. Public opinion in Vietnam was not a factor. The Vietnamese had been carrying out wars of resistance against foreign invaders for centuries, and it had created a prominent cultural feature: a patriotism that infiltrated and encompassed every aspect of life.

The Geneva Accords were signed on July 21, 1954. An additional protocol divided Vietnam into two parts at the 17th parallel and established a six-mile-wide demilitarized zone. Ho Chi Minh's communist government would control North Vietnam and a government headed by Emperor Bao Dai would rule the South, and the Accords called for free elections by July 1956 to reunite the country under a democratically elected government. The U.S. and the South Vietnamese, who had refused to participate in the negotiations, refused to sign the agreement. U.S. Secretary of State John Foster Dulles knew that Ho Chi Minh would win any election that was held. The North had a population advantage; plus Ho enjoyed immense popularity with the nationalists, even in the South.

Dulles then set out to make the best deal he could out of a bad situation. The U.S. was already committed to supporting the non-communist government in the South. Within two months, he got the Manila Pact signed, thus creating the Southeast Asia Treaty Organization (SEATO). The treaty obligated its eight signatories to defense commitments, fighting communist aggression in Southeast Asia. In September 1954, the battle lines had been drawn for the next big war in Indochina.

The first U.S. advisors

In January 1955, the first direct U.S. military aid arrived in Saigon, and on February 12, President Dwight D. Eisenhower's administration sent the first U.S. advisors to South Vietnam to train the struggling South Vietnamese Army. In October, Bao Dai was ousted by his Prime Minister Ngo Dinh Diem in what was widely considered to be a fraudulent election. Diem's chief advisor on consolidating his power was attached to the Central Intelligence Agency. After the election, the Republic of South Vietnam was proclaimed with Diem as its first president.

Meanwhile in the North, Ho Chi Minh had flown to Moscow and readily accepted Soviet aid. The Chinese communists had provided most of his aid to that point. In December, land reform in North Vietnam reached its most radical phase as landlords and land owners were hauled before people's tribunals. There are estimates from several sources that 100,000 people were executed, and thousands more were sent to forced labor camps during one of the worst periods of what came to be known as "ideological cleansings." For the first time, Americans saw a different side of "Uncle" Ho Chi Minh. He was no longer viewed as the beloved father-figure and devoted nationalist leader of a unified Vietnam. They now saw him more realistically as a radical communist ruler who would readily resort to the mass murder of tens of thousands of his countrymen in order to achieve his political goals.

In early 1956, Diem began a brutal crackdown on Viet Minh suspects and other dissidents. The suspects were brought before security committees without counsel, and many were tortured and/or executed. In addition, Diem, who was Catholic, had seized land from Buddhist peasants and given it to his Catholic supporters thereby eroding Buddhist support. He allowed big land owners to retain their holdings, thus disappointing peasants hoping for land reforms in the South. In July, the deadline passed for the unifying elections set by the Geneva Convention and Diem, backed by the U.S., refused to participate. But there was one bright spot for the Vietnamese: on April 28, 1956, the last French soldier left South Vietnam.

In November 1956, a "peasant's revolt" occurred in the North. Several hundred peasants gathered in a market place near Vinh to protest land reforms and ask that some be allowed to migrate to South Vietnam. The next morning, a contingent of North Vietnamese Army (NVA) troops arrived and arrested members of the group. A riot ensued, which turned into an insurrection. That, in turn, was put down with heavy casualties. Thousands of peasants then attacked local government offices, destroying land records and blocking roads. Some of the local militia soldiers joined the rebels and the attacks spread. Ultimately, 10,000 peasants marched on the provincial capital, seizing weapons and forcing party cadres to sign confessions of crimes against the people. It took two reinforced NVA divisions to put down the uprising. The total number of casualties will never be known, but it has been stated that "close to 6,000 farmers were deported or executed." Diem, of course, deplored the massacre in the north. His official press agency was quoted in a Saigon daily: "In the North, the fall of the illegitimate regime is near…As soon as the people's hatred of the communist dictatorship is sufficiently mature for it to succeed in overthrowing it, then general elections which are really free will take place in the whole of Vietnam, and will peacefully bring about the reunification of the country." In 1956, life was not so good either north or south of the 17th parallel.

First U.S. advisor lost

During 1957, Viet Minh guerrillas assassinated more than four hundred South Vietnamese officials, and in October, communist insurgent activity began in earnest with a widespread terror campaign of bombings and assassinations. To facilitate the campaign, Hanoi had organized thirty-seven armed companies in the Mekong Delta. Thirteen Americans working for Military Assistance Advisory Group (MAAG) and U.S. Information Service (USIS) were wounded in terrorist bombings in Saigon.

On 21 October 1957, the first American advisor died in Vietnam. Special Forces Captain Harry G. Cramer, Jr., was killed by an explosion while watching an ambush drill during graduation exercises for the cadre of the South Vietnamese Special Forces. The official Report of Death states: "While engaged in exercise demonstrating principles of vehicle ambush, deceased was in vicinity of man throwing TNT block which exploded while in throwing position." The official Army position is that the TNT block involved was a deteriorated French explosive and caused the premature explosion. However, the two Special Forces medics who attended to Cramer, one of whom was also injured in the blast, state unequivocally that guerrillas fired several mortar rounds at the Special Forces advisors simultaneous with the start of the drill. The medics' account gains credence by the fact that at dawn the next day, guerrillas detonated a bomb outside the bus stop in front of U.S. military quarters in Saigon wounding fourteen U.S. personnel.

Harry Cramer was one of those men without whom our world, and certainly our military, would be a far poorer place. He always strived to be first in everything he did. He was the son of an Infantry captain and the grandson of an Army first sergeant. All he ever wanted to be was a soldier. He was an outstanding student and athlete, and the youngest member of the West Point Class of 1946, graduating when he was barely twenty. He fought in Korea, serving as a rifle company commander, earned the Silver Star for gallantry, and was wounded twice, receiving two Purple Hearts.

In 1953, Harry Cramer became the first West Point graduate to volunteer for the new Special Forces, and in 1956 he was part of a team known as the 14th Special Forces Operational Detachment which was sent to Southeast Asia to help train allied armies to fight communist guerillas. Members of Captain Cramer's team included Master Sgt. Henry Furst, Master Sgt. Frank Ruddy, Master Sgt. Everett White, Master Sgt. Fred Williamson, Sgt. 1st Class Chalmers Archer, Sgt. 1st Class Ray Labombard, Sgt. 1st Class Bobby Newman, Sgt. 1st Class Don Williams, and Staff Sgt. Robert Stetson. In June 1957, Cramer and his NCO team were deployed to South Vietnam to train the new South Vietnamese Army (ARVN) Special Forces unit. He was the first American advisor and the first Special Forces soldier to die there. He would not be the last.

Capt. Harry G. Cramer, Jr., of the 14th SFOD, U.S. Army, was thirty-one years old. He was a resident of Johnstown, Pennsylvania, and was buried in the U.S.M.A. cemetery at West Point, New York. He was survived by his wife Kit and three children: daughters Kainan and Anne, eight and six, and son Harry G. Cramer III, age four.

Buis and Ovnand

By June 1958, the communists had formed a coordinated command structure in the eastern Mekong Delta, laying the groundwork for the armed revolution that was being prepared by Ho Chi Minh and his communist leadership in the north. In March 1959, Ho declared a "People's War" to unite all of Vietnam under his leadership. His Politburo ordered an all-out military struggle in the south, thus officially declaring the Second Indochina War, and in May, construction began on the Ho Chi Minh trail to funnel cadres and weapons into South Vietnam.

In July 1959, over 4,000 Viet Minh guerrillas who had been born in the South were sent from the north to infiltrate South Vietnam and spread terror. On the night of July 8, two U.S. military advisors, Maj. Dale Buis and Master Sgt. Chester Ovnand, were killed in an attack by six Viet Minh guerrillas at Bien Hoa, twenty miles northeast of Saigon. The Americans were part of an eight-man MAAG advisory team attached to a base camp, and were watching a movie in the mess hall with four other men. During an intermission to change the movie reel, the lights were turned on, and the guerrillas attacked with machine guns and assault rifles. Buis and Ovnand were killed, along with two South Vietnamese guards. Buis had been in Vietnam only two days.

PART I

THE LISTENING GAME

CHAPTER 1

THE '60S – DECADE OF DEFIANCE AND DEATH

Arlington Hall—Headquarters of the Army Security Agency
(Photo: U.S. Army Intelligence and Security Command aka INSCOM)

In April 1960, the government of North Vietnam imposed a system of universal military conscription and set in motion a plan to form the National Liberation Front for South Vietnam. The Diem government would call the group "Viet Cong." Meanwhile, on November 11, 1960, there was a failed coup against President Ngo Dinh Diem in Saigon. It was led by Lt. Col. Vuong Van Dong and Col. Nguyen Chanh Thi of the ARVN Airborne Division.

The rebels launched the coup in opposition to Diem's autocratic rule and the negative political influence of his brother Ngo Dinh Nhu and sister-in-law Madame Nhu. They also opposed the politicization of the military, whereby regime loyalists were promoted ahead of more competent officers who were not insiders. Dong was supported in the conspiracy by his brother-in-law Lt. Col. Nguyen Trieu Hong, whose uncle was a prominent official in a minor opposition party. The main link in the coup was Dong's commanding officer Thi, who was persuaded to join in the plot.

The attempted coup caught the Ngo family completely off guard but was chaotically executed. The plotters neglected to seal the roads into Saigon that would keep out loyalist reinforcements, and Diem was able to buy time for pro-regime forces to enter the capital and rescue him. The coup failed when the 5th and 7th ARVN Divisions entered Saigon and defeated the rebels. More than 400 people, many of them civilian spectators, were killed in the ensuing battle. They included a group of pro-Diem civilians who charged across the palace walls at Thi's urging and were cut down by loyalist gunfire.

Dong and Thi fled to Cambodia, while Diem berated the U.S. for a perceived lack of support during the crisis. Afterwards, Diem ordered a crackdown, imprisoning numerous antigovernment critics and former cabinet ministers. Those that assisted Diem were duly promoted, while those that did not were demoted. Diem's regime accused the Americans of sending CIA members to assist in the failed plot.

ARVN COMINT

The Army of the Republic of Vietnam certainly knew of the French intercept and DF capabilities, but they had no expertise or equipment with which to work. When the French Expeditionary Forces were forced to leave Vietnam, they had taken their COMINT organization and most of their equipment with them. The South Vietnamese had initiated their own communications intelligence effort, but it was poorly staffed and equipped. The unit had sixty-five men assigned to it and was commanded by an ARVN Lieutenant. Their first assignment was to set up intercept sites in Saigon and Da Nang.

In 1958, President Diem had requested U.S. assistance for his

COMINT efforts, but President Eisenhower refused. The U.S. was already actively assisting the Vietnamese in other areas, but Eisenhower was afraid of compromising the highly secret code-breaking techniques of the National Security Agency. In 1960, Diem renewed his request, simply asking for new equipment. A few months later, he received an affirmative reply.

JFK's top-secret unit

After John F. Kennedy became President of the United States in January 1961, he recognized very quickly that a major problem for the South Vietnamese Army was poor communications intelligence. The program in place in South Vietnam had progressed little over the past years, and he intended to make recommendations that would improve the situation. The U.S. Intelligence Board (USIB) had reviewed the state of signal intelligence (SIGINT), including COMINT, in Southeast Asia, and of greatest concern was the ineffectual and inadequate DF effort against communist communications. The COMINT missions operating at that time were not delivering the necessary and timely DF information needed to support the military operation. The conclusion reached by the Board was that providing effective DF was the most important support the U.S. could provide to the South Vietnamese in their military effort against the communists.

This time, however, the approach would be different. A panel of high-level policymakers headed by Deputy Secretary of Defense Roswell Gilpatric submitted a laundry list of recommendations to President Kennedy. On the list was a proposal not just to send U.S. equipment to South Vietnam, but an American COMINT unit, and two days later the President presented that list to the National Security Council.

Shortly thereafter, the President approved the entire program, including the COMINT unit, stipulating that the entire project which also included Green Berets and an Air Force special operations unit was to be top-secret. Instead of implementing the program by the usual NSC directive, the program received its formal approval in a memorandum from Secretary of Defense Robert S. McNamara and was established by Presidential Executive Order signed on April 27, 1961. There was to be no public acknowledgement of any part of the program.

Whitebirch and Sabertooth

As part of the newly approved program, two projects were approved and code-named "Whitebirch" and "Sabertooth." Whitebirch would create a seventy-eight-man ASA operational unit to target local communist guerrillas, and Sabertooth would field a fifteen-man team to train South Vietnamese COMINT specialists who would support the South Vietnamese Army.

Additional parts of President Kennedy's "1961 COMINT escalation" included expanding the interception and DF programs already in place covering Vietnamese communist communications targets in both North and South Vietnam and obtaining USIB authority to conduct future operations in full partnership with the South Vietnamese. That would permit the sharing of intercept, DF, traffic analysis, and cryptographic analysis by U.S. agencies with the South Vietnamese to the degree needed for them to launch attacks against the communists. This arrangement heralded a new day in the gathering of communications intelligence in Southeast Asia. It also marked another step in the U.S. commitment to the Republic of South Vietnam.

Whitebirch was authorized three officers and seventy-four enlisted men, and Sabertooth one officer, two warrant officers and twelve enlisted men. Together they constituted the 400th Operations Unit (Provisional) of the Army Security Agency. Its cover identity was 3rd Radio Research Unit (RRU). Within three days, ASA had already identified the personnel it needed and assembled them at its training center at Ft. Devens, Massachusetts. While the personnel were being briefed and provided with some additional advanced training, ASA logisticians were locating and arranging shipment of the equipment that would be required for the mission.

Throughout the Vietnam War, the ASA designated its communications intelligence units as "Radio Research" to hide their highly-classified mission. In addition, the first ASA personnel who were sent to Vietnam carried U.S. diplomatic passports and wore civilian clothing. They posed as military advisors attached to MAAG-V. The Post Exchange at Ft. Devens provided the civilian clothing for the men of the 3rd RRU, but there was little variety to choose from. The standing joke was that they might just as well have worn uniforms because they were all dressed alike. Their medical records were stamped: "If injured or killed in combat, report as training accident in the Philippines."

Another world

The ninety-two crypto personnel arrived in Saigon on 13 May and set up their operation in a heavily guarded compound at Tan Son Nhut Airfield. Only seventeen days had elapsed since the order had been signed creating their unit and its mission, and the soldiers of the 3rd RRU were a different breed. For the first time, a U.S. military unit had been sent to Vietnam as an operational unit. They were not advisors; they were a fully functioning field unit established to provide intelligence to MAAG-V.

Whitebirch, comprised of seventy-eight men operating under the direct supervision of ASA-Pacific and NSA, was organized to intercept enemy communications, break codes, analyze radio traffic, and utilize various methods of monitoring signal intelligence (SIGINT). On 15 May, two days after their arrival at Tan Son Nhut, Phase I of their operation began with manual Morse coverage. ASA was now in business in Vietnam, and throughout the next week, additional equipment continued to come in from ASA units all over the world.

Their mission was conducted in what can only be described as "third world" conditions, in the worst possible sense of the term. Their main operational facility was an old aircraft hangar at the base, which had no air-conditioning. Temperatures inside regularly rose above 100 degrees, and then the monsoon rains came. Water poured through the doors and flooded the entire area to a depth of several inches.

The various operational sections were separated by stacks of C-ration boxes, and the analysts worked at long tables pieced together from plywood and scrap lumber. There were no chairs, so the tables were built high enough that the men could stand while they worked. Of course, the NSA civilian in charge of the operation had somewhat better facilities. He had a desk made of two stacks of C-ration boxes with a piece of plywood on top—and, he had a folding chair. The men were initially housed at the Majestic Hotel in Saigon, until more permanent quarters could be arranged. The enlisted personnel were later moved to a new building that offered more privacy, and the officers resided in a nearby residential area.

Locating the Viet Cong and North Vietnamese Army units by monitoring their electronic communications was the job of the radio DF specialists. That is why their job was so important and why the program was given such high priority. As envisioned by Washington and ASA HQ, ASA units in the field would locate VC units through DF, identify them by traffic analysis, and notify ARVN units in the area who would destroy the target and their transmitters.

The reality, however, was a far different story. Instead, what the men of the 3ʳᵈ RRU found within the hot, damp environs of their old hangar, was a mission totally unlike anything they had been trained for or experienced before. Like the rest of the U.S. Army, they had expected a conventional war, with all that encompassed, and a reliable ally with whom to serve, but what they found was far different. Most of what they had assumed was not true, and most of what they had learned in advance, they had to unlearn. They had to start over from square one and create a SIGINT program that worked within the special environment that was Vietnam. There was no voice intercept, because the VC used no voice communications, and effective direction-finding was nearly impossible. Due to the ongoing weather conditions and the topography of Vietnam, coastal plains rising quickly to high jungle, mountains, and deep valleys, the DF mission proved to be most difficult.

Racing to thwart the North

The primary reason for President Kennedy's decision to move forward with the proposals to bolster South Vietnam's COMINT effort and send the first U.S. units to South Vietnam was a top-secret report that was presented to him along with the April 1961 "Program of Action." The most compelling part of the report was an appraisal of the overall situation on the Vietnamese peninsula.

Almost two years earlier, the Central Committee of the North Vietnamese Communist Party had announced publicly that they intended to smash the government of South Vietnam. That announcement was followed by an immediate increase in the infiltration, subversion, sabotage and assassination activities by the Viet Cong. In September 1960, the North Vietnamese Communist Party Congress reaffirmed their earlier pronouncement, and that was followed some two months later by a military uprising in Saigon. Since that time, a state of active guerilla warfare had existed throughout the country. The number of hard-core VC had increased from 4,400 to some 12,000, and they were reporting an average of 650 violent incidents a month. During the first three months of 1961, casualties on both sides had totaled more than 4,500, and approximately 58% of the country was under some degree of communist control.

The VC had stepped up the pace and intensity of their attacks to the point where the survival of the government of South Vietnam was now in question. If the situation continued to deteriorate, the communists would be able to set up a rival government in one of the areas they controlled and plunge the nation into open civil war. The Viet Cong had publicly announced that they would "take over the country before the end of 1961." President Kennedy believed that he had to help stop the aggression while there was still a chance to thwart the plans of the North Vietnamese, and thus stall the overall communist master plan to subvert all of Southeast Asia.

North Vietnamese COMSEC effort

At the same time the Kennedy Administration was establishing the U.S. COMINT effort in South Vietnam and endeavoring to bolster the South Vietnamese intelligence collection effort, the communist government in Hanoi was establishing a cryptographic system in the South that would make their communications more secure. The initial network was comprised of two units known as Phuong Dong Group One and Phuong Dong Group Two, and cadre and personnel were trained in techniques and equipment in the North. The units then infiltrated into South Vietnam carrying their equipment, various cipher keys, and cryptographic systems on their backs.

Phong Dong Group One was comprised of twenty-nine cryptographic cadre and personnel. They left Hanoi in May 1961 and were in place near Ma Da by the end of July. Their challenge was to create an effective communication security system from scratch; standards were set and models presented, then local initiative was encouraged and different areas developed their own local systems. As a result there was not a system-wide cryptographic code that could be broken like Nazi Germany's "Enigma." Instead, the enemy (South Vietnam and its allies) was confronted by a myriad of widely varying yet similar crypto systems that they had to attack and try to break individually.

Utilizing SIGINT

After the 3rd RRU was operational, an intelligence unit was established at the U.S. Embassy in Saigon to evaluate and determine the best use of the collected material. The J-2 (intelligence) office of MAAG was tasked with the responsibility of creating the evaluation center, and the Special Security Officer (SSO)-Saigon, was in charge of its operation. The SSO also served as the Army's SIGINT advisor to Chief-MAAG concerning the release of COMINT to the South Vietnamese.

At that early stage of the game, SIGINT analysis depended heavily on loaned personnel from the Defense Intelligence Agency (DIA), the Assistant Chief of Staff for Intelligence (ACSI), the Department of the Army, and the U.S. Army Pacific (USARPAC). NSA-Pacific also furnished TDY specialists to help interpret SIGINT, but due to the response shown by CINPAC and the Secretary of Defense, they soon made the decision to permanently assign an NSA specialist to Saigon. Designated as the Resident Intelligence Research Analyst, Vietnam (RIRAV), the individual's affiliation with NSA was classified.

ASA's first DF site, located near Nha Trang became operational on 14 June, and was the first of six fixed sites. ASA personnel manned two more sites at Can Tho and Bien Hoa, and ARVN personnel manned three sites located at Pleiku, Da Nang, and Ban Me Thuot.

Passing muster

In October 1961, General Maxwell D. Taylor, President Kennedy's Chief of Staff, visited the 3rd RRU command center at Tan Son Nhut and inspected the ASA operation. Following his visit, the unit was authorized an increase in strength to 236 men and eighteen intercept positions, a 300% increase in five months. Obviously in spite of having to reinvent most of its operation, ASA was showing the results that Washington wanted to see.

By the time General Taylor came to Tan Son Nhut, the 3rd RRU was producing all kinds of targets for the ARVN. The Americans were locating radio transmitters, weapons and supply depots, VC headquarters and camps of VC soldiers, all in South Vietnam. Finding targets was not the issue, but getting their ARVN "partners" to follow through with their end of the operation was more difficult. Time after time, attacks would be planned by the Vietnamese based on solid SIGINT and COMINT analysis, only to be cancelled at the last minute, or they simply did not happen at all. That type of slipshod, unfocused, "half-assed" military operation was extremely difficult for U.S. military commanders to cope with.

A prime example of the problem occurred in October 1961. Intelligence developed through a variety of sources indicated there would be an important target in the Nam Bo region north of Saigon.

According to J-2 analysis, Viet Cong provincial representatives were going to meet at an unspecified location on 10 October. ASA DF operations for 8-10 October indicated that the meeting site was the village of Moumien, and since it was near a VC headquarters, an ARVN tactical operation was scheduled for 10-11 October. An ARVN armored battalion, two paratroop battalions, and additional infantry units were going to attack Moumien and the VC HQ. ARVN authorities informed MAAG in Saigon that they were going to launch their attack, and then the Americans learned that, for whatever reason, the operation had been cancelled.

Another member of General Taylor's party during his visit to Vietnam was Walt Rostow. Rostow was known as a staunch anti-communist and served as a national security advisor for both the Kennedy and Johnson administrations. Upon the completion of their Vietnam tour, Taylor and Rostow recommended that the President send 8,000 U.S. troops to bolster the South Vietnamese forces.

Harm's way

Poor and ineffective direction-finding continued to be a problem for ASA. In the highest tradition of the U.S. Army, ASA troops worked to solve the problem by mounting PRD-1 receivers on trucks. The PRD-1 is a high-frequency receiver that was designed for direction-finding, and by August 1961, they had begun to deploy mobile teams. That development required ASA operators to move into the countryside to accomplish their mission and ultimately resulted in the first U.S. battlefield casualty.

CHAPTER 2
TENNESSEE HERO

Tom Davis and friends in the field (Photo: © Tom Davis Family)

In many ways Tom Davis was the typical all-American boy, and the typical ASA enlisted soldier. He was born on June 1, 1936, in Livingston, Tennessee, where his father, a World War II veteran, was a pharmacist. Tom grew up there, the oldest of five children, and worked in the family drugstore. In his free time, he loved to hike and hunt in the wooded hills surrounding his home. He went to school at Livingston Academy where he was a good student and earned a letter as a defensive half-back on the Wildcats football team. He was named "Harvest King" his senior year and once wrote in a school assignment, "My ambitions are unlimited, my fate unknown."

After high school, Tom married his high school sweetheart, Geraldine Martin, and then spent three years studying engineering at Tennessee Tech University in Cookeville, which was just twenty miles south of his home. Unsure about what he wanted to do with his life, he decided to forego his senior year and enlisted in the U.S. Army. As part of the enlistment process and throughout basic training at Ft. Jackson, S.C., he was subjected to a battery of aptitude tests, and his scores were very high. As a result, he was selected to join the Army Security Agency and was sent to the ASA training school at Ft. Devens, Massachusetts, to become an RDF intercept operator. By now, he had a baby daughter, and he missed his family.

Tom was perfect for ASA. He had attended college and had grown up in a small southern town where most everyone knew him. A small-town background made it easier for the FBI to complete its extensive background checks, and within a few months, he received his top-level security clearance.

Tom Davis would take his place in history as a member of the original Whitebirch team that President Kennedy secretly ordered into Vietnam. His is the eighteenth name on the original orders, dated 10 May 1961, assigning ASA personnel to the 3rd Radio Research Unit (Provisional) Vietnam. He would be the first ASA soldier to die there.

Tom Davis in Vietnam (Photo: © Tom Davis Family)

The hunted

On 22 December 1961, Davis, along with a Vietnamese driver, was riding in the front seat of an ARVN three-quarter-ton truck equipped with a PRD-1 receiver. He was serving as an advisor to nine members of an ARVN mobile PRD-1 team who were riding in the back. As the group proceeded along Provincial Highway #10 about twelve miles west of their base at Tan Son Nhut, their eyes scoured the rice paddies and brush that obscured the surrounding countryside. They were in an area referred to as "the pineapple region," because it had been the site of a huge French pineapple plantation before the French-Indochina War, and it was known to be a center of communist activity.

Everything seemed routine, but enemy activity had been increasing, and the VC could suddenly appear out of nowhere. Another RDF team had narrowly escaped a recent ambush attempt. Tom and his team needed to get in close in order to locate the insurgent transmitter locations, but about noon, near the old French garrison town of Cau Xang, the routine mission changed, and the hunter became the hunted.

As Davis' vehicle rumbled along the dusty road, there was a loud explosion. The bed of the truck was catapulted into the air by a remote-controlled landmine detonated under the tailgate and landed with a jarring crash. The vehicle veered wildly and continued about thirty yards before careening off the road, coming to rest in a slough at the end of a culvert. The ARVN troops in the back had been thrown into a tangled heap and came under immediate attack by Viet Cong troops armed with rifles, machine-guns, and hand grenades. The insurgents had hidden in the brush along the road and sprung the trap as the truck lumbered by. The men in the bed of the truck were dazed, possibly injured by the explosion, and had little protection as they attempted to escape from the disabled vehicle. Most were unable to mount any defense before being gunned down in the muddy ditch.

Davis sat stunned for a moment as smoke filled the cab and then realized that he was uninjured. He grabbed his weapon and quickly scrambled outside into the total chaos of the attack. The air was filled with the roar of automatic weapons, grenade explosions and the screams of men who had been riding in the back. Realizing the seriousness of the situation, Davis hurled his bag containing top-secret communications codes and other classified materials into the water of a nearby rice paddy to prevent them from falling into enemy hands. He then pulled his injured driver out of the vehicle and dragged him into the culvert where the driver concealed himself in the water beneath the truck.

In a desperate final effort to save his men, Davis screamed for his team to "run for it" and then ran up the gravel road away from the truck. He turned and fired his carbine as he ran, yelling at the enemy; drawing fire to himself and away from his driver and the other team-members, most of whom were probably already dead or dying. At a position some fifty feet in front of the vehicle, he was hit by a bullet to the head and died instantly. He had fired four or five rounds at the enemy before the fatal blow.

Suddenly all was quiet. As the smoke cleared, the VC quickly stripped the fallen soldiers of their weapons and gear, along with the radio equipment that had been mounted on the truck. Within a few minutes, a unit of the ARVN Civil Guard arrived on the scene, but the insurgents had melted into the countryside, and there was no evidence of any Viet Cong casualties. Only the driver whom Tom Davis had saved remained alive to tell the story of his heroism.

An officer from the 3rd RRU and a member of the ARVN general staff arrived on the scene by helicopter an hour after the attack, and the bodies of the dead were removed to Saigon. It was soon learned that VC commanders in the area were fully aware of the mission of the DF teams and had ordered strong action against them because of their success in disrupting guerilla operations. The ASA teams had a target on their backs; the hunters had become the prey.

Dark night in Tennessee

Amy Davis, the wife of Tom's nephew recently wrote: "On a dark December night in 1961, a cab driver made his way toward the Davis residence on East Cedar Street in Livingston. The merry feeling of

Christmas was in the air, but on this cold, wintry evening, the Davis family was celebrating another happy occasion. It was December 22nd, the birthday of Janie, the fourth of five children born to Clarence and Blanche Davis. Adding to the festive mood was the anticipated return of eldest son, Tom who was serving in the Army and due home any time from Vietnam, a faraway place none of them had ever heard of before."

From what they could tell of photos and letters Tom had sent home over the past nine months, the twenty-five-year-old soldier seemed to be in a tropical paradise. But lately, the tone of his letters had changed, indicating a growing sense of uneasiness. In one letter, he had asked his father to send him a .38 Special, as he and his fellow soldiers had not been issued side-arms. In August, he had written to his father telling him of the narrow escape of two U.S. advisors from an enemy ambush: "We became a little more involved in this conflict yesterday...It looks like the bad guys have gotten the word to start giving us hell. It breaks the daily routine even though it could become a bit dangerous. I didn't really get shaky until I realized that I was very lucky. I had worked the night before, and I and another fellow came over the [same] road earlier that morning on our way back to town. So it's just chance that it was Bill instead of us that got hit. Fortunately, nobody was hurt."

"[Initially] he didn't even have a uniform," youngest brother Jack Davis said, of the secret U.S. operation. 'They were required to wear civilian clothes because they weren't supposed to be over there. It wasn't actually a war at that time."

It is ironic that this first U.S. battlefield fatality would be someone who was in Vietnam travelling on a civilian passport. By the time Tom Davis died, however, ASA personnel had been issued battle-dress uniforms and were wearing them when operating in the field.

Jack, who was "eleven going on twelve," remembers when the taxi cab arrived. "The taxi driver brought a telegram and knocked on the door. It was the last day of school before Christmas vacation, and I was sitting at the dining room table. Dad went to the door, and mumbled something and turned around. Then he called 'Mother...something bad has happened'...she ran in and that's about all I remember."

Joe Davis, who had just started a family of his own and lived down the street, remembers getting a phone call from his older brother, Bill. "The phone rang, and he said. 'You need to come up to Mom and Dad's. Tom was killed.'...It was a tragedy no one expected. We were waiting for him to come home," Joe says. "After all, America wasn't at war—not yet. We didn't have any reason to think that he was going to get shot, you know. We just didn't think that way." And nothing much had been in the news, but that would change, soon enough.

A hero comes home

Two weeks later, the body of Tom Davis lay in state in the living room of the house where he had grown up, and many came to pay their respects to him and to his family. A traditional Vietnamese "funeral pall" covered his casket. The gift had been hand-made by some of the South Vietnamese soldiers with whom Tom had worked. It had required many hours of intense labor and the soldiers had gone without sleep in order to finish it in time for it to be shipped to Tennessee with Tom's body. A red sash across the pall reads: "In Memory of James T. Davis from Officers and EM (enlisted men) of the 1st RRC."

Funeral pall hand-made by South Vietnamese soldiers (Photo: © Tom Davis Family)

Spc.4 James T. Davis was buried with full military honors at Good Hope Cemetery, among his beloved Tennessee hills on January 3, 1962. He left behind his young wife Gerrie, daughter Cindy, and a host of grieving family and friends.

Joe Davis says, "Every year about this time, his name pops up and people want to know what happened." Amy Davis continues, "Then the family simply explains that, like so many before and after him, Tom was a young man who served his country—and died in the process. But, most importantly—just like all the other fallen soldiers—Tom Davis lived."

Afterword

In the ensuing weeks and months, those who had known Tom Davis tried to find ways to honor his memory and his sacrifice. The students and faculty at Livingston Academy named the football stadium "Tom Davis Memorial Stadium," and a wildcat (the school's mascot) that Tom had shot and stuffed still holds an honored spot in their trophy case. Technically, the U.S. was not at war, so Army regulations prohibited awarding Davis the Purple Heart, but the regulation was later waived and the family was presented with his medal posthumously.

Davis Station, Tan Son Nhut A.B., Saigon (Photo: © L. Long)

Some two weeks after his death, his fellow ASA soldiers honored him by naming the 3rd RRU's base/living quarters at Tan Son Nhut, "Davis Station" and it retained that name throughout the remainder of the war. VFW James T. Davis Memorial Post 5062 in Livingston, Tenn. is also named in his honor, as is VFW Post 1246 in North Brook, Ill. In 1975, the ASA Training Center at Ft. Devens, Massachusetts, built a new library and named it Davis Library. Clarence and Blanche Davis, Tom's parents, took part in the dedication ceremonies at the school.

"Operation Chopper"

The first U.S. helicopter units had arrived in Saigon on 21 November 1961. They were the 8th Transportation Company (Light Helicopter) and the 57th Transportation Company (Light Helicopter). One of the newly-arrived helicopters had been sent to Cau Xang to bring the body of Tom Davis back to Saigon. Some three weeks later, thirty H-21 Shawnee helicopters of the 57th Trans. Co. ferried over a thousand Vietnamese paratroopers into the pineapple-area for an assault on the suspected VC stronghold and to search out the clandestine VC radio transmitter that Davis had died trying to locate. They were part of what was called "Operation Chopper," and it was the first air-mobile assault mission of the war in Vietnam.

Caught by surprise, the VC troops were soundly defeated, and the mission was successful. The radio transmitter was located, and a number of Viet Cong were killed or captured. "Operation Chopper" is reputed to be the origin of the nickname "chopper" given to helicopters.

By the end of the year, the U.S. was spending over $1 million per day training and supporting the ARVN forces. In his State of the Union speech on January 11, 1962, President Kennedy said: "Few generations in all of history have been granted the role of being the great defender of freedom in its maximum hour of danger. This is our good fortune." A few days later, however, when asked if U.S. troops were involved in the fighting in Vietnam, Kennedy answered, "No."

Operation "Chopper"–12 January 1962 (Photo: U.S. Army)

USAFSS joins the fray

The U.S. Air Force Security Service, NSA's "air wing" arrived in Vietnam in January 1962, some eight months after ASA. The Air Force cryptologists were divided between the U.S. bases at Danang and Tan Son Nhut. Two Air Force VHF intercept vans were flown into Danang and four vans, including an HFDF station, were flown into Tan Son Nhut. The Security Service HF intercept mission was later moved to Danang as well due to better reception. The VHF operation at Danang was less than effective, however, due to the surrounding terrain, so after much haggling with ASA and NSA, the Air Force VHF mission was moved to a new location on Monkey Mountain some twelve miles north of the base.

Finding a safer way

With the deliberate targeting of the mobile teams by the VC, there was an immediate effort to find a safer way to accomplish the Army's DF mission. In response, the ASA proposed to develop an airborne radio direction-finding (ARDF) program, thus allowing for greater mobility and less danger. If they could not do it safely on the ground, maybe they could do it in the air.

Army engineers at Ft. Monmouth, New Jersey, began experimenting with a variety of different aircraft, and first tried the UH-19 (Chickasaw) helicopter. That experiment was short-lived due to turbulence from the copter blades and static produced by onboard electronics, making it an impractical vehicle. The engineers next turned to the U-6A De Havilland Beaver. It was small, had adequate power, was readily available in Vietnam, along with the required maintenance facilities—and it was dependable. It was the same aircraft that had been used by the military as early as 1954 for electronic intelligence (ELINT) missions in Alaska testing Russian defenses.

In early March the first ASA ARDF platforms arrived in Vietnam. Three U-6As had been procured from the Army Signal Corps, and Army transport pilots had been assigned to fly them. The "backseaters" (intercept operators) were manual Morse intercept specialists recruited from the 3rd RRU. A series of controlled tests were carried out using captured VC transmitters that were positioned around the city of Saigon. The tests were so successful that ASA wanted to put the planes into immediate operation. The aircraft seemed to solve most all of the problems that had plagued ASA's DF operation from the beginning, providing both speed and increased security for the technicians. ASA command set about forming a small aviation section that was assigned to the 3rd RRU, and they flew their first live mission on 22 March 1962. The soldiers assigned to the unit soon began referring to it as "TWA" (Teeny Weeny Airlines).

The importance of ARDF had been realized and understood during WWII, but it was not until Vietnam that systems were put in place to realize its full potential. The intelligence that was gathered from the ARDF missions was most useful when it was merged with other forms of intelligence gathered from an array of sources. Those sources included aerial photography, long-range reconnaissance patrols, enemy documents, and interrogation of enemy P.O.W.s. All of that material was collected, sorted, studied, and analyzed by ASA cryptanalysts, under NSA supervision. ARDF quickly became the single most valuable intelligence resource available to the U.S. and its allies, and that remained true during the balance of the war in Vietnam

"Teeny Weeny Airlines" U-6A "Beaver" (Photo: © L. Long)

In April 1962, the U.S. cryptologic community had to consider a long-standing question. Was it preferable to preserve an enemy radio station as a continuing source of intelligence, or consider it a target and destroy it? With the early success of the nascent ARDF program, the issue needed to be resolved quickly. The fact that such a question was being considered would indicate ASA cryptologists were breaking the codes being used by VC transmitters and exploiting the information on a regular basis.

NSA identified sixteen VC transmitters from which ASA was intercepting usable intelligence and then graded them according to their value. They told Saigon that the loss of nine of those stations would constitute a "serious loss of communications intelligence," and three other stations were rated of such high value that they should be considered untouchable.

A few days later, allied SIGINT operations in South Vietnam suffered a major blow when the VC executed a nearly total change in communication procedures on their military networks. The changes were extensive and universal and included ten-day changing call signs, frequencies, and schedules, along with a standardization of format so that all VC messages throughout North and South Vietnam looked the same. It was no longer possible for analysts to identify where messages came from by their local formats. It would take time for the traffic and crypto analysts to recover.

In fact, what happened in April 1962 was the culmination of a two-year program to upgrade and make VC communications more secure, and that upgrade was directly tied to Hanoi's decision to begin the liberation of the South through violent revolution. A major part of their plan was to upgrade all of their cryptographic systems and increase the number of cryptographic personnel and their technical bases in the South.

Through the remaining months of 1962, ASA's ARDF mission matured and continued to prove its immense value. Within four months, the air crews flew 162 missions and identified twenty-three transmitters belonging to approximately sixteen enemy headquarters.

A bitter pill called "Ap Bac"

The village of Ap Bac was located in the Mekong Delta. It had been a communist stronghold since the French colonial days, so it should have come as no surprise when an ASA ARDF mission identified a VC transmitter there in December 1962. It was determined that the transmitter belonged to an unidentified VC unit, and U.S. advisors led by Lt. Col. John Paul Vann used the intelligence to plan an attack.

The ARVN 7th Division, consisting of 2,500 infantry troops, and advised by Lt. Col. Vann, had at its disposal ten H-21 Shawnee helicopters from the U.S. 93rd Trans. Co. (Light Helicopter), five armed UH-1B "Huey" helicopters from the U.S. Utility Tactical Transport

Helicopter Co., thirteen M-113 armored personnel carriers, long-range artillery, thirteen fighter-bombers, and all the napalm they could use. Their mission was to locate and destroy a suspected VC command center at Ap Bac.

VC activity had previously consisted of hit and run attacks, and the old-school American military commanders had always believed if the VC could be forced to stand and fight, they would be soundly defeated. In reality, when the communists stood and fought, they inflicted serious injury on the attacking allied forces.

On 02 January 1963, the ARVN division attacked Ap Bac. The village was well defended with about 350 hardened VC troops, and spies had alerted them that the attack was imminent. They were lying in wait when the ARVN forces moved in. Pinned down by waves of heavy gunfire, mortars, and RPGs (rocket propelled grenades) from a tree line, the ARVN commanders called for reinforcements. Ten Shawnees from the 93rd flew in with additional ARVN troops and the enemy positions were pounded with artillery, but the VC were well dug in and waited out the bombardment.

Downed helicopters on the battlefield at Ap Bac (Photo: U.S. Army)

As the 93rd flew within 200 yards of the VC bunkers, they were engulfed in a massive barrage of gunfire. Two of the Shawnees and one of the escorting armed Hueys went down. As a fourth chopper flew in to rescue the downed crewmen, it was also shot down, and its crew chief killed. Two additional armed H-21s were so badly damaged that they were forced to land further away from the action.

The last two armed Hueys immediately attacked the tree line with rockets and machine gun fire, but the VC gunners held firm and returned fire. An unarmed Huey "slick" attempted to rescue the downed American crews but was shot down, losing a second crew chief in the crash. The U.S. advisors to the ARVN infantry division furiously demanded that the huge South Vietnamese force attack the VC positions, but their commanders refused to join the battle. They were completely cowed by the ferocity of the VC defenders.

As nightfall approached, seven U.S. helicopters had been shot down, with two American crewmen dead. Several more crewmembers were wounded and still trapped on the battlefield. Total U.S. casualties for the day were three dead and eight wounded. In the darkness, the VC quietly melted into the jungle with an estimated thirty-five wounded and twenty killed. The ARVN division lost eighty killed and 100 wounded.

American commanders in Saigon called the battle a victory, and that was echoed by Admiral Harry Felt, Commander of the U.S. Pacific Fleet, and General Paul Harkins, Commander of MACV. They still held the age-old view that saw military progress in terms of territory won or lost, but in Vietnam, such progress was meaningless and such pyrrhic victories of little value. It is reminiscent of the British victory at the Battle of Guilford Court House during the American Revolution in 1781. In its aftermath, British M.P. Charles James Fox echoed Plutarch's famous words by saying, "Another such victory might well ruin the British Army." Discrediting the regime in Saigon, along with its allies, was the communist goal, and one battle had gone a long way toward convincing them they were on the right track. The ARVN alone could not win the war against them. The Americans were going to have to make a tough choice: cut their losses and withdraw, or commit U.S. combat forces to the fight.

"Emulate Ap Bac" became both a communist slogan and a method of operation. Diagrams and descriptions of the battle were sent to all communist forces in the South, and the engagement was studied as a classic model for how the Viet Cong should fight against their better-equipped opponents.

CHAPTER 3
PHU BAI

Phu Bai—"virtually a VC camp ground" (Photo: © L. Long)

During its first year of operation in Vietnam, ASA's efforts had been focused on the VC networks in South Vietnam, but with the growing sophistication of those networks, it became obvious that Hanoi was playing a major role in their day-to-day operations. There was a growing need for current and viable intelligence on North Vietnam with regard to their activities in the South. Information was needed on logistics and their support of the VC, on troop movements in the border areas, on agents operating in the South and Laos, on Chinese involvement in the war, and a myriad of other details.

There was also a growing concern by Admiral Laurence H. Frost, the Director of NSA, that the Whitebirch program was not going well. He felt that joint SIGINT operations with ARVN cryptologists was a bad idea and should be discouraged. He was willing to train and assist the ARVN in conducting its own operation but believed that NSA needed to build a new intelligence gathering site that would be exclusively a U.S. operation. After the massive change in communist communications in April, there was increasing pressure to make that happen, and a preliminary site at Phu Bai was selected.

The site was about twelve miles southeast of Hue and offered easy access to communist communications from both North Vietnam and Laos. The only stickler was getting the South Vietnamese to go along with the plan. General Harkins approached General Nguyen Khanh, who was President Diem's intelligence chief, and he refused. He made what was probably a correct assumption that U.S. intelligence operatives would gather information and then not share it with Saigon. He was certainly aware that new restrictions were being put in place regarding the Whitebirch operation, so he was not inclined to go along with a U.S.-only operation at Phu Bai.

After a month of wrangling, Khanh finally agreed to allow the Americans to build their base, with the understanding that Saigon would receive "relevant" intelligence. A detachment from the 3rd RRU would be situated near the airport at Phu Bai and agreed to work with local airport officials to ensure that their operation would not interfere with air traffic. The ARVN would provide land to accommodate the Americans' new buildings and antenna fields and agreed to provide adequate security around the perimeter area of the new base. Finally, General Harkins agreed that intelligence gathered at the installation "which may have been of value to the government of Vietnam" would be provided to Saigon.

It is ironic, after all of the haggling involved in establishing the new base at Phu Bai, that it was almost immediately considered to be at risk from a security standpoint. It would seem that such concerns should have been considered before the site was agreed upon. MACV was concerned that it could be subject to an attack by conventional forces from the north (either North Vietnamese or Chinese), and NSA thought it was especially vulnerable to attacks by the VC. One NSA official referred to the area as "virtually a VC camp ground."

There was no question the area had seen heavy VC activity, including attacks on local military and police installations and ambushes of ARVN patrols. Admiral Frost conceded to the security concerns by requiring that all secret and top-secret materials be kept to a minimum so that they could be more easily destroyed in case they had to evacuate the base.

Defensive line at Phu Bai–1964 (Photo: © L. Long)

By late summer, construction of the installation and its attendant antenna field was underway, and the ASA detachment had begun to move in, along with a small detachment of U.S. Marines from Pleiku. The Marines were the 4th sub-unit of the 1st Composite Radio Company and were an element of the Naval Security Group (NSG), NSA's U.S. Navy branch. They had deployed from Kaneohe, Hawaii, in January 1962, thus becoming the first unit of U.S. Marines in Vietnam. The Marines' mission was radio-intercept of North Vietnamese naval communications, but their officers were quick to remind them that they were "Marines first," and their additional combat training and advanced infantry training was a welcome addition to the defenses at Phu Bai.

Marines of the 1ˢᵗ Composite Radio Company (Photo: U.S.M.C.)

Construction was completed and the personnel in place by the first of February 1963 and intercept operations began on February 3. In spite of its vulnerabilities, Phu Bai was an ideal site for communications intercept, and ASA was soon reassigning intercept missions to Phu Bai that had been undertaken from other less desirable locations. By the end of 1963 over 200 personnel were stationed there.

ASA operations compound–Phu Bai (Photo: © L. Long)

Meanwhile, back at the ranch

In March 1963, ASA established the 7th RRU located in Saigon. The true identity of the unit was the 101st ASA Security Detachment (COMSEC), and their mission was to determine what information Hanoi and the VC were intercepting by monitoring U.S. communications. Little was known about communist efforts, other than a few references in intercepted VC communications and "intel" gathered from captured VC COMINT personnel.

March also saw the continuing upgrade of the 3rd RRU's burgeoning air wing, with the delivery of seven more RU-6As, code named "Seven Roses." They were joined by two RU-8D Seminoles, code-named "Checkmate," and one RU-8F aircraft.

RU-8D "Checkmate" (Photo: © L. Long)

The RU-6As are described as having "armored protection," and its crews "carried parachutes." But actually, the parachutes served as the back of the crew's seats and were never taken out or repacked. It is also an open question as to what the results would have been had any of the crewmen been forced to use the parachutes, as none of them had been given any instruction on putting the parachute on, successfully exiting the plane, pulling the ripcord, or any other part of the jump process. In addition, the U-6A's armor consisted of a one to two inch steel plate under a cushion the crew sat on.

The RU-8Ds had greater range and speed and were equipped with Doppler radar to allow all-weather operations. But, like everything else in Vietnam, things did not work out as expected. The radar system required continuous maintenance due to the heat and humidity, and if it failed during a mission, the low wings made it difficult to manually mark a location on the map. The aircraft was equipped with the new AN/ARD-15 which offered a sharper null and a better determination of the median null; however, the cockpit located above the wings was more exposed to the sun, and space for the ARDF operator, located behind the pilot, was more cramped.

The delivery of the new aircraft had been delayed when it was discovered that the cranes in the Port of Saigon could not lift the larger aircraft from the deck of the ship. The ship was then sent to the U.S. Naval Base at Subic Bay in the Philippines. A contingent of 3rd RRU, Aviation Section pilots, headed by Major Stanley Frick, the commander of the small section, were sent to Subic to fly the new aircraft back to Tan Son Nhut. During a flight check Major Frick and a Navy mechanic had a hydraulic failure, but the Major was able to land the aircraft, wheels-up, without injury.

Best of the best

On 14 May 1963, exactly two years after their clandestine arrival at Tan Son Nhut Airfield, the 3rd RRU was awarded a Meritorious Unit Commendation by the Secretary of the Army, the first unit to be so honored in Vietnam. The citation reads as follows: "The 3rd Radio Research Unit has distinguished itself by exceptionally meritorious achievement in the performance of outstanding service to the United States during the period 13 May 1961 to 31 December 1962 while engaged in military operations. During this period the 3rd Radio

Research Unit furnished vital intelligence information to the Armed Forces of the United States. The information was secured under conditions of grave danger and was processed and delivered through long and arduous hours of dedicated effort. The brilliant achievements of the 3rd Radio Research Unit have been invaluable to the success of military operations in Southeast Asia and have reflected great credit upon the unit, the United States Army Security Agency, and the United States Army." The order was later amended to also include the "Sub Unit #1, 1st Composite Radio Company, FMF (U.S.M.C.)"

Changing tides

On June 11th, President Kennedy submitted civil rights legislation to Congress and made a nationally televised address to the nation on civil rights, concluding with: "A great change is at hand, and our task is to make the revolution peaceful and constructive for all." The very next day, civil rights leader Medgar Evers was shot in the back by a Ku Klux Klansman at his home in Jackson, Mississippi.

On the same day, a Buddhist monk, Quang Duc, publicly immolated himself in an appeal to Diem for religious tolerance. In the following weeks other monks would follow his example. Madam Nhu referred to the incidents as "barbecues" and offered to "supply the matches." Buddhist demonstrations continued throughout Vietnam.

On Sunday, September 15, 1963, the 16th Street Baptist Church in Birmingham, Alabama, was bombed by the Ku Klux Klan. Four young girls died in the explosion which shocked the nation and galvanized the civil rights movement.

CHAPTER 4

CHANGING HORSES

President Eisenhower and John Foster Dulles greet President Diem
(Photo: National Archives aka NARA)

On 29 October 1963, NSA noticed a higher than usual volume of messages coming out of Hanoi, and that spike in communist communications continued the next day throughout South Vietnam. Something was obviously going on, but what? Forty-eight hours later, President Diem was overthrown in Saigon, and he and his brother, Ngo Dinh Nhu were both executed by ARVN soldiers under the command of General Duong Van Minh.

South Vietnam's Buddhist majority had long chafed under Diem's autocratic rule and unbridled favoritism toward the Catholic minority he represented. It had been an unwritten law of his regime that public servants and army officers would be promoted on the basis of their religious affiliation and loyalty to Diem. That policy had created an undercurrent of bitterness and discontent among those in the military who were passed over as a result. Catholics were also provided their pick of government contracts, tax concessions, American aid and whatever favors the government could provide.

The disaffection between the Buddhists and the Diem regime had been long-running and deep, but the situation worsened in 1963. A series of confrontations and protests that had ultimately resulted in attacks on Buddhist pagodas across the country by South Vietnamese Special Forces loyal to Ngo Dinh Nhu; thousands of monks were arrested, and the death toll was estimated to be in the hundreds. Many across the social spectrum began calling for Diem's removal from power, and numerous coup plans had been considered, but a more serious effort began to take shape after the Kennedy administration and the U.S. embassy in Saigon indicated they were open to the possibility of a regime change.

Documents made public after 2003 provide irrefutable evidence President Kennedy and his advisers played a considerable role in the coup. The administration had been supportive of ARVN military officers who had questioned what the U.S. response would be to a coup, and had openly withdrawn U.S. aid from Diem. Washington had also publicly pressured the Saigon government in a way that made it clear to those plotting against Diem that he was isolated from his American ally.

In addition, at several meetings, Kennedy had CIA briefings and led discussions based on the estimated balance between pro and anti-coup forces in Saigon that leave no doubt the U.S. Government sought the coup against Ngo Dinh Diem, without actually considering the physical consequences Diem and members of his regime might face. The officials, including J.F.K., apparently overestimated their ability to control the outcome of the coup and the generals who staged it.

An audio tape of a top-level White House meeting held on October 29, 1963, just prior to the coup, includes the President's brother Robert Kennedy voicing doubts about how "intimately involved" they were in the coup plans. The fact that the CIA provided $42,000 in funding to the plotters on the morning of the coup would seem to indicate the U.S. Government was more than "intimately involved."

The coup that removed the Diem regime from power prompted an immediate and expected increase in communications activity coming from Hanoi and its minions. The spike in activity two days before the coup is now thought to indicate that the VC probably knew what was about to happen. They had a very sophisticated system of agents in place throughout the south, including the South Vietnamese military and would have been eager to pass along such "hot" information to Hanoi.

American officials had been generally optimistic about the state of affairs in Vietnam. Military operations by ARVN troops with their American advisors and equipment had appeared to dampen the VC insurgency during the past year, and by October, some officials were considering a partial withdrawal of up to a thousand U.S. advisors. NSA, on the other hand, made it clear that their SIGINT operation in Vietnam would need more resources, not fewer.

On November 20, 1963, the first high-level review of the war in Vietnam since the fall of the Diem regime was presented at a conference in Hawaii. Among those attending were Secretary of State Dean Rusk; Secretary of Defense McNamara; Gen. Taylor, Chairman of the Joint Chiefs of Staff; Under Secretary of State George Ball; and National Security Advisor McGeorge Bundy. The group heard Ambassador Henry Cabot Lodge, Gen. Paul Harkins (Chief-USMACV), and their team from Vietnam present a promising picture of the nine-year-old war, indicating it had "taken a turn for the better," and the future seemed to hold "an encouraging outlook." The December 2, 1963, issue of *Newsweek* stated: "So comforting were the reports that the delegates felt able to confirm that 1,000 of the 16,500 U.S. servicemen stationed in Vietnam would be withdrawn by the end of the year" and a 2,000 word communiqué was issued to that effect.

Two days later, shortly after noon on November 22, 1963, President John F. Kennedy was dead. It is the height of irony that some three weeks after Kennedy was sitting at his desk considering the coup that would ultimately kill President Diem, he himself would die a violent death at the hands of an assassin in Dallas, Texas. Lyndon Baines Johnson was now President of the United States.

By year's end, the communist leadership in Hanoi had decided to step up the fight in the South. The 3rd RRU at Tan Son Nhut had 300 men providing intercept, primarily of VC communications, and Phu Bai had an authorized strength of approximately 200. The total number of American military personnel serving in Vietnam stood at 16,000.

Exit strategy or buildup

The communists stepped up their attacks in South Vietnam early in 1964 just as planned, and the Americans continued plans to reduce their presence in South Vietnam, based on the Kennedy Administration's original schedule. The South Vietnamese Army, however, was becoming involved in more and more large-scale battles and was being badly beaten. McNamara and the Joint Chiefs called for the reduction of U.S. advisors by 1,000 at the end of 1963 and then by 50% in late 1964. They planned to be down to about 6,000 by the end of 1965. The 3rd and 7th RRUs' strength would remain the same. The USAFSS 6925th Security Squadron at Danang and the Marines at Phu Bai would stay at current manning if their respective services opted to keep the units in South Vietnam.

On the surface, the picture appeared rosy in Washington. McNamara and the Joint Chiefs seemed optimistic that, militarily, the war would be won, but in private, administration officials admitted that the war was not going well. President Johnson's determination to continue Kennedy's policies led him to follow through with the withdrawal of the first thousand men in December 1963, but it has been described as "largely an accounting exercise." It was questionable whether actual conditions in South Vietnam warranted any withdrawal of troops, and some have expressed doubts that Kennedy would have done so, had he lived.

While Secretary McNamara was endeavoring to draw down the U.S. presence in Vietnam, NSA came to the conclusion that their cryptologic program needed to be expanded dramatically upwards as quickly as possible. By early summer, their plan for a "major augmentation" was approved by the governing authorities, including the Joint Chiefs and Ambassador Maxwell Taylor in Saigon. It called for the expansion of Phu Bai into the major "U.S.-only" intercept site and establishment of a regular NSG detachment in addition to the U.S. Marine SIGINT company already there. The plan also called for the implementation of a full-time aerial communications reconnaissance platform (ACRP) program, a near tripling of intercept positions in South Vietnam by the end of 1964, and doubling intercept positions in Thailand. At that time, there were approximately 1,200 SIGINT personnel in the region, so the "augmentation" would set a new ceiling at just over 1,700 by September. That was an increase of about 45%, and the NSA expansion was well under way by mid-summer.

First ASA casualties—1964

On 09 February 1964, the 3rd RRU suffered two more casualties of the war. Spc.4 Arthur Glover and Pfc. Donald Taylor were killed at Tan Son Nhut Air Base when VC guerillas radio-detonated two bombs buried under the bleachers at an inter-unit softball game. Pershing Field was used exclusively by U.S, service teams, and the bleachers were filled with soldiers, sailors, and MAGV personnel. One of the injured was a female U.S. aid mission employee.

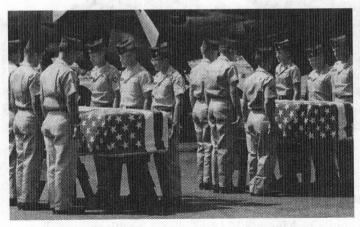

**3rd RRU renders honors to the flag-draped coffins
of Taylor and Glover (Photo: INSCOM)**

Donald Richard Taylor was a communications center specialist (72B). He was twenty-one years old and a native of Harrisburg, Pennsylvania.

Arthur Wayne Glover was a Signal Security Specialist (05G) from Bluff City, Tennessee. He was twenty-four years old and engaged to be married. Just two weeks before, Glover's mother had sent him a package of clothing for the orphaned children he had been working with. Wayne was an orphan himself and had been adopted by the Glovers. He was volunteering at the Sancta Maria Orphanage in Saigon which was being sponsored by the 3rd RRU.

When Saigon fell, most of the Sancta Maria orphans were evacuated to Australia, but those who had mental or physical disabilities were left behind and continued to live in the original orphanage building in Ho Chi Minh City (Saigon). In the years following the war, the Arthur Wayne Glover Memorial Fund was created by the Southeast Asia ASA Veterans Association and proceeds from that fund have helped to support those aging orphans who were unable to leave.

Truck-load of Davis Station's finest—1964 (Photo: © Wayne Robertson)

Big push from the North

In the middle of March 1964, the signal intelligence analysts at NSA began to see a major expansion in communist communication networks across South Vietnam. Two new control stations also came online in Laos, and communications activity exceeded anything they had seen before. They were seeing the first phases of Hanoi's new "Southern Strategy."

After the deaths of Presidents Diem and Kennedy, the Politburo in Hanoi met to consider the situation and determine their plan of action. The decision was made to implement a stronger, more confrontational strategy and to step up attacks on ARVN forces in the South. They felt that now was the time to strike and finish off the South before the Americans became more involved. Politically, Saigon remained in chaos.

By summer, huge caches of Soviet and Communist Chinese weapons and supplies were coming down the Ho Chi Minh Trail through eastern Laos, and Hanoi had ordered the 808th Battalion, the first units of the North Vietnamese regular army (NVA), to head south. A few months later, two units of the 325th NVA Division followed them, and by early 1965, they were positioned just across the Laotian border from South Vietnam's Quang Nam and Kontum Provinces.

There were increased levels of communications and other clues during the summer months, but NSA had no proof that regular army units were moving southward. Then in November, the radio network in Laos that was supporting the troop movements changed its procedures to that routinely used by NVA units stationed outside North Vietnam, and reliable sources in Laos reported seeing NVA troops moving through Laos. The war had just moved into another very dangerous phase.

Westmoreland comes on board

President Johnson was becoming impatient with what he considered a side issue: Vietnam. The war was interfering with his domestic agenda. According to Bill Moyer, the White House Press Secretary to LBJ, the President said, "I want 'em to get off their butts and get out in those jungles and whip hell out of some communists. And then I want 'em to leave me alone, because I've got some bigger things to do right here at home."

In June 1964 Johnson appointed General William C. Westmoreland as Commander, Military Advisory Command-Vietnam. Shortly after arriving in Vietnam, Westmoreland received a letter from Major General William Yarborough, the commanding General of the U.S. Army Special Warfare Center at Fort Bragg. The generals had been friends and classmates at West Point. In the letter Yarbrough provided the following advice: "Under no circumstances that I can foresee should U.S. strategy ever be twisted into a 'requirement' for placing U.S. combat divisions into the Vietnamese conflict…I can almost guarantee you that U.S. divisions…could find no targets of a size or configuration which would warrant division-sized attacks in a military case."

**Gen. Westmoreland and Lt. Col. Owen, C.O., 3ʳᵈ RRU
at the ASA Day celebration, Davis Station, Saigon–
September 1964 (Photo: © Robert Flanagan)**

CHAPTER 5

TRUTH, LIES, AND CONSEQUENCES

The *U.S.S. Maddox* (Photo: U.S. Navy)

There have always been questions about what actually happened in the Gulf of Tonkin on 2 to 4 August 1964. The facts with regard to August 2 are reasonably clear. The destroyer *U.S.S. Maddox* was in the Gulf monitoring radio and radar signals following an attack by the South Vietnamese on two islands claimed by the North. At about 1500 hours, the ship was attacked by three North Vietnamese Navy (NVN) torpedo boats of the 135th Torpedo Squadron.

The *Maddox* had been patrolling along the coast of North Vietnam as part of the CIA's OPLAN 34A. The so-called "Desoto" missions were designed to assist South Vietnamese forces by relaying intelligence and coordinating commando raids against the North. *Maddox* was loaded with a wealth of intelligence gathering equipment and an NSG detachment that had been engaged in SIGINT operations when it was attacked. On board the *Maddox*, Capt. John J. Herrick, commander of the mission, ordered the ship's captain, Commander Herbert Ogier, to have gun crews open fire on the attacking boats and called for assistance from the aircraft carrier *U.S.S. Ticonderoga*, which was providing air support. The *Maddox* hit one of the craft before three U.S. F-8 Crusader jets arrived on the scene to strafe the NVN boats. It was all over in about twenty minutes with one NVN boat sunk and the other two badly damaged. The North Vietnamese had ten casualties, including four dead. There were no U.S. casualties. The *Maddox* was ordered to withdraw from the area and await further instructions.

On August 3rd and 4th, the South Vietnamese Navy using PT boats launched two more attacks against North Vietnamese targets: the radar installations at Cape Venhson and an installation at Cau Ron estuary. The commanders of *Maddox* and *C. Turner Joy* were said to be "aware" of the SVN operation and attempting to avoid becoming associated with it, but Admiral Sharp ordered the U.S. ships to "assert our legitimate rights" and stay close.

In reality, the two U.S. ships were probably part of the South Vietnamese operation. Missions of that type were frequently used to expose radar capabilities and defense communications networks. Knowing that there was an NSG detachment onboard *Maddox*, it is unlikely just coincidental that the ship and its partner were in the area when the SVN attacks took place. In Taiwan, Nationalist Chinese jet fighters would depart the north end of the island on a regular basis and intentionally violate Communist Chinese airspace. All of the CHICOM radar networks and anti-aircraft warning systems would react, and the data was intercepted and recorded by ASA, USAFSS, and NSG units monitoring the exercise. USAFSS Chinese linguists at Shu Lin Kou A.B. in Taiwan would also monitor the voice communications of the communist fighter units that scrambled to intercept the intruders. NSA had been launching such missions against the Soviets since 1946.

The second event on the night of 04 August has been the primary subject of conjecture, argument, accusation, Congressional investigation, and scorn for much of the past four decades. At approximately 2000 hours, the *Maddox* intercepted messages that gave Capt. Herrick "the impression" that his ship and *C. Turner Joy*, were going to be attacked again by six NVN PT boats. Herrick called for air support from the *Ticonderoga,* and eight Crusaders were dispatched to assist the *Maddox.* The weather was poor, and the night was pitch-black. Neither the pilots nor the ship's crew ever saw an enemy craft, but at about 2200 hours, sonar operators reported detecting torpedoes approaching. The destroyers were turned to maneuver out of the presumed path of the torpedoes and began to fire blindly into the night. At one point the *Turner Joy*'s guns were pointed at the *Maddox.*

When the incident was over some two hours later, U.S. officers reported sinking "two, possibly three North Vietnamese craft." In fact, no one on the U.S. ships or planes was certain that they had seen any sign of the enemy or detected any enemy gunfire. The storms in the area had created freak anomalies affecting both radar and sonar, and their readings were confusing at best. Capt. Herrick went on record immediately, voicing his doubts about the reported sinkings to his superiors and urging a "thorough reconnaissance in daylight."

The result of the two Gulf of Tonkin incidents, the real one and the alleged one, were enormous and of great historical significance. A "grim-faced" President Johnson appeared on nationwide television to denounce the attacks in international waters and to inform the American people that he was ordering air strikes against North Vietnamese naval facilities. Defense Secretary McNamara, who had pressed for the President to bomb the north in the past, knew that the August 4th attack claim was in doubt, but did not tell the President before Johnson went on the air to give his address.

Johnson thought he had the latest intelligence and did not know that part of what he was telling the public was of questionable validity. In his published work, *Essay: 40th Anniversary of the Gulf of Tonkin Incident*, John Prados states that in a telephone conversation on the morning of August 4th, McNamara had told the President that the *Maddox* was "allegedly to be attacked tonight." McNamara and the President went on to discuss what retaliation they could carry out for the attack (that had not happened), including bombing targets in North Vietnam. An hour later, when McNamara called in the first report that the alleged attack had begun, he had already prepared a list of options. This would seem to indicate that McNamara had advance knowledge that the "alleged" attack was going to take place, which opened up a whole new set of questions.

In less than a week, President Johnson sent a joint resolution to Congress referred to as *The Gulf of Tonkin Resolution*. It would give the President authority, without a formal declaration of war by Congress, to take all necessary measures to repel attacks against U.S. forces and to take all steps necessary for the defense of U.S. allies in Southeast Asia, including the use of military force. It passed almost unanimously, and the Johnson administration used that resolution as a blank check to begin a rapid escalation of U.S. military involvement in the war.

Within the U.S. government, and throughout forty years of historic speculation and political posturing, no clear picture of what actually happened the night of August 4, 1964, had been revealed, until 2002. NSA officially maintained that the second incident occurred, but NSA historian, Robert J. Hanyok, in his journal *Spartans in Darkness: American SIGINT and the Indochina War, 1945-1975*, came to the conclusion that "no attack happened that night." Hanyok maintained that midlevel NSA officers had deliberately skewed the evidence. While researching his work, he found a pattern of uncorrected mistakes, altered intercept times, and legitimate evidence that had been selectively lifted out of context, which convinced him that the material had been deliberately distorted. He concluded that it was done, not for political reasons, but to cover up earlier mistakes, and that neither top NSA officials nor President Johnson knew that the information was incorrect.

Many historians believe that the Johnson Administration would have found reasons to escalate military action against Hanoi, even without the Gulf of Tonkin incident, but apparently Johnson had his own doubts about the second attack. He is reported to have told George Ball a few days later: "Hell, those dumb, stupid sailors were just shooting at flying fish!"

Hanyok's in-house journal was published in 2000, but was classified by high-level NSA policy makers who determined that the information was too sensitive to be made public, and the book remained classified for two more years. Hanyok and other government historians pressed to have the information released, and NSA relented in 2002.

Commander James B. Stockdale, who led the flight of Crusader jets from the *Ticonderoga* on August 4th, saw no enemy. He later wrote: "There was absolutely no gunfire except our own, no PT boat wakes, not a candle light let alone a burning ship. None could have been there and not have been seen on such a black night." Stockdale also remarked on the situation: "I had the best seat in the house from which to detect boats, if there were any. I didn't have to look through surface haze and spray like the destroyers did, and yet I could see the destroyers' every move vividly."

Ironically, Vietnamese communist histories may provide the final bit of evidence regarding the alleged second attack. North Vietnamese radar had tracked the *Maddox* for days prior to 2 August, but the ship had not crossed into North Vietnamese territorial waters. Ho Chi Minh told the Politburo in Hanoi, "We need to be prepared, but we will not attack first. If they attack, we will retaliate immediately." General Giap agreed with him. Le Duan, one of the younger, more aggressive members of the Politburo ordered an attack anyway, through military channels on 2 August. Later that day, the order was countermanded, probably by Ho Chi Minh, but it arrived too late to stop the action. The NVN torpedo boats had already been sent to attack the ship. In the face of "Uncle Ho's" great displeasure, it is unlikely that a second attack would have been ordered two days later.

Marines in the house

Phu Bai offered its Marine NSG unit a forward area for intercepting North Vietnamese naval communications. The Marines were especially interested in NVN reactions to U.S. Navy patrols in the Gulf of Tonkin, so it is not surprising that on 2 August 1964, it was Marine operators who accurately foretold of a pending attack on the *U.S.S. Maddox.*

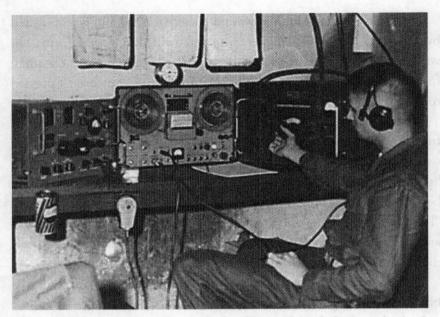

1st Composite Radio Company work area (Photo: U.S.M.C.)

Roger Trussell was on his first tour in Vietnam in August 1964 and was stationed at Det. J, 3rd RRU in Phu Bai. On 02 August, Trussell and two other ASA 058 operators were manning Morse intercept positions in a 292 van. On that particular day, there were three other positions manned by Marines from the 1st Radio Battalion (formerly the 1st Composite Radio Company). One of the Marines, a Lance Corporal, noticed something unusual in the traffic he was monitoring and yelled for a "cryppy" (cryptanalyst). A Marine analyst, Sgt. York, scanned the intercept, immediately ripped the carboned paper off of the machine, and jumped out of the van yelling "Critic!"

The message was from a "Swatow-class" patrol boat, the T-142 to the North Vietnamese naval base at Port Wallut and stated: "[WE] HAVE RECEIVED THE ORDERS. [T]-146 and [T]-142 DID USE [unreadable] HIGH SPEED TO GET TOGETHER [PARALLEL] WITH ENEMY FOLLOWING LAUNCHED TORPEDOES."

"We later learned it was orders for the North Vietnamese boats to attack the American ships in the Gulf of Tonkin," Trussell says. Some minutes after the Morse message was intercepted, the North Vietnamese station switched to voice, and they could hear gun fire in the background.

The station at Phu Bai issued a "critic" (critical message) that alerted all of the relevant commands and the *Maddox* that it was about to be attacked. Phu Bai also added that there were four boats (T-142, T-146, T-166, and T-135) engaged in tracking the "enemy" which was assumed to be "the current Desoto mission." The last paragraph of the intercepted message indicated that the NVN facility at Port Wallut was acting as the shore-based "coordinator/director" for the ongoing surveillance of the "enemy" vessel.

Former Marine Tom Dague was a Morse intercept operator assigned to the 1st Radio Battalion and was "on post" when the *Maddox* was attacked. Dague says, "I think I was there in late 1963 or early 1964, so I guess it was still 1st Radio Company when I got there. When we went to Phu Bai, I think there were fourteen of us that worked side-saddle with 3rd Radio Research (ASA) until about July, and then we moved into our own building next door. Nobody knew why we did that until just before the Gulf of Tonkin, and then they told us what our mission was. We watched the [Desoto] ships all the way up the coast until they went into the gulf and stirred up some shit. I guess I can say I witnessed the start of the war that followed."

Tom continues, "I was there for the Gulf of Tonkin. We monitored the North Vietnamese radar stations on the Gulf for the whole event, including vaporizing them. I think I was on for about thirty-six hours and got mad when they tried to relieve me. I'm sure this isn't classified anymore but my target's call sign was GSHT ["Gee-shit"]. I can still hear him [GSHT]. He came up a week later with a new call, but I nailed him the second he hit the key."

David Ollman was a Marine cryptanalyst and says, "While I was not involved in the incident, I can relate some of the history. I met the Marine who intercepted the attack message....I cannot recall his name, but I do know that he received a Bronze Star for his work. As for 'Sgt. York,' that was Master Sgt. York…as a Sgt. I worked with him at Ft. Meade (where we became friends), Vietnam, and 2nd Radio Bn after we both returned from Vietnam. He was one of the best 'cryppies' ever and was a real mentor to me…He was on his second tour and running the cryptanalyst shop in Da Nang when I got there in July 1967. He showed me the ropes, sent me to Phu Bai to work with the Army for a few days, and then let me work while he built a computer in his spare time. We worked together as cryptanalysts many times, and in one of our conversations, he confirmed to me the Tonkin Gulf intercept…"

Jack Bowditch was a Marine stationed at Phu Bai in 1964. Bowditch recalls another Marine named Red Katz taking him to the back room and showing him a message that Katz had intercepted about the attack on the *U.S.S. Maddox*. The message had been badly garbled, but the cryppy had copied enough traffic to recognize it as an attack message. When monitoring the motor torpedo boats, the analysts looked for what was called a "stutter group" at the beginning of the message. Attack messages began with a five number code group such as 00000 or 11111. They had broken the code and could read the messages.

The Marines of the 1st Composite Radio Company and Det. J, 3rd RRU ASA at Phu Bai were recognized for their efforts and their success during the Gulf of Tonkin Incident. They were awarded the Meritorious Unit citation for their actions.

Circle the wagons

On 01 November 1964, The Viet Cong launched a fierce pre-dawn rocket and mortar assault on Bien Hoa Air Base, located twelve miles north of Saigon. It was the first direct attack by the VC against an American installation in Vietnam. A squadron of B-57 bombers was grounded, with five destroyed and fifteen more seriously damaged. The attack resulted in the deaths of five Americans, two South Vietnamese, and nearly a hundred other casualties.

Gen. Maxwell Taylor had been named U.S. Ambassador to South Vietnam by the Johnson Administration in July. He stated that the attack was "a deliberate act of escalation" and called for an immediate and appropriate reprisal. The Joint Chiefs called for a series of retaliatory strikes, but the attacks were never ordered. The government in Saigon had been in total disarray since the overthrow of the Diem regime and was extremely unstable. The U.S. Presidential election was two days away. It was feared that retaliatory attacks could have a negative impact on the political situations on both sides of the Pacific, and President Johnson dismissed all recommendations for retaliation against North Vietnam. He was expected to win the election, and was taking no action that might sway public opinion against him.

Senator Barry Goldwater was running on the Republican ticket against President Johnson. Goldwater tried to make the war in Vietnam a campaign issue, charging that the Democrats were leading the nation blindly into "Lyndon Johnson's war in Vietnam…American sons and grandsons are being killed by communist bullets and communist bombs…and we have yet to hear a word of truth about why they are dying." But Goldwater's message failed to resonate with the American people. On November 3rd, LBJ received 61% of the popular vote and 486 of the 538 Electoral College votes. It was already known among the ASA rank and file in the 3rd RRU that U.S. combat troops were being sent to Vietnam.

Armed and dangerous

On 01 November 1964, the designation of Detachment J, 3rd RRU, was changed to the 8th RRU, and as the base grew, it became an ever increasing security problem. The location was near the Phu Bai Airport in a flat open area of sand dunes. NSA's expansion meant increased numbers of military personnel and large amounts of valuable and highly classified equipment in an exposed area. That compounded the risk that the 8th RRU would become a prime VC target.

New bunker construction—Phu Bai (Photo: © James McInnes)

ASA took what steps it could to ensure the physical security of the base. They established and maintained radio contact with the nearby ARVN National Training Center, which normally had at least one ARVN regiment in residence. There was also an ARVN division and corps headquarters, a U.S. Marine detachment on-call to augment the security force if needed and the 34th ARVN artillery battery was just down the road.

Sandbag detail at Phu Bai—1964 (Photo: © James McInnes)

Late in November, a group of combat trainers arrived from the Delta area in southwestern South Vietnam. Most of the ASA troops had not had weapons training since their basic training some years earlier, and it is doubtful that any of them had been exposed to advanced weapons training. These men were the cream of the intellectual crop. They had been hand-picked for their intelligence and analytical abilities; they were not combat soldiers.

Weapons training at Phu Bai (Photo: © L. Long)

Over the course of several days, all of the ASA soldiers received instruction in the use of the new M-14 "battle rifle," the M-60 machine gun, and the M-79 grenade launcher. The unit also received three armored personnel carriers (APCs) equipped with .50 cal. machine guns. In addition to all the new training and fire power, other defensive measures were put in place; barbed wire fences were erected, mine fields were laid out, and bunkers were built for a perimeter defense. They were as prepared as time, terrain, and manpower would allow.

AUTHOR'S NOTE: Letter to Gary Blackburn from Lonnie Long, 26 November 1964, 8th Radio Research (APO 158), Phu Bai, South Vietnam—

"I got your letter several days ago after it was forwarded from Taiwan. Yes, I'm in Vietnam and it's hell. I'm in the northern part of the country outside of a town called Hue. I work straight days and train every night. I'm the .50 cal. machine gunner on an armored personnel carrier. The VC haven't bothered us yet but frankly we expect to be hit before the first of the year. We are about 400 strong and well trained [this may have been wishful thinking]. *There is absolutely nothing to do in town or on base and we cannot go out after 6:00 p.m. because the VC controls the area at night."*

New APCs at Phu Bai–1964 (Photo: © James McInnes)

Christmas in paradise

In December, eighty ASA soldiers from the 8th RRU were fortunate enough to be flown to Da Nang to see Bob Hope who was making his first trip to Vietnam. His troupe included the irrepressible Jerry Colona, guitarist Bob Jones, comedian John Bubbles, and of course the GI favorites: Anita Bryant, Janis Page, Anna Maria Alberghetti, Jill St. John, and Miss World, England's Ann Snyder. Anita Bryant closed the show with "Silent Night." There was not a dry eye anywhere.

On Christmas Eve, the Viet Cong bombed the Brinks Hotel in heavily fortified Saigon. It was also known as the Brinks Bachelor

Officer's Quarters and housed U.S. Army officers. Two Americans were killed, an officer and an NCO, and fifty-eight injured, including American military and Vietnamese civilians. The VC detonated a car packed with 200 lbs. of explosives that had been parked beneath the hotel, intending to show that they could strike anywhere, at any time, and that the Americans were just as vulnerable as anyone else.

On Christmas Day, Ambassador Taylor sent Washington a message: "Hanoi will get the word that, despite our present tribulations, there is still bite in the tiger they call paper, and the U.S. stock in this part of the world will take sharp rise. Some of our local squabbles will probably disappear in enthusiasm which our action would generate." However, President Johnson refused to act. Most of his advisors favored retaliation and the introduction of U.S. combat troops, but Rusk and McNamara were opposed. In the end, Johnson declined to act, saying that an escalation during the Christmas season would be inappropriate and could damage public morale.

PART II

1965–THE YEAR OF TOTAL COMMITMENT

CHAPTER 6

FIRST BIRD DOWN

"Capt. Carlisle...Lt. Col. Owen, Commander of 3rd RRU and assorted others can be seen clustered about the remains."–Robert Flanagan (Photo: U.S. Army)

On 14 January 1965, the 3rd RRU lost its first aircraft. The U-6 Beaver, piloted by Capt. Ray McNewel with DF operator Spc. Dan Bonfield, was flying an ARDF mission over an area northwest of Saigon when it was allegedly shot down by the Viet Cong at 10:32 a.m. They are sure of the time because Dan Bonfield's watch was crushed and stopped during the ensuing crash, but there is some question as to what caused the crash. McNewel put out a "mayday" call and piloted the aircraft into a deadstick landing on the Michelin rubber plantation. As the aircraft smashed through the trees, the wings were sheared off, and the fuselage rolled over on its side as it slid to a halt.

The plantation was located about halfway between the Cambodian border and Saigon, and was an important VC base and staging area; there were always Viet Cong in the vicinity. After the crash, Capt. McNewel pulled the injured Bonfield out from under his radio gear and managed to drag him clear of the wreckage. They were already coming under fire from VC troops who had seen the plane come down, and Bonfield was seriously hurt.

McNewel and Bonfield were able to get to some cover, and then local villagers arrived to help them. The villagers were not sympathetic to the VC activity in the area and hid the two Americans under a hut until the danger had passed. They then led them to friendly forces who took Bonfield to a hospital. Bonfield spent several hours getting his mangled right arm patched up before being transported back to Davis Station at Tan Son Nhut.

Another ASA soldier, Randall A. "Randy" Nicholas, was a DF operator flying in the same area with Capt. Carlisle in a new RU-8F. He remembers, "[We were] at 30,000 feet checking out the cabin pressurization when we heard the 'mayday' call and subsequent crash. Never have I gone from thirty-k to 500 feet so fast." He continues, "We did what we could to coordinate the rescue. Thank God he [Dan] was alive and 'well' after the rescue. Dan and I were good friends..."

Dan Bonfield's arm was badly injured, and a few days later he was flown to a hospital at Clark Air Base in the Philippines to recover. When he was finally discharged from the hospital, he was sent to Valley Forge, Pennsylvania, where he stayed until March 1965 and then on to Homestead Air Force Base, Florida, to finish out his enlistment. He was discharged in July 1965.

The official investigation by NSA concluded that the plane was not "shot down" but had experienced engine failure. Dan Bonfield, however, believed and maintained for the rest of his life that the plane was shot down.

As a side note, Roger Trussell states, "The captain that Nicholas is talking about was Capt. Carlisle from Arkansas, one of my favorite pilots. He later landed a Beaver on Michelin rubber plantation and shot several holes in the wing so we could continue drawing hostile fire pay.

MACV had threatened to cut off our hostile fire pay because we were not reporting any hits. What a character!"

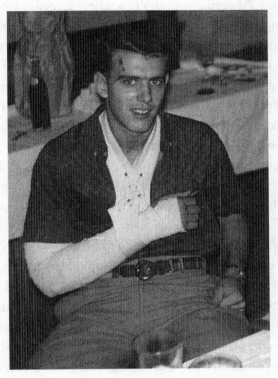

Dan Bonfield after plane crash–January 1965
(Photo: © Wayne Robertson)

Randy Nicholas says, "Capt. Carlisle, what a guy. He served as an enlisted man in the Korean War. In 1972, my wife and I went to Germany to visit her mom and dad who were stationed there. While there, we went to the officer's club one night, and who is there but… Carlisle, still a hot-shot and still a pain in the ass. During that night, one of Carlisle's young hot-shot pilots, who was in uniform, wanted to give me his wings when he found out that as operators we were not authorized wings. Carlisle said to him, 'Son, when you have flown as many combat missions as Nick and I have, then you can give away your damned wings.'"

Turning up the heat

In February, the VC stepped up their attacks on U.S. installations. Before dawn on 7 February, 300 VC soldiers staged a bloody raid on the MACV compound at Pleiku, lobbing dozens of mortar rounds into the barracks area. Simultaneously, sappers penetrated the perimeter of nearby Camp Holloway placing charges on or near most of the aircraft. The attacks lasted about fifteen minutes and resulted in eight killed, 126 wounded and twenty-five aircraft damaged or destroyed. Twelve hours after the attack, President Johnson launched "Operation Flaming Dart" to bomb selected targets in North Vietnam. A total of forty-nine U.S. fighter-bombers from the U.S.S. Coral Sea and the U.S.S. Hancock attacked the North Vietnamese barracks in Dong Hoi, just north of the 17th Parallel [the DMZ]. The next day, the President ordered the withdrawal of all U.S. dependents from South Vietnam.

On 10 February at 8 pm, the Viet Cong struck in Qui Nhon, setting off 100 lbs. of explosives under the Viet Cuong Hotel, which was being used to house the enlisted men of the 149th Transportation Detachment, U.S. Army. The powerful charge was detonated on the first floor of the building causing it to collapse and "pancake" the floors, each on top of the next, trapping many of the men in rubble thirty feet deep. It took days to dig everyone out. The final casualty toll was twenty-three U.S. soldiers dead, twenty-one injured and fourteen Vietnamese injured. In response, President Johnson ordered an even larger attack against the North Vietnamese. A combined force of about 160 U.S. and South Vietnamese fighter-bombers launched "Flaming Dart II," targeting Chap Le and Chanh Hoa, also located just north of the 17th Parallel.

February 19 brought another attempted military coup against General Khanh. Although there was hesitation and opposition in Washington to another regime change, the coup had been encouraged by U.S. Ambassador, Gen. Maxwell Taylor. Taylor and Khanh had developed an intense personal hatred for each other which had made it nearly impossible for them to work together. Taylor had asked Khanh to voluntarily step down from his leadership role, and Khanh had responded by threatening to expel Taylor from the country. He had also launched a media campaign against the ambassador. Taylor had threatened to cut off military aid, thus upping the stakes with Khanh, but that was not going to happen because South Vietnam could not survive without it, and that was not considered to be in the best interests of the U.S.

Taylor told Washington: "I can well visualize the necessity at some time of using full U.S. leverage...to induce our Vietnamese friends to get Khanh out of position of commander-in-chief and to install their very best governmental line-up." The coup ultimately failed, but General Khanh was forced to accept a vote of "no confidence" by the Armed Forces Council in Saigon, and a new military/civilian government was put in place led by Prime Minister Dr. Phan Huy Quat, a moderate Buddhist.

Khanh was ordered to leave the country and agreed to go if given a dignified send-off to save face. The other generals arranged a ceremonial farewell at Tan Son Nhut on February 24. Military bands played, and Ambassador Taylor met him at the airport. The foes managed smiles and handshakes for the media cameras. To make the coup "appear as much as possible the doing of the Vietnamese themselves," Taylor had made no public statement after Khanh's ouster on orders from the State Department. Khanh then left as ambassador-at-Large for a meaningless world tour, starting with a report to the United Nations in New York City.

February also saw the onset of Operation Rolling Thunder, America's sustained bombing campaign against North Vietnam. It was given government approval and officially started on 24 February 1965, though the first attack did not occur until 2 March when 100 U.S. and South Vietnamese planes attacked an ammunition base at Xom Bang. It was to be a demonstration of America's near total air supremacy and was initiated in an effort to demoralize the North Vietnamese people and undermine their government, but it did not achieve the results that President Johnson and his advisors envisioned.

CHAPTER 7
THE MARINES HAVE LANDED

U.S. Marines land at Da Nang (Photo: U.S.M.C.)

On 01 January 1965, U.S. troop strength in Vietnam had stood at 23,000 men, and during the first quarter, U.S. casualties averaged twenty-five KIA and 152 WIA per month, but all was about to change drastically. On 08 March, the 9th Marine Expeditionary Brigade commanded by Brig. Gen. Frederick J. Karch landed at Da Nang. One battalion arrived by air, and the other battalion, in full battle dress and armed with M-14 rifles, landed at China Beach. The 3,500 U.S. Marines were the first battalion-sized deployment of U.S. combat troops in South Vietnam. Their sole mission was to defend the American air base at Da Nang and prevent the kind of attack that had killed eight Americans at Pleiku airfield the month before, but their arrival was indicative of something far more significant. The American advisory role in the war was transforming into a much more direct and active role by the U.S.

military. By the end of March, two more Marine battalions would be authorized for deployment to South Vietnam and would secretly prepare for the first American offensive actions.

As U.S. combat troops began to arrive in Vietnam, there was a feeling of optimism. Although the average soldier or marine was apprehensive about combat, there was a prevailing belief that they would take care of the VC in short order and be heading back home soon. The possibility of losing the war was not even a consideration. These Marines were the best of the best. They were part of the greatest military power the world had ever seen. Who could stop them?

As American forces came into the country, they were not alone. The first South Korean infantry units had arrived in Binh Dinh province on 26 February 1965, with more to follow, and the Prime Minister of Australia, Sir Robert Menzies, announced he was sending an infantry battalion along with an armored personnel carrier troop, a signals troop, and a logistic support company. They would eventually be joined, in various capacities, by soldiers from New Zealand, Thailand, and the Philippines. Nationalist China (Taiwan) wanted to be included, but there were major problems involved, including the centuries-old antipathy of the Vietnamese toward Chinese of any variety within their country and the possibility of drawing Communist Chinese ground troops into the fray. Nationalist Chinese contributions would be very limited and low key. By June U.S. military strength in Vietnam reached 52,000; the 1st Battalion of the Royal Australian Army arrived at Vung Tau, and construction began on the giant U.S. Navy base at Cam Ranh Bay.

Limited war or limited leadership

In spite of the Johnson Administration's determination to escalate U.S. involvement in the war in Vietnam, there was no indication that the President or his advisors had any real understanding of the goals or long-term aims of Ho Chi Minh or the North Vietnamese leadership. In his book *This Time We Win, Revisiting the Tet Offensive,* James S.

Robbins wrote: "The U.S. conducted a limited war against an enemy with unlimited objectives."

In a speech at Johns Hopkins University in April 1965, President Johnson stated that he sought to "convince the leaders of North Vietnam, and all who seek to share their conquest, of a very simple fact: We will not be defeated….Armed hostility is futile. Our resources are equal to any challenge. Because we fight for values and we fight for principles, rather than territory or colonies, our patience and our determination are unending."

Unfortunately, the noble rhetoric of Johnson's speech would have little positive impact on Hanoi, at least not from the U.S. viewpoint. The President had just forfeited the strategic initiative to the North Vietnamese and their Communist bloc supporters. He did not tell them that they would be defeated; only that they could not win. It was now up to Hanoi to determine when the fighting would end, and they would have ample opportunity to test American resolve and to determine if the patience of the American people was a durable and long suffering as the President envisioned.

Enter the direct support units

On June 25th, the 404th ASA Detachment was deployed to Bien Hoa in support of the 173rd Airborne Brigade under the cover designation of Detachment 1, 3rd RRU. This was the first direct support unit (DSU) to be deployed in Vietnam, and it would alter the way the ASA supported the war.

The ASA direct support units were intelligence-gathering units that were attached to regular Army units and presented a wide-ranging number of challenges. Traditionally the supported command would provide the attached unit with food, fuel, ammunition, etc., and if the arrangement was to be long term, their responsibility was expanded to include personnel assignment, promotions, awards, training, equipment replacement and military justice. However, when the ASA, and more importantly NSA, became involved, tradition was no longer a consideration. The arrangement between the ASA DSUs and their supported commands had entirely new rules.

ASA/NSA retained control over the personnel assignments and day to day administration of the DSUs. All of their personnel held such high security clearances that only ASA administrators could have access to their records. They also made it clear that they were in control of the mission assignments and tasking of their units, which put them immediately at odds with the commanders of the supporting commands. The radio research detachments were frequently placed in the impossible position of trying to respond to both their ASA mission and the combat mission assigned by the commanders of their supported units.

ASA's primary justification for maintaining control of their units was that they required special protection and special direction. Most of the supported commanders had no experience or any real understanding of how to use the ASA units, so ASA felt that they must retain control in order to successfully accomplish their mission; however, logistically it was a nightmare. If the units were on the move, and many of them moved frequently, it was nearly impossible for ASA to maintain contact with their DSUs, so they were largely on their own. Lost personnel records, missed promotions and awards, and the lack of other normal administrative support was just a small part of the problems that this "army within an army" created.

There was also the problem that the DSU's actual mission was so highly classified that the information they collected was designated "special intelligence" and was often filtered by NSA/MACV. As a result, they were unable to share the information directly with the units they were assigned to support. One of the true delights in the life of a young ASA soldier in the field was to tell lieutenants, captains, majors, and even higher ranking officers that they were not allowed in the ASA operations tents, bunkers, or vans. Those areas were strictly off limits to those who did not have "the need to know."

NSA was primarily focused on strategic intelligence, so any tactical intelligence that might have been of benefit to the supported commanders was usually outdated by the time it was filtered through Ft. Meade and made its way back to the field in Vietnam. Sometimes, when the unit the DSU was supporting finally got back the "intel" it had produced, it was marked: "From a Usually Reliable Source." Frequently, the only intelligence firebase or garrison commanders received from their DSUs was the inference that an attack might be underway when the ASA team hurriedly tore down its antennas and prepared to move out. It should be added, however, that as the smaller DSUs worked in the field with the units they were supporting, many of the ASA soldiers found ways around the structured relationships, and established informal channels of communication that were beneficial to all concerned.

And it got bigger

On 24 July the first U.S. aircraft was shot down by a surface to air missile (SAM) over North Vietnam, and on 28 July, President Johnson addressed the American people on national television. He said: "I have today ordered to Vietnam the Airmobile Division and certain other forces which will raise our fighting strength from 75,000 to 125,000 men almost immediately. Additional forces will be needed later, and they will be sent as requested." General Westmoreland had requested forty-four additional combat battalions, and the President had approved his request. The war was escalating at a rapid pace.

The August 6, 1965, issue of *Time* magazine reported that a grey-hulled U.S. troop transport had slipped into Cam Ranh Bay, "its decks aswarm with the 'Screaming Eagle' of the U.S. 101st Airborne Division…" In a display of buoyant optimism, *Time* stated: "Since the onset of the summer rains two months ago, the stain of red domination has spread swiftly; the communists now control 65% of the countryside and fully 55% of the country's 16 million population….U.S. intelligence estimates place the number of communist combatants in South Vietnam at 145,00 to 165,000."

Time also made reference to the operations of the 8th RRU at Phu Bai: "Pivotal to the U.S. strategy is the necklace of enclaves…Phu Bai, ten miles southeast of the ancient Buddhist center of Hue, is the northernmost of the strongholds. From its bulbous Hill 225, a battalion of U.S. Marines under the command of Lt. Col. Woodrow 'Roughhouse' Taylor guards a 6,000 ft. airstrip and an adjoining installation known as 'the Radio Research Unit.' which is believed to be engaged in jamming North Vietnamese radar, monitoring communist radio traffic, and guiding air strikes against the North." Obviously, *Time* had no clue with regard to the true mission and purpose of the RRUs that had been operating very effectively in South Vietnam for over four years.

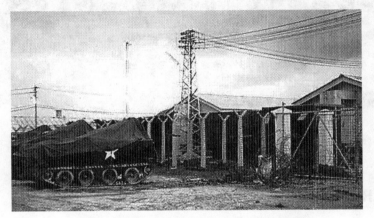

Det J, 8th RRU (Photo: © James McInnes)

What the *Time* article failed to mention was that Phu Bai had also gotten bigger and better. ASA's expansion of the 8th RRU included a headquarters and a headquarters company with enough security guards to man eleven guard posts twenty-four hours a day, in addition to a 221-man service company for operational control, radiotelephone collection, processing, operational maintenance and logistical support. When everything was operational, it would greatly increase their coverage of targets in North Vietnam and Laos.

To limit budgetary and construction restraints, ASA used prefabricated trailer units complete with generators and hardware. Their only real concerns were site preparation, roads, security fencing, exterior utilities and concrete slabs for the main buildings and power plants. The expansion was virtually complete by the middle of May.

Canvas Castle Motel—Air conditioning, wall-to-wall pallets, floor show nightly! (Photo: © L. Long)

3rd RRU's ARDF makes *Saigon News*

On 06 August, the English-language edition of *Saigon Daily News* reported an interesting story. With the headline "V.C. Divisional HQs in Cambodia" and datelined "Saigon, Aug. 5 (UPI)," the first paragraph read: "The Division's sanctuary was tracked down by secret radio detection equipment aboard American surveillance planes. The new equipment was put to use after the Americans lost track of the 325th's headquarters. They were formerly able to pinpoint within a few hundred yards the location of the communist radio transmitters."

"Reliable American intelligence sources" had told UPI that "the Reds" had shifted the headquarters of the NVA 325th Division to a Cambodian hideout about 270 miles North of Saigon. This is a portion of an article that Lonnie Long clipped from the Saigon Daily News in August 1965. Considering the highly classified nature of the 3rd RRU's mission, it is surprising that this information was released to UPI or any other press organization.

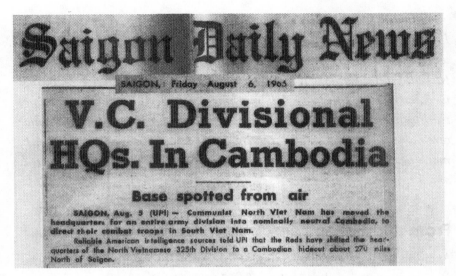

Saigon Daily News (Photo: © L. Long)

Now you see'em—

MACV (Military Assistance Command-Vietnam) Command History states that on 09 August 1965, four USAF B-57 Canberra light bombers were presented to the South Vietnamese Air Force.

Martin B-57B "loaned" to V.N.A.F.–August 1965 (Photo: U.S. Air Force)

PERSONAL OBSERVATION From Lonnie Long: "One morning as I walked out of the back gate at Davis Station onto the flight line, on my way to our aircraft, I observed several B-57s that had been flown in and parked. Over a period of the first few days of August, the U.S.A.F. markings were removed and the V.N.A.F. markings applied. As that was happening, workmen were constructing bleachers. A few days later, I walked by a major ceremony with a lot of fanfare. The next day, I observed the V.N.A.F. markings being removed and replaced by U.S.A.F. The B-57s departed, and I never saw them again."

From another voice

Aviation blogger Dr. J. P. Santiago of Dallas/Ft. Worth, Texas, seems to corroborate the observation of L. Long. Dr. Santiago maintains an aviation trivia blog, and on August 16, 2010, he wrote: "It wasn't until August 1965 that the formal announcement was made that the B-57 was going to be operated by the V.N.A.F. At a formal ceremony on 9 August 1965 at Tan Son Nhut, a U.S.A.F. B-57 was flown in and repainted with V.N.A.F. insignia and a prominent South Vietnamese flag on the tail. The 'U.S. Air Force' titles were removed but were obvious from the shiny areas left behind where the lettering had been buffed off. This B-57 was displayed with all the various armament stores it could carry, including one inadvertently armed 500 lb. bomb.

"Before the ceremony, three dual trainer B-57Cs were flown in from Clark A.B. in the Philippines and repainted with V.N.A.F. markings. General Ky, who by now was the premier of South Vietnam, and the previously trained pilots were given quick familiarization training to perform a fly-by during the ceremony. Having taken off before the ceremony, each pilot had an American instructor in the back seat. During the formation fly-by, Ky himself had to relinquish control of 'his' B-57 to his instructor, as he had not been present during all of the previous day's familiarization training. After a spirited fly by and landing, once the B-57Cs landed and were at the far end of the runway and out of sight of the assembled guests, the U.S.A.F. instructor pilots climbed out of their back seats and the three jets were taxied to the ceremony area by their V.N.A.F. pilots and Premier Ky, which, of course, had the desired propaganda effect. As soon as the ceremony ended, the three B-57s had their U.S.A.F. markings reapplied and were flown back to Clark A.B."

CHAPTER 8

THE 3ᴿᴰ RRU-AVIATION SECTION AT WAR

One of the original 3ʳᵈ RRU Beavers–Tail #682 (Photo: © Al Russo)

On 18 August 1965, the U.S. Marines launched the first major military operation involving U.S. ground forces in Vietnam: Operation Starlite. Earlier in the month, the 3ʳᵈ RRU's Aviation Section, flying routine ARDF missions over northern South Vietnam, had picked up a heavy volume of VC Morse code radio transmissions coming from just south of the Marine air base at Chu Lai. By mid-August, the ASA aircraft had discovered the source of the transmissions and identified the VC unit sending them. The transmitter belonged to the HQ of the two-thousand-man 1st VC Regiment, which was secretly gathering its forces on the Van Tuong Peninsula, fifteen miles south of Chu Lai. The information was forwarded to General Lewis Walt, Commander of the 3rd Marine Amphibious

Force, who immediately launched a combined land-air-amphibious operation aimed at surprising and destroying the VC Regiment.

The operation commenced with the onshore landing of the 3rd Battalion of the 3rd Marine Division. At the same time, the 2nd Battalion of the 4th Marine Division flew into landing zones to the west. The battle was hard-fought as the Marines moved from one VC defensive position to the next, but within a few days, the remnants of the VC regiment were pinned down along the coast and destroyed by a combination of ground fire, air strikes, and naval artillery.

By 24 August, the Marines reported that they had destroyed two battalions of the VC regiment, killing an estimated 700 VC troops. The Marines' losses were substantial as well due to the fierceness of the fighting, with forty-five men killed and over 200 wounded. Two Medals of Honor were awarded, the first of the Vietnam War.

Despite the heavy losses, NSA considered the success of Operation Starlite to be SIGINT's most important accomplishment in Vietnam up to that time. The ARDF units had proven to be a key factor, not only in identifying the initial threat but also in helping to bring about the U.S. victory. General John McChristian, Chief of the MACV Intelligence Staff, and General Walt both acknowledged that SIGINT had been indispensable in the operation. McChristian called SIGINT "the confirming catalyst which led to our decision to act," and Walt termed it "a clinching factor in the decision to launch this operation."

Unfortunately, despite the U.S. victory, SIGINT gathered over the next few days would indicate that the majority of the 1st VC Regiment had managed to escape from General Walt's trap. In addition, according to a declassified NSA history, radio intercepts showed that "within two days of the battle, the 1st VC Regiment's radio network was back on the air."

Supply & demand

During the summer of 1965, the ASA struggled to meet the demand for their talented "spooks." The war was escalating and expanding at an incredible pace. At the same time, ASA was rapidly establishing, manning, equipping, and training new units as quickly as possible and deploying them to the war zone. Some detachments were formed from existing division support companies so that they could be deployed with the first combat units sent to Vietnam. The first complete ASA DSU to be deployed was the 10th Radio Research Company, supporting the 1st Cavalry Division which arrived in September 1965. The 10th RRU had been assigned to the 1st Cav at Ft. Benning, Georgia, and was reorganized as an air mobile unit like its division.

The second RRC to arrive in Vietnam was the 11th, which deployed from Ft. Campbell, Kentucky, to join the 1st Infantry Division. They were later augmented with an ASA detachment that had deployed earlier with a brigade of the 1st Div.

As each of the units arrived, they were assigned to the 3rd RRU and also attached to the tactical unit they were supporting. The same procedure was followed with most of the RRUs that were deployed, and at its peak, more than 20 RRCs were providing direct support to tactical units in Vietnam.

Summer back home

In July, The Animals released "We Gotta Get Outta This Place." Although it only reached number-thirteen on the U.S. charts, it would become an anthem for the troops in Vietnam. It is still known as "the Vietnam anthem," and every lousy band that played in any military club in the Far East in the late 60s had to know the song.

On August 6, President Johnson signed into law the sweeping Voting Rights Bill. That was the same month the Watts Riots raged for six days in Los Angeles. Fourteen people died, and over a thousand were injured; 3,400 were arrested.

To win, or not

In October 1965, Ambassador Henry Cabot Lodge asked Henry Kissinger to come to Vietnam and provide an assessment of how long it was going to take to pacify the country. After two weeks there, Kissinger delivered a very insightful prognosis: "We have involved ourselves in a war which we knew neither how to win nor how to conclude....We were engaged in a bombing campaign powerful enough to mobilize world opinion against us, but too halfhearted and gradual to be decisive.... No one could really explain to me how, even on the most favorable assumptions about the war in Vietnam, the war was going to end."

While Kissinger was in Vietnam, Ronald Reagan was running for Governor of California. Reagan believed that it was immoral to get into any war if we were not going to make every effort to win it as quickly and effectively as possible, and he summed up in a campaign speech: "If you ask a man to lay down his life for his country, the least you can do is to tell him that he has the right to win....It's silly talking about how many years we will have to stay in the jungles of Vietnam when we could pave the whole country and put parking stripes on it and still be home by Christmas. It's ridiculous to trade bombers for bamboo bridges. If the President is pursuing this thing with all his might to put an end to it as quickly as possible, then I'm behind him. But, there are indications that he is not pursuing it with all his might."

Meanwhile the ASA expansion continued

Co. B, 313th Army Security Agency Battalion was first deployed to South Vietnam under the cover designation of 11th Radio Research Unit and was under the command of the 3rd RRU (53rd USASA Special). They were based at Bien Hoa as a DSU of the 1st Infantry Division.

On 10 August, Detachment 4, 3rd Radio Research Unit was deployed to Vietnam to support Field Force-Vietnam, located in Nha Trang. It would be deactivated on 3 May 1966 and redeployed on 28 July 1968 as the 407th Radio Research Detachment.

On 16 September, Co. C, 313th ASA Battalion arrived under the cover designation 10th Radio Research Unit and was under the command of the 53rd USASA Special (3rd RRU). The unit was a DSU to the 1st Cavalry Division and was located in An Khe-Camp Radcliff.

The unit would be reassigned command, 313th ASA Battalion on 10 April 1966 and redesignated 371st Radio Research Co. on 15 October 1966.

AUTHOR'S NOTE: Letter to Gary Blackburn from Lonnie Long, 15 October 1965, "I have 23 days left in the Army. I have about 12 more missions to fly and I'll be glad when that is over. Towards the end it begins to worry you just a little. I took a .30 cal. round in the wing yesterday from ground fire."

Siege of Plei Me

On 19 October 1965, the 33rd Regiment of the 325th NVA Division and Viet Cong troops attacked Plei Me Special Forces Camp in the Central Highlands 215 miles north of Saigon. They were supported by the 32nd NVA Regiment, which was put in place to ambush any reinforcements that might attempt to reach Plei Me's defenders. The outpost was manned by twelve Green Berets and 350 Montagnard tribesmen. There had been significant ARDF fixes of enemy troops moving into the area during the previous week and fixes the day before indicating NVA forces in close proximity to the camp, so the attack was not entirely a surprise.

Plei Me Special Forces Camp (Photo: U.S. Army)

The NVA troops initially overran the post but were repelled by its defenders and U.S. gunships, setting up a siege situation. The next morning, a group of 250 ARVN Rangers led by U.S. advisor Maj. Charles Beckwith arrived by helicopter and helped to reinforce their position. During the siege, the Green Berets and their allies repelled numerous enemy attacks, assisted by air strikes and C-130 airdrops of munitions, rations, and medical supplies. The siege was finally lifted with the arrival of an ARVN armored column on 25 October and the U.S. 1st Air Cav on the 27th.

Beyond Plei Me

On 04 November 1965, ASA Staff Sgt. Robert Townsend of Royal Oak, Michigan, was fatally shot in the chest by a VC sniper near Plei Me. Sgt. Townsend was serving with the 371st RRC supporting the 1st Cav. He had been in the Army for almost twelve years, serving in France and Ethiopia, and had shipped out of Ft. Benning, Georgia, eleven weeks earlier with the 1st Cav. He was twenty-nine years old and was the ASA's fourth casualty in Vietnam.

Robert Franklin Townsend had graduated from Royal Oak High School in 1954 and had married Mary Edwards in 1960. They had three children, Richard age four, Katheryn age two, and Daniel, eleven months.

Bloody Ia Drang

With the Special Forces camp secured, General Westmoreland decided to seize the advantage and sent in the 1st Cavalry Division to "find, fix, and defeat the enemy forces" that had attacked Plei Me. That decision resulted in the Battle of the Ia Drang Valley a few weeks later. It would prove to be the war's bloodiest battle to date.

During the first two weeks of November, the 1st Cav, under the command of Maj. Gen. Harry Kinnard, continued to pursue elements of the NVA division that had attacked Plei Me. As the 325th NVA Division retreated deeper into the Ia Drang Valley, it was shadowed by five ARDF aircraft tracking the locations of its radio signals and its subordinate regimental commanders. The information ASA provided General Kinnard's commanders enabled his forces to move up the valley by helicopter and continuously attack the retreating division. Early on 14 November, a tactical SIGINT intercept team attached to the 1st Battalion, 7th Cavalry, intercepted a transmission indicating that an NVA battalion was trapped at the base of the Chu Pong Massif. Acting on this information, 7th Cav helicopters dropped 450 men, commanded by Lt. Col. Hal Moore, at a landing zone in front of the Massif; their mission was to destroy the enemy force.

Unfortunately, SIGINT can sometimes be wrong or misinterpreted. Col. Moore soon discovered that he was not facing an NVA battalion, but two full regiments of the 325th Division, some 2-3,000 NVA regulars. Two days of bloody fighting followed, much of it hand-to-hand, but when it was over, both of the NVA regiments had been decimated. NVA losses were 1,238 killed and twenty captured. U.S. losses were 250 dead and 358 wounded. What remained of the NVA units retreated across the border into Cambodia.

The intercept team's SIGINT and analysis during the Battle of the Ia Drang Valley was not a total success. Declassified NSA reports indicate that at least four times during the battle, ARVN and U.S. units were ambushed by large NVA units, and SIGINT had been unable to detect the attacks in advance. The lesson that should have been taken away from there is that SIGINT is an imperfect intelligence source if used without corroboration. It needed supporting intelligence from agents, P.O.W.'s, and captured documents to verify and focus the information. Unfortunately, that lesson was not learned by senior U.S. field commanders in Vietnam.

Tommy Franks, ASA cryptanalyst

Without a doubt, ASA's most famous code-breaker, if only for a little while, was now-retired General Tommy Franks. During his last week of basic training at Ft. Leonard Wood, Missouri, Franks received orders to the ASA cryptanalysis/code-breaking school at Ft. Devens. He said that "talent scouts had come to Ft. Leonard Wood searching for recruits who'd scored well on the aptitude tests. I might have been a terrible student in Austin, but I wasn't stupid. In fact, I'd managed to rack up some of the best test scores in my brigade." The recruiter had told him that he could not tell him much about the job until his security clearance was complete, but "it involves some of America's most sensitive intelligence."

"Holy Shit," Tommy Franks thought, "James Bond, Agent 007, martinis, shaken, not stirred. A shoulder holster under my dinner jacket, maybe I'd have to seduce beautiful Russian spies. This was a much better deal than chasing coeds and sneaking into drive-in movies."

Pvt. Tommy Franks—1965 (Photo: U.S. Army)

Franks soon discovered, however, that training to be a cryptanalyst did not involve any of the exciting things he had envisioned. There were no baccarat tables, dinner jackets, or beautiful Russian spies at Ft.

Devens, only long hours and hard work. In October 1965, the school was operating around the clock to meet the demand for qualified intercept operators and analysts. The ASA was pushing students through the school on double twelve-hour shifts, and glamor was in short supply.

General Franks says that during the first few days of class, cryptanalysis seemed like "an impossible challenge," but he finished the course. He volunteered for the Ft. Devens color guard and graduated from the program. A short time later, he applied to OCS and was accepted. He had decided he wanted to be in the "real" Army.

Pfc. Franks was selected for the Artillery and Missile Officer Candidate School at Ft. Sill, Oklahoma, and received his commission in 1967. A few months later, the new 2nd Lieutenant was sent to Vietnam as an artillery officer with the U.S. 9th Infantry Division, where he earned six awards for valor and three Purple Hearts.

PERSONAL NOTE From Lonnie Long: I talked to Tommy Franks after his book came out. He flunked out of the University of Texas; I almost flunked out of Wake Forest. He married a Tri-Delta; I did too. He went into the Army and ASA at Ft. Devens, and I did too. I pointed out to him that we had a lot in common, except for that "general" thing.

Somebody's listening

To test U.S. communications security (COMSEC), the 7th RRU furnished a monitoring team that augmented the RRC assigned to the 1st Cav soon after they arrived in Vietnam. They were to listen in on friendly transmissions and see how much the VC or NVA might learn from them. The COMSEC unit monitored almost 11,000 transmissions over a three-week period as the Cav made its initial deployments and found little cause for concern. They recommended a few COMSEC improvements but saw no major problems.

Soon after the monitoring team completed their analysis, 1st Cav became embroiled in the Battle of Ia Drang Valley. During the battle, the COMSEC teams continued to listen to over 28,000 more transmissions and found that security was almost totally ignored in the heat of battle. The only codes they used were unauthorized, homemade ones that could be easily broken by the NVA; actual army codes and encryption devices were never put into practice. "Ia Drang" greatly alarmed NSA officials, who asked their contractors to design new equipment that would automatically scramble the sound of a voice on the radio.

Heading home (Photo: © L. Long)

PERSONAL NOTE From Lonnie Long: I departed Vietnam on 07 November 1965 after 15 months of duty and over 350 ARDF missions in U6 Beavers and U8 Twin engine Beechcraft.

When I arrived in Vietnam in August 1964, there had been around 18,000 American advisors in-country. When I departed, there were 180,000 of our troops including major combat units. Since 1958 the U.S. had lost a little over 600 killed and suffered over 6,000 wounded. The war had changed dramatically. In the first quarter of 1966, shortly after my departure, 1,700 American troops would die. And things had changed at home as well. On November 2nd, Norman Morrison, a thirty-one-year-old Quaker pacifist, set himself ablaze at the Pentagon just below the window of Secretary of Defense Robert McNamara. On the 27th, 40,000 protesters surrounded the White House. On the same day, President Johnson announced a massive increase in the number of American troops in South Vietnam from 180,000 to 400,000.

ARDF successes

By December, U.S. troop strength in Vietnam had reached 181,000, with more on the way. President Johnson suspended bombing in the north to try to induce the communists to negotiate, but they perceived only weakness in his actions.

The ASAs airborne effort against the VC in the south was so successful that it became MACV's primary source of information for planning attacks. MACV had requested seven additional DF-configured planes with operational and support crews at mid-year, but with the escalation of the war, those were not enough to meet the demand for intelligence. MACV needed enough planes to deploy airborne DF throughout all of South Vietnam, and by year's end, they had requested fifteen more planes along with the personnel to operate and service them. That would bring the total number of airborne DF platforms in South Vietnam to thirty, and swift approval was anticipated from the Joint Chiefs and the Department of the Army.

Hunger for more

As 1966 began, ASA's lengthening list of successes in the expanding war quickly led to an increase in the number of targets they were asked to monitor and for more and better quality intelligence. MACV needed to know where enemy units were located and where they were heading, what the NV Air Force was doing, and the location of their SAM sites, about weapons and munitions shipments from China and the Soviet Union, civil aviation, and NV Naval operations; the list increased daily.

The ASA was producing a steady stream of usable intelligence about the North and the VC units operating in the South by exploiting their cipher systems, combined with traffic analysis and DF data collected by their ARDF flights. According to a declassified NSA history: "American and allied cryptologists would be able to exploit lower level communist cryptographic systems, that is more precisely, ciphers and codes used by operational and tactical-level units, usually regiments and below, on an almost routine basis."

Another bird down

On 15 December 1965, ASA lost another aircraft. An RU-6A (#53-2833) from the 3rd RRU in Da Nang crashed while flying a mission in support of Operation Harvest Moon. The plane's crew consisted of its pilot, Maj. David H. Moffett; copilot, Chief Warrant Officer Cisco; DF operator, Spc.4 James E. Hoppa.

According to Jim Hoppa, the crew was flying in support of U.S. Marines engaged in a search operation through the valley south of Da Nang. "About an hour into our mission we were flying near some mountains southwest of Da Nang, and we encountered some ground fire," Hoppa said. "Evidently we sustained a hit in the engine, which caused us to lose all oil pressure, and eventually the engine seized up. Initially Major Moffett attempted to fly to a landing strip at Chu Lai, but once the engine quit, he attempted to glide it to a landing on a small road that traversed through some rice paddies. Obviously…we did not make a successful landing." The plane hit a water buffalo, cart-wheeled, and landed upside down.

Hoppa continued, "After escaping the wreckage and subsequent fire, we spent about half-an-hour evading the Viet Cong. Eventually two USMC helicopters that were escorting a convoy south of our location noticed the smoke from our crash and came to investigate. While one laid down ground cover, the other rescued us and then returned us to our Da Nang detachment. Thankfully…[the] crew members only sustained minor cuts and bruises." Maj. Moffett, Chief Warrant Officer

Cisco, and Spc.4 Hoppa were all awarded Purple Hearts for the injuries they sustained in the crash

1966–The "Boo"

Pathfinder with dipole antennas on horizontal stabilizers (Photo: U.S. Army)

In January 1966, the 146th RRU took possession of a one-of-a-kind De Havilland RCV-2B Caribou (Serial #62-4147) code-named "Pathfinder." The "Boo" had a high-frequency ARDF system installed in it and flew with a much larger team than the airborne units already in service. Capt. George Roney was the aircraft commander.

Richard McCarthy tells about an incident during one of Capt. Roney's last missions north of the DMZ. Spc. McKay was the crew chief, Sgt. First Class Franklin was the 05K (SIGINT/non-Morse interceptor), and there were two linguists on board. There was also a 05H, a second 05K and a warrant officer 4 flying copilot. McCarthy had his window covered to help keep the aircraft cooler and began to hear "backfiring," so he contacted the captain. Captain Roney's curt response was: "Backfiring my ass! Look out the window."

When McCarthy looked out his window, he saw antiaircraft fire exploding all around the plane. Another crew member reported "the sky was red with tracers going by." McCarthy grabbed his flak jacket to sit on as he felt the plane turn and move back across the DMZ. Capt. Roney complained that the plane was "steering sluggishly" and requested permission to land at Dong Ha.

The aircraft landed without incident and the crew piled out to look at the underside of the plane, which had been peppered by .30 cal bullets. None had penetrated the skin of the aircraft; however, it looked like someone had pounded the underside of the plane with a ballpeen hammer. As the ASA team crowded beneath the plane, several Air Force crewmembers approached and were staring at the tail. That was the first indication the Pathfinder crew had of the 37mm AA damage to the tail. There was a huge hole in it.

Caribou's tail with 37mm AA damage (Photo: Robert Taylor)

Capt. Roney gave the crew the option of returning to Phu Bai in the Caribou, or riding in an SAR (search and rescue) helicopter that would accompany them; every man climbed back aboard the Boo. McKay, the crew chief, was an avid sport parachutist. He put on his parachute and spent the trip sitting on the tailgate of the Caribou waving to the crew of the SAR chopper as it trailed along behind.

In August, Capt. Charlie Dexter took over as commander and flew Pathfinder missions until March 1967. "Our great crew chief, Spc. McKay, remained with Pathfinder," says Dexter. "We then flew it the rest of that year, turning it over to the U.S.A.F. in late April 1967." Dexter continues: "Pathfinder was virtually the only Caribou in the U.S. Army inventory...I even had painted under the Pilot's window 'Owned and Operated by the U.S. Army;' which was our way of ribbing the U.S.A.F. since I had to take it to them for maintenance...Pathfinder was a very unique and amazing plane."

According to Dexter (who is a retired colonel), Pathfinder's unique equipment included: "A Decca Navigation system; a Marconi Doppler Radar system; a Sperry C-12 Compass system; an early generation auto pilot; four RDF/Operator console stations; two air turbine generators externally mounted under the wings to augment the heavy power load needed; a KY type teleprinter for secure data link air-to-ground communications; an old WWII bombsight mounted on the cabin floor to visually update exact ground locations; an infrared camera for verifying DF located enemy positions; and a small Polaroid camera for taking instant pictures of the pilot's instrument panel for NCOIC posting on the large DF map-board mounted on the port bulkhead."

Col. Dexter continues: "The actual Pathfinder crew consisted of eight: Pilot (me), copilot (rotated among several different 224th Avn. Bn. twin engine qualified pilots), a master sergeant mission NCOIC, four highly skilled ASA linguist/RDF operators, and one aircraft crew chief; totaling eight, not six or seven as often reported elsewhere. Occasionally, I took an extra crew maintenance specialist when the aircraft or equipment needed inflight analysis and/or repair.

"We operated virtually all over Vietnam from Saigon to Davis Field Station at Hue/Phu Bai. Most mission flights were four hours in duration with an occasional six or seven-hour ones after refueling. Contrary to popular belief, we did more than 'just troll' and went after specific enemy organizations/locations, even calling in artillery and naval gunfire on specified targets. We occasionally violated the Cambodia and Laos borders, and the DMZ when chasing important targets, but it was not our routine or normal intent to do so, and those accounts claiming otherwise are more than likely just 'old war stories' told by the uninformed or by wannabies."

Richard McCarthy says, "The Caribou was a good system…It was noisy like all Caribous, and due to the weight it was carrying, [it was] even slower in the climb than most. I can't remember if it flew the standard four-hour mission or stayed up longer. Everything that was painted OD and flew at low altitudes was hot. The Boo had the advantage of space so you could at least stand up occasionally. Many times the tailgate was left up for cooling, but this was stopped when one of the 'Phyllis Ann' crews (Air Force EC-47 ARDF team) lost some top-secret materials out of an open door. Other than the Master Op (DF team-leader) and the TA (traffic analysis) guy, the crews were flexible. I flew on it a few times, but didn't like it; not because of the system, but because of the similarity to field station work. The most disconcerting thing about the Boo was [that] due to the long fuselage, you really got slammed around when it was working a target. When we had to turn the Boo over to the Air Force… all the mission gear was stripped out of it and put in a conex container. Somebody probably bought a complete set of mission gear at a government auction years later, and is still trying to figure out what it is."

Another man down

On 17 February, 2Lt. William Leatherwood of the 8th RR Field Station was killed during a courier run when the Marine helicopter he was riding in crashed after take-off from Phu Bai airfield. The helicopter lost power at about 300 feet altitude, crashed mid-runway, and burst into flames.

William E. Leatherwood, Jr., had just celebrated his twenty-sixth birthday three weeks before. He was from Carrollton, Alabama.

ASA's buildup continues

The signal intelligence that ASA provided quickly surpassed all other intelligence sources in its quality, timeliness, and accuracy. Its ability to find and track the movements of the NVA and VC units operating in South Vietnam made opposing and destroying them immeasurably easier.

Jim Lairson, an ASA "ditty-bopper" (05H) assigned to the 8th RRU at Phu Bai recalled an incident in February 1966. The traffic he was intercepting indicated that the VC combat unit he was assigned to monitor was moving toward Phu Bai. He says: "The (VC) operator I was copying got frustrated with (his) control and switched from coded to plain text. Our translator was standing behind me, and I typed 'Phu Bai' on the paper. I got the word. There were three battalions of Viet Cong coming at us." A standby force of U.S.A.F. fighter-bombers was called in immediately, and the approaching force was decimated, thus averting the threat.

Coincident with the buildup of U.S. forces in Vietnam, ASA units were arriving as quickly as they could be assembled and trained. On February 13, Company A, 303rd ASA Battalion was deployed to Cu Chi in direct support of the 25th Infantry Division. It would be redesignated the 372nd RR later in the year.

In March, the 303rd and 313th ASA Battalions arrived. The 313th RRB HQ landed in-country on 15 March 1966 with the cover designation of 13th RRU and was located in Nha Trang. Their cover designation would be changed to the 313th on 03 May, and they would be reassigned command to the newly designated 509th USASA Group on 1 June.

The 372nd ASA Co., which originated as part of the 303rd ASA Battalion, was redesignated as the 16th RRU. It was later reorganized and redesignated as the 372nd RRC and supported the 25th Inf. Div., operating in Kontum, Tay Ninh, Dau Tieng, Nui Ba Dinh, Go Da Hau, and Trang Bang, among other places.

The 303rd ASA HQ Co. arrived on 12 April under the cover designation of the 17th RRU and was assigned to the 53rd USASA Spec. Ops. Command (3rd RRU). They were located at Long Binh, II Corps. They would be reassigned to the 509th USASAG in June, and their cover designation changed to the 303rd RRB.

The 303rd had a long and storied past. The unit had served in five

WWII campaigns including Normandy and the Battle of the Bulge. It had been reactivated on 22 September 1950 and served with distinction throughout the Korean War, being deactivated in 1955. With the buildup in Vietnam, the 303rd was activated again on 15 June 1962 at Camp Wolters, Texas. Due to its location and the large number of "Texas boys" in the unit, it had adopted the nickname: "The Longhorn Battalion."

On 02 April 1966, Staff Sgt. John Hoffman of the 3rd RRU was killed when a weapon accidentally discharged. He was a native of Philadelphia, Pennsylvania.

According to the *Philadelphia Inquirer*, Hoffman's military career spanned ten years, and he specialized in "communications monitoring and code interception." The twenty-eight-year-old staff sergeant served in Germany from 1959-1962 and was sent to Vietnam in 1965.

John D. Hoffman was assigned to the 7th Replacement Company when he was killed. He was married and had two sons.

CHAPTER 9

SPRING RAID ON TAN SON NHUT

ASA barracks at Davis Station (Photo: © Gary Spivey)

In the early morning hours of 13 April, 1966, a VC unit penetrated the thirteen-mile defense perimeter around Tan Son Nhut airport and shelled the field with mortars for over four hours. ARVN troops and U.S. security guards finally drove off the attackers, killing eighteen of them. One U.S. RF-101 reconnaissance jet was badly damaged in the attack. The guerrillas returned that same night and resumed the attack, but security guards stopped them, killing eleven more. During the initial attack, Staff Sgt. Donald Daugherty of the 3rd RRU was killed by shrapnel from a mortar shell.

Duncan L. Daughtry recalls: "I was there that night. I had been in-country for about three days. We landed on Easter Sunday, just in time to be hustled over to sunrise services. I flew over on Tiger Airlines. There was a guy by the name of Bryan Eskell who came over with me. We were joking about what to expect when we got in-country. Bryan jokingly told me that we would be in-country three days and would be hit. The third round would have my name on it. I was asleep when the first rounds began to drop. Someone came around and asked if we had any ammunition. I said, 'Ammunition hell, I don't even have a gun!' He told us to go to the armory and get a weapon, which we did, but we still didn't have any ammunition. The next morning, I found out that Sgt. Donald Daugherty (his name was 'erty' while mine was 'try') was killed by an incoming round…I was one of those assigned to clean up the blood that was all over the sidewalk and also all over the barracks floor where he had been pulled in. I gave Bryan hell the next day and told him I didn't want to hear any more of his predictions or the VC wouldn't have to kill him, I would. That is one night I will never forget."

Tino "Chui" Banuelos described the scene in this way: "Prior to the April 66 mortar attack at TSN, all weapons and ammo in the 3rd RRU had been locked into conex boxes at Davis Station. When the mortars started falling, people were trying to break into the conex boxes to get weapons. The guy with the key for the locks had gone to Saigon for the evening. The 7th RRU, however, had weapons and ammo locked in our three-quarter-ton 'offices' in the motor pool. When the guys in the 3rd RRU got the conex box open, they found grenades. They had to break open the lock on the second conex box to get to the weapons and ammo. I was doing a 'nug' (new guy) thing and was just standing outside of the hootch watching guys run around in circles. Actually my left leg was running but my right leg was standing still. I saw the flash of the mortar that landed inside Davis Station killing Sgt. Daugherty and heard the cries of 'Medic!' John Giles got me moving by slamming me in the shoulder and yelling in my face, 'Get in the bunker!'"

Phil Panuco remembers: "I was sent TDY from the 104th ASA Det, Torii Station, in March 66 for 90 days. On the night of the attack, I didn't want to run in the dirt from the hootch to the 7th RRU compound in my bare feet, so I put my socks and boots on. By that time I was the last person going through to the compound. The main entrance to the ASA compound was guarded by some RRU personnel manning an M-60 machine gun and some M-14 rifles. They didn't know who I was (I didn't work with them) and they told me to freeze and identify myself. I almost shit in my pants thinking I was going to get killed by my own people. I didn't look white because of my brown Hispanic skin. After convincing them who I was, I then reported to the 7th RRU Ops hut."

John Crafton recalls: "I remember that night. I was running to the barracks to grab my gear and in the pitch dark ran into a large stack of lumber. Instead of going around the stack I climbed right over it and tumbled off the other side. The next morning I looked at that stack of lumber and wondered how I managed to do that."

Roger Wightman says, "John Giles was really upset after that attack because one of the unlucky guys…died in John's arms…John Saltar was the first one to the arms room and had to bust off the lock to get in. Some lieutenant was yelling at him about destroying government property until the round landed near the water purification plant. John said the first weapon he passed out was a Montagnard crossbow."

Allan Rubin tells his story: "The night we were mortared, I was sitting at the back gate opening to the airfield in my shorts with some buddies drinking beer when all hell broke loose. We jumped into the ditch and watched some of Ky's Skyraiders get hit and a couple jets. I remember crawling to a bunker next to the barracks, and we were all saying prayers….Guys were crawling out of the NCO club 'cause our MP's were shooting down the road at anything that moved. They even shot at the ambulance trying to get in the compound….When the armorer finally made it to the arms room, sometime later, he was handing out rifles and belts of ammo; there were no loaded clips. Also we set up a machine gun position at the opening at the rear of the compound that led to the airfield, and when it was light in the morning they realized they had put the ammo belt in the machine gun backwards…so much for ditty-boppers. By the way, Staff Sgt. Daugherty was in my bunker when the mortars began to fall. We were in the last bunker west, which was near the west wall at the end of the compound and the nearest to the airfield wall where the opening was to the airfield, and I remember that when the lull in the shelling began, Sgt. Daugherty thought it was over and said he was going to go to the arms room for a weapon. I remember telling him, along with others with me, to stay put and wait awhile, but he was adamant. He exited the bunker and began running down the sidewalk when the shelling started again, and he was killed instantly when a shell struck the sidewalk where he was running. I further remember that all I could think of was I needed a cigarette, and I stupidly crawled out of the bunker and into my barracks to retrieve them, then crawled back to the bunker. I probably should have been a statistic also, but we did do some dumb things when we were younger. The rest of the guys sure appreciated having the cigarettes though. I remember after the shelling, as we all left the bunkers, someone stupidly lit off a string of firecrackers, and we all dove for the bunker, again. Talk about stupid!"

Lloyd Moler was part of the group at the back gate, too. "Don (Daugherty) and I had been friends in Chitose (Japan, 12th ASAFS) before we came to Davis Station in 1965. We, along with several more guys, were sitting on the sandbag bunkers between the back of Davis Station and the landing pad for the helicopter unit behind us. We were out there watching the Phantoms take off and enjoying a few beers. When the incoming rounds started, we weren't sure exactly what was happening. The rounds were hitting mostly around the flight line down toward operations. Once it dawned on us what was going on, Don took off towards the orderly room and the arms room. I took off with a couple of guys behind him. We ran down the sidewalk from the back gate alongside a barracks building. As soon as Don made the turn at the end of the barracks, a mortar round hit about six feet from him. He was only hit by one piece of shrapnel that I saw. That was all that was needed. I have never seen so much blood in such a short time in my life. Somebody herded us out of there, and they were trying to take care of Don. I ran to the arms room to try and get my weapon. [It was] mass confusion. I finally got a weapon and some ammo and was put out on the trench line behind the motor pool. The next morning, we had a formation in the motor pool to count heads. One guy asked his sergeant if he could go to the medics. The sergeant kinda went off on the guy until the guy told him that he had been hit in the back with shrapnel. Apparently he was lying in bed just inside the barracks that Don had been killed in front of and he had been splattered with all kinds of shrapnel. They rushed him to the medics….By the way, the attack came right after the U.S. started air strikes on Hanoi."

William R. (Bill) Wilson still remembers that night, too. "I was a Spc.4 working rotating shifts at Whitebirch. The night of the attack, I was in skivvies about to go to the midnight movie when the first rounds hit. My hooch was on the opposite side of the compound, across the road from the EM [Enlisted Men's] Club from where the round hit and killed Don. A few of us were standing around our hooch when we could hear the incoming rounds on the flight line. We headed for the bunkers then to draw our weapons. I was there when it was discovered that the keys were in town. After some work on the doors we got our arms and were assigned posts. A couple of us were at the head of a drainage ditch behind the motor pool area. After daybreak, we were formed up in the MP—many were in skivvies, steel pots, and flip-flops with M-14s! I bet [we were] a truly awesome sight."

Donald D. Daugherty was a twenty-nine-year-old Morse intercept operator (O5H) from San Diego, California. Daugherty was survived by his mother, Lorraine.

PERSONAL NOTE From Lonnie Long: "Death and war are never to be taken lightly. However, most of the things that happen are more like an episode of 'M*A*S*H' than the John Wayne war movies we grew up watching. The men of the Army Security Agency were different from most of the Army. In order to qualify for ASA they had to test in the top 10% of the Army, but most of them would tell you that they were superior in loving, drinking, smoking and generally avoiding anything military. On the night of the attack on Tan Son Nhut/Davis Station, the ASA weapons were locked in a metal conex; the soldier with the keys was out on the town. What else can I say?"

Changing perceptions

As the summer of 1966 approached, the American people were becoming less and less supportive of the Johnson administration's policies in Vietnam. Public perception was that President Johnson was not trying to win the war, and there was little stomach for the mounting costs, both in money and in American lives. According to polls taken at the time, the vast majority of Americans favored an all-out escalation to defeat the North Vietnamese.

CHAPTER 10

WILD BLUE YONDER

EC-47s on Phu Bai ramp—1967 (Photo: U.S.A.F.)

In 1966, the U.S. Air Force Security Service formed ARDF squadrons at Tan Son Nhut Air Base, Nha Trang Air Base, and Pleiku Air Base to conduct EC-47 direction finding operations. The pilots, copilots, navigators, and flight mechanics were assigned to the 360th, 361st, and 362nd Tactical Electronic Warfare Squadrons (TEWS), and the Morse intercept operators, linguists, analysts, and equipment repairmen were assigned to the 6994th Security Squadron and its detachments.

The first operational base for Det. 1 of the 6994th was Nha Trang A.B. on the southern coast of South Vietnam. It was activated on 1 July 1966 and most of the airmen assigned there lived off-base in Nha Trang City. The Det. 1 crews flew SIGINT intercept missions ("Project Drill Press") from Phu Bai with the support of ASA's 8th RRFS. Drill Press had a unique mission and an even more unique working arrangement. The

Air Force crews lived with the Army, receiving tech support, translation, analysis, and reporting for their SIGINT intercept from the 8th RRU, and primarily supported the U.S. Marines in their operations along the DMZ. It was an unusual arrangement, but it worked.

The Air Force used two EC-47s for their missions out of Phu Bai. Their configuration included three HF radio positions and one VHF radio position along with three 292s (Morse interceptors), one 203 (linguist interceptor), and one 202 (analyst), all of whom were USAFSS enlisted men. The 292s and 202s were permanently assigned to the 6994th; the 203s were TDY from the 6988th at Yokota (Japan) initially and later from the 6990th at Kadena (Okinawa). The front-end crews were from the 361st. The Director of Intelligence with the 3rd Marine Division said 90% of the useable intelligence they received about enemy activities in the DMZ was derived from Drill Press missions.

Interior of EC-47 showing intercept and analyst positions (Photo: U.S.A.F.)

Airman 1st Class Darwin Bruce was one of the airmen assigned to the 6994th at Phu Bai. Bruce says that Operation Drill Press, "a collection only mission," originally had ten 292s (Morse intercept) and two 202s (analysts), but those numbers soon increased. "During the first couple of months, the Drill Press Ops office was a forty-foot van parked behind the base comm center at Tan Son Nhut, near the flight line.

"...About mid-August, we began making trips to Hue-Phu Bai and working with the 8th RRU ("8th Rock and Roll") in the DMZ and Ah Shau Valley areas. After about three weeks of living in tents at Da Nang and commuting..., the Army gave us permission to quarter at Hue-Phu Bai. The first nights, we stayed in a very small building next to the Phu Bai medical clinic. The medics had a pet monkey on a dog chain living in a dog house next to the walkway to our small building; the monkey would jump each of us as we returned to check for candy or gum in our pockets.

"After about a week, they gave us more spacious quarters in an old barn away from the Army area. The barn was basically a huge open-bay type storage building with smudge pots for heat during the cool rainy season. We lived there for the rest of the time I was in the unit. We still had bunks at Tan Son Nhut and got down to Saigon once every three weeks while the maintenance types pulled PM (preventive maintenance) on the airplane."

Darwin Bruce continues: "Our daily routine started at 'oh-dark-thirty' when I rose, showered, and went to the 8th RRU ops building and prepared the bag (cheat sheets, 'brain,' and check lists) for the mission. I left the bag with the ASA guards and met the rest of the crew at the chow hall. We then took our weapons carrier back to ops to pick up the bag with the classified and then to the flight line. We unlocked the plane, pushed it out and turned it before starting the engines to keep from blowing sand and dirt into the local M*A*S*H unit. Most of our missions were about six to seven hours; however, on occasion we'd... stretch things a bit."

Bruce recalls one incident during a "firefight" in the DMZ when the USAFSS aircraft became the "on-scene commander" for a couple of shoot-downs of U.S. F-4s and a U.S. Navy F-8. "The first two F-4 crewmen didn't make it," he says. "The second F-4 crew bailed out and had two good chutes. The F-8 who came in to help suppress the enemy fire got shot up, too. He came alongside of us with flames traveling along the dorsal fuel tanks and made it back across the river to safety before ejecting."

On a lighter side, Bruce tells about some of the airmen at Phu Bai purchasing four small refrigerators at the Post Exchange and taking them to Saigon where they were sold at a profit. The money was then used to "buy more booze for trading at Phu Bai. The Army had refrigerators, but couldn't get much booze," he says. "The refrigerators were like gold in Saigon. The booze came in handy when we had to get a mortar bunker built in Phu Bai next to the barn. The ASA commander didn't like it when he found out that we [had] traded booze for Navy CB labor. He wanted to see U.S.A.F. personnel out there in the hot sun digging holes in the ground."

"During my tenure and flights," Bruce says, "we had fires on board five times, all due to small arms fire. One day, as we flew into Da Nang with the starboard engine on fire…the Da Nang controller asked that we not set down until we passed more than half of the runway to keep from possibly 'messing up the runway.' He continues to say that when the planes were damaged or needed repair, their 'parts depots' were…a broken V.N.A.F. C-47 that sat at the end of the Phu Bai runway…The V.N.A.F. plane was an empty shell when I got finished requisitioning parts from it." Staff Sgt. Darwin Bruce left the 6994th SS in April 1967.

In August 1966, a USAFSS EC-47 plane flying an ARDF mission near the DMZ (over Quang Tri Province) intercepted the largest number of NVA transmitter fixes they had ever encountered. The Air Force team had located the NVA 324B Division which was trying to escape back across the DMZ after being mauled by the U.S. Marines a few days earlier. A B-52 Arc Light mission was called in, and the area was saturated with a carpet bombing of high-explosives and napalm. Hundreds of NVA troops died in the attack. On 29 September, the Director of Intelligence for the U.S. Pacific Command said without the work of the Security Service EC-47s and that of "more sensitive intelligence (SIGINT), we would be completely in the dark about the enemy situation in the DMZ."

During the seven years that the 6994th and their TEWS flight crews flew missions over South Vietnam and Laos, thirty-six airmen were KIA. One airman was killed in a ground attack, and the remainder died with the loss of six planes and their crews. When the planes went down, there were few if any survivors.

The 6994th had more combat casualties than any other Security Service unit in Vietnam and was one of its most decorated. The EC-47 reconnaissance missions were top-secret, unarmed, and extremely dangerous. The 6994th unit history sums it up best: "It was inevitable that some men would sacrifice their lives for what had to be done." The back-end crews, like their ASA counterparts, were all enlisted volunteers and the cream of the crop. For decades their stories have been locked away in NSA's vaults, their contributions unrecognized and their sacrifices unremembered.

The 224th Aviation Battalion

The 224th AB (RR) was activated at Tan Son Nhut A.B. near Saigon on 01 June 1966; its first C.O. was Maj. John D. Rieser. The battalion had four subordinate companies: the 138th Avn. Co. (RR), located in Da Nang (I Corps Tactical Zone); the 144th Avn. Co. (RR), located in Nha Trang (II CTZ); the 146th Avn. Co. (RR), located at Tan Son Nhut (III CTZ); and the 156th Avn. Co. (RR), located in Can Tho (IV CTZ). The 1st Avn. Co. (RR) ("Crazy Cats"), based at Cam Ranh Bay Naval Air Station was added on 3 July 1967 and directly supported MACV. The battalion's tactical callsign was "Lonely Ringer."

At the time of its inception, the unit boasted a total of six aircraft and 159 personnel, but it expanded quickly. Within three years the number of ASA personnel assigned to the battalion and its subordinate companies stood at 1,066 with a total of eighty aircraft. The aircraft consisted of eighteen RU-6A, thirty-eight RU-8D, sixteen RU-21D, six RP-2E and two RU-1A. All of ASA's fixed-wing aircraft in Vietnam were assigned to one of the five subordinate companies. The 224th participated in fifteen campaigns and pioneered the introduction of Special Electronic Mission Aircraft (SEMA) to the battlefield.

Jerry Laney of the 156th Avn. Co. (RR)–224th AB (RR), Can Tho
(Photo: © Jerry Laney)

CHAPTER 11

HARRY LOCKLEAR'S STORY

RU-6 Beaver in flight (Photo: © Robert Flanagan)

On 6 August 1966, a U-6 Beaver on an ARDF mission crashed northwest of Saigon near the Cambodian border. The area was known to contain logistical bases for the VC 9th Infantry Division and was of particular interest to NSA. The DF operator on board was Harry Locklear, who remembers the event like this:

"Captain Mike Wolfe and Chief Warrant Officer 4 Cairns were the pilots on the mission. Neither one had been in-country a week; this was the first mission for both of them. The reports say we suffered 'engine failure.' The fact is, bullets were hitting the cowling around the engine. I tried to tell them; I yelled 'ground fire,' but before they could understand me, the engine quit, and down we went.

"We were lucky. There were rice paddies down there, and as we hit the ground, we hit a paddy dike…it knocked the front of the Beaver upward; then we slammed into about two feet of water, [and the] plane broke in half.…I figured I was gonna die.

"A Bell OH-13G helicopter came flying over in response to our distress signal, and I stepped out of the jungle to wave at it. The pilot motioned me back into the jungle and then flew a couple hundred yards across the open paddies to the other side, checking on our safety. He turned and hauled ass back to us, and circled twice, giving me hand signals. He held up his left hand with the 'V' sign, then took his thumb and index finger and made a cupping motion, meaning 'C'–'VC.' They were on the other side, and he saw them. He came around again and motioned for me to get my ass back inside the jungle.

"The pilot then turned and flew back across the clearing to recheck [on the VC]. He was only flying about 200 feet off the deck, and I was worried about that. Not all VC were bad shots, especially not the ones in…[our] area. They were hard-core cadre up there. The helicopter got to the other side and made a turn to come back. About half way through his turn, he got hit with a shit-load of ground fire. Crashed! Burned! Dead! The only good thing that came out of it was that the [helicopter] pilot had relayed the coordinates to where we were laying up, and about an hour later, a Chinook (CH-47 helicopter) from the Big Red One came in with guns blazing and picked us up.

"While [we were] waiting to see if the VC would come first, or someone to get our asses out, I suddenly remembered our instruction on the care of the KY-7 and KW-7 (top-secret encryption/decryption equipment onboard the plane): 'Bring it back, or you don't come back.' While sitting there in the brush, I realized that when I…[left] that aircraft, I had left mine inside. Oh shit!

"The aircraft was directly in the middle of the large open field, 100 meters from the jungle on our side and about 100 meters from the jungle on the other side. I told Captain Wolfe that I was going to get my KY-7. He gave me this strange look and then asked me if I could do him a favor. It seems that his flight helmet had sentimental value, as his wife had bought it for him as a birthday present the year before. He asked me if I would bring it back, too. I said 'ok' and hauled ass out into the open.

"I got the KY, went around and got the Captain's helmet, figured 'so for, so good,' and turned to run back to the tree line. Then, all hell broke loose. I heard the beating of the tandem rotors of the Chinook, and the VC opened fire on me from the tree line across the field. The Chinook flew over me, with the crew members motioning for me to run, …hurry, hurry, and hurry! The VC had two automatic weapons trying to zero in on me, and as I ran, I just had to laugh, 'cause they just had to be such bad shots. The bullets were zinging into the rice paddy about five or six feet on either side of me and cutting an 'X' in the water ahead of me where they crossed paths.

"About halfway back to the jungle, I saw the Chinook sink down to hover-height, and Wolfe and Cairns ran around and jumped in. The door gunners were throwing slugs at the tree line behind me, and I was running as hard as I could, I thought. Then, one of the VC shooters decided not to 'lead' me so much, and a bullet zinged across my left wrist, burning like hell. I am sure I looked like some cartoon character when I jumped, climbed out of that water, and really started to run. It was like I was going across the top of the water. I remember Wolfe, Cairns, the gunners, and even the pilot of the chopper screaming and waiving for me to get my ass there in a hurry—pulling for me, cheering me on, and all the while [they were] trying to dodge those bullets."

The machine gun had opened up on the helicopter, blasting off the passenger door and damaging the main rotor, but Harry kept running. "When I got to the aircraft, I knew that I didn't have time to stop, put the helmet and KY in the bird, and then climb in. That LZ was too damn hot. I came out on dry ground, ran up a little rise, and then just took flight. I jumped, packages and all, and dived head first into the chopper. My big nose led the way, scraping some of the skin off of it. By the time I rolled over, we were up and airborne, and the gunners were still returning fire."

The chopper made it as far as An Loc, but the weather had closed in, and the ASA crew would not be able to get back to Tan Son Nhut until the next day. Capt. Wolfe called in the location data on their crash site so the local artillery commanders could destroy the downed plane and prevent the enemy from acquiring the highly-classified mission equipment which still remained on board.

Harry arrived back at his barracks the next day, still muddy, tired and happy to be "home." The other soldiers wanted to hear about what had happened, so Harry told his story, and concluded by saying that when the machine gun bullets were whizzing past his head and blowing the door off the chopper, he had thought, "Shit!" and almost stopped and walked. "I didn't think we were going to get off the ground again."

Harry with pilot's wings–1970 (Photo: © H. Locklear)

CHAPTER 12
THE DIGGERS OF NUI DAT

Australian intercept operators in the "set room" at Nui Dat
(Photo: Denis Hare-pronto@au104.org)

During the first week of August 1966, the Australian 547 Signal Troop, a radio-intercept unit at Nui Dat in Phuoc Tuy Province, identified the radio call sign of the 275th VC Main Force Regiment. They were under the control of the VC HQ5 Division and were new to the area. The Aussies were also able to fix the location of the VC regiment's transmitter. The intercept team thought their intelligence coup would excite interest at Headquarters Company, 1st Australian Task Force (ATF). In the Troops opinion, it "should have stirred the possums," but the command staff was indifferent.

Part of the problem was that the headquarters staff did not understand the significance of the information they had been given. Another factor was that only four individuals were authorized to know the source of the information, so HQ did not give it the credence they might have otherwise. The SIGINT capabilities and successes of the Australian Signal Troop were as closely guarded as were ASA's radio research units. Their compound at Nui Dat was surrounded by barbed wire, and only those with the highest security clearance and the "need to know" were allowed inside. SIGINT was never revealed as the source because they did not want the enemy to know the extent to which its communications were being intercepted and analyzed. As a result of this obsessive concern for secrecy, sources of information were obscured and in some cases led to crucial command problems when field commanders did not have access to the information.

Task Force HQ received huge volumes of U.S. intelligence, but much of it was too narrow in scope to be of value, and South Vietnamese intelligence was always suspect due to the conflicting information it contained. The tradition-bound commanders had always relied on reports from patrols and still had a tendency to do so. Most paid little deference to "electronic warfare."

Toward the end of July, the Aussie troop had noted a significant increase in radio traffic from the east, suggesting to their analysts that something was brewing. On the same day, the unit had located the 275th Regiment's transmitter near Xuyen Moc. The transmitter then moved toward their base at Nui Dat in regular stages, taking sixteen days to move seventeen kilometers, to a location near Long Tan. That was only five kilometers away from the Australian base, so two weeks into the month of August, 1st ATF HQ finally paid some attention to what the 547 Signal Troop had to say.

The Royal Australian Army taskforce had arrived in Vietnam over a ninety-day period from April to June 1966 and were constructing their base on high ground amid old French rubber plantations. The VC leadership, which had controlled the area, planned to lure the Australians from their base and inflict a defeat that would be politically unacceptable in Australia. During the early morning hours of 17August, with some 2,500 men in the field, the VC 275th Regiment, supported by at least one NVA battalion and elements of the VC's D445th Provincial

Mobile Battalion, launched a heavy attack of recoilless rifle and mortar rounds on the Nui Dat base. They assumed the Aussies would send out companies to sweep the area, and they would ambush them. Twenty-four Australians were wounded in the early-morning attack. The Australians, however, were aware of the large VC force due to the radio intercepts of the previous two weeks. They had sent out patrols but had been unable to locate the main body of the enemy force.

Mismatch

On 18 August, after some minor skirmishes with smaller enemy squads, D Company of the 6th Royal Australian Regiment with 108 men (105 Aussies and three New Zealanders) located an enemy force near the Long Tan rubber plantation at about 1600 hours. They thought they had encountered a VC company and launched an attack. During the ensuing firefight, one Aussie platoon chased a squad of VC soldiers in among the rubber trees and ran straight into the enormous mass of the VC 275th Regiment and their support units. In the midst of a torrential monsoon downpour, the enemy corps attacked with a barrage of mortars, machine gun and small arms fire. Half of the Australian platoon fell to the ground, either dead or wounded, and the remaining soldiers were pinned down by the hail of enemy fire.

The Australians responded with their regular arms, regrouped into a defensive position and called in artillery from the batteries at Nui Dat. The available artillery included two Australian batteries: the 105th and 103rd Bty RAA with twelve 105mm howitzers, one New Zealand battery: the 161st Bty RNZA with six 105mm howitzers, and a U.S. artillery battery: A Bty, 2/35th Howitzer Battalion with six 155mm M109 howitzers. The artillery fire was non-stop, with sixty rounds-per-minute striking the huge enemy force during the peak of the battle.

The VC and NVA forces were attacking the small Australian unit with human-wave assaults. The enemy soldiers would rise up out of the mist and charge in groups of forty to fifty at a time, and when they were beaten back, another forty or fifty would rise up and charge forward through the pouring rain. One of the Aussie sergeants said that as a new wave of enemy troops came charging forward through the downpour, some of the earlier wave would rise up out of the muck and mist, and move forward with them. It was like the dead were coming back to life, and they just kept mowing them down.

Royal New Zealand Artillery battery (Photo: U.S. Army)

By 1700 hours, D Company was running out of ammunition and enemy support units were moving to encircle their defensive position. The Aussies kept pleading for relief, tactical air support, and resupply, but to no avail. Close air support was impossible due to the weather conditions. Shortly after 1700, two helicopters piloted by volunteers, managed to locate the small unit amidst the smoke and fog and deliver a load of ammunition, but the unit's true salvation had been the constant artillery bombardment of the enemy ranks. At one point, the plight of D Company was so dire that its commander was calling in artillery rounds on top of his own position in order to slow the VC onslaught.

At this crucial time, a most significant event occurred. The Task Force Commander, Brigadier O. D. Jackson, contacted the O.C. (officer in charge) of the 547 Signal Troop, Capt. Trevor Richards, and asked for his assessment of the enemy force attacking D Company. The Commander could not chance losing his entire base in order to save one company. Richards quickly produced a detailed report and analysis of the situation, thus providing the Commander with the invaluable information he needed to make the difficult decisions.

Soldier of the Royal Australian Regiment (Photo: U.S. Army)

In the meantime, B Company, 6th RAR, which had been out on patrol was on its way back to base. The Commander contacted the company and ordered it to move to the battle area on foot "with the greatest possible speed." A Company was also ordered to move out in support and at about 1800 hours, was loaded onto the armored personnel carriers of the 1st APC Squadron. The APCs crossed a flooded stream and headed toward the battlefield, but soon encountered the Viet Cong D445th Battalion which was massing to attack D Company from the rear. The seven armored vehicles loaded with Australian infantry caught the VC battalion completely by surprise and slicing through the middle of the enemy force, were able to break through to relieve D Company. B Company also moved into the area, converging with the other Australian companies at the same time.

The Australian armored cavalry had arrived at the most critical part of the battle. The enemy forces were moving to encircle and crush the small unit and its remaining sixty-six able-bodied fighters, but the arrival of the armor, the infantry reinforcements, and the nonstop artillery barrage had turned the tide. Darkness was settling across the area, and the large enemy force simply disappeared into the surrounding countryside, taking many of their dead and wounded with them. One of the survivors said, "One minute it was total pandemonium, and the next minute it was total quiet." The Battle of Long Tan was over. The Aussies secured their area, set up a defensive perimeter against a possible counter attack, and using the lights from the APCs to illuminate a landing zone, brought in helicopters to remove their dead and wounded.

Aftermath

Sunrise the next morning revealed how badly the huge enemy force had been decimated by the allied artillery bombardment. Their commanders had obviously underestimated the effectiveness of the batteries at Nui Dat. Some 245 VC and NVA bodies were still strewn among the broken rubber trees, and estimated enemy casualties were 500 KIA and over 1,000 wounded. The Australians had eighteen KIA, seventeen from D Company and one from 1st APC, and twenty-four wounded. After the Battle of Long Tan, neither the Viet Cong nor the NVA ever again made a serious attempt to challenge the "Diggers" of the 1st Australian Task Force for control of Phuoc Tuy Province.

Once again, SIGINT had provided an early warning and tactical information that could have been derived in no other way. What might have been a serious defeat, both politically and in lives lost, became a major victory for Australian and allied forces, and the services of the 547 Signal Troop had finally won the recognition and respect they deserved. What had heretofore been viewed as the Australian "agency" that just passed on U.S. intelligence quickly and quietly began passing its own intelligence back to U.S. sources as well as the Australian Task Force. The SIGINT/EW unit no longer played an intermediary role but became a trusted source of information for other agencies during the remainder of their years in Vietnam.

547 soars

Former 547 trooper Mike Conaghan says, "Our people decided in '66 that we needed our own ground-based DF systems—either ARDF or something like the PRD-1. This was to ease our reliability on U.S. usage which was not always available at certain times. ARDF was decided to be the benchmark for us as we were rather short on personnel in the theatre. We had, at max strength, thirty-two personnel on base. That included operators on the sets, processing, clerk, comcen (communications), etc."

Cessna 180A–1968 (Photo: Denis Hare-pronto@au104.org)

The Weapons Research Establishment (WRE) in South Australia was tasked with developing and field-testing an Australian system. The new equipment, consisting of a receiver with a copper-wire "aerial" that trailed out of the aircraft, was tested in mid-1967. The aerial was reeled in and out of the plane using a fishing reel. It was simple, but effective and accurate. The system was mounted in a Cessna 180A aircraft, piloted by a 161 Independent Reconnaissance Flight pilot, and the Troop commenced ARDF operations in August 1967. "I was the first

ARDF operator to serve with the Troop," Mike Conaghan says, "and very proud of the fact and the results that we were getting."

In 1970, the 547 upgraded its ARDF equipment and installed it into the new Pilatus Porter aircraft. The upgrade proved to be a major improvement for both ARDF operators and technicians and was used successfully until the unit ceased operations in December 1971. Conaghan concludes by saying, "The last eighteen months, in Vietnam, we also flew a second aircraft. It was often tasked by U.S. (MACV) and operated way up into the border areas."

Pilatus Porter–1970 (Photo: Denis Hare-pronto@au104.org)

547 afield

With the 1st ATF deploying forward into the field, it became necessary for the 547 Signal Troop to also deploy and operate with its parent unit. An ACV "armoured command vehicle" (APC) was allocated to the 547, but it was not the typical ACV. The Troop's vehicle was fitted and wired with the necessary communications equipment to convert it into what was required for their mission: an "Armoured Communications Vehicle." The ACV was also equipped with a special "jenny" (generator) for power. That was something the regular APCs did not have. That allowed the 547 representatives in the field to provide timely information and replies to any questions the staff might have.

Bob Harland, who served with the 547 says, "[The ACV] was a bit of an experiment in the beginning, but ended up quite useful….We actually were in a convoy returning from FSB Picton and ran into a bunch of Chicom mines. Lost a tank, two tracks, and a dustoff chopper that was coming in to carry the dead and wounded out—now that put a buzz up the C.O.'s arse—the call came back, 'I don't care how you do it, but get that track (the ACV) out of there. The trip home was at best frightening, following the remaining tank through the boondocks, and having to sit on top of it!"

The troopers found out many years later that there were high explosives installed under the "cypher gear" in the ACVs. That is similar to the thermite panels ASA installed on its Explorer systems and the thermite grenades that were available to destroy cryptologic equipment, thus preventing it from falling into enemy hands.

ACV "Callsign 85D" dug in at FSB Colorado–
January 1970 (Photo: © Bob Harland)

Bob Harland continues, "I got to go out in the track 85D every time it went out. [The] 3 Cav didn't trust us with their toy, so we had to take…[drivers] along—buggered if I know what they did all day—they weren't allowed in….It was like being in an oven [inside the ACV]. Your guys at [FSB] Colorado did us proud—they dug a bloody great hole for us to back the ACV into, then put a nice tin roof on it, then sandbagged it—it was like the Hilton in the end. Cheers!"

Jon Swayze, Bob Harland, Dennis "DJ" Dean, Unknown (Photo: © Bob Harland)

547 update

In May 2012, a headline appeared on the daily news website of the Australian Broadcasting Company: "Secret Vietnam War radio unit in line for medals." The Australian Government had announced an independent inquiry into whether members of 547 Signal Troop should be awarded medals for their service in Vietnam. The 547 had served both on the ground at Nui Dat and also in the air flying ARDF missions in light airplanes over Phuoc Tuy Province.

In 1968, the unit was commanded by Maj. Peter Murray, and he welcomed the inquiry. Murray said, "The fellows who did that work have not been recognised over the years, and they did something which made a significant contribution to Australia's military effort in Vietnam....Their covert work saved many Australian lives, and to this day the unit still holds top-level secrets."

The long-term problem has been that the work of the 547 was so top-secret that some forty years after the end of the war, there are still few people who know of their efforts and their successes. "I'm amazed really that over the period of the Vietnam War probably over 200 or 300 men went through that unit, and I have not known of a single occasion of one of them ever discussing publicly what he did, other than the very, very close family, maybe their spouses," Murray continued. "But even then they couldn't say very much and still retain the secret."

"Chaps" of the 547 Signal Troop: Harry Lock, Des Williams, Tony Luck and Bob Harland (Photo: © Bob Harland)

Much of the information about the mission of the 547 has been declassified in the years since the war ended. The equipment they used is on public display in museums in both Australia and the U.S., but the men were so thoroughly trained to maintain their silence and not discuss anything pertaining to their work that they still find it difficult to discuss. "Absolutely we do [hold secrets], Maj. Murray said. "There is a great deal which is not ever discussed. We discuss it sometimes amongst ourselves, but these chaps just got so imbued with the need for secrecy…it's just they don't have big mouths."

CHAPTER 13
330TH RRC SAILS IN

The 330ᵗʰ RRC at Engineer Hill–Pleiku–1966 (Photo: © Larry Hertzberg)

On 19 August 1966, the 330ᵗʰ Radio Research Company arrived in Qui Nhon after twenty days at sea aboard the *U.S.S. Gaffey.* They moved by convoy to Pleiku and established their base at Engineer Hill. Jim "Sakk" Frankenfield was among the ASA soldiers who were on board the *Gaffey* and later wrote: "Many of us arrived at Ft. Wolters, Texas, around May and June of 1966. Since the entire unit was being transported to Nam by ship, everything had to be prepared for shipment. All vehicles, vans, mess gear, supply items, etc. had to be secured to be sent on [the] ship. We had an advanced party (about twenty men) led by Staff Sgt. Wilder that left about two weeks before the main group for Nam. Their job was to secure the area for our new home and begin to transport and set things up for when the rest of the company arrived."

When the unit arrived on Engineer Hill at Pleiku, they were informed that another unit had moved into the area assigned to the 330th. Their only recourse was to secure a different site and set up a security perimeter. They also learned that all the equipment they had not carried with them had been loaded onto the wrong ship and was headed for Italy. In addition, there were six or eight of their troops accompanying the equipment across the Atlantic. The ship developed engine problems in Italy, so their equipment and men were delayed arriving in Vietnam for nearly three months. In the interim, the 330th's encampment consisted of two tents someone had "borrowed" from the infantry; the soldier's individual pup tents, their individual weapons, and the uniforms they had brought with them. They had no vehicles, none of their larger tents, no mess gear, and none of the equipment they needed to do the job they were sent there to do.

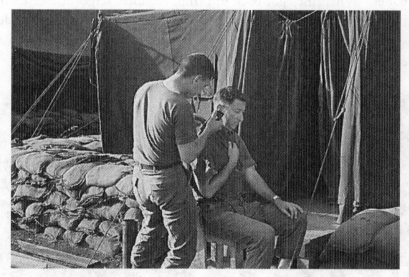

Not quite high-and-tight (Photo: © Larry Hertzberg)

"Staff Sgt. Dubrowski volunteered…[our] platoon to be the 'scrounge platoon.' We would go out in the day and look for things that the company needed, and then at night, we would all go out and 'borrow' them. At first, we did very little duty during the day, but were out most of the night. We signed for anything we could during [the] day, using any signature (since the Army likes signatures), and then stole everything we could get our little hands on and transported it at night, most of the time. If we couldn't transport something, we stole something that we could transport it with."

The unit lived on C-rations for months until the "scroungers" had "borrowed" enough items to actually set up a mess tent in which to cook. When the mess sergeant discovered that he could at least double the company's allotment of food by taking Sakk Frankenfield and Joe Weir along to the ration point, they got the job permanently. On their first run to get rations, the two had realized that if one of them kept the guard busy, the other one could keep loading the truck. "Since we already had a lot of practice in 'borrowing,' it was easy," Frankenfield said later. As they left, the guard told them "it didn't look like that much on paper." When they got back to camp, the mess sergeant told them that if they would accompany him on all the ration runs, they would "never have KP" and would have "free access" to the storage tent for a snack whenever they wanted it. Life was good.

Filling sandbags at the 330th (Photo: © Larry Hertzberg)

Sakk continued: "Our first club was a large tub full of ice and beer and a few sodas. In about five or six months, the club made about $10,000, and we were able to buy (and steal) enough lumber, coolers, etc. to build a real club....One thing anyone in ASA could do was put the brewskis away! That club may be the one that so many enjoyed for many years after when they arrived at the 330th RRC.

"We ran several convoys to An Khe and Qui Nhon for supplies every few weeks. That usually turned out to be a big road rally all the way down and back. I happen to hold a record for damaging five deuce-and-a-halfs on the return trip of one convoy. I was kindly greeted by First Sergeant McKillip that day and became his personal slave for almost two weeks afterward, one of the contributing factors preventing me from ever getting my Good Conduct Medal."

It sounds like the men of the 330th spent most of their time drinking and playing, but they also worked. They cleared brush, dug bunkers, filled sandbags and pulled guard duty, both in the company area and on the perimeter. They also worked hard on the mission they were sent there to do. They were just never permitted to talk about it.

Soldiers of the 330th RRC reporting for guard duty (Photo: © Larry Hertzberg)

"We acquired some 'ops' from Phu Bai after about three months in country to help us get going on our mission," Frankenfield said. "They were some of the best ops in the country. Some [of their names] were: Larry Koza, Adam Adatto, Dave Miller, Bob Soppe and Bruce Keaton. Joe Weir (one of the 20-men advance party for the 330th) began working with Miller on the 'spy net,' and they put much of it together with a lot of hard work. I had the honor and pleasure of working with Bruce 'Buz' Keaton on another project. He was probably the best op seen by many, and he was a great influence on me during his stay there. There were many great men there doing all the jobs required of them [to the best of their abilities]."

Some of the soldiers at the 330th left after about ten months and joined ARDF crews: Al Adatto, Bob Soppe, and Sgt. Ron Morris went to the 156th Aviation Co. Joe Weir and Sakk Frankenfield moved to the 146th Aviation Co. Those that transferred had to have been in Vietnam a minimum of six months, had to extend their time for another tour, and had to be "rated rather high," according to Frankenfield. At the time, ARDF was the "high-priority" mission, so even though the C.O. of the 330th did not want to lose all of the men at one time, he had little choice in the matter. Frankenfield stayed with the 146th for two years. The last year, in addition to flying regular missions, he did much of the training for the new ops coming in.

Jerry Laney and uncle, Lt. Col. Ike Laney, in front of new barracks—1968 (Photo: © J. Laney)

In spite of its rocky start, the 330th RRC compiled a distinguished record in Vietnam, earning twelve campaigns, four Meritorious Unit Commendations, and two Vietnamese Crosses of Gallantry with Palm.

AUTHOR'S NOTE: James "Sakk" Frankenfield passed away November 28, 2007.

ASA soldiers continued to die

On 19 August 1966, Pfc. Dennis Bahr of the 303rd RRB was killed in a vehicle crash. He had been in Vietnam approximately three months.

Dennis Keith Bahr was a military policeman and was from Columbus, Nebraska. He was nineteen years old.

On 25 September, Capt. James Stallings, Commanding Officer of the 337th RRC was killed in an ambush. David N. McDonald, formerly of the 409th ASA RR Detachment had met Capt. Stallings when he was TDY to the 337th. He was told that Capt. Stallings was killed by a claymore mine while returning from a PRD1 site. Sgt. 1st Class Morris who was travelling with him dragged him from the M151 (light truck) to cover, not knowing he was already dead. An ARVN unit behind them said they received small arms fire from the trees. The driver, Thomas Herring lost his right leg, and Sgt. Morris received a Silver Star for his actions.

James D. Stallings was thirty-four years old and from Carthage, Tennessee. He was buried at Arlington National Cemetery.

Letter home

On 15 October 1966, a twenty-five-year-old ASA lieutenant named John Cochrane wrote a letter to his parents. It was his third wedding anniversary, and in the letter he said:

"Tonight...I am awaiting an attack. Yes, that's right....Your only son, who you didn't raise to be stupid, is 11,000 miles from home, sitting here beneath a shaded Coleman lantern on top of a hill awaiting a visit from friend 'Charley.'

Here I sit, so afraid that my stomach is a solid knot, yet laughing, joking, kidding around with the eighteen troops with me—even writing a letter to the folks back home as if I haven't a care in the world. What I really want to do is load up these men…and get out of here. I don't belong here. Neither do these men. This isn't our war…It doesn't make sense. I refuse to believe God created a human being, let him live for twenty years on this Earth just to send him to some foreign land to die…

I have offered every excuse in the book, but I know why I am here and why I couldn't be any other place. The reason is because I do believe we should be here and I do believe that…basic principles are enough for a man to die for…We are here because we actually believe that our country is good enough to fight, and even if necessary, die for. All we ask is that some good come out of it…

Now you may think this is all written in a highly emotional state, and if fear is considered a highly emotional state, and it is, then you are right. But I have sat here this night and looked in the faces of eighteen young men–the oldest is twenty-eight–and I have talked to them about their homes and families and wives and sweethearts…

I have had to sit here and direct them about what action they would take and what they would do if 'Charley' does pay us a call, and I have had to tell them that once it starts, there can be no giving up–no relenting even if it's to the last man, because of the information they have had access to…I could read on their faces the fear, the doubts, and the anger…

As they asked their questions, I could feel the tension they were feeling as they asked me what they should do–or where the machine guns should be deployed. And I was scared–not because of death, because I have accepted the Lord and I know where I will spend Eternity–but because I also had to assume the responsibility for eighteen other lives– and that takes guts–lots of them…

All precautions have been taken, and double-checked. If he comes, he will have a fight on his hands. If he doesn't come, then we will all walk around with sheepish looks on our faces telling those around us that we really weren't afraid. But it's not tomorrow, it's right now, and it's dark, and he is out there—we can hear him...

It is times like right now that we search our souls and are able to see our faults and shortcomings...Here I am alone—only I can make the decision. I have to be right. If I am not, then men will die—good men with families and girlfriends and mothers and fathers...

Charley is...a formidable enemy...I will kill him if I get the chance because he does not agree with me. That is what war is all about. A simple disagreement, yet we, the most civilized of God's creatures, have to resort to shooting and killing to settle this simple disagreement. Reminds me of that passage from Psalms, 'What is a man that Thou are mindful of him?' That may not be exactly correct ...but the thought is still there.

It really seems that God has turned his back on mankind when one is in a situation like this. With all of the intellect and intelligence and scientific discovery He has endowed man with, it boils down to two soldiers on opposite sides, sworn to kill each other...

I am going to take one last look around and then I am going to try and get some sleep. If all goes well, I will finish this tomorrow. Thank goodness I can call on God at a moment like this.

Much Love, J"

John Cochrane and his eighteen ASA soldiers survived that night. The next morning, as he finished his letter, he wrote, "I wonder if I will ever know what makes man work. What causes him to do the things he does?"

On 24 October 1966, six days before he was to join his wife, Elaine, in Hawaii for R&R, John Cochrane was killed by a sniper near Xuan Loc.

David McDonald says, "When I was in the 409th, 1st Lt. Cochrane was the operations officer and my OIC. I remember that day very well. The detachment commander, Lt. Cochrane, and an acting sergeant, who was driving, left the Long Binh staging area in search of PRD1 sites.

When out of sight of the staging area, the Captain told the Sergeant to get in back and let him drive. That placed Lt. Cochrane in the passenger seat. Somewhere south of Xuan Loc, in the vicinity of what was to be the 11th ACR compound, a sniper fired two shots. The first went through the oil filter, stopping the engine. The second shot went through the windshield [killing Lt. Cochrane].

"There are pictures showing the only visible damage to the M151 is a hole in the windshield. I guess the reason I remember it so well is that the Captain chewed my ass out for not knowing that the sniper was there. Hell, we usually could not pin-point the regiments, let alone a single VC. The Captain proceeded on to the 303rd…while we at the detachment had to contact Lt. Cochrane's wife who was enroute to Hawaii."

In December, President Johnson read portions of Cochrane's last letter home to a group of wounded Vietnam veterans who were attending the Christmas tree lighting ceremony at the White House. After reading the letter, Johnson said, "I have known many brave men and wise men, but I wish I had known Lieutenant John Cochrane. Then I would have known the best of men."

John Floyd Cochrane was a Signal Security Officer with the 409th RRU. He was a native of Dearborn, Michigan, and was twenty-five years old. He and his wife, Elaine, had been married for three years. John Cochrane was buried at Arlington National Cemetery.

ASA loses another Beaver

On November 15th, Capt. Harry Ravenna of the 138th Aviation Co. took off from Dong Ha in a U-6A (Beaver) after filing a VFR flight plan at Da Nang. On board with him was Marine Cpl. John Keiper assigned to Helicopter Attack Maintenance Squadron 16, Marine Air Group 16, which was based at Dong Ha. Keiper assisted in the maintenance of aircraft temporarily based at Dong Ha.

At approximately 1430 hours Capt. Ravenna made radio contact with Da Nang. He said: "Lonely Ringer 723 (aircraft #541723), heading

125, 3000 feet, estimating Da Nang at 40, request radar, presently on instruments." Da Nang could not locate the aircraft on radar and requested his position. Ravenna radioed that he was forty-five nautical miles from Dong Ha. Da Nang requested that he contact Dong Ha, and he acknowledged that request, but that was the last contact with the aircraft.

It is believed that the plane went down in the Hi Van Mountains in South Vietnam, half way between Da Nang and Hue, but due to the hostile threat in the area at the time, an extensive search was not possible, and the actual crash site was never located. A later investigation concluded that if the plane had continued on its original course, it would have impacted with the side of a mountain in that vicinity. Capt. Ravenna and Cpl. Keiper have never been found and are still listed as KIA/BNR.

Harry M. Ravenna III was from San Antonio, Texas. He was a graduate of St. Mary's University and had graduated from OCS at Ft. Sill, Oklahoma. He was twenty-nine years old at the time of the crash.

John Charles Keiper was from Renovo, Pennsylvania, and had enlisted in the Marine Corps in 1963. He was twenty-one years old.

Former ASA intercept op David Adams of Tucson, Arizona recently wrote: "I was stationed in Da Nang when we were called the 3rd RRU Det. J. I was there from June 1965 until December 1966. I was a Morse intercept operator and flew in U-6s and U-8s. I flew with Captain Harry Ravenna on his flight from Da Nang to Dong Ha. His mission was to fly me to Dong Ha where we were supporting the Marines. The weather was terrible, and we barely got into the Dong Ha airfield. The Marine (Keiper) that was lost that day was on his way home on emergency leave due to a family emergency."

1966 winds down

As 1966 closed, U.S. forces stood at 362,000 with an additional 50,000 from Australia, New Zealand, and the Republic of Korea. ARVN regulars totaled 315,000, in addition to about 300,000 regional and self-defense forces. NVA forces numbered 114,000, including about 46,000 regulars and an additional 320,000 Viet Cong.

Operation Cedar Falls

Sunday, 8 January 1967 saw the launch of the war's first major U.S.-ARVN combined operation and the first U.S. corps-size operation. Cedar Falls deployed 32,000 troops against the notorious Iron Triangle, 20 miles north of Saigon.

The intelligence compiled prior to the start of the operation was amazingly accurate. Not only was it correct regarding the movement and activities of major VC units, it had also pin-pointed the locations of many VC installations and facilities. According to *Time* magazine, about 88% of the enemy installations uncovered during the operation were within 500 meters of where U.S. intelligence had suggested they would be located. That intelligence came from ASA intercept.

The main objectives of Cedar Falls were to engage and eliminate enemy forces, destroy their base camps and supplies, remove all non-combatants with their possessions and livestock to "strategic hamlets," and completely destroy four villages that had been long-time VC strongholds. After the area was free of civilians, it would become a free-fire zone, and anything that moved within that twenty-five square-mile area would be a target.

Extensive underground tunnel complexes were uncovered, including what was described as an "underground city" on the Triangle's western flank. It was probably the headquarters of the VC 4th Military Region, which included Saigon. It was heavily booby-trapped and contained maps and diagrams of hotels and billets in Saigon that housed Americans. They also found detailed plans for the VC suicide attack on Tan Son Nhut Airport, along with office equipment, medical supplies, and officers' side-arms.

The complete U.S. arsenal was authorized and applied. The area was intensively bombed, followed by flame-throwers and chemical warfare (defoliants and tear gas). And then came the land-clearing Rome plows. The media reported there was little actual fighting, as most VC troops had fled into Cambodia, but seventy-two allied soldiers died and 337 were wounded during the course of the operation. The destruction was extensive, and about 7,000 refugees were created. The VC later returned to rebuild their camps, which were used to launch attacks on Saigon during the Tet Offensive in 1968.

Another soldier dies

On 8 March 1967, Sgt. 1st Class John Stirling was killed during a mortar attack on the detachment at Tan An. Sgt. Stirling was assigned to the 335th RRC, and his MOS is listed as "Light Infantry." He died of multiple fragment wounds during the mortar attack.

John F. Stirling was a native of Los Angeles, California and was married with one son, Rodney. He was thirty-five years old with sixteen years of military service and was buried in the cemetery at Ft. Devens, Massachusetts.

The war on paper

In April 1967, Defense Secretary McNamara asked the CIA to provide an objective assessment of how the war was going in Vietnam. The results were not what he had hoped to hear. He was told that VC strength was about 500,000; the air campaign over North Vietnam was not achieving the necessary results; and the U.S. pacification programs in the South were totally mired down.

MACV in Saigon was furious. Gen. Creighton Abrams, Westmoreland's second in command, sent a cable stating that: "This is in sharp contrast to the current overall strength figure of 299,000 given to the press here….We have been projecting an image of success over the recent months…when we release the figure of 420,000-431,000, the newsmen will immediately seize on the point that the enemy force has increased about 120,000-130,000. All available caveats and explanations will not prevent the press from drawing an erroneous and gloomy conclusion as to the meaning of the increase."

A meeting was finally convened between the CIA and MACV in Saigon in September. MACV depicted the VC as sick, hungry and frightened, low on ammunition and declining in numbers. At the conclusion of the rancorous six-day meeting, George Carver of the CIA met privately with Gen. Westmoreland, and MACV got everything it wanted. The VC order of battle was slashed beyond all recognition to get the numbers where MACV wanted them to be. NVA and VC regular forces were cut only a few thousand, but support units were cut by 50%, and the VC infrastructure disappeared altogether with a simple stroke of the pen. In its final form, the document showed total Viet Cong capabilities at just over 188,000 to 208,000. In his book *Who The Hell Are We Fighting?* author Michael Hiam said the report was "nothing less than the prostitution of intelligence."

National Security Advisor Walt Rostow sent a memo with the report stating that the new estimate showed "a substantial reduction in guerrillas," "a slight reduction in main force units," and "a fairly good chance" for a decline in the Viet Cong infrastructure. Rostow concluded that "Manpower is the major problem confronting the communists."

Back at Langley, George Allen, Deputy Director of Vietnamese Affairs, read the report and said it "damn near made me puke." Allen would later testify that "the production in late 1967 of a 'misleading' intelligence estimate on enemy strength in South Vietnam was part of a broader 'self-deception' by the Administration of President Lyndon B. Johnson regarding progress in the war." He also reported that the White House had tried to "head off mounting public opposition to the war" through a "massive public-relations campaign to influence, exaggerate and misrepresent." Allen had described the doctored numbers as "making a mountain out a molehill" and said that "the production of this dishonest estimate was only a small part of that bigger issue, that bigger exercise by the Administration, which in fact, caused its loss of credibility." The ultimate result was that "neither Congress, nor members of the Administration, nor the population was prepared for the psychological impact mounted by the communist forces on an unprecedented scale" during the Tet offensive in January 1968.

The spoken word

In May 1967, Ellsworth Bunker arrived in Saigon to replace Henry Cabot Lodge as U.S. Ambassador. May also marked the first detection of unsecured communist HF voice communications in the A Shau Valley. ASA cryptologists had been trying to intercept communist voice communications since they first arrived at Tan Son Nhut in 1961, but had been unsuccessful up to that point. ASA hoped that the voice communications would help to locate units infiltrating from the North into South Vietnam.

Once the HF voice communications were detected, voice interception quickly developed into a large-scale operation involving ASA, Air Force Security Service and Naval Security Group cryptologists. The amount of intercept was greater than the linguists from all three services could handle, and a program to use native Vietnamese was begun to fill the gap. Initially, however, the intercept, consisting mainly of Hanoi's air defense network, was of little value.

It was not until October that a breakthrough occurred, when an operator on an RC-130 intercepted a communication on an LVHF (Low Very High Frequency) voice network. It was encrypted, but readable, and contained mostly logistics information. The communication was between communications-liaison stations located along the infiltration route south of Thanh Hoa, North Vietnam, and the large logistic-billet complex around Vinh, North Vietnam, which provided support for the troops heading into South Vietnam.

In November, the communists began sending voice reports on the movement of military troops heading south, and from November to February 1968, cryptologists identified over fifty groups moving south. Other intelligence sources were able to ID most of the groups and their destinations. Then, in February, the situation got even better. The North Vietnamese changed their system of numbering the groups to a four-digit system; the first number identified the group's destination. Using information from other sources to verify their findings, it was now possible not only to accurately estimate the number of NVA soldiers infiltrating into the South but also to know where they were heading. This intelligence bonanza became known as the "Vinh Window," named for the city of Vinh located along the northern portion of the Ho Chi Minh Trail.

Before the Vinh Window, such information was derived almost totally from P.O.W. interrogations, but after March 1968, it was based on SIGINT, and P.O.W information was just used for verification and to fill in small gaps. Thanks to the efforts of ASA and its crypto partners, Washington now had a view of North Vietnamese activities that it had never had prior to that time.

The Vinh Window intelligence was limited in the amount of geographic information it contained, so it was difficult to know where an identified enemy group would be located at any given time, but in the end that was not of any great importance. On March 31, 1968, President Johnson stopped all air strikes north of the 20th parallel, hoping to lure Hanoi to the conference table for peace talks, and then on November 1st, all air strikes against North Vietnam ceased. Whatever advantages could have been derived from the "Vinh Window" intelligence would never be realized. ASA and its associates could only listen and watch as NVA troops and supplies continued to pour into the South to no tactical advantage.

CHAPTER 14
CRAZY CATS & LEFT BANK

P2 Neptune at Cam Ran Bay–1967 (Photo: U.S. Army)

The 1st Radio Research Company (Aviation), known as "Crazy Cats," was deployed to the Naval Air Station at Cam Ranh Bay in June 1967 as the fifth subordinate company of the 224th AB. There was a good reason why an Army aviation unit was stationed with the U. S. Navy; they were flying six converted P-2 Neptune aircraft. Most of the planes were being retired by the Navy, and only an NAS could provide the spare parts necessary to support their operation.

The planes had been procured from a storage facility and flown to General Dynamics in San Diego to be electrically outfitted. The ASA configuration was designated RP-2E and was the largest aircraft in the Army fleet at that time. It was the first time since 1948 that the Army had operated a four engine aircraft, and they had never operated one with jet engines. Army ground crews trained at NAS Jacksonville, Florida, and the pilots trained at NAS North Shore in San Diego, California.

The aircraft were modified with pole antennas, and all five were fitted with SIGINT gathering systems. Three were equipped with radio jamming systems. The right-side bomb bay door was sealed, and the area was filled with electronic gear and a turbine generator for additional equipment power. Behind the cockpit were five intercept/op positions, each about thirty inches wide, and five tape recorders to record the intercepted traffic. Behind the "op" positions was an observer area large enough for men to stand up, and there were two hanging bunks for use on long flights.

The aircraft departed the U.S. on 23 June 1967, and all but one arrived in South Vietnam on 30 June. Aircraft 485 made at least three attempts, but had to turn back for various mechanical reasons. She became known as *The Burbank Boomerang*. Aircraft 492 was used for pilot training and was called *The Bounce Bird* due to its hard landings. Other Crazy Cat aircraft were named *Miss Conception*, *Miss Carriage*, and *Old Faithful*.

Vietnam-era blood chit (Photo: U.S. Army)

Originally promoted by Gen. Westmoreland for electronic "jamming" of enemy HF and UHF radio transmissions, their primary use became HF/VHF Morse and voice intercept. NSA decided it was more productive to listen and intercept enemy communications than to disrupt them. Aircraft 429 flew the first mission on 12 July 1967. The next day, 429 slid off the runway at Pleiku when one of its engines failed to reverse. No one was injured, but the plane caught fire and was out of service for over two months while being repaired.

There was normally one mission per day with a crew of twelve to fourteen. The crew wore uniforms with no name tags, rank or IDs. They carried "blood chits" (documents with a U.S. flag and a statement in several languages indicating that anyone assisting the bearer would be rewarded) like those carried by the Flying Tigers in WWII.

"Crazy Cats" at Cam Ranh Bay–1968-69 (Photo: U.S. Army)

The crews were made up of three to seven operators, a mission controller, and an equipment repairman. There were also Vietnamese voice-intercept ops and three pilots, due to the length of the missions. Their primary area of operation was the Ho Chi Minh Trail (Laos), and the aircraft stayed at its assigned location for eight to eight-point-five hours at an altitude of 8,500 to 10,500 feet. All intercepted transmissions were hand-recorded and taped; on their return flight they would drop off the intelligence at Da Nang while refueling. Sixteen hours after their morning departure, they would arrive back at Cam Ranh Bay.

Project "Left Bank"

In the summer of 1967, the 1st Cavalry Division provided three UH-1D "Huey" helicopters and pilots in a joint effort with ASA. Its direct support unit, ASAs 371st RRC provided ops and intelligence gathering systems, and a unique partnership known as "Left Bank" was born. The 374th RRC, supporting the 4th Infantry Division, also took part in the ASA collaboration. Left Bank was unique in the respect that it was under the direct operational control of the division commanders.

ASA operator in a Left Bank helicopter (Photo: INSCOM)

The 1ˢᵗ Cav's three Left Bank Hueys, named *The Good, The Bad,* and *The Ugly,* were originally equipped with a direction-finding system, a radio finger-printing position, and a voice recorder. The RFP was later eliminated when it was deemed ineffective due to excessive vibration, which actually made the remaining two systems more effective.

What made Left Bank so successful was the combining of the DF platform with the firepower and mobility of airborne warfare. If the Left Bank pilot located a "fix," he hovered over the area at canopy level looking for evidence of troop movement or enemy installations; if he spotted enemy personnel, he called in an Arc Light mission (B-52s), gunships, or troops. During January 1969, Left Bank was responsible for six B-52 strikes, multiple artillery rounds, and troop insertions that resulted in over 300 enemy KIA. Lt. Col. Donald E. Grant, C.O. of the 303ʳᵈ RR Bn said, "Left Bank went out, obtained a target, and then became a small command center in the sky directing the attack. In fact, the Cav became so reliant on this technique that when the Left Bank was no longer available their effectiveness was severely hampered."

The Ugly, one of 1ˢᵗ Cav's original Left Bank Hueys (Photo: © Carlos Collat)

Sad day for ASA

On 8 October 1967, seven members of ASA's 8th RR Field Station were killed when their aircraft crashed shortly after take-off from Phu Bai airfield. All of the soldiers had completed their tours of duty in Vietnam and were returning to the U.S. The C-130 crashed into a mountain near Phu Loe. There were no survivors. The dead included:

Spc.5 William L. Stewart, Jr., age twenty-four, of Williamsburg, Virginia.

Spc.4 Robert D. Nelson, twenty-one years old, of Knoxville, Tennessee.

Spc.4 Ronald A. Villardo, twenty-one, of Sacramento, California.

Spc.4 Richard G. Feruggia, twenty-two years old, of Cedar, New Jersey.

Spc.4 Terrance H. Larson, twenty, of Cody, Wyoming. Terrance Larson was buried at Arlington National Cemetery.

Spc.4 Joseph P. Rowley, twenty, of Cumberland, Maryland. Joseph Rowley was buried at Arlington National Cemetery.

Spc.4 John D Saville, Jr., twenty, of Cumberland, Maryland. John Saville was buried at Arlington National Cemetery.

All but one of the soldiers had arrived in Vietnam together. Rowley and Saville were both from Cumberland, Maryland, where they had been born four months and one day apart. They both died on the side of a mountain in Vietnam on the same day twenty years later.

The Air Force C-130B was assigned to the 773rd Troop Carrier Squadron, 463rd Troop Carrier Wing, based at Clark A.B., Philippines. There were a total of five crew members and eighteen U.S. servicemen as passengers on the plane when it departed Phu Bai for the short hop to Da Nang. The weather was described as "horrific" with low clouds, ground fog and rain. About ten minutes into the flight the aircraft hit Thon Canh Duong Mountain, an 1850 foot peak, about 150 feet below the summit. When the wreckage was located two days later the rescuers discovered that all aboard had been killed. The death toll in the crash was eight soldiers, six airmen, five Marines and four sailors.

Rumble of distant thunder

As early as the summer of 1967, there had been talk of a major communist attack coming within the next few months. Robert Pisor had reported in the *Detroit News* in August that there were rumors in Saigon of a "massive, country-wide military strike" coming soon.

On 25 October, the Central Committee in Hanoi passed Resolution 14 calling for a General Offensive/General Uprising in the South, and on November 13 a copy of the order was captured in Quang Tri Province by the 101st Airborne. As a result, by late November, the CIA station in Saigon had produced a report entitled "The Big Gamble." In the report, they asserted that the communists were changing their strategy and planning a major attack.

MACV was initially skeptical of the report, but Westmoreland later concluded that a nationwide attack was possible. However, he thought that the North Vietnamese objective would be to grab areas along the frontier and in the northern part of the country. U.S. intelligence and MACV had hard evidence of where and how the impending offensive was going to take place about two months before Tet, but they made little use of the information.

Operation MacArthur

From 03 November to 22 November 1967, one of the bloodiest battles of the war took place near Dak To. Dak To sat on an infiltration route into the Central Highlands used by the VC and NVA operating out of Cambodia. During early November, U.S. troops from the 173rd Airborne Brigade and the 4th ID attacked NVA fortifications along the ridgelines. The 173rd was supported by the 404th RRD, and the 4th ID included Det. 1, 374th RRC.

By the third week in November, the battle had centered on Hill 875. Gen. Westmoreland ordered in over 300 B-52 missions and 2,000 fighter-bomber sorties to destroy the defensive positions of the 174th NVA Regiment that was dug in there. On 19 November, U.S. troops began to ascend the hill, and the battle raged for four days, complete with air strikes, napalm, and hand-to-hand combat. Late on the 22nd, the NVA retreated from the area, and the next morning U.S. soldiers claimed the summit.

Three Medals of Honor were awarded following the eight-day battle, and both battalions received the Presidential Unit Citation. The NVA Regiment withdrew into Cambodia with 1,500 to 2,000 dead and 3,000 wounded. U.S. casualties numbered 285 killed and 985 wounded. The 404th RRD and 374th RRC, along with other radio research units were acknowledged for their contributions to the victory.

More ASA losses

On 26 November 1967, three ASA soldiers from the 335th RRC were killed on Highway 4 near Xom Dua when the quarter-ton vehicle in which they were traveling was ambushed by the VC. The truck was hit by an enemy B40 recoilless rifle round at close range, followed by small arms and mortar fire. Those killed were:

Sgt. 1st Class Robert D. Taylor, forty years old, was a native of Santa Monica, California. Robert Taylor was an EW/SIGINT non-Morse interceptor 05K.

Sgt. Diego Ramirez, Jr., twenty-two years old, was from El Paso, Texas. Diego Ramirez was a radio teletype operator 05C.

Spc.5 Michael Paul Brown, twenty-two years old, was from Hazleton, Pennsylvania. Michael Brown was a Viet linguist 98G.

On 30 November, Sgt. Jose Miranda-Ortiz died in an accident. **Jose L. Miranda-Ortiz** was a 04C (expert linguist) with the 330th RRC. He was thirty-one years old and from Rio Piedras, Puerto Rico.

The gathering storm

By December 1967, U.S. troop levels had reached 485,000, including 332,000 U.S. Army and 78,000 Marines. The Politburo in Hanoi had passed a resolution moving the revolution in the South into the "phase of winning decisive victory," and traffic on the Ho Chi Minh Trail had surged by 200%. Hanoi offered to "talk after a bombing halt." The Tet holiday was approaching, and few U.S. or South Vietnamese officials believed that the NVA and VC would attack during Tet. The Tet holiday symbolized the "solidarity of the Vietnamese people," and the general belief was that enemy attacks at that time would be deeply resented by the South Vietnamese people, thus hurting the communist cause. Gen. Westmoreland said later, "I frankly did not think that they would assume the psychological disadvantage of hitting at Tet itself, so I thought it would be before or after Tet." In previous years the communists had used that time period to resupply.

More ASA planes go down

On 4 December 1967, Capt. Douglas Kelly and Warrant Officer 1 Robert King of the 138th Avn. Co. RR were killed when their RU6-D crashed north of Da Nang. Sgt. Melvin "Joel" Jorgenson, the senior 05H operator on the flight, was severely injured but managed to drag Spc.5 Tim Brown, the other 05H operator, from the burning wreckage. Jorgenson's head had hit the R-390 radio equipment. He was also reported to have had "shrapnel wounds" and a broken ankle.

Brown said later, "We spent about four hours on the ground before we were picked up by air rescue choppers. Both Joel and I were taken to the Naval Support Activities Hospital at Da Nang and later 'medevaced' to the 249th in Japan. I spent two months in the hospital in Japan and then returned to the 138th to complete my tour. I only saw Joel once while we were in the hospital, so I don't know how long he was there."

Joel Jorgenson had several operations and had a plate inserted in his head to repair his shattered skull. He was later awarded the Soldier's Medal in a ceremony at Ft. Devens for his heroism in December 1967.

The criteria for the medal states that the soldier's performance "must have involved personal hazard or danger and the voluntary risk of life under conditions not involving conflict with an armed enemy." It is the highest honor that an American soldier can receive for an act of valor in a non-combat situation and is equal to or greater than the level which would have justified an award of the Distinguished Flying Cross had the act occurred in combat.

Douglas J. Kelly was twenty-nine years old and from Salisbury, Massachusetts.

Robert D. King was from Marshalltown, Iowa, and was thirty-nine. King was the intercept-equipment repair technician on the mission.

AUTHOR'S NOTE: "Joel" Jorgenson recovered from his injuries and remained in the U.S. Army, retiring with the rank of Sergeant Major. He died in Fairfax, Virginia, on July 21, 2006, at the age of sixty-six and was buried at Arlington National Cemetery.

The second crash of December

On 29 December 1967, an RU8-D crashed on takeoff killing Warrant Officer 1 Milton Smith and Warrant Officer 1 Jonathan Shaffer. The soldiers were both assigned to the 138th Avn. Co. RR but were TDY to the 8th RRFS and crashed within 100 meters of the 8th RRFS compound.

Milton W. Smith was twenty-three years old and from Belt, Montana.

Jonathan P. Shaffer was twenty-two and from San Mateo, California.

Away from the war

On December 4, 1967, the *Denver Republic* printed one of the strangest stories to come out of the Vietnam War. Stephen J. Shlafer, twenty-five, of Springfield, New Jersey, came to Vietnam as an ASA Vietnamese linguist in 1963, serving for one year. He became intrigued by the country and its people and remained there after his discharge, enrolling at Van Hanh University under a University of Michigan scholarship.

Three years later Shlafer, who was Jewish, "walked three times around a Buddhist pagoda…then went inside to pledge himself to a life of celibacy. He emerged a full-fledged Buddhist monk with the name Thich (Venerable) Thien Hien." Shlafer, who had his bar mitzvah confirmation at thirteen, talked with reporters later in Gia Dinh. He appeared with the traditional saffron robes and shaved head, outside the small cell where he would live. He said, "I wrote my parents today to tell them, 'Today, I am becoming a monk.' They knew I was going to do it. They haven't said too much about it. When I was a kid, I was a Torah scriptures reader in the synagogue. I don't think they're excited about this. They probably think it's another one of my wild schemes."

AUTHOR'S NOTE: After a long journey that took him to many other parts of the globe, Thich Thien Hien eventually returned to his native shore. In the early 1980s, Dr. Stephen J. Shlafer, M.D. finished his medical residency, opened his practice in Mill Creek, Washington, and would become a well-respected pediatrician.

Flashes of lightning

On 5 January 1968, U.S. 4th Infantry troops operating near Pleiku captured a copy of "Urgent Order Number One." The highly-classified NVA order outlined the planned attack on Pleiku during Tet by a VC battalion and an NVA regiment.

Early in January the U.S. Embassy in Saigon issued a press release on the General Offensive/General Uprising document that had been captured in November. The release noted that Hanoi had ordered "the entire army and people of South Vietnam to implement a general offensive and general uprising in order to achieve a decisive victory for the revolution." The Associated Press reported that the embassy had "distributed a translation of what it described as a captured enemy notebook saying the opportunity for a general uprising was within reach in South Vietnam." The implication was that "this was not as significant as it sounded," but there were those who understood the significance of the plan and its implications. The *South Carolina Chronicle* ran an editorial that stated: "The Viet Cong confidently expects to win, not through defeating America's armed forces, but through a general uprising in Vietnam, plus considerable inside help from soul mates in the United States."

Hanoi was planning on stirring up things in Vietnam so that there would be an uprising in the South, and the antiwar movement in the U.S. was gathering momentum. Between the two, they saw an opportunity to bring about the withdrawal of U.S. troops and the formation of a coalition government. That, of course, would lead to a complete communist take-over of the country.

On 17 January 1968, NSA sent out the first of a series of intelligence bulletins regarding recent SIGINT analysis. According to the bulletin, it was "likely" that various NVA units were preparing to attack Kontum, Pleiku, Darlac, Quang Nam, Quang Ngai, and Binh Dinh Provinces, as well as the city of Hue. On the 20th, documents were captured that contained plans for attacks on the cities of Ban Me Thout and Qui Nhon, and there were indications of increased enemy activity in the areas around Saigon.

CHAPTER 15

THE *PUEBLO* INCIDENT

U.S.S. Pueblo (AGER2) (Photo: U.S. Navy)

On 23 January 1968, the *U.S.S. Pueblo*, a Naval Security Group ELINT/ SIGINT collection ship was boarded and seized by North Korea. The incident occurred less than a week after President Johnson's State of the Union address and a week after the start of the Tet Offensive. The U.S. Government and *Pueblo's* Captain, Commander Lloyd M. Bucher, always maintained that the ship was in international waters, but the North Koreans claimed they had strayed into their territorial waters. Jerry Laney, who was assigned to the 330th RRC at Pleiku from September 1967 to August 1968 says, "We were in direct contact with the Pueblo during the incident. Not many people know that."

Lt. Steve Harris, the officer in charge of *Pueblo's* NSG detachment said: "We had retained on board the obsolete publications and had all good intentions of getting rid of these things but had not done so at the time we had started the mission. I wanted to get the place organized eventually, and we had excessive numbers of copies on board...only a small percentage of the total classified material aboard the ship was destroyed." The North Koreans acquired an intelligence treasure-trove, including top-secret cipher machines that were immediately removed from the ship and flown to Moscow.

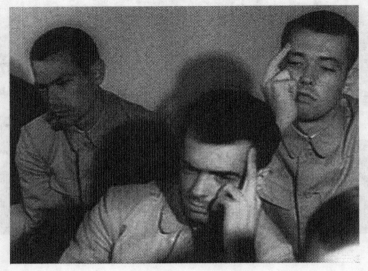

**Sailors Steve Ellis, Brad Crowe and John Shilling
express sentiments (Photo: U.S. Navy)**

During the ensuing months the *Pueblo*'s captain and crew were subjected to both mental and physical torture, and that became even more severe when the North Korean authorities figured out that the U.S. sailors in their staged propaganda photos were giving them the classic "finger."

After repeated North Korean threats to execute the entire crew as spies, the U.S. State Department relented and issued a public apology, a written admission that the Pueblo was spying, and assurances that the U.S. would not do it again. One sailor, Duane Hodges, had been killed during the attack, but the remaining eighty-two crewmembers were released on 23 December 1968. As soon as the last man crossed the DMZ into South Korea, the U.S. verbally retracted the apology, the admission, and the assurance.

The *U.S.S. Pueblo* is still in the custody of the North Korean government. It is moored along the Taedong River near Pyongyang where it is proudly displayed as a trophy for "anti-American education" as decreed by Kim Jung Il. The ship remains a commissioned ship of the United States Navy and is the only U.S. ship held captive by a foreign power.

VC campaign in Saigon

On 24 January 1968, MACV Joint Intelligence received an ARVN report that the VC were planning to launch an immediate political campaign in Saigon. The campaign would include "armed propagandists dropping leaflets, displaying flags, setting up slogans, beating drums, and radio broadcasting." The report also claimed that the VC were planning to move large amounts of sub-machine guns and grenades into the city and had given instructions to "annihilate military police." This was an unusual rumor and should have alerted analysts that the VC were planning some sort of action in the near future.

At the same time, Saigon learned that a Laotian army outpost near the South Vietnamese border had been overrun by NVA forces using tanks. Some 6,000 refugees from the attack, including remnants of the Laotian 33rd Royal Elephant Battalion were heading for the Special Forces camp at Lang Vei, west of Khe Sanh. U.S. reconnaissance later spotted five tanks moving toward the South Vietnamese border. By the next day, U.S. forces were preparing for an attack on their base at Khe Sanh, and Westmoreland had requested permission to begin planning an amphibious landing north of the DMZ to relieve pressure on Khe Sanh.

Classification: "SECRET SAVIN"

On 25 January, ASA/NSA issued a "SECRET CODEWORD 'SAVIN'" report entitled "Coordinated Vietnamese Communist

Offensive Evidenced in South Vietnam." In that report, NSA analysts stated that SIGINT "during the past week has provided evidence of a coordinated attack to occur in the near future in several areas of South Vietnam." The analysts said that the "most critical areas" were probably the northern half of the country, but there was some evidence that communist units in the Nam Bo area might also be involved. The Nam Bo area included Saigon, Ben Hoa, Tay Ninh, and Vung Tau. They believed that the "major target areas" for the NVA offensive would be the western highlands, the coastal provinces, and the Khe Sanh and Hue areas.

The report provided more than just a generic warning of planned attacks; it provided specific details about the location of attacks and the recent movements and identity of the NVA/VC units.

The following is an example of the kind of intelligence provided: "Coastal Provinces of MR 5-SIGINT indicates that elements of the PAVN [NVA] 2nd Division and HQ, MR 5 currently located in the Quang Ham-Quang Tin Province border area are in an attack posture. The possible PAVN 2nd Division Forward Element has been maintaining tactical control over the division's three regiments since 31 December, a procedure indicative in the past of Vietnamese Communist offensives. Additionally, the possible HQ, PAVN 21st Regiment, PAVN 2nd Division was located on 22 January, 9 km southwest of Tam Ky city. Collateral information indicates that an attack by elements of the 21st Regiment is imminent in this area. [MR5 included Da Nang.]

"MR Tri-Thien-Hue-SIGINT reflected a renewed Vietnamese communist interest in the Hue area. On 29 January HQ, MR TTH was located near 16-25N 107-21E (YD 5115), approximately twenty-six km west-southwest of Hue. Other units located in the general Hue area included the possible Hue Municipal Unit located near 16-18N 107-36E (YD 778030) on 8 January; one possible subordinate of the Hue Municipal Unit located near 16-25N 107-26E (YD 606171) on 17 November; HQ, PAVN 6th Regiment located near 16-26N 107-20E (YD 491173 on 12 December; and a possible battalion of the PAVN 6th Regiment located on 10 January near 16N 107-13E (YD 376301)."

The report goes on to identify increased activity in the Nam Bo region which included Saigon, Tay Ninh, Bien Hoa, Phuoc Long, and specified movements of element of the 9th NVA Light Infantry Division, the 5th LID, the VC 274th and 275th Regiments and many more. The detail of this five-page, single-spaced legal paper was exceptional. However, there was one thing missing. ASA/NSA had not been able to identify the timing of the attacks.

The U.S. and South Vietnamese commanders had the information about the enemy's plans and intentions and had taken some steps to counter them, but the policymakers still refused to accept that the communist plans had any real chance of succeeding. They were considered to be too flawed to be taken seriously; too large an undertaking and would divide the enemy forces, leaving them without reserves, and costing them the mobility that had been the guerrillas' primary strength. The erroneous conclusion was that the enemy had no chance of winning; therefore, such an operation was unlikely to take place, and the call for a general uprising was dismissed as just so-much propaganda.

AUTHOR'S NOTE: This report was released by NSA without redaction on January 10, 2011 as a result of a Freedom of Information request (FOIA Case #63653) submitted by Lonnie M. Long.

The storm breaks

On 29 January 1968, communist forces launched a mortar attack on Da Nang. More attacks followed after midnight on January 30. The 18B NVA Regiment hit Nha Trang with 800 troops and was defeated by ARVN forces in less than a day. Six cities were assaulted by an estimated 2,000 troops in the early morning hours, but most had been contained or driven off by daybreak. According to North Vietnamese history, "the offensive broke out simultaneously in sixty-four cities, villages and hamlets, and regions of the countryside." They attacked Saigon and other cities to the south twenty-four hours later.

CHAPTER 16

HOLIDAY IN DA LAT

**The center of Da Lat—theater, Modern Hotel and
market place (Photo: © Ken Thompson)**

Da Lat, the "city of a thousand pines," with its winding roads and clear streams, flowering trees and mist-filled valleys, was one of the garden spots of the Central Highlands. It was also called the "city of eternal spring" and was considered to be a vacation spot for both sides during the war. It was a great place for R&R and soldiers of all persuasions had been known to spend time there, enjoying the cool temperatures and quiet, comfortable lifestyle. No one expected the war to come to Da Lat.

In January 1968, Warren Galinski and Dick Spinner were part of an ASA "Monitor Mission" team that had been fortunate enough to go TDY to Da Lat. They were assigned to the 2nd Platoon, 101st RRC. They had just finished their mission and were due to fly out of Da Lat the next day.

"We were staying in downtown Da Lat at the Modern Hotel," "Skip" Galinski says, " …We had a lot of beer left over, and we were making a good attempt at getting rid of it [before we left town]. The hotel was in a little valley, and the center of town was above most of the buildings. If you walked out onto the flat roof, you could look out at the main part of the town. I know there was a large movie theater, a bunch of restaurants and a market. There was a large concrete set of steps that ran from the base of the hotel up toward the theater. That evening the Vietnamese were doing a lot of celebrating by shooting off fireworks everywhere." It was the first night of the Tet holiday.

Rude awakening

"I remember someone shaking me awake in the middle of the night," Galinski continues. "They were all excited that we were being mortared. I sat up in bed and was trying to tell them that they were crazy; nobody ever did any fighting in Da Lat. This was a resort town for both sides. Just after saying that, a round went off just outside the hotel, and I knew it was not fire crackers. I quickly got out of bed, and we went up onto the roof to check it out. In hind sight, that was not the smartest move because the roof was lighted, and we were easy targets for anyone in the area. For a few minutes we watched the airport [a few miles away] being shelled, and it was quite a show. I believe a mortar round went off in the market that made us realize we should not be on the roof."

As daylight broke, the weary soldiers were still peering out of their upper-level windows and soon realized that the town was filled with what appeared to be North Vietnamese regular army troops. Their hotel was completely surrounded. "It appeared they just drove in and took over the town," Galinski says, "They had to know that we were in the hotel because our truck was parked outside in plain sight."

Sometime later, the young men left their room and were relieved to discover that they were not the only Americans in the hotel. There were two U.S. Army majors with a radio there with them, and the officers were in contact with MACV. Word was spreading fast that something big was happening, and Da Lat was not the only place under attack. MACV instructed the group to observe the enemy force and keep them posted as to what was going on in the center of the city. Since the NVA solders were showing no interest in attacking the Americans, they were told not to start a firefight. "So, we did what we did a lot of in the Army," Skip says, "we sat around and waited and watched."

Da Lat—"The city of eternal spring" (Photo: © Ken Thompson)

As the men watched the street, a few of the local citizens began to venture out of their homes, and the enemy troops started to harass them for sport or entertainment. "I remember this poor kid riding his bike up the main street that ran parallel to our hotel and straight toward the movie theater," Galinski recalls. "…The movie theater was filled with NVA troops, and I believe it was one of their main strong points in the city. As the boy rode his bike toward the theater, the NVA troops yelled at him and he stopped his bike and got off. There was some conversation between the troops and the boy. He then left his bike in the middle of the street and walked to the side and sat down on the concrete steps out of the line of fire. He stayed there for a while but must have worried about his bike being in the middle of the street. He got up and walked back to his bike, picked it up, and was about to wheel it to the side of the road when the NVA yelled at him to stop. Instead of leaving his bike and going back where he was safe, he sat down next to his bike; for some reason he did not want to leave his bike, and this cost him his life. He was not sitting but for a few minutes when one of the bastards in the movie theater fired one shot and killed the kid for no reason."

Mouse trap

Galinski continues: "It was a short time after the boy's death that a group of four ARVN 'White Mice' (military police) drove up the same street toward the movie theater. They acted like they did not know the city had just been taken over by the NVA. I remember we had one of the guys watching the street, and he tried to warn them of the danger on top of the hill. They just waved at him and continued on up the street. They came alongside the body of the dead boy and stopped to look out at him. I was watching from my window, and I just knew that they were in a world of trouble. All of a sudden, the jeep with the four Vietnamese cops in it just blew up. At first I did not know what had happened, but soon realized that they had just been hit with an RPG round. I thought to myself, there is no way anyone survived that blast, but I was wrong. From out of the smoke came three guys running like hell back down the street in the direction they came from. Needless to say, the NVA opened up on the three men with automatic weapons, and I witnessed bullets striking the pavement all around the three runners."

"To this day, I don't know how they managed to avoid all the lead that was hitting around them, but they did. They never stopped running until they were out of sight. It seems the driver of the jeep took all the blast from the RPG. As the smoke cleared from around the jeep, you could see that the shell had folded the jeep like an accordion. The driver...was not killed immediately. He laid in that tangled mess for a long time and just screamed. I was hoping that the NVA would at least put the poor guy out of his misery, but the bastards just let him scream until he finally died. I know a lot of us in that hotel were getting real mad and frustrated because we were under orders not to shoot."

The Fight

Late in the morning, the majors were informed by MACV that they were going to launch a counter-attack on the NVA force in Da Lat with ARVN troops and APCs. The APCs had twin .20 caliber machine guns mounted on revolving turrets and were formidable weapons against ground troops. The majors told MACV that the NVA troops were armed with RPGs, and the bulk of the force seemed to be holed up in the local movie theater. It was going to be up to the small U.S. force in the hotel to keep the NVA in the theater pinned down so that they could not use the launchers against the APCs.

Before the attack started, one of the majors assigned each of the ASA soldiers a target to kill when he gave the order. "I was given the job to shoot an NVA soldier who was standing next to a building about 150 yards away from me," says Galinski, "I was stationed in a bathroom and was looking out a small window. I remember we had to wait for what seemed like forever before the order to fire came.

"Being in the ASA meant we did not do a lot of shooting with our weapons; I for one could not remember the last time I even fired my weapon, and I had been in-country for over a year and a half. Well, the order came, and I fired my first shot at a real live person. Not surprising, I missed. I hit the wall of the building he was standing next to. I only missed by a few inches, but that gave him time to bring his rifle up and point it in my direction. My next shot did not miss, and I was relieved that he did not get a shot off. I remember looking around for other targets after my man went down, but could not find anyone still standing. A minute ago, the streets were full of NVA, and now nobody was around. I was pumped up and looking for something to shoot at when I saw an NVA soldier lying down on some steps leading to the local market. At first I thought he was dead, but took a shot at him anyway. My bullet hit the cement steps right next to his head, and he immediately sat up. I believe a lot of us in the hotel saw this guy sit straight up, and a bunch of us fired about the same time. This was the first time I ever saw what a bullet from an M-14 could do if it hit someone in the head. I had trouble sleeping for a long time after Tet. I kept picturing someone shooting me in the head; not good.

"We did a lot more shooting that day," Galinski says, "and we killed a lot of NVA when they tried to escape the attacking ARVN. When the shooting was over, and we were being evacuated from the hotel, there was a funny moment. The owner of the hotel had put a chain with a padlock around the two main glass doors. An ARVN soldier ran up the steps and tried once to open the two glass doors. The owner of the hotel was waving at him to wait until he unlocked the chain. The ARVN did not want to wait and instead used the butt of his rifle to shatter the doors. I thought it was funny at the time, but I'm sure the hotel owner did not see the humor in it

ASA soldiers Galinski and Spinner were both honored for their heroism during the Tet Offensive. Skip Galinski was awarded the Army Commendation Medal for heroic action, with "V" device for "valorous actions in direct contact with an enemy force." Dick Spinner earned the Bronze Star Medal for heroism, with "V" Device for valor.

And the storm raged

Radio Research and Military Intelligence units across the South had warned their support combat commanders that attacks were coming, but MACV could not or would not put the big picture together until it was too late. Fortunately, the NVA offensive lost some of its tactical advantage due to a simple time change. Hanoi had changed the North Vietnamese lunar calendar in August 1967 from the traditional China Standard Time to Indochina Time, and their military planners did not catch the time discrepancy until it was too late. The offensive was set to begin after the first day of the lunar New Year. Most NVA units in the areas adjacent to North Vietnam used the new calendar and attacked on January 30, but the VC and NVA units from the

South were still using the old calendar and attacked on January 31. The result was a number of scattered attacks to start the offensive in place of the single huge coordinated attack across the country that they had envisioned.

The 404th RRD had analyzed and accurately predicted an attack on the cities of An Khe and Tuy Hoa a week before Tet. They were a support detachment for the 173rd Airborne Brigade, so the 173rd was well prepared to defend against the attacks when they came. Several hundred VC were killed attacking 173rd positions near Phu Hiep village and hundreds more died fighting the 173rd and Co. D, 16th Armor in hand-to-hand combat in Tuy Hoa city. Because of their advance preparations, Tet was not a big event for the 173rd. What was left of the enemy force gave up and faded into the jungle.

Task forces from the 173rd were sent to relieve Special Forces camps at Kontum and Dak To and then on to the Pleiku-Ban Me Thout area. Two-man LLVI and ARDF relay teams from the 404th RRD were sent with them.

During the Tet Offensive, Tuy Hoa was the only major city in South Vietnam whose defensive perimeter was not penetrated by enemy forces. The 404th was later cited by the commanding general of the 173rd Airborne Brigade for providing the early warning that prevented enemy success there.

According to Jim "Sakk" Frankenfield, who was an ARDF operator with the 146th Aviation Co., RR, "When Tet happened, it was really a mess. We were flying double missions much of the time, trying to keep up with the action. It was getting hard to keep the planes in good flying condition and hell to pay if any of us didn't meet our take-off times.

"The flight crews had limited resources and everyone was beat. For the first few months, there were more 'hits' (fixes) than we could handle, much of the time. We soon got a bunch of FNGs (f***ing new guys) in for our replacements and had to get them trained. Many of the FNGs were sharp operators and really fit in well. We also got some "lingies" for another special mission for our outfit. They flew their missions in the Otters with one of the regular ARDF operators."

A tornado instead of a typhoon

The numbers of Viet Cong and NVA forces estimated to have been involved in the Tet Offensive varied widely, depending on who was doing the counting, what their agenda was, and whose "nether regions" they were trying to protect. MACV's numbers were always suspect. They were narrowly focused and designed to provide whatever image Saigon wanted the American people and the current U.S. administration to see. Some historians have suggested that the offensive was "a simultaneous assault by 80,000 communist troops against fortified cities and towns throughout South Vietnam" and that "the offensive was quickly suppressed." Other writers have said that such numbers are "sheer nonsense."

MACV estimated that 85,000 troops were "committed" during the offensive, but as usual, it is a good idea on practice to check the fine print. They are only talking about their somewhat meager estimate of the number involved in the assault on the major towns and cities. That was only one small part of the total picture.

The full time frame of what is referred to as the "Tet Offensive" was two weeks in January and February of 1968. At the same time the cities were being attacked (by the 80,000 to 85,000), nearly every major allied base and supply facility in Vietnam was attacked or bombarded, Khe Sanh was under siege, hundreds of rural hamlets were attacked, and allied troops being moved in response to the offensive were actively blocked and delayed by enemy units in the field. MACV's estimate does not include any of the VC or NVA forces involved in those other actions. Former CIA analyst George W. Allen believes the total numbers may have been "as many as 400,000 including hamlet militia troops integrated into main force and local force units." Allen also states that "unfortunately, no intelligence service in Saigon or Washington undertook a comprehensive postmortem study of this matter to establish in detail the identity, strength, and specific activities of all enemy forces committed during this politically decisive campaign." To sum it all up, those in power, both in Saigon and in Washington, did not want to know the true numbers and certainly did not want the American people to know the true numbers because they were way out of line with earlier figures that had been presented to the media and the U.S. public.

Militarily, the Tet Offensive was a disaster for Hanoi and the Viet Cong. The VC, who did most of the fighting and dying, suffered a tremendous setback. The South Vietnamese people did not rise up in support of the offensive, and the Saigon government survived, actually gaining strength from the ordeal.

But ironically, it was a brilliant political victory for Hanoi, within the U.S. Its greatest impact was on the American public. The Johnson Administration had access to all of the intelligence and had known about the buildup but had made the foolhardy decision not to share it with the American people. The administration had chosen to emphasize the good news coming out of Vietnam. Secretary of State Dean Rusk had told the *Washington Post* that "the war was being won by the allies" and that it "would be won if America had the will to win it." The President had also provided several reasons for optimism in his State of the Union address on January 17. The American public was ill-prepared for the attacks when they came. It mattered little whether or not Hanoi actually achieved its objective.

The Hue Massacre

Overall support for the war quickly turned more negative, and the antiwar movement gained momentum, spurred on by the news media. During Tet, communist forces that are reputed to have reached 12,000 had captured and held Hue for twenty-six days. While in control of the city, they had rounded up local businessmen, landowners, ARVN military reservists, college professors, students, and other young people. Estimates of the number killed during the "Hue massacre" vary widely, but over 2,000 unmarked graves were later excavated, and thousands more were missing and never found. Many were clubbed to death or buried alive. The American people never heard about it, because the U.S. media chose not to cover it.

Hue massacre interment (Photo: U.S. Army-NARA)

Truong Nhu Tang was appointed VC justice minister soon after the massacre and understood that he needed to assure "the Southern people" that a communist victory would not bring about a bloodbath. "Large numbers of people had been executed," Tang wrote later, including "captured American soldiers and several other foreigners who were not combatants...Discipline in Hue was seriously inadequate [and]...fanatic young soldiers had indiscriminately shot people. [The massacre was] one of those terrible spontaneous tragedies that inevitably accompany war."

Hanoi officially denounced those who had been executed as "hooligan lackeys and captured VC documents boasted that thousands of "members of reactionary political parties, henchmen, and wicked tyrants" [had been eliminated]. One VC document boasted of 3,000 killed, while another reported 2,867 executed. The after action report of one VC regiment stated that its units alone had killed over a thousand of Hue's citizens, but it received little attention in the American press.

Head shots

When General Nguyen Ngoc Loan, South Vietnam's National Police Commander, executed a VC colonel by shooting him in the head during the Tet Offensive (1 February 1968). News media referred to it as "the shot seen around the world," and the photo won a Pulitzer Prize for photographer Eddie Adams. The VC officer, Nguyen Van Lem, is reputed to have been commander of a VC death squad that was rounding up and executing South Vietnamese National Police officers and/or their families. It was determined later that Lem had been caught dressed in civilian clothing near a ditch which held the bodies of over thirty policemen and their relatives. Some of the bodies were close friends of General Loan's, including several of his godchildren, but that did not matter to the antiwar movement or their supporters in the media. The photo was front-page news world-wide and was presented to show the brutality of U.S. forces and their allies in Vietnam. Photographer Adams later apologized to Loan for destroying his reputation and said, "The guy was a hero."

In addition to the public impact of Tet, there was the psychological impact on the U. S. Military. They had been told for months that they were winning the war, and suddenly the fight had erupted, almost simultaneously, on all fronts. Over 1,500 Americans had been killed and another 7,700 wounded. It seemed that everyone knew someone who had been killed or injured.

Although Hanoi's political objectives were achieved, the cost was disastrous for their military forces. The media focused its attention on the number of U.S. losses and not the estimated 45,000 to 50,000 communist battlefield deaths that occurred during the same period. More NVA and VC troops died in two weeks than the U.S. lost during the entire Korean War, and the media ignored the story. The number of enemy wounded was never revealed, but the total is estimated to have been in the range of 150,000 to 250,000. The Viet Cong never recovered from their devastating losses during Tet, and their numbers were gradually replaced by "volunteers" from North Vietnam. In the border areas, all fighting was taken over by NVA regulars.

Hitting home

The Johnson Administration was impacted too. It had lost credibility and was unable to convince the American public that Tet had been a major defeat for the communists. On February 23, the U.S. Selective Service announced a new draft call for 48,000 men, and on February 28, Robert S. McNamara, the man who had overseen the major escalation of the war in 1964 and 1965, stepped down as Secretary of Defense. One month later, on March 31, 1968, President Johnson announced a unilateral bombing halt during a nationally televised address and then stunned the nation by announcing that he would not seek re-election.

In spite of public assurances, General Westmoreland seems to have also been seriously affected by Tet. He later admitted that the offensive had allowed Hanoi to inflict "a psychological blow, possibly greater in Washington than in South Vietnam." Within a few months, he would be replaced as Commander of MACV by Gen. Creighton Abrams, his Deputy (10 June 1968).

Fuel for the fire

In response to the Tet Offensive, Gen. Westmoreland requested an additional 206,000 more U.S. troops, including airborne. He asked for the entire 82nd Airborne Division from Ft. Bragg, North Carolina, but President Johnson would only give him one brigade. The unit's advance party departed Pope A.F.B. by plane on February 13, 1968, and the rest of the Brigade and all their equipment departed on Valentine's Day. The Commander-in-Chief flew to North Carolina to speak to the paratroopers, wish them well, and see them off.

3rd Brigade-82nd Airborne Div.-Chu Lai-February 1968
(Photo: Staff Sgt. Luis Dacurro-U.S. Army-NARA)

My Lai

On 16 March 1968, Co. C of, the 11th Infantry Brigade, 23rd Infantry Division (Americal) committed the worst U.S. atrocity of the Vietnam War when they murdered 300-500 Vietnamese civilians in the hamlet of My Lai.

The Americal Division had been created with soldiers moved from various other units in February 1967, and named for a division from WWII which had served in New Caledonia (American Caledonia). The atrocity did not come to light until 1969.

The "bastard stepchild"

By 1968, the direct support units (DSUs) were being referred to as the "bastard stepchildren" of ASA in Vietnam. They were under-manned, poorly equipped, and barely supported. The men who served in the units had to beg, borrow, or steal whatever they needed to accomplish their missions. Someone said, "We, who have done so much, with so little, for so long…can now do anything, with nothing, forever." Methods of communication, operations, equipment and material supply, and command structure that would have been unheard of in more traditional military organizations were not unusual at all within the DSUs. That was the only way in which they could function successfully and do their job, which was to provide daily intelligence to the combat units to which they were assigned. Providing daily intelligence was also made more difficult due to the fact that so-called "special intelligence" (SI) could only be released to a small number of senior officers who were cleared to receive it.

The units were also a dangerous place to work because they were usually in the middle of the military action in which their combat unit was currently involved, and most ASA personnel had only a minimal amount of basic weapons training. The 404th RRD (Abn) was attached to the 173rd Airborne Brigade (Separate) and epitomized the worst, and in some ways the best, of the DSUs in Vietnam. The U.S. Army rated its units each month according to four categories of readiness. Before June 1967, the detachment operated out of the Bien Hoa military complex near Saigon and supported the 173rd as they conducted operations in the surrounding area. Then in June, the 173rd was "temporarily" deployed about 300 miles north to the Central Highlands. That "temporary" assignment lasted for four years. After departing Bien Hoa, the 404th was rated (readiness condition) C3 for six continuous months. C3 means the unit was ready for combat but with "severe deficiencies." In mid-January 1968, the detachment's commander reported it was C4 or "combat ineffective," and it was reported to be in that condition for about three subsequent months in early 1968.

The 173rd was the first major ground combat unit of the U.S. Army to serve in Vietnam and by 1968, MACV had designated it to be the "reserve unit," moving it all over Vietnam in support of other units. If there was a problem, the 173rd was sent in to help. They were even moved to Khe Sanh to support the U.S. Marines. Their supply lines had trouble keeping up with their constant moves, and the ASA soldiers of the 404th were at the very bottom of the food chain.

The 404th was commanded by a captain, assigned two lieutenants, authorized two sergeants first class, two staff sergeants, four sergeants, and fifty-seven enlisted men for a total of sixty-eight. In early 1968, there was not a single noncommissioned officer among the approximately forty men assigned to the unit. Most days, about fifteen men were at their base camp, wherever that was, and the rest were deployed with their combat units. The fact that most of the men did not wear rank, insignia or shoulder patches did not indicate their involvement in covert intelligence operations, but only reflected the fact that the supply system could not keep up with the constant mobility of their unit. No one knew where they would be from one day to the next, and that was the least of their concerns.

The 404th was allocated eighteen trucks to haul men, supplies and equipment, and had seventeen generators, all of which required regular maintenance to keep them operational twenty-four hours a day. In January 1968, only two of their eighteen trucks were operational, and one of those could only be driven forward because the rear driveshaft was missing. Five of the vehicles were missing altogether; several others had missing engines, broken axles, wheels, driveshafts, belts, and/or frames. One truck was missing both its bed and cab, but had a working engine and transmission. The driver sat on a wooden box to drive it, and they used it as a tow truck. There were also trucks with inoperable brakes, punctured radiators or fuel tanks, and missing gauges—and the condition of the available tires made driving any of the vehicles an adventure. There may be various ways to describe the unit's plight, but the acronym "SNAFU" seems to sum it up best. (For those who have not served in the military, SNAFU translates as "Situation normal, all f***ed up.")

Of the seventeen generators on the detachment's books, six were missing and could not be accounted for, and nine were sidelined for parts, leaving only two that were operational, and they were constantly overloaded resulting in frequent breakdowns. Power outages caused their communications and intercept positions to be out of service about half the time, contributing to their C4 rating. Other factors also contributed to their operational problems, including teletype equipment that was twenty years old and unsuitable for combat operations anywhere but especially in the heat and humidity of Vietnam.

The 404ᵗʰ RRD (Abn) at Phu Hiep–1968 (Photo: U.S. Army)

Due to poor logistics, only three percent of the unit's spare parts and replacement parts were being received. The fact that the unit continued to function at all can only be attributed to the outstanding young men who went about their jobs on a daily basis with little more than spit, baling wire, and lots of ingenuity. Among those outstanding and ingenious young men was an ASA private named Edward W. Minnock, Jr.

CHAPTER 17

THE WIZARD OF TUY HOA

Tuy Hoa, Phu Yen Province–1968 (Photo: © John M. Taylor)

Ed Minnock was an Army "brat" who enlisted in September 1966. During basic training, he was selected for ASA and shipped out for Ft. Devens in his native Massachusetts. After completing his training, he deployed to Vietnam as a member of the 404th RRD (Abn), in support of the 173rd Airborne Brigade. His father, Edward W. Minnock, Sr. was a Military Intelligence Army Sergeant Major and was also serving in Vietnam.

By March 1968, nineteen-year-old Pvt. Minnock was an acting Operations Sergeant, a position normally filled by a sergeant first class with much more experience. During Tet, the 173rd Brigade's task forces had been sent to relieve Special Forces camps at Kontum and Dak To and then to the Pleiku-Ban Me Thout area, and the 404th RRD had sent support teams along with them. Minnock was in charge of four other privates operating a make-shift radio-intercept site set up in a tent, and they were the only team left at the base camp. The nearly-empty fortification was located near Phu Hiep village, about five miles south of Tuy Hoa. The men's job was to monitor enemy communications in Phu Yen Province and be on the lookout for enemy activity that might pose a threat to Tuy Hoa City. The small unit had been on its own since January with few supplies and no transportation, and Minnock rarely communicated with the battalion HQ. His primary method of contact was hitchhiking on helicopters and vehicles or walking.

The city of Tuy Hoa had continued to be a primary communist target. It was a provincial capital with a host of government offices, ARVN military targets, and a number of U.S. targets, including a huge U.S. Air Force base that housed the most important F-100 wing in South Vietnam. The area was also crowded with thousands of refugees that had pushed their way into the city during the Tet Offensive a few weeks before.

Ed Minnock, Jr., and Ed Minnock, Sr.–Thanksgiving in Vietnam–1967 (Photo: © Sharon Minnock)

On 27 March 1968, Minnock began to notice a difference in the "pattern" of the enemy communications that his team routinely monitored. He sensed that a major operation was being planned and began to analyze and reanalyze huge amounts of data. He asked his fellow privates to focus their efforts on the event he saw developing and to provide him with as much material as they could. By the 31st, he and his team had heard enough. Using the collected data, his intuition, and insight, Minnock produced a comprehensive tactical analysis predicting which units would make up the enemy force, the size of the force, the time of the attack, the routes the force would take during their advance and withdrawal, and their primary targets. Those targets included the U.S. airbase, an ARVN artillery battalion, the city prison that held a large number of VC prisoners, and two important bridges. The attack was going to happen in the next ten days.

Up the chain

Private Minnock attempted to report his findings up the chain of command within the 173rd Brigade, but his efforts did not go well. The lower-level officers would not take time to listen to him, and the rear-area colonel who had just arrived in-country was not impressed with him or his "wild" theories. Minnock had made the mistake of assuming that he was briefing a senior officer with a certain amount of intellect and experience, but soon learned otherwise. He outlined his facts and the reasons for his prediction of the upcoming attack; he suggested possible courses of action, but because of the highly secret nature of his work, he was not able to explain the source of his information. The colonel perceived a mere private who could not possibly know anything of value and dismissed the young man with a stern lecture about the proper use of the chain of command.

Rejected, but determined to find someone who would listen to him, Minnock sought out the commander of the 26th ROK Regiment, the Korean unit based at Tuy Hoa. The 26th Regiment was preparing to deploy its 3,000 Korean infantrymen in a search-and-destroy operation that would leave Tuy Hoa City lightly defended. Stopping the operation was not a matter to be taken lightly by either the unit commander or the ASA private who asked to see him.

Ed Minnock did not intentionally attempt to deceive the Korean commander. Even as a child he had been highly ethical, and his military father had raised him to respect authority and rank. Most of the soldiers in both the 173rd Brigade and the 404th RRD wore no rank or name tags on their uniforms, so it was not readily discernible whether Minnock was a private or an officer. The Korean colonel did not ask. It was all in the attitude. Ed Minnock had no shortage of attitude and confidence. The commander listened to Minnock's report, observing his demeanor, commitment, and mastery of the facts. Above all, he was impressed by the young man's conviction and command of the situation. This young American was obviously a leader who knew his business. The Korean assumed that he must be an officer and never questioned it.

The 26th ROK Regiment of the "Tiger" Division in Vietnam (Photo: U.S. Army)

Taking action

Believing what Minnock told him, and quickly grasping the full implications of it, the commander knew what he had to do. He called his MACV advisor, explained the situation, and advised him that he was changing his regiment's operation "to kill many NVA." The colonel's plan was not to intercept the NVA on their way into Tuy Hoa, but to parallel their routes, allow them to move into the area, and then spring the trap. He ordered complete radio silence; all communication would be by courier until the operation was complete. There could be no chance that the enemy would learn of the plan.

Minnock's next step was to find a way to defend the main bridge into the city in case some of the NVA troops got past the ROK infantry. The bridge was normally protected by a few ARVN soldiers, but they could not stop determined NVA regulars. Minnock went to see the Army captain who commanded D Squadron, 16th Armor, a unit of the 173rd Brigade. The captain was recuperating at the Phu Hiep base camp where Minnock's team was located, and he knew him slightly. The private explained the situation to the captain and told him about the ROK commander's redeployment. He urged the captain to help block the bridge with his armored personnel carriers. The captain contacted his commander, the same newly-arrived colonel who had refused to listen to Minnock earlier, and the C.O would not authorize the move. He also refused to recall the 3rd/503rd Infantry from a training exercise in an adjacent area.

M-113 APC with three machine gun turrets (Photo: U.S. Army)

After some deliberation, and understanding what the consequences would be for him if Minnock was wrong, the D/16ᵗʰ captain followed his gut instincts and did it anyway. He parked his unit's dozen APCs side-by-side with their twelve .50 cal. and twenty-four 7.62mm machine guns trained on the only approach to the bridge.

Three days before the attack, Pvt. Minnock encountered an old and trusted acquaintance. Capt. John Moon was from the 173ʳᵈ Brigade's Military Intelligence Company and had recently returned to Phu Hiep to check on the intelligence situation. Minnock was already putting the pieces of his plan into place, but he could always use more help and support. Moon listened to Minnock's analysis, appraised the situation, and suggested they try to disrupt the 5ᵗʰ NVA HQ as they prepared to command their forces.

Capt. Moon knew that prior to the attack, the 5ᵗʰ NVA would deploy its command and control into a hidden complex of bunkers that existed southwest of Tuy Hoa City. Military Intelligence had determined approximately where the HQ complex was located, but the problem was how to get to the system of caves and tunnels that were fortified under fifteen feet of earth and logs.

Twenty-four hours later, Minnock and Moon managed to launch a barrage of 200 high-explosive shells, compliments of the ROK, ARVN, and U.S. Army artillery. The Air Force then dropped drums of a napalm-like mixture, ignited it, and followed up with 500 lb. bombs. The secret command and control complex was completely destroyed. How the two accomplished that feat is open to conjecture and probably better left to history.

The battle

Early on 05 April, the 95ᵗʰ NVA Regiment began to deploy its three battalions in a three-pronged attack, exactly as Minnock had predicted. By late on the 6ᵗʰ, each of the enemy battalions had been flanked by the 26ᵗʰ ROK and was outnumbered three-to-one by the Koreans. The NVA troops were terrified of the huge Koreans, and for good reason.

The ROK infantry soldiers were trained in martial arts, used only rifle, bayonet, knife, and hand-to-hand combat, and they took no prisoners. When the battle was joined, only about fifty of the 1,000 enemy soldiers escaped the carnage. The survivors ran from the battlefield, charging toward Tuy Hoa's main bridge—and straight into the machine guns and M-16s of the D/16th Armor. Every man died. The only enemy survivors were seventeen members of the VC 85th Local Force who had entered the city disguised as civilians, and they were later captured. The 95th NVA Regiment had been annihilated.

After the battle, American and Vietnamese generals arrived from all areas, and were happy to accept praise for the victory, but it was the Korean colonel who came looking for Ed Minnock. He wanted to find the brilliant "American captain of intelligence" who had single-handedly "outfoxed" the NVA generals. When the pieces were finally put in place, Pvt. Edward Minnock and the 404th RRD were credited with the victory, along with the destruction of the 5th NVA Division Headquarters. Minnock was awarded the Bronze Star Medal for his efforts.

The Legion of Merit (Photo: U.S. Army)

The commander of the 26th ROK Regiment was still not satisfied, however. He contacted Brigadier General Richard J. Allen, the Commanding General of the 173rd A.B. to personally thank him for the help of the 404th. When the general fully understood what Minnock had done and how he had done it, the Bronze Star was rescinded and the Legion of Merit was awarded. The award was presented by the commander of the 313th ASA Battalion, with the endorsement of General Allen, Brigadier General Leo H. Schweiter and the commanders of ASA-Pacific and the Army Security Agency.

Recognition

Pvt. Edward W. Minnock, Jr., became the first U.S. Army private in history to be awarded The Legion of Merit. The Legion of Merit is awarded for exceptionally meritorious conduct in the performance of outstanding services and achievements and is one of only two U.S. military decorations to be issued as a "neck order" (the other being the Medal of Honor). It is typically awarded to general officers and colonels occupying command or very senior staff positions. It may be awarded to officers of lesser rank and senior enlisted personnel, but that is rare. It is even rarer for a Legion of Merit to be awarded for exceptional achievement in combat, but one was: to a nineteen-year-old ASA private from Massachusetts.

When he heard that his award had been upgraded to the Legion of Merit, Minnock replied, "Sounds like a (expletive) French award. I'd rather keep the Bronze Star." One must also consider what the consequences might have been had Pvt. Minnock been wrong. He was already a private, so he was not risking much in the way of rank, but he would almost certainly have faced consequences for his actions, and might have cost the careers of the officers who had supported his efforts. Fortunately that was not the case.

Ed Minnock was inducted into the Military Intelligence Hall of Fame at Ft. Huachuca, Arizona in 1990. Sharon Minnock, Ed's sister says: "I know my Dad was always very proud of Ed, but Ed Jr., was also very proud of his Dad. Minutes after being inducted into the Hall of Fame in 1990, I was congratulating him [and] he told me he felt bad. He thought our Dad, who had spent thirty years in military intelligence and retired an E-9, the highest rank achievable as an enlisted man, should be getting the honor [and] the recognition; not himself who had only served a few years."

Dr. Ed Minnock, Jr. (Photo: Sharon Minnock)

AUTHOR'S NOTE: Ed Minnock, Jr., passed away August 2, 2011.

More and bitter losses

On 25 March 1968, Capt. John Casey of the 371st RRC was killed by mortar fire when Camp Evans came under attack.

John Michael Casey was twenty-three years old and from Sparta, Tennessee. He was a 1962 graduate of White County High School and had attended Middle Tennessee State before attending OCS. Casey had completed one tour in Vietnam and extended for another six months. He had been home on leave in January and was killed two months later. Eight of his high school classmates served as his pallbearers.

On 30 March 1968, Spc.4 **John Francis Link**, the dedicatee of this book, died in a field hospital eighteen kms northeast of A Luoi. John was twenty-three years old and from Ottumwa, Iowa. He was a proud member of Det. B-52 (Project Delta), 5th Special Forces Group.

The King riots

On April 4, 1968, Martin Luther King, Jr., was assassinated in Memphis, Tennessee. Riots broke out in dozens of cities across the nation. The D.C. riots lasted five days with crowds as high as 20,000. The District's 3,100 man police force was overwhelmed, and 13,600 federal troops were brought in. There were U.S. Marines with machine guns on the steps of the Capital and units of the 3rd Infantry Division guarded the White House.

On April 5, rioting reached within two blocks of the White House before the mob was repelled. By the time rioting ended on April 8, twelve people had died; 1,097 had been injured; over 6,100 had been arrested; 1,220 buildings (including 900 stores) had been torched; and damages topped $27 million. That was the equivalent of $160 million in 2012.

With the destruction and closing of businesses, thousands of jobs were lost, and the economy of Washington's inner city was devastated. Many of the hardest hit areas did not recover for over thirty years.

Crazy Cats again

On 14 April 1968, Aircraft 531 took off from Cam Ranh NAS at 0530 for a day-long mission. The plane turned over Hue and arrived on station. At 0715 hours, 47mm anti-aircraft fire hit the left wing in the area of the wing flap and aileron. The hit missed the fuel vane in the wing, so there was no fire. The aircraft was able to fly back to Cam Ranh and land safely. It was later painted with a Purple Heart.

Death of another ASA hero

On 13 May 1968 Spc.4 Christopher Schramm was killed south of the DMZ at Thua Thien in Quang Tri Province. He was in a convoy en route from Phu Bai to Camp Evans when several of the trucks struck land mines. Schramm dismounted to help fellow soldiers who had been wounded and stepped on a mine.

Chris was from Fairless Hills, Pennsylvania and in a *Philadelphia Inquirer* article dated May 18, 1968, his father said, "He was to have gone on a seven-day leave to Taiwan on May 15—his first leave in nineteen months. Another day and a half and he might have made it." The family requested that their son's body be accompanied home by his first cousin, Sgt. Joseph McFadden who was stationed in Japan with the U.S. Air Force.

One of eight children in a family of Pennsylvania steel-workers, Chris was unsure what he wanted to do with his life. After high school, he took a job with U.S. Steel at their Fairless Works and attended a Catholic seminary for a short time but soon made the decision to join the Army "because I owed it to my family…my country to do what I can to make this a better world." After exhaustive testing, Chris was selected for ASA, and upon completion of his specialized 05D training at Ft. Devens, he was assigned to Taiwan where he served for a year.

As time neared for Chris to return to the States, he had to make a decision. He could return to the States for probable duty in a regular Army unit or transfer to another foreign post in order to remain in ASA. In late summer 1967, a call came out for volunteers to go to Vietnam, and he was the first to volunteer, stating that he wanted to "help save other soldiers' lives." He had told his parents, "I volunteered for Vietnam because there's a job to be done." Originally assigned to a land-based unit, he later transferred to the 371st where he was involved in communications intercept and ARDF as part of Project Left Bank. Chris Schramm's MOS was 05D20-EW/SIGINT identifier.

Christopher Joseph Schramm was posthumously awarded the Bronze Star Medal for heroism with "V" device for valor, two Air Medals with twenty Oak Leaf Clusters for meritorious service while participating in aerial flight, and a Purple Heart. He was a member of the 371st Aviation Co. RR, DSU of the 1st Cavalry Div. He was twenty-one years old and is buried at Resurrection Cemetery, Cornwell Heights, Pennsylvania.

CHAPTER 18

DEATH ON THE BLACK VIRGIN

Daybreak on Nui Ba Dinh (Photo: U.S. Army)

The French called her "La Montagne de la Dame Noire," The Mountain of the Black Lady or Black Virgin Mountain. It was named for Ba Dinh, a young Vietnamese girl who according to legend, fell in love with a soldier, was betrayed and threw herself off the mountain to her death. Because of its strategic location, the mountain had always been of value militarily. The Japanese had occupied its summit during WWII, and then it was occupied in succession by the Viet Minh, the French, the Viet Cong, and the Americans.

In 1967, NSA determined that there was a need for more and better radio-intercept of targets in Cambodia. That was due to large numbers of NVA and VC troops traversing to and from bases they had established across the Cambodian border. Hoping to find an effective location, ASA began conducting a test at Nui Ba Dinh in Tay Ninh Province.

Nui Ba Dinh was a perilous outpost, accessible only by helicopter when the weather permitted. Space was limited to a two-acre, boulder-strewn camp on top of "the rock," and frequent rain driven by winds topping 80 mph made living and working conditions there barely tenable. The test ran for four days, limited by weather conditions, but produced favorable results. After analyzing the quality of the intercepted traffic, NSA decided to establish a semi-permanent intercept site on top of the mountain. By May 1968, ASA had a team from the 372nd RRC at Cu Chi established in the "pagoda," a stone and mortar structure at the peak of the mountain. It was the only truly "secure" building on the mountain, housing the ASA operation and their top-secret equipment, and shielding their highly classified mission from prying eyes.

The "pagoda" with its antenna array on Nui Ba Dinh
(Photo: Capt. Ronald H. Tinnell—U.S. Army)

The mountaintop installation was technically under the jurisdiction of the 25th Infantry Div., but it primarily housed a radio relay station for the 125th Signal Battalion. Other military units also sent communications teams to the mountain to relay their messages if they were within the 25th Infantry Division's area of operation, and A-234, a Special Forces team with about thirty men, was located on the mountain to provide radio relay for S.F. and V.S.F. units throughout the III Corps area.

The 25th ID had a company in place to provide camp security, but the camp's best defense was believed to be its location, and there was little in the way of additional fortifications. A series of log bunkers mounted on stilts and a single strand of concertina wire was hardly designed to stop a determined force of Viet Cong. Special Forces had expressed concerns about Nui Ba Dinh's defenses several months earlier, but nothing had come of it. Over the past year, those defenses had gradually become weaker, and the VC had probed the camp several times in the summer and fall of 1967. The Americans held the very top of the mountain, but the 3,000 feet of crags, crevasses and caves that constituted the sides of the mountain belonged to the VC.

Nui Ba Dinh bunkers and reservoir (Photo: Capt. Ronald H. Tinnel—U.S. Army)

The attack

What has been referred to as the "Nui Ba Dinh massacre" began on a clear night at 2145 hours on 13 May 1968. The ASA installation had only become operational the week before, and the night crew was on duty inside the pagoda. Sgt. 1st Class Beeson was in charge, and he along with Spc.4 Goldberg was monitoring NVA communications. The rest of the ASA team had been released for the night and would be back early in the morning. Morse intercept ops Jeff Haerle and "Smitty" Smith had gone to their barracks; Spc. Brocato and one of the other ops had gone to the chow hall for a late meal. Living conditions on the Rock weren't great, but the food was exceptional, so that helped morale.

Some of the Green Berets were in their team house watching Jimmy Durante on TV when they heard loud booms, and they assumed it was a mortar crew firing illumination rounds. But then the noise began to get louder; they heard dirt and shrapnel hitting the roof, and they knew something was wrong. The peaceful night had exploded into a wild melee of noise and flame. Rocket propelled grenades and 82mm mortars struck the bunkers and main buildings, throwing out huge waves of rocks and shrapnel and setting some of the buildings on fire.

Per standard procedure, only half the defensive bunkers were manned at one time, and that alternated from day to night. The manned bunkers opened fire with automatic weapons and machine guns, but several were quickly knocked out by mortars. A large enemy force moved up to the helicopter pad where a command post was established with communications and a mortar team to protect it. A smaller enemy force moved up the slope toward the pagoda at the top of the mountain. Other small squads of VC reached the crest of the hill and spread out, placing satchel charges on the operations building, officers' quarters, and other major buildings.

Upon hearing the mortar blasts, Beeson and Goldberg quickly barricaded the already locked door of their stone fortress and began to destroy their classified materials. Sgt. Beeson radioed Capt. Carter, the commanding officer of the 372nd RRC at Cu Chi and advised him that they were under attack. The C.O. requested a report every five minutes and instructed the sergeant to destroy his top-secret equipment as quickly as possible.

A few moments later, there was a loud banging on the door. The two Americans had already moved their heaviest pieces of furniture against the door. Grasping their carbines, they put their backs to the furniture and pushed with all their might as the enemy troops attempted to batter their way in. The heavy, reinforced door held. Suddenly automatic weapons fire came through the small high windows and bullets pinged around, ricocheting inside the stone walls as Beeson and Goldberg scrambled under one of the heavy metal work tables. That was followed by two loud explosions as the generator and the antenna array on the pagoda roof were blown with satchel charges. The interior of the stone building went pitch black. The lights were gone; the radio was gone; all the two men could do was hunker down and wait for whatever was to come next.

Nui Ba Dinh helipad with bunkers and camp buildings (Photo: U.S. Army)

The large enemy force at the helipad split into smaller groups and moved up the left side of the camp covered by a mortar barrage. They placed additional satchel charges and tossed hand grenades into the mess hall, barracks, and the officers' and enlisted men's clubs, some of which were already on fire from the shelling. The building housing the Special Forces A-Team was destroyed when an RPG round hit the butane tank attached to it. Nearly all of the U.S. soldiers within the camp were unarmed and trying to hide in the darkness.

The Special Forces and infantry troops manning the bunkers continued to fight as long as they could hold out and then fell back to regroup. Several of the Green Berets who had been forced out of their bunkers moved to the reservoir area and found about fifteen to twenty very young soldiers hiding there among the rocks. Most of the youngsters had been rousted out of bed when the attack began and were not fully clothed; some were only wearing boots and boxer shorts, and several were wounded. They were clearly terrified; some were crying, and they had a total of four weapons among them. Most of the men were signal corpsmen with no infantry training and no combat experience, so the Green Berets took charge.

A defensive perimeter was established with their minimal armament, and they treated the wounded with the limited supplies at hand. One of the Berets had a portable radio and managed to contact Katum and the 25th Infantry Div. He was told that AC-47 "Spooky" gunships were on the way to assist them. Spookys were U.S. Air Force fixed-wing aircraft that were used only at night, due to their slow speed. The planes were armed with three Gatling guns and would fly over an enemy force dropping flares that lasted for three minutes, emitting 750,000 candlepower of light. The Green Berets then settled down with their young charges to wait for help to arrive and for daylight to come.

Another group of U.S. infantry and Special Forces soldiers had regrouped in one of the destroyed bunkers and set up a defensive perimeter, but they were afraid to fire, because they could not identify their targets. They were also low on ammunition. They could hear the VC troops calling to each other as they searched the destroyed bunkers and walked around the camp shooting the American wounded. One U.S. soldier left the bunker and managed to get to an ammo bunker near the pagoda. He grabbed an M79 grenade launcher and two cases of grenades and made his way to another bunker where he was able to place intensive fire on the enemy mortar position at the helipad. The VC troops began to leave the area shortly thereafter. The time was 2330 hours.

Light and fire

At about the same time, light-fire teams arrived over the mountain. A Huey gunship arrived from the 17th Air Cav, and the first Air Force Spooky and flare ships from the 5th Air Command Squadron arrived to attack the enemy force. They drew heavy anti-aircraft fire from the base of the mountain. The weather was still clear, and the gunships attacked the sides of the mountain, blasting the area outside the perimeter of the camp with their mini-guns. The pilots wanted to prevent any further infiltration of enemy troops into the area and hoped to hasten the retreat of those opting to leave. The gunships were guided by a lone radio operator who had survived the VC attack and still had an operable radio.

A second Spooky arrived in the area at 0100, but within thirty minutes the mountaintop was shrouded in dense fog, and it became more difficult for the planes to assault the terrain, even with good illumination. They continued to receive moderate to heavy AA fire from the sides and base of the mountain, and at 0200 hours, steady rain moved in that would last for several hours. In spite of the weather, the gunships remained on task until their ammo ran out at 0230. The flare ship remained in the area continuing to drop flares until the weather eventually forced it to return to base.

Meanwhile, Special Forces at Det-B HQ at Tay Ninh were putting together a rescue operation. They were loading helicopters with ammunition, medical supplies, food, water, blankets and a generator and planned to move out at first light. They had received a message from one of their men on the mountain stating that all but one building and most of the defensive bunkers had been destroyed. They needed help badly, but no one could get to the mountain before morning due to the fog, rain, and fierce winds.

For the most part, the American troops on the mountain remained in place during the night. They were wary of moving about in the misty blackness due to the gunfire from the Spookys, and the assumption that there were still VC in the area. The darkness was total, except for the eerie glow of the flares as they were fired into the swirling fog. Then the pitch dark returned.

At first light, small battered groups of survivors began to emerge from the destroyed bunkers and the reservoir area. It had been a long night. The soldiers were formed up into three squads and sent to secure the helicopter pad, check the camp for any remaining VC, and carry the dead and wounded to the landing pad for evacuation. Several of the bodies were booby trapped, including the bodies of dead VC, so the soldiers had to be extremely careful in their task. It was still raining and very cold in the gusting wind.

Sgt. Beeson and Spc.4 Goldberg heard American voices and pulled the furniture away from the door of the pagoda. They moved outside, and Goldberg joined the crew that was searching for the wounded and the dead. He and Beeson were concerned about the other members of the 372nd who had left the pagoda shortly before the attack. The camp was almost totally destroyed, along with all of their food and supplies. There were only mounds of black smoldering rubble where the barracks had stood. Sgt. Beeson remained at the pagoda to ensure all classified materials had been destroyed or secured and to await an ASA security team that he expected to arrive shortly from Cu Chi.

Relief flights

The first helicopters from Det-B arrived about 0700. Two Green Beret medics arrived with them and were working with two medics who were stationed on the mountain to tend to the wounded. The resident doctor had been killed in the attack. The first chopper to come in had sustained damage from automatic weapons fire as it approached the top of the mountain, and one of its crewmen had been wounded. Greenberg learned that Haerle had been shot to death. Smith had been seriously burned in the barracks fire, but he would survive. Brocato had spent a cold and frightful night hiding in the rocks, but was otherwise ok. He and Greenberg joined the detail carrying bodies to the helipad.

When the first helicopters arrived, there was some confusion. Groups of young soldiers were standing around the pad. They were muddy and cold; many were clad only in wet shorts, and a few were barefooted. Some of them appeared to be in shock and tried to climb onto the choppers before the more seriously wounded could be loaded. They were junior enlisted, many of whom had just arrived in-country, and they wanted "off the mountain." They were ordered to leave the aircraft, and the wounded were then taken aboard. It was a difficult operation for all involved.

Helicopter pad on Nui Ba Dinh (Photo: U.S. Army)

The second group of helicopters brought in food, clothing, medical supplies, communications equipment, more blankets and a case of whiskey. The landing zone was congested with the newly delivered equipment and groups of young infantry soldiers milling around talking to each other. Most of the wounded had been evacuated, but the hillside surrounding the pad was still littered with the bodies of those who had fallen the night before, and many were badly mutilated. A senior Special Forces officer who had arrived on the scene realized that the sight of the bodies was having a detrimental effect on the young enlisted men and ordered that the bodies be covered until they could be transported off the mountain. He also organized a carrying party to move the bodies to the helipad and had as many as possible loaded onto the choppers for transport to the U.S. Army base at Tay Ninh West.

By 0900, the perimeter of the camp had been secured using the available camp personnel who had been fed, clothed, and resupplied. The rain had stopped, and the sun was breaking through the high clouds. Work crews had been assigned to erect tents for temporary housing and storage facilities and to move the materiel under cover before the next rain storm moved in. The new communications equipment had been hauled up to the pagoda area.

The ASA security team had arrived, dismantled their classified equipment, and made a complete sweep of the pagoda's interior. The 372nd RRC had lost one man and had another critically injured. If not for the quick thinking of Beeson and Goldberg, they might have lost much more than that. NSA now considered the location to be too dangerous and insecure for their highly secret operation, and it would be terminated.

After the pagoda was cleared, the new radio apparatus was moved inside and set up. It was the only building left to protect the equipment from the always threatening weather. By early afternoon communications had been restored, and a relief company of the 2/22 Infantry, 25th I.D. was airlifted to the mountaintop to reinforce the camp's defenses.

The final U.S. toll on Nui Ba Dinh was twenty-four killed, thirty-five wounded, and one taken prisoner by the VC. Pvt. 1st Class Donald G. Smith was knocked unconscious during the initial mortar attack and carried away by the VC. He was released on 01 January 1969. Three of the Green Berets from A-324 were awarded Bronze Star Medals for their heroism during the attack.

Buck's tale

Buck Buchanan, who served as a repairman on the PRD-1 and PNH-4 equipment, was based at Cu Chi with the 372nd. He had spent time at Nui Ba Dinh and knew the layout and the intercept operators who worked there. He monitored the attack from Cu Chi that night and was part of the ASA team that flew to "the rock" the next morning. The company commander had put him in charge of removing and evacuating the top-secret radio-intercept equipment back to Cu Chi.

Buchanan recalled his time on the mountain and the attack. He had also known most of the Green Berets who were assigned to Nui Ba Dinh. "There were twenty-eight or so S.F types there. They were B-Team support types with a black captain C.O. and a wild man for a first sergeant," he said. "There were other signal types up there who ran microwaves and other jumbled up signal gear. The S.F. types were weapons, medical, signal operators and admin type guys. I knew all of them fairly well, and none of them were authorized to go near our detachment's shit in the pagoda. The S.F. C.O. was always trying to get us to tell him what we were doing up there. We'd B.S. him all of the time, and Jerry Gainous, the other repairman with me, told him one afternoon that we monitored submarines operating off the coast.

"There weren't many American heroics that night," Buchanan continued. "We only found two VC/NVA bodies, and they had been killed by the Korean generator repairman for PA&E who'd killed them with an M-60 he'd bought on the black market. [Some sources suggest he was CIA.] Sgt. 1st Class Beeson was trapped in the pagoda with a Spc.4 operator through the whole performance because everybody else had gone back to…the mess hall, the club or the barracks. Capt. Carter (C.O. of the 372nd) and I listened to Beeson on the radio while the AK's were being shot through the window. He was destroying the gear and the documents."

"Capt. Carter wanted a sitrep (situation report) every five minutes. Beeson continued to xmit until the 292 antenna on the back of the pagoda was blown up at about 2200 that night. Writing this right now has made my pulse go up by leaps and bounds…

"Haerle and a big guy named Smitty were trapped under the barracks. As it burned down around them, Smitty said the last thing Jeff did was tell him he couldn't stand being burned to death, and he was going to try to make a run for it. He made it as far as a big rock next to the trail leading up to the pagoda. There was a huge pool of blood on the rocks of the trail, and there were forty to fifty AK-47 casings right there. According to what they told us that morning, the survivors who were still on the hill said that the bad guys went around and fired into every American body that they could find. It was pretty obvious that is what had happened to Jeff there by that rock.

"I spent almost forty-eight hours on that (expletive) rock after we flew back in, and I would say that there was probably less than one brass M-16 casing for every 200 copper-colored AK casings along the trails and up at the pagoda. The piles of NVA brass made the walk up and down the path from the pagoda to the chopper pad treacherous because it was like walking on marbles.

Buchanan continued: "To say that Nui ba Dinh was a loose goose operation was an understatement. Even during the worst of the Tet 68 Offensive, it had never been hit either by indirect fire or ground attack. They (Special Forces) told me that the last time they had been hit had been in the middle of the summer of 1967 and that had been only a few mortars. That night [of the attack] we were so poorly trained, poorly led, stupid and naive that we walked around without our weapons and other accouterments because we were so sure that the mountain was impenetrable. Most of the time [when working at Nui Ba Dinh] I left my iron hat, rifle, and flak vest at the pagoda rather than…carrying it around. At any given time, there probably weren't more than 110-120 guys up there. That night there were ninety-nine Americans on the Black Virgin Mountain.

"I'd gotten back [up there] the next a.m. before all of the walking wounded WIAs were off the mountain. The 25th Infantry Division [had] put in two companies of grunts from the 2/22 Triple Deuce (Golden Dragons) on the mountain as soon as the fog and the smoke dissipated enough to land H-model Hueys on the pad. When I got there a couple hours later, it was still cool enough that the flies hadn't started buzzing around the blood pools. So I'm positive that there weren't any people from the ASA up there before our C.O., the security officer, and us 'numb-nuts' arrived. Because I [had] worked at the pagoda before the attack, Capt. Carter demanded that I be in charge of 'evac-ing' the equipment back to Cu Chi.

"There are only two dates out of the 716 days I spent in RVN that I remember: 0245–31 January 1968, the minute that the Tet of 68 began while I was on guard duty on the east perimeter of Cu Chi base camp and 13 May 1968."

AUTHOR'S NOTE: Ted T. "Buck" Buchanan was born and raised in Sheridan, Wyoming. After leaving the Army, Buck graduated from the University of Wyoming with a B.S. in Range Management and an M.S. in Entomology. He worked for the U.S. Dept. of Agriculture, Soil Conservation Service.

While in the Army, Buck's MOS was 33B radio maintenance/33D tape recorder repairman. He served two tours in Vietnam, December 1967-October 1968 with the 372nd RR Co. and June 1969-June 1970 with the 8th RRFS at Phu Bai.

Jeffrey William Haerle was a Morse intercept operator (05H20) and was TDY from Torii Station in Okinawa. He was assigned to the 372nd RRC and was killed in action on top of Black Virgin Mountain, Tay Ninh Province, South Vietnam, on the night of 13 May 1968. He had been in-country twenty-eight days and was ten days short of his twenty-second birthday. Jeff was from Minneapolis, Minnesota, and is buried at Ft. Snelling National Cemetery in Minneapolis.

Four days later—another man down

Spc.5 Samuel Martin was a member of the 101st RRC and was killed by a land mine on 17 May 1968. His brother, Sgt. John David Martin, a veteran of eighteen months in Vietnam had started his second tour of duty there in April. Sammy had served eighteen months in Vietnam, then seven months in Germany. Like his older brother, he had started a second six-month Vietnam tour in April.

Len Nagel said: "I was TDY with Sammy on that fatal day. He had volunteered to go on a 'search and destroy' mission with a MACV major. Both were killed when someone hit the trip wire and set off a 'bouncing betty' anti-personnel mine. I still can remember hearing the chopper and someone asking if I…[knew] Sammy Martin. I remember saying 'Yes, I know Sammy.' That's when I identified his body."

Samuel Calvin Martin was twenty-one years old and from Greensburg, Kentucky. John Martin escorted his brother's body home for burial. Sammy was buried on a hill in the Greensburg Cemetery with full military honors. Ft. Knox provided pallbearers and a rifle squad for the service, and Greensburg businesses closed during the service to honor him. Sammy Martin was posthumously awarded the Bronze Star for bravery.

Robert F. Kennedy assassinated—June 5, 1968

Early in June 1968, Robert Kennedy had been locked in a tight battle with Eugene McCarthy in the California Democratic Primary. As Kennedy entered the Ambassador Hotel through the kitchen to attend a victory celebration, he was gunned down by Sirhan Sirhan, a young Palestinian immigrant. Sirhan hated the Senator for his support of Israel. Kennedy died twenty-six hours later at Good Samaritan Hospital and Sirhan Sirhan was convicted of the murder. He was sentenced to life in prison for the crime.

And during the same month

Newsweek - June 17, 1968: "Paris be damned, there's still a lot of war here," growled a U.S. infantry officer in Vietnam last week. During the week that ended June 1st, 438 U.S. soldiers were killed, bringing the total American dead during the month of May to more than 2,000-the highest monthly total of the war.

Hanoi named Le Duc Tho, a member of the North Vietnamese Politburo to represent its interests at the Paris Peace Talks.

27 June, the U. S. command in Saigon confirmed that U.S. forces had begun to evacuate the military base at Khe Sanh due to "a change in the military situation."

Lt. Col. Richard A. McMahon denounced the body count as a "dubious and possibly dangerous" method of determining the enemy's combat potential.

Crazy Cats Aircraft 531 used up another of its nine lives when it blew a tire while landing in Da Nang and almost flipped over.

CHAPTER 19

A DIFFERENT KIND
OF ASA SOLDIER

**ASA's Green Berets–Soldiers of the 403rd RR SOD
(Abn) in Vietnam (Photo: INSCOM)**

It is a little known fact that some of ASA's Direct Support Units were Special Forces qualified. They were the soldiers who made up the ASA Special Operations Detachments (SODs). It was an anonymous writer of ASA SOD history who penned the following: "In the history of mankind, there are fleeting moments of time when, by fate or good judgment on the part of someone, a group of people are brought together at the most appropriate time and place to form extraordinary military units. One such fleeting moment of history, was the formation of an extraordinary military unit called the United States Army Security Agency Special Operations Detachment…."

All ASA SOD members were three time volunteers: first, each man volunteered for the Army Security Agency; second, each volunteered to serve with the new ASA special ops detachments; and third, each volunteered and successfully completed the U.S. Army Airborne Training School at Ft. Benning, Georgia as part of his qualification for the Special Forces training program at Ft. Bragg.

These soldiers were physically conditioned from completing the arduous airborne training and annual physical testing required of all special ops units. In addition, most were subjected to forced marches with full packs, morning runs up to three miles, and a variety of special training courses in SCUBA, cold-weather survival and skiing, Jump Master and HALO parachute, infiltration and extraction, and extensive weapons training. Active participation in volunteer academic training was also encouraged for enlisted troops. These ASA soldiers were a special breed.

Low-level voice intercept team from the 403rd SOD (Photo: INSCOM)

The men of the SOD units were extraordinary soldiers who progressed to rate among the most highly trained and proficient enlisted men in the U.S. Army, and their records speak for themselves. They served their country with distinction and honor, and one sobering fact underlines the high degree of their training: of the hundreds of men who served in the ASA SOD units in Vietnam from 1966 through 1970, many of whom were involved in active combat roles and were awarded medals for valor, there was only one killed in action.

On 23 July 1968, Sgt. Thomas Tomczak was killed in Kontum Province when a mortar malfunctioned. Tomczak was assigned to the 400th SOD (Abn), 1st SFG in Okinawa. He was in South Vietnam on a TDY assignment with the 403rd RR SOD (Abn) at the time of his death. His MOS was 05H (Morse intercept-Airborne Qualified)

Thomas James Tomczak was twenty years old, a proud Green Beret, and from New Berlin, Wisconsin. He was buried at Holy Sepulchre Cemetery, South Milwaukee, Wisconsin.

Travis C. Bunn—Military Intelligence Hall of Fame

Master Sgt. Travis C. Bunn (Photo: U.S. Army)

Travis Bunn began his long and very successful ASA career in 1958 when he became a member of the 320th U.S. Army Security Agency Battalion in Bad Aibling, Germany. When ASA joined the counterinsurgency effort in 1961 and created the direct support units, Travis was one of the first to volunteer as a member of the 10th Special Forces Group (Abn.) He instructed Special Forces teams in the application of security and counterintelligence techniques for clandestine, covert, and overt operations, and provided ASA support for Special Forces operations. In 1963, he was appointed as an instructor at the Special Warfare School at Ft. Bragg, North Carolina.

In 1965, Sgt. Bunn was promoted to the NCOIC of the ASA SOD, Operations and Training in Panama, and was charged with planning, organizing, and supervising the training of special ops teams involved in ASA and Special Forces operations. He was also an instructor for both U.S. and Latin American forces at the U.S. Army School of the Americas. During his time in Panama, Travis Bunn developed security measures and life-saving operations that became standard procedures for all Special Forces teams.

In 1967, Bunn was assigned to the 403rd SOD in Vietnam as a Special Forces/ASA team leader. Once again, he enjoyed great success in his work. He recruited, trained, and led a company of Montagnards in combat operations in the central highlands and supervised a team of twenty soldiers in ASA and Special Forces operations.

In 1969, Sgt. Bunn became the Morse collection NCOIC at the ASA Field Station in Herozenaurach, West Germany, and increased productivity to a level beyond national standards. When their operation was combined with Augsburg, Bunn personally oversaw the move, ensuring no loss of productivity, and in 1974, was named the Acting Sergeant Major of the 402nd SOD, 10th SFG. In July 1977, he returned to Panama as Acting Sergeant Major of the ASA Southern Command before retiring later that year.

During Master Sgt. Bunn's remarkable twenty-year career, he earned the Silver Star Medal, the Legion of Merit, the Bronze Star, and two Purple Hearts. His time in service was marked by devotion and love for his job, his initiative and creativeness, and his sense of duty. He was inducted into the Military Intelligence Hall of Fame in 1992.

The fighting 403rd

The 403rd RR SOD (Abn) was the DSU for the 5th Special Forces Group. Their unit had arrived straight from Ft. Bragg, North Carolina, in September 1966 with fifty-one men as part of the effort to restructure the intelligence capabilities of the 5th SFG. Although subordinate to the 509th RRG ASA in Saigon, the 403rd was headquartered with the 5th Special Forces Group in Nha Trang. At full strength, their personnel would ultimately be deployed to some eighty-five locations in support of 3,500 Special Forces troops across Vietnam. The men served in their capacities as highly trained SIGINT operators and also performed duties as members of Special Forces based on operational needs. They were a rare hybrid, bred by the necessities of a brutal war.

403rd SOD Plei Ku to Kontum courier run–1968 (Photo: INSCOM)

CHAPTER 20

THE BATTLE OF DUC LAP

Guarding the approaches to A-239 (Photo: © James Alward)

All wars contain acts of heroism that go unnoticed by the public; that is especially true if the war is unpopular. That does not, however, lessen the valor of the men who fight those battles. In August 1968, a battle took place at a small remote Special Forces camp forty-two miles from Ban Me Thuot near the Cambodian border. Not many Americans have heard of the Battle of Duc Lap or the story of the men who fought so valiantly to survive it and to save each other. It is the modern day equivalent to the Battle of the Alamo, only with a better outcome, barely.

The Duc Lap Civilian Irregular Defense Group (CIDG) Camp (known as A-239) was of critical importance because it was located at the crossroads of two main enemy infiltration routes from the Ho Chi Minh

Trail in Cambodia and Laos into South Vietnam. The remote outpost was authorized some 650 Montagnard soldiers, along with their families, eleven South Vietnamese Special Forces (LLDB) soldiers, and a ten-man detachment of U.S. Special Forces advisors. It also included three members of ASA's top-secret 403rd RR Special Operations Detachment (Abn): Staff Sgt. Danny Hall, Sgt. James Alward, and Spc.5 Donald Childs. All three soldiers were Special Forces-qualified, in addition to their ASA training as Morse intercept operators, and Alward, who was TDY from the 400th SOD in Okinawa, was also a Thai linguist.

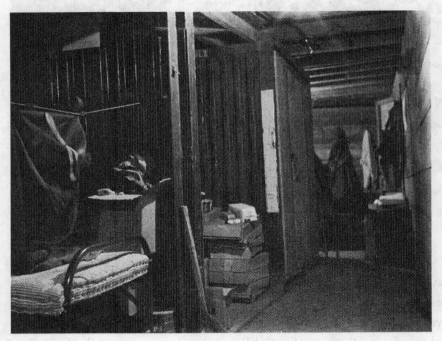

Childs' underground quarters and "radio room"—Duc Lap (Photo: INSCOM)

As with all of ASA's operations in 1968, the mission and intelligence gathering effort of the 403rd at Duc Lap was highly classified. That would seem to have been difficult within such a confined and close knit group as the small Special Forces contingent assigned to A-239, but Jim Alward says it was not a problem. "The three of us worked and slept in an underground bunker. There were four eight-by-eight steel conex boxes linked together with a walkway and buried under fifteen-or-twenty feet of logs and dirt. Danny Hall and I lived in the first box; the second box was used as a store room for medical supplies; Don Childs lived in the third box and the fourth one was our 'radio' room. I would think Danny Shepherd would've had access to the medical supplies, but absolutely no one ever came down there, other than Danny Hall, Don and me. I'd guess the C.O. and XO had been briefed; others may have had a general M.I. (military intelligence) idea, but they never asked what we did, and we never talked about it. All of that was above my pay grade anyway. Danny Hall had a reel-to-reel tape recorder and a couple of music tapes. He played 'Little Green Apples' by Roger Miller night and day. When I hear that song, I will always think of mud and incoming."

Alward and Hall's luxury bunker—"mud and incoming" (Photo: INSCOM)

The ASA team at Duc Lap had noticed a significant increase in the volume of enemy communications they were intercepting during the middle of August. They had passed that information up the line to NSA, but the traffic was all encrypted Morse. They had no way of knowing what information it contained or the significance of it. They forwarded the mass of raw data through the usual channels for others to analyze. "We never got feedback, of course," Jim Alward says.

Hell breaks loose

It was about 0100 hours on a moonless night when a distant rumble awakened Lt. William Harp, the Special Forces A-Team commander at Duc Lap. Half his available team was on duty, while the rest were sleeping in well-fortified bunkers deep within their hilltop compound. Master Sgt. Ted Boody was the NCOIC and writing a letter to his wife; radioman Sgt. Mike Dooley, a talented cartoonist was drawing pictures to send to his five-year-old son back home in California. The other team members had been playing cards or reading. They heard the dull rumbles too, like far-off thunder, and knew that a mortar attack was taking place somewhere in the distance. Opening the reinforced door of their team house, they saw flashes of light off to the west toward subsector headquarters. It was Friday, 23 August 1968.

"I MUST BE GETTING OLD, I DON'T FEEL AS ELITE AS I USED TO..."

SSG M. DOOLEY ©

Cartoon by Mike Dooley—August 1968
(Staff Sgt. Michael B. Dooley-U.S. Army)

"Everybody up...get outa bed!" Harp yelled. Don Childs, Danny Hall, Jim Alward and team medic, Sgt. Daniel Shepherd were among those sleeping when the alarm was sounded. The men dressed quickly and headed to join the rest of the Green Berets in the team house. A message was coming in from Duc Lap Subsector Headquarters. The headquarters was under heavy attack and needed help. Team Sergeant Boody put in a call to B-Team HQ at Ban Me Thuot to inform them of the attack, and the rest of the team headed for their assigned defensive positions.

Jim Alward crouched low in the first 81mm mortar pit and peered into the black night, wondering where his CIDG helpers were. Sgt. 1st Class Howard Blair, a light weapons expert and one of the older members of the team, was assigned to the second 81mm pit. "Shep" Shepherd, the medic, was helping him, and Sgt. 1st Class Harold Kline, a radio op who was TDY from Det. B-57 (Project Gamma) in Nha Trang, was manning the third position. Kneeling beside him was Don Childs, the "short-timer" who had only six days left before he rotated back to the States.

Suddenly, mortar rounds and B-40 rockets exploded inside the barbed wire surrounding the camp. The sound of automatic weapons and small arms fire split the night air, and the Special Forces team members could see the flashes of enemy guns in the distance. Two Montagnard helpers climbed into pit number one beside Alward and began to hand him rounds. It looked like it was going to be another long night.

Childs and Kline were firing a constant stream of anti-personnel rounds to the north and east, while Danny Hall and Sgt. Roland Vas were on the 4.2 inch mortar throwing out illumination rounds for the Montagnard troops who were manning the trenches around the perimeters of the camp. Mike Dooley was at his usual position in the 57mm recoilless rifle pit. The attack intensified, and B-40 rockets were hitting the camp every two minutes. The 81mm teams were firing about twenty to thirty rounds-per-minute, and continued firing until their mortar barrels overheated. They quickly cooled their weapons with water and began to fire again, a procedure that was repeated for over two hours.

Spooky had been overhead almost from the beginning. The aircraft's three Gatling miniguns fired at a rate of 6,000 rounds per minute and during a three-second burst placed a projectile every six feet over a fifty-two-yard area. The NVA were terrified of them, and with good reason; they could decimate a large force in one slow pass.

When the Spooky pilot returned to his base at Pleiku, he wrote the following account: "Things looked bad for Duc Lap Special Forces Camp A-239—Receiving mortar and rocket fire—Old Spooky came in like gang busters and stopped the rocket and mortar attack—When old Spooky 23 went back to base, Camp A-239 receiving light small arms fire—Left that up to Spooky 42—Another thankful customer…"

U.S. Air Force Spooky with Gatling guns blazing (Photo: U.S.A.F.)

At about 0300 hours, the attack let up. Lt. Harp assumed that the VC or NVA had a company of 150 to 200 troops around A-239 to prevent them from sending help to district headquarters. He talked with Capt. Bao, the LLDB (ARVN Special Forces) commander, and they decided to send out the CIDG recon platoon at first light to sweep the local village for enemy activity. If all was clear, they would attempt to get a relief force through to the district compound.

The team did not expect A-239 to be hit again, but they resupplied all positions with ammo, just in case. At 0430 hours, Sgt. Boody sent a message to Ban Me Thuot informing them that enemy contact had broken off at 0300. Three Montagnards and one dependent had been wounded. That would be the last direct message A-239 would send for four days.

At 0600, the Montagnard recon team headed out through the main gate to sweep the village. Suddenly, rockets and mortars exploded on both hills of the camp, and the recon soldiers began to pour back through the gate, running for the safety of the fortified compound. On top of the main hill, a mortar exploded near Sgt. Vas, and he fell to the ground bleeding profusely. A second round struck a short distance from Sgt. Blair, knocking him down. Dazed by the blast, but not seriously injured, Blair crawled to his feet. Realizing that Vas was badly hurt, he began to drag the wounded sergeant toward the medical bunker and called for help. Lt. Anthony Ayers, the team executive officer, ran to help with rounds bursting all around. Another mortar round exploded nearby, and a fragment struck Ayers in the jaw. Now there were two casualties. Boody came on the run, got the wounded men down into the bunker and placed a tourniquet on Vas' torn arm while Blair applied pressure to the wound. A vein had been hit, and there was blood everywhere. Vas was in serious condition; Lt. Ayers had a deep facial wound, and his uniform was soaked with blood. Both needed medical attention immediately. Shep Shepherd was near the camp dispensary by the main gate when the new attack began. Boody called him on the radio and told him to come to the medical bunker immediately. "Vas has been hit bad," he said, "Ayres is also wounded."

Medic, Sgt. Dan Shepherd (Photo: Spc.6 Eugene M. Randon, U.S. Army-NARA)

As Shepherd hurried up the curving mud road toward the medical bunker, mortars began to explode near the top of the hill. The enemy "walked" the shells down the road, and then back up making it impossible for anyone to use the rutted trail. Shepherd crouched behind some sandbags for a moment to see if the barrage would stop, but knew he needed to get to Vas. Cutting away from the road, he made his way down to the motor pool and along a protective trench behind the store building. Suddenly he stopped when he spied the men from the CIDG recon patrol huddled and hiding their heads in their hands.

"Get up and shoot back," Shepherd yelled, but they stared at him blankly and did not move. Shepherd, who was small and blonde, and was teased by his team-mates as "the boy next door" and "a kid headed for his first prom," seemed to visibly grow in stature. He strode over to the cowering lot, physically picked each man up and threw him into the defensive trench. "Find something to shoot at, dammit!" he roared, and they hastily began to fire their weapons.

Resuming his trek, Shepherd arrived at the medical bunker and efficiently began to treat the wounded men. He inserted an IV and bandaged Vas' arm, then dressed Ayers' wound. Lt. Ayers, with a huge bandage on his jaw, was soon back out on the 106 recoilless rifle grimly firing away at rocket positions; Sgt. Boody was loading for him. Lt. Harp was trying to contact Ban Me Thuot, but to no avail. He could hear them, but he could not answer back. The mortar barrage that had injured Vas and Ayers had also destroyed their antenna. Outside, mortars and rockets continued to pound the camp, and small arms fire poured in from the brush and overgrown fields to the north. There was no further discussion of sending a relief squad to the district compound. The Special Forces team had their hands full atop A-239.

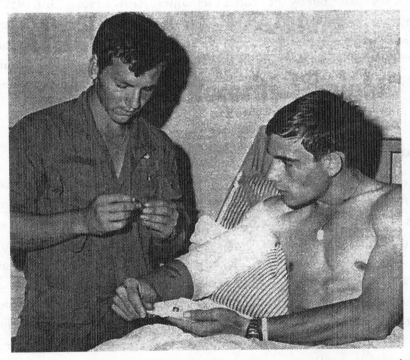

Shepherd looks at shrapnel removed from Vas' arm (Photo: U.S. Army)

When the camp was attacked, it was nowhere near full-strength. It had a total of twelve Green Berets, including the three ASA ops, six LLDB soldiers, a CIDG Combat Reconnaissance Platoon with thirty-five soldiers, seventeen Montagnard "M.P.s" who guarded the main gate, and 220 CIDG regular troops: 163 in 1st and 2nd companies on the main hill and fifty-seven in 3rd and 4th companies on the smaller hill at the north end of the camp. That was a total of 290 soldiers available for defense. The remainder of their forces, including most of 3rd and 4th companies and their Green Beret advisors were out on normal patrol duties along the Cambodian border. Most of the Montagnards also had their families living with them inside caves and bunkers that had been dug within the trench lines that guarded the hill.

The Special Forces team had no way of knowing that by daybreak, A-239 and its 290 defenders would be under siege, not by a VC or NVA company, but by the North Vietnamese Army's Hong Linh (95C) Regiment, some 1,500-2,000 well-trained regular infantry, and they were supported by units of the 320th Regiment and the 8th Battalion 66th Regiment, all elements of the NVA 1st Division. With its various support units, the combined enemy force in the Duc Lap area totaled some 4,000 troops.

A deadly race against time

With the first morning light, U.S. Air Force tactical aircraft had arrived on the scene and attacked the enemy positions. About 0930, Jim Alward was standing outside the team house watching the jets perform and admiring the pilots' expertise. During one strafing run, he saw an F-100 Super Sabre sweep in low, and then watched in amazement as its afterburner flamed out and a black dot popped out, sprouting a parachute. The plane continued on its path, exploding in a ball of fire as it collided with another hill to the north. The pilot had ejected safely, but had parachuted down perilously close to enemy-controlled territory near the village. There was no time to lose.

Tactical air support over Duc Lap—23 August 1968 (Photo: © James Alward)

Grabbing his carbine, Mike Dooley jumped into a jeep and careened down the hill toward the front gate. The FAC overhead was contacted to provide gunship cover, then Boody, Alward, Hall and Childs joined other members of the team in a second jeep and a three-quarter-ton truck as they sped after Dooley. Shepherd was in the dispensary near the front gate as Dooley arrived in a cloud of dust. Dooley was yelling at the M.P.s to move the concertina wire they had strung across the road in front of the gate, and they rushed to obey him.

When Shepherd learned that a jet had been shot down, he grabbed his weapon and medical kit and jumped into the jeep with Dooley. The other two vehicles had caught up, and after loading a half-dozen CIDG soldiers in the back of the truck, the ragtag caravan sped out the gate and down the road toward the pilot's landing area. They had not been fired upon, so far.

As the vehicles slid to a halt beyond the village, Dooley and Childs jumped out and raced across an open field toward the billowing parachute. The others covered their flanks and watched for enemy troops. Small arms and AK-47 fire was beginning to whistle through the trees at the edge of the field. Enemy soldiers were closing in fast, intent on completing their coup over the American F-100 and its pilot.

From the hill-top compound, observers could see NVA soldiers moving in from the west to cut off the return route of the rescue vehicles.

In the meantime, the rescuers had not found the pilot. The Americans had fanned out and were searching the surrounding area when Hall and Shepherd stumbled over him hiding in the brush at the edge of the woods. The pilot would later confess that he had almost shot Dooley as he came running down the trail, fearing that he was the enemy. But now, they had to get back to their compound. Bullets were whining through the brush like angry hornets, and the volume of gunfire was increasing.

Suddenly, two U.S. helicopter gunships appeared on the scene. Rising like huge dragonflies over the clearing, their miniguns sliced through the foliage and formed a steel wall around the small band of soldiers. The men hurried back up the narrow path, half-dragging the young pilot to their vehicles, and with the gunships providing cover, they sped back to the relative safety of their fortified camp.

Moving underground

Friday morning, 23 August 1968—Front row: Howard Blair, Harold Kline, possibly Hall, Lt. Harp, Top Sgt. Boody and unknown CIDG— Back row: Unknown, Dan Shepherd, Roland Vas, a bandaged Lt. Ayers and unknown CIDG (Photo: © James Alward)

The B-Team commander and his staff had flown in from Ban Me Thuot at first light to help coordinate A-239's defense. He had instructed his helicopter crew to transport ammunition and supplies into the camp from Ban Me Thuot as quickly as possible. The crew had also evacuated Vas and Ayres, transported the rescued pilot, 1Lt. Julius J. Thurn, back to his unit at Phan Rang, and brought in the B-Team XO, Maj. Roland Greenwood, who would coordinate with the Mike Force companies coming to reinforce the camp's defenses.

The weather had completely cleared, and the sky was blue for the first time in days. The 202nd Mobile Strike Force (MSF) from Pleiku was airlifted by helicopters to a location just north of the camp, but was driven back by entrenched NVA infantry and forced to withdraw back to the landing zone. At 1500 hours, some three hours later, the 204th MSF was dropped by helicopters at the same LZ. The two companies linked up and moved west, setting up a defensive perimeter on high ground overlooking the battlefield. From there, the Special Forces advisors with the units had a clear view of the besieged camp and were able to call in airstrikes and gunship attacks on suspected NVA positions.

**Mike Dooley, Don Childs, Blair, Hall and Shigeo
Umeda (Photo: © James Alward)**

During the afternoon, mortar rounds and rockets continued to fall on the camp sporadically, and sniper fire came in from a corn field and weed-filled gully off to the west. NVA troops could be observed digging in near the eastern perimeter of the camp, and there was continuing fear of an enemy ground assault on the main gate. Danny Hall and some of the other team members picked off a few enemy troops using M-16s with sniper scopes, and Dooley zeroed in the 57mm recoilless rifle on suspected NVA rocket positions.

The Green Berets spent much of their time preparing for the ground attack they expected to come that night. Chopper crews braved enemy antiaircraft fire again and again in order to strengthen the camp. Landing on a helipad near the dispensary, they brought in food and medical supplies, water and ammo. Only two of the camp vehicles were still serviceable, a jeep and the three-quarter-ton truck, so hour after hour, Hall, Alward, Childs and Shepherd sped the vehicles up and down the rutted red hill loaded with supplies. Ammunition was restocked at all the positions, and food supplies were laid in. At about 1500 hours a huge Chinook helicopter descended over the saddle area between the hills and delivered a load of badly needed 105mm ammunition. Harp and Boody assumed that the camp was in for a rough time, but they were as prepared as they could be, under the circumstances.

Toward evening, Childs and Hall were standing near the team house and heard a strange whistling sound. "What's that?" Childs asked. Both of them ducked behind a barricade and watched an explosion down the hill in front of the trench line. "Maybe it's a 122," Hall said. Then they heard the whistle again, followed by another explosion. That time it was further up the hill. "I swear that is artillery fire," said Childs. During the course of the next twenty minutes or so, about ten more rounds hit and worked their way up the hill, blasting huge holes in the bunkers and trenches. No one seemed to have been killed or hurt, but the barrage was an ominous sign of worse to come.

Bunkers and trenches at Duc Lap (Photos: © Ken Thompson)

The team had moved everything they thought they might need into the underground bunkers. A few mattresses had been placed on the floor on the chance that someone had a few minutes to rest. The team was well-stocked with food. "Mostly we ate C-rations," Alward said, "but I don't think many of us were that hungry...The whole time I had maybe three or four cans, some ham, a couple of cookies and chewed some gum."

Their most serious problem was water. There was no well within the camp fortifications; all water had to be transported in. To conserve what little water remained, the team members drank warm beer until they ran out of it on Saturday. It didn't taste that great, but it quenched their thirst.

As the sun set on Friday night, a steady barrage of mortars and rockets began to hit the camp; Danny Hall joined Jim Alward and his two Montagnard helpers in 81 pit one. Shep Shepherd was with Blair in number two. Kline and Childs were manning the third 81mm position. Dooley and Sgt. Shigeo Umeda were on the .50 caliber machine gun. The barrage continued to increase in intensity until near 2100 hours when there was a brief lull.

Losing ground

In the meantime, under cover of the trees north of the camp, the NVA commanders readied the first wave of their attack on the smaller, lightly-defended north hill. At 2100 hours they launched a heavy mortar and rocket barrage. That was followed by a ground attack preceded by troops with bangalore torpedoes to blow breaches in the concertina wire surrounding the camp. After repeated human-wave assaults, the enemy troops overwhelmed the small fortress with its fifty-seven Montagnard defenders and their families. Radio transmissions coming in from the north hill had reported "Beaucoup VC!" over and over, but based on past experience, Lt. Harp thought they were exaggerating. There were no Green Berets or LLDBs assigned to that end of the camp, so he had no way of verifying what was actually going on there.

About 2300 hours Top Sgt. Boody left the main bunker to check the defensive line and take some beer to his men when automatic weapons fire zinged near his head. He dropped to the ground and crawled to the pit where Childs and Kline were operating. AK-47 rounds were hitting all around their location. Dooley and Umeda also began to receive sniper fire at their location. "Wonder where the hell that's coming from?" Dooley asked. He put down his 57 and moved around the perimeter past Shep and Blair to the 90mm recoilless where he continued to watch for the flash of enemy guns. The sniping continued to plague the men in the trenches and firing pits on the main hill, and they kept their heads down. About midnight, Childs learned from an LLDB soldier that the north hill had fallen and was in enemy hands. They were being sniped at from their own northern fortifications.

The NVA troops had not only swarmed over the north hill, but had also seized control of much of the saddle area between the two hills.

About 0100 hours, most of the survivors of the 3rd and 4th companies of Montagnard soldiers and their families straggled up within the inner perimeter of the main hill. A few more would make it across the next morning, but out of the original fifty-seven soldiers, only thirty-five had survived the enemy onslaught.

More hell

Childs and Kline had continued to fire from pit three until 0200 when they ran out of ammo. The other two pits were running low, too. Childs climbed over to the sandbag wall to look out at the northern hill, and suddenly a B-40 rocket exploded nearby. Something struck him hard against the back of his hand. "My hand, I can't move it!" he yelled. With his other hand, he managed to call Shep on the radio, and a few minutes later the medic jumped down into the trench beside him. The skin was unbroken, but the hand was numb and Childs could not move his fingers. "You'll be all right," he assured Childs, "[It's] just a slight fracture."

Blair and Shepherd had returned to the tactic operations bunker (TOC), and Blair was trying to get some rest. The firing stopped for about an hour, and Blair dropped off to sleep; then the mortars began to fire again. Shepherd shook the older man awake and said, "They're hitting us again. Let's go…" As the two men settled in to begin launching illumination, an enemy mortar round exploded nearby, and the rounds kept coming; one hit the medical bunker, and another blew off the side of an ammo bunker. Blair was crouched in the trench line opening canisters of illumination when a third round hit the lip of the mortar pit in which Shepherd was working. Shep was slammed to the floor of the pit, and Blair was blown out of the trench and into the pit on top of Shepherd. Blair screamed, "My arm!" and was holding the back of his head. Shepherd did what he could to stop the bleeding and then dragged the wounded man into the medical bunker. Fortunately, the wound was not as serious as it first appeared, but Shepherd made Blair stay in the bunker to rest and went back to the mortar pit to resume firing illumination. The time was 0300 hours.

Childs time

Sometime later, Childs' hand was feeling better, so he decided to leave pit three and see what was going on around the area. "Besides," he mused, "I better save my ammo for when Charlie gets to our wire…" It was still very dark as he made his way down the side of the hill to the 60mm pit which was assigned to the LLDB. The pit appeared to be abandoned, but when he jumped down into it, there was a small Montagnard man huddled deep in a dark corner. "Where is everybody?" he asked, but the little soldier just stared blankly. He was obviously terrified and probably spoke little or no English. Childs settled into the pit and began to fire the 60mm mortar.

When the NVA captured the north hill, they had also captured two 57mm recoilless rifles, complete with ammunition. Now the Americans were receiving fire from their own 57s. Childs always had a solution for everything; sometimes it was not the most rational solution, but it was a Childs solution. Spooky was overhead; Childs began to fire the 60mm at the 57, so the enemy gunner would shoot back at him. Spooky was supposed to see the muzzle flash and unload on the enemy. In Childs' mind, it was a simple fix to a serious problem, as long as he didn't get nailed by the 57.

Sometimes Childs' radio would malfunction, and the other team-members would think the lanky kid had been hit. Mike Dooley had gone looking for Childs on several occasions when he had not responded to a radio call. Dooley could never be sure what was going on with Childs, but he was always sure that if there was action taking place, Childs would be in the middle of it.

By that time, the sky in the east was turning a deep shade of red. Umeda was still on the .50 caliber when a 57 round exploded nearby, and he jumped into a bunker. He thought he heard someone cry out; it sounded like Childs' voice, so he called Boody on the radio.

Boody tried to contact Childs, but received no answer. "We looked all over for Childs," Boody said. "Suddenly he comes up on the radio. He's directing Spooky to put fire on the hill."

The time was 0600, and the red sky was giving way to pink and yellow on the horizon. Heavy weapons fire was pounding the area where Childs was located. Each time he fired, he received a new wave of mortar and automatic weapons fire.

"This is Childs," the young man called.

"What the (expletive) are you doing?" Boody asked. "We've been looking all over hell for you."

"I'm down by the 60," Childs answered, "Things are getting hot over here. I think they got me bracketed."

"All right, listen," the top sergeant said in his most patient manner. "Get your ass back up here while you still have one." There was nothing but silence. "Do you hear me Childs?" the sergeant roared. "I'm ordering you to leave there!"

"Look," Boody said, resuming a more reasoned tone. "I'll call Spooky in for two runs. Let him go the first one. When he starts the second, you move your ass fast up the hill, all right?" There was still no response. "Do you hear me, Childs? This is an order!"

"Okay," Childs said, as he continued to fire mortar rounds. Spooky made his first run with his Gatlings blazing. "He never hit that hill," Childs fussed, and he continued to fire the mortar at the enemy target. He waited for the second run, all the time telling the plane overhead, "Closer, closer!" and that time Spooky hit a bull's eye, destroying the 57.

Childs motioned to the small Montagnard still crouched in the pit and yelled, "Come on!" The terrified man just shook his head and did not move. Childs yanked off his extra gear, jumped out of the pit, and sprinted up the hill, running as fast as his long legs could carry him. Automatic weapons and small arms fire nipped at his heels throwing up showers of red dirt all the way to the top. Fighting for breath, he threw himself into the command bunker as ground fire continued to rake the area. Sgt. Boody glared at Childs for a split second and then turned his attention to more important matters.

Saturday

The NVA attack had continued to push forward at daybreak. At one point, their troops had come within 150 feet of the TOC on the main hill before being beaten back by small arms fire, mortars and helicopter gunships. When the attack was broken, the enemy took terrible losses retreating back to the bunkers atop the north hill.

Reconnaissance later on Saturday confirmed that the northern half of the camp was totally in NVA hands. A Montagnard radio operator, along with four other CIDG troops had hidden in a small bunker on the enemy-controlled hill during the attack the night before and he had communicated throughout the night with the LLDB commander. The radioman had provided information about enemy forces, called in fire on NVA gun placements, and even called in fire on the position where he was hiding. His last message said that enemy soldiers were clearing nearby bunkers, tossing in grenades and firing AK-47s. Nothing was heard from him or his companions again.

With Childs' return, the team members gathered in the tactical ops bunker to discuss the overall situation. The night-long attack had ceased as the sun rose, but no one knew what to expect next. "We didn't know if we were going to be extracted at this time, which sounded like a very good idea to us," Childs said. "The situation looked pretty hopeless... We were getting our shit ready, waiting for the word on what to do. We didn't know...what Charlie was planning, but we knew he held the other hill, and it wouldn't...[take] too much effort to get our hill, at least I didn't think so. I knew the Yards were pretty undependable, even with their own lives at stake."

As of noon, A-239 had suffered eighty casualties, and over fifty of those were KIA. The overall strength of the camp was about 200. Lt. Harp still had no idea how many NVA they faced on the other hill, but he was sure that his team did not have enough manpower to retake it on its own. The Green Berets had been told that help was on the way. They just had to stay barricaded in their camp, stay alive, and wait.

Any additional supplies would have to be airdropped. The concentrated enemy firepower was now so intense that helicopters could not get in.

The second 57

The main compound was under constant attack by enemy troops who had moved into bunkers at its northern perimeter during the night. In addition to the 57s, the enemy had captured two .50 caliber machine guns, a 3.5 inch rocket launcher, and a number of mortars. With no American leadership present, the Montagnards had made no effort to destroy any of their weapons. Fire from those captured 57s had been so intense on the 81mm pit three that no one could get near it, and a direct hit had finally destroyed the mortar. Childs had managed to eliminate one of the captured 57s, but the enemy force still had the second one, and it was a devastating weapon.

Danny Hall, Mike Dooley, and Shep Shepherd grew tired of sitting in the ops bunker and went outside in the sunshine. The three men crawled up over the sandbag fortifications where they had a clear view of the enemy-held hill and could survey the battlefield spread out below them. The enemy gunfire had ceased after the last bombing and napalm runs by the Air Force F-4s and F-100s. The area below them was littered with NVA bodies, burned and bloating in the midday sun. It was a horrific sight.

Suddenly Hall said, "Look, isn't that a 57?" There was no mistake; directly across from their position, on top of a bunker on the northern hill, stood the remaining captured 57 recoilless.

"Let's knock it out," Dooley said with a grim smile. He and Shepherd climbed down and disappeared into the operations bunker. They returned quickly with several LAWs and an M-79 grenade launcher. They fired at the 57, but it was beyond their range. Dooley then attacked the rifle with the .50 caliber machine gun, but no luck. Howard Blair, who was recovering from his shrapnel wounds, had followed Dooley and Shepherd back from the ops bunker, and he had an idea. He climbed down and ran over to the 105mm howitzer crew.

Montagnard 105mm howitzer crew at Duc Lap (Photos: © Ken Thompson)

Blair had helped train the Montagnard crew and knew them personally. One tall slender young man named Lah-Nhi spoke English and had learned the procedures especially well. Blair now pointed at the captured 57, and Lah-Nhi nodded with a smile. The crew turned the big gun; Lah-Nhi adjusted the artillery piece for direct fire, and two shells later, the last 57 was no more.

The 202nd

At 0900 on Saturday, the 203rd MSF was airlifted in to the Duc Lap area with the other two Special Forces companies already on the ground. The three companies joined up and launched a three-pronged assault on the enemy. The 202nd was on the right flank, the 203rd was on the left, and the 204th was in the middle. About noon, the three companies encountered entrenched NVA forces near the camp, and air strikes were called in on the north hill. After the strikes, the three Mike Force units continued their drive with the 202nd in the lead. The 204th was in the middle and the 203rd was further back.

About 1230 hours, as the 202nd neared the camp, they saw a sign:

"Welcome to Camp Duc Lap," and beneath it were sprawled the mangled remains of several NVA soldiers. "Some welcome," their commander thought. Then, as they reached the main gate, automatic weapons fire swept across the trail behind them, along with mortars and B-40 rockets. The 204th was immediately pinned down, the Montagnard soldiers seeking cover wherever they could find it. The 202nd was hit by small arms fire and mortars, too, but their main problem was they could not get through coils of concertina wire that were piled in front of the camp gate. The Montagnard leader of the 202nd, along with Vinh, an LLDB lieutenant, and Capt. David Savage, an Aussie commander, struggled to remove the wire. Suddenly Savage was hit; he slumped forward and fell to the ground. Sgt. John Wast, a Green Beret platoon leader, called in an airstrike in an attempt to suppress the enemy fire.

With the barriers finally cleared, and carrying their wounded, the men of the 202nd lurched forward through the opening. Inside the gate the Montagnard M.P.s were providing good cover fire for the soldiers as they ran inside the fortifications. Numbering only seventeen men, the M.P.s held their position throughout the entire battle. Armed with only two BARs, a pair of Thompson sub-machine guns, and a few carbines, they kept the entrance gate open for relief troops to enter, despite being surrounded by enemy troops the entire time.

The 202nd, with its fresh group of Montagnard fighters, a contingent of LLDB troops, and members of the Australian Army Training Team (Aussie advisors) were inside the compound, but the other two companies were forced to withdraw due to intense enemy mortar and automatic weapons fire. Falling back to the trench line and suffering heavy casualties, the commanders made the decision to withdraw the 203rd and 204th to the previous night's position so they could resupply and medevac their wounded away from the battlefield. The 204th commander thought he had lost about 50% of his men, but did not realize that some of his Montagnard troops had merged with the 202nd and were now inside the camp.

Dooley and Shepherd were manning the machine gun by the innermost gate on the main hill. Shepherd asked Dooley if he'd like some peaches.

"Sure," said Dooley, so the medic walked up to the team house to get a can he had stashed there. When he came out, Green Berets and Mike Force troops were coming up the hill.

"I couldn't believe it," Shepherd said, "I was really glad to see them. We shook hands, laughed and joked. They wanted to know what was going on…I talked with them for a while, then I headed back to Dooley in the machine gun pit."

Danny Hall had been up in a mortar pit and watched the 202nd advance through the mortar and automatic weapons fire. "They came up through the main gate," he remembered, "about ten people at a time, around to the side, down by the motor pool, then through the fence and all the way up the hill. They'd gather around the team house and ask where they could go." The 202nd provided the defenders with welcome reinforcements, and morale soared. Maybe the coming night would be a little easier. The newly arrived soldiers immediately manned the bunkers and trenches facing the enemy force on the opposing hill. The time was 1500 hours, and the day had just gotten brighter, for a brief moment.

Getting personal

The non-stop NVA assaults, complete with mortars and B40 rockets, had continued throughout the day. Attempts to get choppers in with supplies and to pick up the wounded had failed due to heavy anti-aircraft fire. One of the choppers had sustained a direct hit. The Americans were running out of ammunition, medical supplies and water. Airdrops were attempted, but most of the supplies fell outside the perimeter of the camp and were impossible to recover due to enemy fire. Resupply was critical and without it, their overnight survival was doubtful.

Shepherd knew that there was a water bag near the dispensary, so he told Dooley to get the jeep, and he ran into the team house to get some five gallon water cans. Suddenly, a shell exploded into the side of the building, slamming him to the floor and spraying the young medic's back with shrapnel. For a few moments he lay stunned and unable to move, and then Dooley was there. With Dooley's help, he slowly got to his feet and managed to make his way into the medical bunker. A Montagnard nurse inserted an IV into Shepherd's arm as Dooley dressed his wounds and helped him down onto a cot.

An hour later, someone was shaking him yelling, "Wake up, Kline's been hurt bad!" Shepherd struggled to clear his pounding head and mumbled, "Let me sleep," but the voice was insistent. "Kline, Umeda, and the Major, they've been hit." Now alert, Shep Shepherd struggled to his feet and made his way out of the medical bunker.

Around 1600 hours, Kline and Umeda had been standing outside the ops center bunker discussing the siege with Major Greenwood and several Vietnamese officers. Without warning, a B-40 rocket exploded in front of them, and the entire area was immediately sprayed with automatic weapons fire and additional rockets. A Montagnard artilleryman with the group was killed outright.

Lawrie Jackson, an Australian Warrant Officer grabbed Umeda who was screaming deliriously, dragged him to the top of the TOC stairs and ran to get more help. All the injured were hauled into the bunker, and then Shepherd came in, quickly surveying the bloody mass of soldiers.

Alward, who had been in the TOC resting, was seated on the floor quietly holding Kline cradled across his lap. Kline's legs were sprawled awkwardly across the floor.

"How is Kline?" Shepherd asked.

"Dead, I think," Alward answered.

The medic knelt down beside the still body of the sergeant and opening Kline's vest, checked his vital signs. "Yes," he said, turning away for a moment. Straightening his shoulders, Shep rose to his feet and began to treat the other men.

The first Green Beret at Duc Lap had just died.

Surviving the night

B-40s continued to hit the camp that evening and late into the night. Shepherd tended the wounded; Major Greenwood and Umeda both had serious leg wounds. If they could not be evacuated to a hospital,

Greenwood would probably lose his leg, or worse. Boody and Harp tried to get a "dustoff" (unarmed medevac helicopter) into the camp and called in strikes by the Spookys. From 2300 until after midnight, four dustoffs tried numerous times to land at the camp, but the enemy fire was so intense it was impossible. The effort was reluctantly called off.

Dooley was on the .50 caliber machine gun. He would sit out in the dark and watch for the muzzle-flash of enemy guns. When he had their location spotted, he would fire tracers with the machine gun to mark the spot, and Spooky would fly in to finish the job. Dooley and Spooky made a good team and their game plan continued until early in the morning.

The other Americans were joined by the Aussies from the 202nd to man the mortar pits. Lawrie Jackson was with Jim Alward for a while in 81 pit two. They kept putting up illumination rounds for the Spooky aircraft flying overhead but were running low on ammo. Every thirty minutes or so, Alward would stop and let the mortar cool down. Danny Hall finally came and relieved Jackson for a break.

Don Childs was on the 3rd mortar with Barry Tolley. "Why don't ya git some sleep?" Tolley asked the exhausted youngster.

"Don't be silly," Childs said, but the Aussie kept insisting. Finally at about 0300, Childs left for the ops center bunker, hoping to find a place to stretch out.

During the night, Air Force Major George Finck volunteered to fly the first-ever C-7 operational night drop. Flying through a hail of ground fire from all sides, and guided by tracers and one white light to ID the tiny drop zone, the pilot delivered pallets of ammunition and water. No one slept much that night. The Americans were expecting another night attack, and even with the reinforcements from the 202nd, there were doubts about whether or not they could withstand it.

Around 0500, Dooley and Sgt. Wast crawled out to 81 pit two. They relieved Alward and Hall who went into one of the bunkers and tried to get some rest. "Man, I could go for a cold beer...," Wast said.

"Just a glass of water would do for me," Dooley replied. For the next thirty minutes there was quiet. Dooley could hear a cricket chirping somewhere near, and birds were chattering in the predawn darkness. Maybe the battle was over, and the enemy had retreated.

"Look!" Dooley said. A green flare had soared high into the air, and that was followed by a red flare.

"Wonder which of those damn Yards is fooling around with the flares," Wast said to himself. His answer was swift and deafening as a mortar round exploded beside the pit in which the two men crouched. Both soldiers scrambled for a nearby bunker as more rounds struck the area throwing up huge lethal sprays of shrapnel and dirt.

Wast sat against the wall inside the bunker, braced against the violent explosions; Dooley stood in the doorway like he was watching fireworks on the 4th of July.

Sunday mourning

It was Sunday morning, and the NVA had just launched another predawn human-wave assault on the main hill. Their attack was timed to begin during the brief break in air cover between the Spookys who ruled the night and the daylight fighter-bombers with their bullets and napalm. This time the enemy commanders attacked from the north hill and brought up a company from the southwest. An airstrike was called in, but many of the enemy troops were concentrated in a gully off to the side of the two hills. The planes missed them in the darkness. The attacking force broke through to the inner perimeter and captured four bunkers at the base of the main hill just outside the inner trenches.

As the wave of NVA troops swarmed up the slope toward the command compound, they were observed by one of the Special Forces advisors with the battered 204th He called in artillery fire, and the newly-arrived U.S. heavy artillery had an immediate and devastating impact. The NVA forces slowed their attack, ground to a halt, and then were forced into a disorderly retreat with heavy casualties as artillery shells burst all around them. The attack had lasted about thirty minutes, but it had seemed much longer. With the light of day, the team could see the bodies of enemy dead within their perimeter wire on the southeast slope. They were only fifteen feet from the CIDG machine gun bunker that controlled access to that side of the camp. The Montagnards had held their ground, and their .30 caliber machine gun and grenades had been deadly effective.

After Danny Hall had left his mortar pit earlier in the morning, he had been unable to sleep. He was exhausted, but too keyed-up to lie down for long. He was in the communications bunker when the dawn attack began and quickly ran out. Grabbing his M-16 and an M-79 grenade launcher, he began firing at anything he saw moving on the north hill. Mike Dooley was now in mortar pit two, but as the attack increased in fury, he gathered some Montagnards and crawled to the 57 recoilless rifle pit on the perimeter. It had no overhead cover and was exposed to enemy fire.

Jim Alward was resting in another bunker when a Montagnard came running in to tell him that an American had been shot. Shepherd had finally allowed himself to collapse in the medical bunker, but jumped awake when Alward called him on the radio. "An American's been hit," he said. "One of the Yards just came running in."

"Who is it?" The medic asked.

There was a pause, then Alward said quietly, "God, I hope not—but I think it's Dooley."

"Which bunker?" Shep asked.

"I don't know," Alward replied.

Shepherd grabbed two cans of albumin and asked John Wast to go with him. The two men crawled up behind the team house but could see no sign of anyone. It was just becoming daylight, and the shadows were still deep and dark. The two then crawled to a small trench partway down the hill, and Shepherd happened to look up. Mike Dooley was lying face down, slumped over a pile of 57mm ammo. He called the young soldier's name, but there was no answer. Hurrying to the body, he checked for a pulse or a heartbeat, but there was nothing, only the now quiet morning. A heavy stream of dark blood oozed from a large perfect hole behind Dooley's right ear.

The 57mm pit where Mike Dooley died (Photo: © James Alward)

Fighting back tears, Shep Shepherd sank to the ground and sat there for a moment staring at the body. Suddenly, another wave of rockets began to strike the camp. The young medic gently pulled the body of his buddy down inside an empty bunker where it would be safe and out of the way. When the battle was over, Mike Dooley would be going home.

The sun was rising, and it looked like it was going to be a golden day. For a brief moment, silence again filled the valley between the two battle-scarred hills. There was a pause, a drawing in, and then there was a roar of pure rage that seemed to grow from out of nowhere and expand outward until it filled their entire world. Again and again, the ground shook and convulsed, and high above, so high that no one could see or hear them, the bomb-bay doors on the B-52s continued to open and silently release their deadly loads upon the NVA strongholds around Duc Lap.

CHAPTER 21

THE SIEGE OF A-239

The lower-south perimeter of A-239–1968 (Photo: INSCOM)

The death of Mike Dooley was devastating for the Green Berets at Duc Lap. Dooley was the funny guy, the cartoonist. Michael Dooley was the one man who could boost their morale during the darkest times, make them laugh and forget their fear, if only for a few moments. But now Dooley was gone.

"Danny Hall and I went down later and got his body out of the bunker," Jim Alward recalls. "It was a hard thing to do."

But on that terrible Sunday morning, there was no time for grief. There was only the continuing fight to survive and hope that help would arrive before it was too late.

The panic

At 0800 hours, under ever-increasing pressure from renewed attacks by the enemy force and frightened by an errant napalm strike near their positions, some of the Montagnard soldiers began to withdraw from the last inner trench, taking their wives and children with them. Alward and Jacko Jackson were in mortar pit two and saw several CIDG come running up the hill with no weapons. "What's going on?" Alward shouted.

He asked an interpreter to find out, and the interpreter said, "They quit! Drop weapons. Run." Alward called Harp and Boody in the ops center and told them what was happening.

"Get them back into position," Boody yelled. But those few were just the beginning of a human tide. All of the Montagnards appeared to be pulling out, dropping their weapons, leaving their positions in the lower perimeter and heading up the hill.

Don Childs was on the south side of the hill and saw what was happening. He fired several shots over their heads, but the Montagnards neither saw nor heard anything in their terror that would slow them down. Nothing at the top of the hill could be as frightening as what they had been experiencing at the bottom of the hill. They continued to push upward toward the compound at the top, dependents and all. If the NVA realized for a moment the Montagnards were in full retreat, the battle was over. The Green Berets would be standing naked with no defensive lines between the enemy forces and their last redoubt.

"It was our asses if we didn't get those people back into position," Alward said. The Americans, the Aussies, and the LLDBs all began to yell and push the Montagnards back down the hill. Alward grabbed one of the men who had helped him in the 81mm pit. The man spoke broken English, and Alward told him that if the soldiers did not go back into the trenches they were all going to die. He pushed the man toward the panicked troops and then walked toward other groups of CIDG soldiers waving his arms and yelling for them to get back down the hill.

The Green Berets finally realized that the Montagnards' main concern was their families, so they allowed them to move their dependents into the bunkers and pits inside the compound, and that seemed to defuse the situation. With a mixture of coaxing and threats, Childs reestablished his perimeter on the north slope of the camp and then had all the dependents from his CIDG group move into bunkers near the TOC, ordering them to stay there. When that was accomplished, he patiently explained to his Yards that if they did not hold the perimeter, the whole place would fall, and they would all die. Everything depended on them.

Montagnard families living in the trenches at Duc Lap (Photo: © Ken Thompson)

Back in the ops bunker, the officers were discussing their overall situation and the alternatives with some of the team members. If more reinforcements did not arrive soon, the camp could not hold out. The huge NVA force had completely surrounded A-239 and was tightening its grip. Sergeant Boody talked about possible escape routes and where the enemy lines were thought to be weakest. If the camp was overrun, survivors might be able to fight their way out and hook up with the additional MSF companies that were trying to get to the camp. He had Sgt. Shepherd bring in thermite grenades and pass out two to each Green

Beret so that the mortars, 57s, and other weapons could be destroyed if the camp had to be evacuated. Nothing would be left intact for the NVA to use against them later. In addition, the ASA team would have to destroy all their classified materials and the intercept equipment in their bunker complex if there was any chance of it falling into enemy hands.

The most difficult part of their worst-case plan was what to do with the two severely wounded Americans from the B-40 attack. Neither Greenwood nor Umeda could walk; both were in constant pain. If the NVA overran the camp, carrying them was not an option. Major Greenwood had a fully-loaded pistol and an M-16. He was propped up in a corner of the medical bunker and kept his weapons pointed at the door. Umeda held a loaded .45 across his chest, waiting for whatever was to come. Neither soldier was going to let the NVA take him alive and intended to take as many with him as he could.

Never say die

Childs reported in at the ops center about 1000 hours, but impatient with all the negative talk, picked up his radio and headed back to the Montagnards on the northern slope. Failure was not in his DNA, and he refused to consider the possibility.

"With no energy or illusion, we knew that our last battle would soon be upon us," Childs says. "We'd been ordered to E&E (escape & evade) out at the right moment, but that meant leaving the wounded, and Boody left that as a personal decision. I didn't intend to leave, but I don't know what anyone else's decision was."

At the base of the hill within the inner wire were several bunkers. Childs knew that the enemy had moved into them during the last attack and suspected they were still there, using them to fire at the CIDG positions. He decided, on his own, to retake the bunkers and establish some Montagnard soldiers there in order to have an early warning when the next big ground attack was launched. Maybe then his "Yards" would be able the stop the enemy force before they got inside the inner perimeter. Childs was always thinking and planning, and doing. That was what concerned his superiors.

The LLDB "bac-si" (medic), Sgt. Le Van Lai, came over to talk to Childs about the bunkers. Childs had never liked the man. He was a bit stocky but about average build for a Vietnamese. The young man had long black hair and a narrow brimmed hat perched on the back of his head. He was missing a couple of front teeth and always seemed to have a sarcastic look on his face. Childs thought he was a bit of a "cowboy," but he had been told that the man knew martial arts and could beat the hell out of anybody around. The bac-si was willing to go with him, so Childs rounded up ten Montagnards, loaded up with grenades and a LAW, and led his tiny band of commandos down toward the bunkers.

Childs fired the LAW, blowing up the first bunker, and then simply climbed over it, sliding down the other side onto the ground. As he looked back up the hill, he realized that his valiant band of Yards was cowering just outside the gate. He yelled for them to come with him but knew that it was going to be strictly his show. Only the bac-si was going to go with him; the CIDG soldiers were not going to be of any help. He tossed his radio back to the combat interpreter and told him that if he got hit, to call on the radio and get someone down there to help him. "I knew Shep would be down," he said, "at least I hoped so."

Childs then sneaked over to the far side of the next bunker. The barrel of an AK-47 was sticking out of a gun port and waving around. He quietly pulled the pin on a grenade, waited a couple of seconds and dropped it inside. The bac-si dropped one in from the other side at the same time, and they ducked down low as the charges exploded. Moving to the left, the tall lanky American and the "cowboy" Vietnamese destroyed two more bunkers with grenades.

During the few minutes all that action was taking place, there had been sporadic sniper fire from the north hill, but suddenly the firing increased greatly with automatic weapons fire. It was coming not only from the hill but also from the gully off to the side, and they were caught in a dangerous cross-fire with little in the way of protective cover.

Looking back up the hill, Childs saw the Montagnards moving back up the hill away from the action. At that point, Childs assumed he and the bac-si were in serious trouble. They had used all their grenades and had only their personal weapons.

Suddenly, about fifteen feet in front of their position, three NVA soldiers poked their heads up out of a shell crater and started toward them. Two of the soldiers were armed with AK-47s. Childs quickly switched his M-16 to fully automatic and shot at them. He did not know if he hit all three or not, but that was the last he saw of them.

Childs and the bac-si began to slowly work their way back up the hill. One would put down covering fire while the other moved in turn, and foot by foot, they made their way safely to the top. On the way up, they saw two B-40 rockets and launchers lying off to one side, but the ground fire had become so intense they could not get to them. The two men were already carrying extra weapons they had picked up from the destroyed bunkers.

Childs and the bac-si tried to get some of the Montagnards to go back down with them to retrieve the B-40s, but none were willing to go, so the two headed back down the hill alone. They had just jumped behind a mound of earth near the rockets when automatic weapons fire began to zero in on them again. Each man, in turn, tried to reach the rockets, but their efforts were met with a hail of bullets. Childs finally decided the B-40s were not worth their lives and told the bac-si they would try again later. He jumped up and dashed back up the side of the hill with AK-47 fire raking the entire area.

The bac-si was following behind him when a burst of gunfire hit him in the back, and he collapsed, sprawling in the red dirt. Childs got to the top, turned around looking for the young Vietnamese, and saw him lying on the ground. He called down, and then had the interpreter call down, but the young man did not respond. Childs could see some slight movement from him, so he assumed he was wounded, but still alive.

In the meantime, Alward had been looking for Childs. He was worried because he had not seen or heard anything out of him in over an hour, and Childs had a penchant for finding trouble. With Childs, no news was usually bad news.

Childs radioed the command center, and Sgt. Boody answered. Some of the other team members had come in to eat and were listening to the conversation. "This is Childs," the voice said.

"Where the hell have you been?" Boody asked.

"I'm down on the forward slope," Childs said, "The Vietnamese bac-si's been hit."

With a slight pause Boody said, "All right, just stay where you are."

Childs replied, "Okay," and then turned to the interpreter beside him. "Get those Yards to fire away and cover me," he said, and he ran back down the hill.

When he got to the medic, he found a hole in his back through the lungs. There was a whistling sound when the bac-si struggled to breathe, and blood was oozing from the corners of his mouth. He was in a great deal of pain. Childs tried to inject him with morphine but was not able to get the injector to work correctly. He also tried to cover the wound with plastic; each time he moved there was a hail of automatic weapons fire that pinned him down on the side of the hill. Childs attempted to pull the injured man, but he was dead weight, and he was only able to move him about ten feet. It was obvious no other help was coming, so he stopped pulling and ran back up the hill.

Childs radioed the TOC again, and Sgt. Boody answered. "This is Childs," he said.

Boody was furious. "Where the (expletive) have you been?" he stormed. "If I get my hands on you, I'll choke you. I'm ordering you to stay where you are."

Boody and Childs had been assigned together before on another A-site and had had a run-in, so the Top Sergeant knew what he was dealing with. Boody was a career Special Forces NCO, a professional soldier. Childs had always believed that Boody did not consider ASA soldiers to be real Green Berets.

Don Childs had been determined to prove himself to the point of wild recklessness. "[There had been] an ongoing difference of opinion between me and Boody about the SODs being SF (or not)," Childs insists.

"He's a big overgrown kid," Boody said later, "a real problem child. Any other time and I would have court-martialed him…I just knew he was going to get himself killed."

"I can't get the bac-si," Childs told him, "I can't get him; he can't move, and the Yards won't move either. I've got to go back."

In his best "fatherly" tone, the top sergeant said, "If he's really hurt and can't get up, look, no sense in losing your own life."

At that point, Lt. Harp grabbed the radio and said, "Childs, get your ass back in the perimeter!"

"No sweat," Childs said, and then asked if they could get a TAC airstrike in the middle of the saddle area.

In a few minutes, the Air Force jets swooped in, but their bombs fell on the north hill. The jets came in several more times, but the ordinance still did not fall in the area that would provide cover for a rescue. Finally, in total desperation, Childs began to remove his gear, and with only his .45, he started back down the hill. Everyone in the command center knew what he was going to do, and every man knew there was no way in hell anybody could stop him.

Childs was already running full-tilt down the hill, straight into the teeth of the enemy guns. As he ran, one thought kept running through his mind: "Childs, you stupid shit, if you go down there again, you're going to get (expletive) killed."

He got to the wounded man and managed to pull him up over a little ridge into a slight depression. Ground fire was pinging all around them. The young American rested for a moment trying to summon his strength for a last final effort. He took a deep breath and then sagged low with the realization that he could do no more. He was totally exhausted. His hands relaxed their grip on the bac-si's shoulders, he closed his eyes, and his body seemed to melt into the side of that hateful red hill.

Slowly Childs stirred and forced his limbs to move. Sniper fire continued to kick up the dirt around them. He pulled the bac-si behind a log and tried to make him comfortable then wearily made his way back up the hill. He would not desert the man on the forward slope. He found some smoke grenades and "persuaded" two Montagnards to go after the bac-si. He threw the grenades down the hill creating a wall of dense smoke between the wounded man and the enemy guns and then fired cover with a .30 caliber machine gun. The two Montagnards managed to drag the man up to the edge of the perimeter where they dropped him on the ground and ran. Somewhat revived, Childs rushed down, grabbed the medic's body, and hauled him up and inside the fortified compound.

Two other CIDG soldiers helped Childs place the man on a makeshift stretcher and carry him to the medical bunker. Shepherd led them inside and immediately inserted an IV into the man's arm. He gave him a shot of morphine, and the bac-si smiled weakly with a flash of his missing front teeth. A half hour later, the young Vietnamese was dead.

So what had Childs and the bac-si accomplished with their bravado, aside from blowing up a few bunkers and capturing a few weapons? In truth, most of the Special Forces A-Team members had thought they were finished, everyone that is but Donald Childs. He would not stick around to listen to their discussion about being overrun. It was not in his nature to quit, or even consider losing. The escape plans and thermite grenades, Umeda with his loaded .45, and the wounded major propped up in the bunker with his guns like Jim Bowie in *The Alamo*, were all signs of defeat. But a gangly Morse intercept op who wasn't a "real" Green Beret, and a tough little Vietnamese medic that no one liked had taken the fight to the NVA, and nobody talked about losing the battle again.

The 513th and the 522nd

By midday on Sunday, enemy forces had begun to work their way around the inner system of trenches on the main hill. The sustained attack on the camp was so great that Lt. Harp notified his superiors that without additional reinforcements, the outpost would soon fall.

Only the top of the hill and the southern side were still controlled by the Americans and their allies. The three ASA soldiers had destroyed the classified materials and intercept equipment within their fortified ops bunker. "The situation was so critical we could not wait any longer," Jim Alward says.

For the most part, the advisors within the main compound spent their time trying to keep the CIDG forces calm and focused on holding what little territory they still maintained. "Let's go up and try to snipe off a few of the bastards," Shepherd told Alward, so they got their weapons and climbed to the bunker above the TOC.

"Shepherd covered the bunker at the base of the hill and I took another one that we knew was sniping at us," Alward said. "We couldn't see anything, but we knew they were there."

The indomitable Childs headed back toward the northern perimeter to make sure his Montagnards were still in place. "We were almost out of M-79 grenades, regular grenades, and mortar ammo," Childs says. "I stayed down there, trying to quiet the people down because I knew Charlie would be coming up that night, and I wanted these people to make a good showing. I figured we could take enough of them along with us that they [the NVA] might not be able to make it into the compound."

Boody and Harp remained at their post in the TOC calling in air strikes. For almost two hours a dozen F-100s pounded the north hill and saddle with all the destructive fire power at their disposal. Spreading blankets of flaming napalm 250 feet long and fifty feet wide, the planes would come over in sets of three. "When the third pair was done, another three would be waiting stacked up," Lt. Harp said. It was impossible for the massive NVA force to launch an effective ground attack as long as the F-100s were in control of the battlefield.

The C.O. of 5th Special Forces Group had decided to extract the 204th due to its heavy losses, and as replacements had sent in the 201st MSF from Pleiku and the 513th and 522nd MSFs from Nha Trang. The 513th and 522nd had combat assaulted into the area at 0940 hours. Moving from the southwest side of the main hill, the two fresh Mike Force companies managed to make their way nearly unopposed into the camp at 1300 hours. They had plenty of cover, and the NVA did not spot them moving up to the perimeter. The southern side of the main hill was not visible from the north hill where most of the NVA forces were concentrated. The 513th deployed its troops around the top of the hill, and the 522nd filled in just below it in the trenches.

Alward and Shepherd were still up in the fire arrow bunker sniping at the north hill. "I was feeling okay," Alward remembers. "Twenty minutes before had been the low point. The Americans were getting together, ready to make the big stand…and give Charlie his money's worth…I was getting some rounds off and no one was shooting back at me. Danny [Shepherd] and I had been talking about what we wanted to do if we got out of this mess, and I told him I wanted to live long enough to dance at my granddaughter's wedding. We both laughed."

"Alward," Boody yelled, shaking the young man's sense of contentment, "Get your ass down here; they're coming up the hill."

"Oh baby," Alward thought, "my times over. Just give me a fresh load of ammo. We'll give 'em a fight anyhow."

Don Childs recalls, "Gathering up for what I knew in my heart was going to be a one-way trip my concerns were on my shitty jam-prone M-16, and 'too bad I didn't have more grenades.' I intended to grab the first AK[-47] I could take."

"Where are they coming from?" Alward asked.

"Up the southwest," Boody replied. "It's the Mike Force."

"That was my one big happy moment," Alward remembers. "There we were planning our last stand, and that beautiful Mike Force comes up the hill. That was just pure happiness."

"As we were up and starting out the door," Childs says, "just as suddenly came clarification that it was Mike Force at the gate, and we were relieved– against all odds. This had to be the happiest moment of my life."

Full circle

Contrary to the lightened mood on top of the hill, the situation was becoming ever more serious. Enemy forces were moving further around the western side of the main hill, and the Americans would soon discover that the NVA had moved troops back into all the bunkers Childs and the bac-si had cleared out earlier that morning. They were also continuing to fight their way around the eastern trenches of the main hill and were within 600 feet of closing off all hope of additional reinforcements getting in or of anyone getting out. The A-239 compound would soon become an island in the midst of the massive NVA force.

Capt. Trimble, the Mike Force commander asked Lt. Harp what he needed. "We've gotta have that hill back," Harp stated.

Trimble replied: "We were sent here to take the [north] hill, and that's what we'll do." In a hastily called meeting, the American and allied commanders decided that the best defense was an aggressive offense. The combined Mike Force units were going to do what the enemy commanders least expected—launch an immediate surprise attack on the other hill.

The plan of attack called for the 513th MSF composed of tough Nung troops to begin the battle by re-seizing Childs' bunkers. The ethnic Chinese Nungs, known for their fighting skills, would then take up firing positions on the north side of the main hill and lay down a base of fire upon enemy positions on the north hill. At the same time, four platoons from the 522nd MSF composed of Rhade, Raglai, and Jarai Montagnards would assault the NVA-held hill from two sides. Capt. Trimble hoped that the NVA would focus on the bunker attack staged by the Nungs and be surprised by the 522nd platoons moving in on their flanks. Prior to the assault, the hill was saturated with extensive air strikes and artillery from 1400 to 1430. During that same time period, the 201st was air-lifted into the area, replacing the mauled 204th, and quickly made its way toward the south slope of A-239.

Just as the 513th and 522nd began their assault on the enemy stronghold at 1430, the Montagnards of the 201st and their Green Beret advisors streamed through the gate and into the command compound. The M.P.s at the gate had seen the additional Mike Force approaching and had run to open the gate and remove the barbed wire strung in front of it. They waved the additional reinforcements in as they arrived at the camp.

The 201st joined the 1st and 2nd platoons of the 522nd, and the combined forces charged straight up the hill, moving through enemy small arms fire with little resistance. Bomb craters and the wreckage of destroyed bunkers littered the saddle and the sides of the hill. Coils of concertina wire were entangled with the burned bodies of NVA troops, exploded sandbags, twisted metal and all kinds of trash. The smell was horrendous, a mixture of putrefaction, cordite, and charred meat. It clung to everything, and the men could taste it on their lips and the roof of their mouths as they ran. Thick smoke cloaked the sides of the hill. It seemed to seep out of the very earth and was filled with a fine red powder that settled on their arms and coated the sweat on their faces. Huge areas of soil had been scorched black. Milky globules of napalm residue dotted the dirt and bunker tops. This was truly hell on earth. Back in the world, young men were just heading home from their Saturday-night dates, but here on a beautiful Sunday afternoon, other young men were going to die to retake a garbage dump.

The enemy commanders were caught completely off-guard. They had not expected to be attacked and certainly were not prepared for an all-out assault. The momentum of the MSF assault forced the NVA troops back through the eastern perimeter wire in wild disarray. One of the retreating enemy platoons was caught in the open and completely annihilated by machine gun and M-79 fire.

For the next five hours the four Mike Force companies fought their way, bunker by bunker, slowly, painfully, bloodily. The Nung and Montagnard soldiers fought well, led by their Green Beret advisors. One young American medic charged an NVA bunker alone with a pump-action shotgun, blasting away until he could get close enough to toss in a hand grenade. Another Green Beret medic crawled toward an NVA bunker as his company commander covered him with a machine gun and then tossed in a grenade. The primary fight occurred within the saddle between the two hills and in the bunkers and trenches to the east. Supported by devastating strikes from tactical air and helicopter gunships, the American-led troops would carry the day.

Lt. Harp and Sgt. Boody remained in the command center, calling in the artillery and air support and keeping headquarters apprised of how the battle was going. The rest of the A-239 team and the Aussies had moved to Childs' northern slope when the assault began. Alward, Shepard and a few others were firing from a sandbag bunker. "We began peppering away at the enemy," Alward said. "This lasted until we got the word that Mike Force didn't want us to fire because we might hit some of them. So we just knocked off, sat back, and watched those sweet mothers take that hill."

When some of the NVA troops tried to escape past the camp toward the end of the battle, the camp personnel helped to stop them. "They saw the Charlies starting to leave the bunkers and trenches," Boody said, "[and] they were picking them off like flies."

"When the hill was finally taken," Jim Alward said, "we began receiving B-40s from the village. There must have been two B-40 teams, but their rounds weren't reaching the usual targets…We were well aware that the village was cluttered with Charlie, so we called air strikes on them…They had started off at first simply trying to get the guy with the B-40; then they decided the village itself was lousy with Charlies, so they really worked it over. After that we spent the rest of the day just walking around, checking the bunkers and making sure the Yards were okay. We had to watch they didn't get too happy and run around wild."

On the back side of the hill, 1st and 2nd platoons worked their way around the trench line rooting out the remaining NVA troops. No prisoners were taken. The Montagnards and Nung troops, having suffered casualties due to bypassed NVA snipers, simply shot all NVA, wounded or not, as they advanced. The successful assault was over by 1900 hours as the Green Beret-led troops swept the north hill, the surrounding bunkers and trenches, and moved their wounded back to the command compound.

The defensive positions were reorganized and strengthened for an expected enemy counterattack, but none came. Although sporadic mortar and rocket fire was heard in the area, it appeared that the outpost was no longer in danger of being overrun. Huge Chinook helicopters flew in with supplies and ammunition, and evacuated the dead and wounded. There were now six Mike Force companies at the Duc Lap camp. Five companies spent the night within the fortifications, and the sixth stood guard outside the perimeter.

At about 2300 hours, an NVA soldier who had "played dead" rolled a grenade into a bunker where three Mike Force troops were standing guard, wounding the men. Two other MSF soldiers ran up the hill to a bunker where they believed the enemy soldier was hiding and tossed in several grenades, collapsing the bunker and burying anyone who was inside. Shepherd and Childs were in the main compound treating the wounded, and Shep was asked to come and tend to the newly injured men. Two of them were serious enough to require hospitalization; one of them died the next morning.

Just before dawn on Monday, 26 August, Shepherd was awakened by a barrage of gun fire. A sizeable group of NVA had been spotted trying to escape; Spooky and gunships were called in. Artillery was also requested on the unlucky enemy unit. Later in the day, a recon sweep would reveal thirty NVA bodies strewn where they fell, the last remains of the once proud regiments that had attacked Duc Lap.

Enemy body count and removal after the battle—Duc Lap (Photo: INSCOM)

Honors and honored

ASA Green Berets Danny Hall, James Alward, and Donald Childs were all awarded the Silver Star Medal for "gallantry in action," Bronze Star Medals with "V" device for valor and Purple Hearts for their wounds. With customary modesty, Jim Alward says: "I was also awarded the Purple Heart, apparently for a very minor, maybe shrapnel nip by my right eye. Bled like hell but I don't recall anyone noticing. Don't know when or who put me in for the PH." The Bronze Star was for rescuing the Air Force Reserve pilot, Lt. Thurn.

Alward and Hall in Nha Trang after the battle—"We were still in the same uniforms we had worn throughout the battle," Alward says. "We had not shaved or bathed for a week. We were a mess." [Sgt. Maj. William West, Alward, Hall, Col. Ira C. Owens, C.O. of the 403rd SOD. As a Lt. Gen., Owens would later serve as Deputy Chief of Staff for Intelligence, Oct. 1991–Feb. 1995] (Photo: © Jim Alward)

According to the after action review written by Capt. Joseph P. Meissner, 5th SFG historian, out of the original twelve-man Special Forces team at A-239, two were KIA and nine were WIA. In addition to Alward, Childs and Hall, Lt. William Harp, Sgt. Michael Dooley, Sgt. Harold Kline and Sgt. Daniel Shepherd were all recommended for Silver Star Medals and Bronze Star Medals with "V" device. Undoubtedly there were many more medals awarded to the men who fought and died in this battle.

In addition to Kline and Dooley, six more Green Berets with the Mike Force units died during the attack and retaking of the north hill. Jim Alward says: "Without the reinforcements from those Mike Force units—and all thanks and love to the incredible air support—the camp was gone. When the MSF guys broke through, we were down to six live/not severely-wounded Americans—the three of us (ASA), the camp commander, first sergeant and medic, [and] none was named Rambo."

Jim Alward would return to Vietnam for another "much less active" TDY in 1969, when he served with a Can Tho B-Team and a Delta A-Team.

Col. Harold Aaron, Commander, 5th S.F.G., awards Staff Sgt. Danny Hall, Sgt. James Alward and Spc.5 Donald Childs Silver Star Medals for their part in the defense of Duc Lap. (Photo: INSCOM)

The Battle of Duc Lap is only one of many operations in which men of the 403rd RR (SOD) took part, and the unit received a host of awards and decorations. Contrary to the usual stereotype of the ASA soldier as an "unlikely warrior," many of those awards were for heroism in combat, including four Silver Stars, twenty Bronze Star Medals with "V" Device, and fourteen Army Commendation Medals with "V" Device. Twenty-four 403rd Green Berets received the Purple Heart and one, Thomas Tomczak, gave his life.

Danny Hall, Jim Alward and "the indomitable" Don Childs (Photo: © James Alward)

As the Battle of Duc Lap proved, ASA soldiers in Vietnam had the characteristics required for success in conflict: discipline and courage under fire. Jim Alward, Don Childs and Danny Hall, Green Berets of the 403rd SOD, personified the best of the Army Security Agency and the best of the U.S. Army.

"AINT NO DANGER—NEVER WAS" (Photo: © Ken Thompson)

Long hot summer of 1968

The 1968 Democratic Convention met in Chicago, and antiwar protesters were determined to disrupt it. Mayor Richard J. Daley and the Chicago police were just as determined to prevent the disruption. The protesters numbered 10,000, and they were met by 23,000 police and Illinois National Guardsmen. Vice President Hubert Humphrey had most of the delegates' support, but the Democratic Party was deeply divided: over the war, the draft, and over the crises that had exploded in cities and on campuses across the nation.

August 28 became known as the day of the "police riot." It began in Grant Park where the majority of the demonstrators were massed, but soon spread throughout the city, and it was nationally televised. Tom Hayden, a leader of S.D.S. (Students for a Democratic Society), a radical "New Left" political group, encouraged the protestors to move out of the park. He wanted to make sure that "if they were gassed, the whole city would be gassed, and if their blood was spilled, it would be spilled all over the city."

The amount of tear gas used was so great that it hung in the air surrounding the Hilton Hotel where the Vice President was staying.

The scene of the Chicago Police charging the screaming protesters as they chanted "kill, kill, kill" became one of the most infamous images of the convention. The entire debacle took place under the television lights with the crowd shouting, "The whole world is watching!" The liberal media made sure that the American people saw it all through their sympathetic eyes, but polls later showed most Americans backed the Mayor and the police and approved of their actions.

While protesters marched in Chicago and elsewhere, young men continued to die in Vietnam. On 10 September 1968, Sgt. Richard Jernigan died of complications from malaria. He was twenty-five years old and from Pecos, Texas.

An eight-year Army veteran, Jernigan had already completed two tours in Vietnam with the 101st Airborne before beginning his third tour on 12 July 1968. He was assigned as a mechanic for the 415th RRD operating in support of the Americal Division. He died from viral pneumonia at the 2nd Surgical Hospital in Chu Lai two months later.

Richard L. Jernigan's younger brother, Sgt. Frederick Jernigan, served as escort for his brother's body when it arrived back in the U.S. Richard Jernigan was buried at Ft. Richardson National Cemetery, Ft. Richardson, Alaska, with full military honors.

Thank-you note

On 24 October 1968, Col. Joseph E. Fix III, Commander of the 1st Brigade, 4th ID, wrote a letter of commendation to the 313th RRB and the 374th RRC in praise of Det. 1 of the 374th. Col. Fix wrote:

"I wish to commend Det. 1, 374th RRC for the outstanding performance of service they have given me while in direct support of the brigade...25 April to 24 October, 1968.

"During the above cited period Lt. Phillip R. Bernstein, Lt. Dennis P. Coyne, and Sgt. Patrick A. Dunn kept me informed daily on the situation in my area of operations. Because of their research, study, analysis, and complete understanding of the forces in this area, I was able to accomplish the assigned mission much more effectively.

"The complete professional manner in which the personnel of Detachment 1 conducted their mission, and their exhibition of exceptional versatility over a broad spectrum of combat activities brings credit to these men, their operations, and the United States Army."

Election '68

On November 3, Richard M. Nixon was elected the 37th President of the United States. Nixon had just 43% of the popular vote, but a sizeable majority of the electoral votes. He selected Henry Kissinger as his National Security Advisor and proceeded to pursue "an honorable end to the war." Nixon believed that it was essential, both politically and for the national morale, to maintain the position that the U.S. effort in Vietnam had been a success, and the South Vietnamese could survive "on their own." Kissinger assured the press that Nixon was "following a carefully thought-out strategy on Vietnam" and that the peace talks were going "as we had expected."

Laff-a-minute

In December, ASA deployed the first of its sixteen U-21D Laffing Eagle platforms. They were designed to perform both DF and airborne collection, but developmental delays of the V-Scan DF system forced it to be employed initially for VHF voice and HF manual Morse intercept. Laffing Eagle was capable of recording low-level voice intercept which could be passed on by courier to an analysis center or by secure voice to a DSU. The aircraft could also pass on targeting data to nearby ARDF platforms.

Laffing Eagle gave ASA its most efficient collection platform. The Ute was a smaller, newer, and superior aircraft to the old P-2E Neptunes (Crazy Cats) and was more flexible because it did not have to be deployed near a particular base.

CHAPTER 22

THE LONG WAY HOME

Along the Cambodian border (Photo: © Larry Hertzberg)

It was 12 February 1969, a bright blue afternoon with just a few clouds in the sky as the RU-1A Otter of the 146th Aviation Co. lumbered along the border of Tay Ninh Province, South Vietnam and the "Parrot's Beak," a chunk of Cambodia situated at the southern end of the Ho Chi Minh Trail. The slow-moving plane and its crew of four were less than thirty-five miles from their takeoff point at Tan Son Nhut Air Base near Saigon.

Cruising smoothly at 3,500 feet, the drone of the plane's engine was interrupted only by the occasional conversation of the crewmembers as they went about their mission of locating and intercepting the communications of NVA and VC units that were known to be operating along the Cambodian border. Then, without warning, the aircraft's single engine exploded.

RU-1A Otter (Photo: U.S. Army)

After a bright orange flash, smoke and flames began to pour back through the cowling into the cockpit, and the ungainly aircraft started to lose altitude. The pilot, the company commander of the 146th, Maj. Querin Herlik switched to the rear fuel tank as the copilot, Warrant Officer 2 Laird Osburn, hit in the face, arm and side by shrapnel and burned by the flames, managed to shut off the fuel supply from the damaged forward tank, close the throttle to put out the fire, and call "mayday" on the emergency channel. Maj. Herlik called for the crew to put on chutes ("as we were at 3.5 and in danger of burning") as he was scouting for a landing site. The aircraft had been traveling in a westerly direction at about 100 knots, and Herlik turned the aircraft southward to attempt a forced landing. Herlik shut off all switches and engaged full flaps. As the plane descended rapidly in a nose-low spiral descent, he picked a dry rice paddy as the most likely landing site for the glide path they were on, but there was a dike the front wheels could hit. Out of concern that the struts directly under the plane's cabin might impale the crewmen if the force of impact was great enough, the pilot forced the plane down in front of the dike and bounced over it. In the business-as-usual style of most military pilots, Maj. Herlik's journal reads: "Touch down made fairly smoothly after emergency descent. A/C bounced slightly, Osburn and I got on brakes hard when it settled second time. A/C stopped undamaged."

"I don't remember any big bump," recalls Jack Fisher. "It seemed like an unremarkable landing to me. I guess everything is relative."

"I would estimate that the RU-1A traveled approximately one mile from the place it was hit," Herlik says. The plane's engine had been hit by one round from a large caliber antiaircraft gun, destroying its carburetor and forcing it down to its surprisingly unremarkable landing. There was just one factor that made the event far from "unremarkable." They had crashed in eastern Cambodia and were surrounded by some 300 heavily-armed Viet Cong and North Vietnamese Army troops.

Some forty years later, the memories for Col. (Ret.) Querin "Quin" Herlik and former ASA Spc.5s John "Jack" Fisher and Robert Pryor are still vividly clear and traumatic. "We were in South Vietnam in the 'Angel's Wing' area, when [we were] hit," says Pryor.

Fisher concurs, "Our coordinates were 110117N, 106214E, which is just inside the Vietnam-side of the border, near the village of Go Dau Hau."

Fisher and Pryor were the two intercept operators on board the intelligence-gathering Laffing Otter aircraft. Fisher was a Morse intercept op, and Pryor was a Vietnamese linguist. "We had two intercept positions in the Otter," Fisher says, "one Morse and one voice, one behind the other, both seats facing forward with radios on our right. As we were going down, I figured the only thing I could do was clear the scrambler once we came to rest, and no further chance of communicating was possible. (The scrambler was a device used to make their communications undecipherable by the enemy.) I thought the scrambler was too heavy to carry, and there were no thermite grenades available to destroy it. That was the only piece of equipment I was really concerned about [falling into enemy hands]." As the plane made its descent, Fisher and Pryor quickly stowed all of their classified documents into a canvas flight bag.

Pryor placed the scrambler into the bag, too, saying that he would carry it when they got on the ground.

Down and out

After the plane came to rest, the two Spc.5s made their escape out of a rear door and were immediately pinned down by small arms and rocket fire. Osburn came around to them from the front of the plane, and tried to get the emergency radio/beacon to work, but to no avail, and the gunfire was getting closer. The enemy force was converging on the aircraft and its crew from all sides. Herlik first thought they might be in the middle of a fire fight, as the troops on one side seemed to be positioned in opposition to the troops on the other, but he soon realized both sides were zeroing in on them. Small arms fire began to hit all around them, and seemed to be mainly targeting the Otter. Each officer had a standard issue .38 caliber revolver in a pistol belt, and the two enlisted men each had an M-16 rifle and one bandoleer (seven magazines) of ammunition. That was their total armament. This was to have been an intelligence mission, not a combat mission, and they were not Marines.

Jack Fisher continues: "After Pryor and I got our M-16s out of the back of the plane, Warrant Officer Osburn took my weapon right out of my hands. I don't know why; maybe he sensed some reluctance on my part, or his Green Beret training took over. Maybe he knew he had no chance with a handgun, plus he figured he would be better with the rifle than me. Then again, my face probably showed that I was scared shitless, as we used to say back then. I was not cut out for infantry, although I had qualified 'expert' with the M-14 in basic training. I had never even fired an M-16, and there is a lot of difference between shooting at a target and shooting at a person, especially when they are shooting at you."

In an effort to avoid capture, the flight crew had spread out in different directions. Osburn went around to the other side of the plane, and Pryor crouched down behind it. Fisher moved into a low spot about twenty-five feet from the rear door of the plane, and crouched there, without a weapon. The pilots had received E&E (escape and evasion) training while in flight school, and Maj. Herlik had crawled to a small wooded area about 100 feet west of the aircraft. "My E&E training was scheduled for the following month, March 1969, and I had been flying since 1967," says Fisher. "Good old Uncle Sam!"

From his vantage point, Herlik could see large groups of troops moving in on the plane and other troops moving through and around the wooded area where he was hiding. He changed position several times to avoid capture, but the entire area was so overrun by the enemy that escape was impossible. On two occasions, he shot and killed single enemy soldiers who came within twenty feet of him, using his revolver. Shortly after that, he saw two U.S. Air Force F-100 jets make low runs over the downed Otter. That caused some of the VC soldiers to seek shelter in the very spot where Herlik was hiding. Realizing he was about to be captured or killed, he quickly buried his wallet, dog tags, and the major insignia from his collar. He was soon confronted with four VC armed with AK-47 rifles pointed straight at him. He threw down his revolver and was seized by those four, plus about eight additional VC soldiers who were in the immediate area. The soldiers took his shirt, along with his wrist watch, a survival knife and a small notebook. They could not unfasten his pistol belt, and when Herlik put his hands down to do it, a VC hit him in the back with a rifle knocking him to his knees.

At the same time, lines of enemy troops continued to advance toward the beleaguered crewmen near the plane. After the two bandoleers (280 rounds) of M-16 ammunition were exhausted, Fisher could hear Pryor and Osburn calling back and forth verifying there was no more ammunition. "It seemed to me like the plane was the main target," he continues. "It took the most rounds and caught on fire again before we were captured. There were even a few RPG (rocket propelled grenade) rounds shot at it, along with lots of small arms fire."

"The firefight lasted about twenty-to-thirty minutes," Pryor says, "until we ran out of ammo." When he saw they would not be rescued,

Pryor threw the heavy bag with the scrambler and classified materials under the burning plane, making certain he was successful in his effort to destroy the materials.

U.S. planes were still circling the area as the Americans were being captured. There was an observation plane and jets that flew low trying to ascertain the status of the besieged Americans, but a barrage of gunfire kept them at bay. A fellow ASA op in the area at the time, Merrill James "Sakk" Frankenfield, later wrote: "We had an Otter get shot down in Cambodia with four crewmen aboard. One of them [was] one of my best friends, John Fisher. I was in the area next to them when they were shot down, and no one could get close. The VC were everywhere, and small arms fire was too thick for the Hueys or Jets. They had a firefight for about thirty minutes, before being overwhelmed."

Fisher says, "I saw the young NVA soldiers hold their AK-47s straight up in the air, firing with the guns kicking off their knees, all in unison, when they heard the planes approaching close. It was like they thought that if they got enough lead up in the air over a wide enough area, a plane was bound to get some rounds into it." There would be no miracle rescue, on that day. The embattled crew was on its own.

All over

Fisher and Pryor were soon surrounded by a large number of young-looking Vietnamese soldiers brandishing AK-47 rifles. The soldiers appeared to be fifteen or sixteen-years-old and moved in from all sides as the two young Americans raised their hands and awaited their fate. The soldiers roughly patted them down and began taking their wallets, fatigue jackets, and Fisher's boots. They even wanted their pants for souvenirs. "When they wanted my pants, I finally balked," Fisher says.

Pryor, the Vietnamese linguist, heard the enemy troops talking and says, "They were in the 1st NVA Division based inside the Cambodian border. Most were in uniform, some were in better uniforms than others. They were talking about the airstrike on our downed plane and [said] that one of our crew had been killed. I am absolutely certain that the troops who captured me were NVA. When they were taking their propaganda photos, the troops were dressed in crisp NVA uniforms, and when one of my two captors was told to 'look more serious,' the young soldier pushed on the bayonet so hard that it cut my neck."

Maj. Herlik was brought in by another group of soldiers, his arms bound with rope, but the men did not see Osburn. He had disappeared, and considering the intensity of the gun battle that had just concluded, they could only assume the worst. The crewmen had seen VC bodies on the ground and thought they had killed at least six and wounded eight or more of the enemy.

The three Americans were bound with rope, put into separate "spider-holes" some distance from the plane and kept under close guard until evening. Fisher was placed in a hole in front and approximately 100 feet to the right of the downed plane. "The hole had two entrances," Fisher says, "kind of a square 'C' shape. A young guard was between me and either entrance. He kept offering me a cigarette, 'ARA' brand if I recall correctly. I'd never heard of it. I kept telling him that they made me sick. I had smoked heavily for six years and had developed a chronic cough, so I had finally managed to quit. After they offered me the cigarettes about four or five times, I thought, what the hell am I worrying about a cough for? Gi'me a (expletive) cigarette!"

The VC soldiers continued to take pictures in and out of the holes. "Most [of the photos were taken] with soldiers pointing AK-47s or RB-40s at my head," Herlik said. From his hole, Herlik could hear and identify different types of aircraft in the area, including helicopters and jets, U-8 Seminoles, and an OV-10 Bronco. He also heard heavy automatic weapons fire and assumed that VC or NVA soldiers were firing at the U.S. aircraft that continued to circle overhead.

Maj. Herlik learned later that the two U.S. Air Force F-100 jets that had buzzed the RU-1A wreckage could not destroy the downed aircraft because they had finished their bombing runs and were out of bombs. Because the crash site was in Cambodia, the executive officer of the 146th (Maj. Herlik's second in command) had to go to General Creighton Abrams, Commander-MACV, and explain the nature of the flight and the classified material that was onboard the plane. Gen. Abrams then gave his personal permission for a bombing run into Cambodia to destroy everything. That was accomplished by using A-1E Skyraiders which dropped incendiary bombs on the wreck site, destroying the aircraft's classified equipment and materials.

As darkness settled over the area, Fisher, Pryor and Herlik were pulled from the camouflaged holes and taken into a densely wooded expanse south of the plane-crash site. The men were photographed, again, and given a congealed rice bar wrapped in green leaves, along with a cup of warm water. They were kept apart and put into hammocks which, surprisingly, had mosquito nets wrapped around them. After a brief rest, the three, escorted by about fifteen guards and with a VC lieutenant in charge, set out on a night march through the jungle that lasted for hours. The lieutenant told Maj. Herlik that his name was Le Van and that he was from Tay Ninh, the province they had been flying over when they were shot down. They left the first camp about 1900 hours on February 12.

The first long night

The men had their hands tied behind their backs, and each one had a rope tied to him that was attached to a guard. Escape was not an option. Just staying alive through the long night was the main concern of each man. During the night, Herlik recalls passing through a stream which was waist-deep and fifty or sixty feet across. He was worried about being shot at by a U.S. helicopter or bombed by a B-52. He had seen a chopper with a searchlight on it when they were crossing the river and assumed it was American. Fisher says, "We walked in line and were guided along the route past checkpoints. They would shine a flashlight for our group to aim toward. We heard a .50 caliber [machine gun] sound off during the night, and later, in the firelight [near a village], I saw a homeowner shot point-blank in the face. I guess he was not a sympathizer." When combined with the plane crash, the ensuing fire-fight, which the three had miraculously survived, their capture and forced-march through the pitch-black jungle, chances of survival during that first terrifying night must have seemed very remote—and "scared shitless" must have seemed mild by comparison.

Overnight, the men were moved to some type of VC training camp, and they assumed they were in South Vietnam. They arrived at the camp at about 0400 and were totally exhausted, both physically and emotionally. The prisoners were given a breakfast of rice, tea, coffee and cookies, and were allowed a brief rest. They were kept apart in camouflaged holes with their arms bound behind their backs and not permitted any kind of interaction with each other. They were interrogated separately by Le Van and tried to respond with the standard Geneva Convention response of "name, rank and serial number."

"[The interrogator] held his hands out like the old Allstate TV commercial," Fisher says. "He was telling me that my life was in his hands. He was maybe thirty years old, wore a khaki uniform with a pith helmet, and spoke English. When I was being taken back to the location where I was being held, I passed Pryor who was being taken to his interrogation. In order to have some consistency to our stories, I quietly said: 'transportation,' which is the type of unit that I had told the interrogator we were in. Just before passing Pryor, I had noticed a Caucasian man standing off to the side in front of some storage containers."

Later that day, the three men were allowed to clean up and take a sponge bath. They were then taken to a site where a large tent was pitched and made to kneel down on both knees beside one another along the front edge of the structure. An older gray-haired man came in, and after some show of respect by the Vietnamese soldiers, Le Van introduced him as a VC major. He sat at a table in the tent. The Americans were each given cups of water and told to take it with both hands. They were then asked to print their names on a piece of blank paper, and Maj. Herlik refused. "At that point," he says, "one of the VC soldiers put a gun to my head, spun the chamber, and after a nod from the VC major, pulled the trigger. I heard the hammer click on an empty chamber, and I decided that I would do whatever they asked, as long as it did not compromise our mission." The VC major accused the United States of a long list of war crimes against the Vietnamese people. All of the proceedings, including the prisoners "allegedly signing documents" were filmed with a movie camera for propaganda purposes. They were also filmed marching through the jungle with their hands in the air and were told they would be going to a P.O.W. camp.

Jack Fisher had only a vague idea of what was going on. "I never learned the [Vietnamese] language," he says, "other than some curse words, and a few basic words. [I was a] typical immature kid." Pryor presumably understood most, if not all, of what he heard, but he did not let the Vietnamese know that. "He played dumb when prompted to move, sit, etc., by the guards," Fisher recalls, "and got a rifle butt or two as a result. I understood from their gestures what they wanted me to do. I received no ill treatment from them....One of the men, possibly in his forties,...brought me a cup of cold water with a slice of lemon in it; he had some scarring on his face, and I wondered if it was from a burn caused by our napalm. He didn't treat me with any animosity, though."

After the propaganda session, Herlik and Fisher were turned over to a VC medic. Herlik's feet were badly blistered and Fisher, whose boots had been taken by a VC soldier when he was first captured, had walked all night in his socks. "My feet didn't last too long with only socks," Fisher says, "so they gave me a pair of Ho Chi Minh sandals, which I still have today."

On the road again

At about 2100 hours on 13 February, the three prisoners and their captors departed camp number two and marched all night, again. Their feet were very sore and blistered. "I was told NHANH LEN!" Herlik says. "Walk faster! Keep walking faster, or be shot!" During that night, they encountered about 350 to 400 NVA troops dressed in black uniforms and armed with AK-47 rifles. Herlik thought the soldiers were headed in the direction of Saigon. The VC moved the Americans about fifteen feet off the trail on which the NVA soldiers were marching.

"I remember hearing our B-52 strikes in the distance, like rolling thunder, but far enough away to not be a threat," recalls Jack Fisher.

"We walked as much as twenty-eight miles during the night," Pryor remembers. "We moved to a different camp, slept, were interrogated, ate, and [then] moved again at night." Ironically, Pryor should never have been on the 12 February mission along the Cambodian border. He had been temporarily assigned to the 146th for two months. "I was due to rotate back to CONUS (Continental U.S.) in six days and was checking out of the 146th to return to my own unit (82nd Airborne, at a forward base, thirty miles ENE of Saigon)," he says. "When I got to flight operations to sign out, the operations sergeant said they needed another crew member for the C.O.'s flight and that he would sign my release when the flight returned." Pryor continues, "I had been flying the new Queen Air platform with air-to-ground teletype prior to this flight. Before that, I had flown Cessna O-2As with the Air Force out of Da Nang. [I had] put in over 100 hours over North Vietnam at 1500 feet in an FAC (forward air controller)." And all that had been accomplished without a scratch.

After marching for about seven hours, they arrived at a wooded area where the VC soldiers seemed to be searching for something. The soldiers searched for about an hour for what the Americans thought would be an underground P.O.W. camp. The VC finally seemed to give up and allowed the prisoners to lie down on their spread-out hammocks. At daybreak, the men were moved about 100 feet under a canopy of jungle until sometime in the afternoon, while the VC sent out patrols. It was Valentine's Day, 14 February 1969.

At the new camp, for the first time since they were initially captured, the three Americans were placed in the same large hole. While together, they took the opportunity to fabricate a mutual cover story they could use to hide the true nature of their mission. They prepared the simple statement that when shot down, they had been on a supply mission, carrying items such as barbed wire, C-rations, etc., in Tay Ninh Province. Fisher and Pryor were identified as crew chiefs. When Lt. Le Van questioned them again, later that afternoon, he seemed to accept the story which the three men told him. "We were [also] lectured by a major about our crimes and how the people of Vietnam were going to win the war," Herlik reported. "We were told [again] we were being taken to a P.O.W. camp.

Later that day, the prisoners were blindfolded and led about 500 meters in a westerly direction, where the blindfolds were removed. They were then led another 1500 meters due west to a small village of thatched-roof huts where they saw mostly women and children. There was also a large red and gold Buddhist temple, which was about forty feet tall. They were allowed to sit down and were given water, while the villagers were called out to look. "Some children with sticks were chased away," Herlik says, "most just looked and laughed."

"We were marched up to the side yard of an unusually modern, painted concrete-block house," says Fisher, "and made to stand side by side. The apparent owner of the house, and a few more Cambodian communist sympathizers, paused in front of each of us." To young Fisher, it appeared as if it was an auction, and the men were bidding on them. "They laughed among themselves," he says, "and with the NVA." Maj. Herlik later described "an argument between an unidentified Cambodian lieutenant and Lt. Le Van. He (the Cambodian) demanded that Lt. Le Van turn us over to him," Herlik says. "There was a brief argument, with me in the middle of a tug-of-war."

Salvation

Pryor recalls, "A Cambodian unit pulled up in jeeps and personnel carriers." One of the jeeps had two or three men in it, and the Americans were told to come with them. As they boarded the vehicle, a man in the front passenger seat turned around, trying to assure them he was a Cambodian officer and they were safe. He told them he had gone through pilot training in Texas, but they were unsure they could believe him. The Americans had been told repeatedly they were going to a P.O.W. camp, and they were concerned this was some kind of ruse.

From the small village, the prisoners were taken to a border outpost where they were turned over to a Cambodian army captain whose name sounded like "Fernandez." They were then transferred to a larger vehicle resembling an English Land Rover and proceeded on to the Cambodian provincial capital of Svay Rieng, accompanied by the Cambodian captain and five Cambodian soldiers armed with a U.S. M-16 rifle and AK-47s. Herlik said, "During the trip, Fernandez made a comment about us being shot down in Cambodia. That remark really surprised me, as I [had] never even given it a thought. I then realized why we were being taken to Phnom Penh to see the general staff and what political implications were involved." The crewmen of the RU-1A Otter of the 146th Aviation Co. RR, Army Security Agency were at the center of an international incident that would involve major world leaders and the President of the United States before it was resolved.

They arrived at Svay Rieng at about 2100 hours. It had been a long day in what had become an extremely long and grueling week, both physically and emotionally. The three men were taken to a hospital within a military compound and were briefly interrogated by Capt. Fernandez. He questioned the prisoners together and recorded their conversation on a tape recorder. He told them that a Mig-17 had shot down their RU-1A, but Maj. Herlik did not believe it, thinking it was "some form of propaganda....[Fernandez] was disappointed when we insisted that we were shot down in South Vietnam," Herlik says. "We were introduced to a [Cambodian] Air Force captain and lieutenant who told me that they were the two who shot us down in their Mig-17." None of it made any sense. It was all like a very bad dream."

The Americans stuck with their cover story and were soon allowed to wash and eat. They were allowed to bathe in a bucket, had their blistered feet dressed, and were given a meal of steak, ham, liverwurst, pepperoni, bread, soup, coffee and beer in glasses with ice. They finally began to believe they might be safe, or at least were in less dangerous circumstances than they had been since their crash, two long days and nights before.

After their interrogation, a Cambodian lieutenant brought Maj. Herlik the unbelievable news that Laird Osburn was alive and being treated for his shrapnel wounds and other injuries at a French hospital about 100 miles away. He showed Herlik a newspaper article with a photograph of Osburn clipped from a Svay Rieng provincial newspaper. He could see blood on Osburn's shirt in the picture. As the three crewmen settled in for the night at the Cambodian military hospital, they were afraid to believe it was true. It would take more than words and a clipping to convince them Osburn was alive.

Early, the next morning, the Americans were allowed to use a French-style water closet in a police station across the street, and Maj. Herlik saw a newspaper on a desk. It had the same photo of Osburn that he had seen the night before and two other photos, one of their plane's engine and one of the left wing. He was able to read enough of the article to substantiate his belief that his crew was involved in a major international incident. The crewmen were soon put back aboard the Land Rover with their Cambodian guards and left Svay Rieng for the 127 km drive west to the Cambodian capital of Phnom Penh. The side-curtains on the vehicle were drawn, so the Americans could see little of the surrounding terrain during their trip.

Capitol hill

When the prisoners arrived in the city, they were taken to the Chief of State Complex (CSC), General Staff Cambodian Army. Maj. Herlik, as the ranking (and only) officer of the group, was taken directly to the office of a Cambodian Army colonel, where he met several other military officers, including an army major, an air force major, and Lt. Lim Ny of the Cambodian Army. While there, Herlik was again questioned and responded with the crew's fabricated story about carrying supplies. The Cambodians insisted Herlik and his crew had landed in Cambodia and wanted him to admit he had done so. He responded, quite honestly, that he was not sure where he and his crew had landed; it was possible they had landed in Cambodia. That seemed to satisfy the Cambodians, and they did not bring it up again. Lim Ny later told Herlik the Cambodian Army colonel and major, along with himself, were Cambodian intelligence personnel, and the CSC was a Cambodian intelligence agency.

"We were interrogated [by Cambodian authorities]," Robert Pryor, says. "They accused us of bombing civilians, and prompted us to make statements to that effect. They even had a guy who claimed to be the pilot that had shot us down, but we didn't cooperate."

Maj. Herlik reported "they were confronted by the Cambodian Air Force captain who claimed to be the one who shot down Herlik's plane." He also reported that "in the open yard (adjacent to the 'intelligence' building), there was a two-and-a-half-ton truck which carried the engine, left wing and right wing, [and the] horizontal stabilizer [of their Otter]."

Later that morning, the prisoners were taken from the CSC to Chroy Changvar, an island just north of Phnom Penh. Jack Fisher recalls: "As we drove through the capital, we passed a memorial which had various captured war equipment, [an] old tank, anti-aircraft [guns], etc., and I saw the remains of our plane. It was obviously our plane, due to the dipole antennas on the front of the big wings, not to mention the fresher O.D. [olive drab] paint."

The three were taken to a facility that is believed to have been the Cambodian Naval Training Center. "[It was] on an island in the Mekong River," says Robert Pryor. Lt. Lim Ny told the men some other captured Americans and a South Vietnamese prisoner had been held there for over a year and had just been released by Cambodian Prince Norodom Sihanouk for Christmas 1968.

The men spent two nights in what Fisher calls a "warehouse." Maj. Herlik says, "It may have been a converted hangar or warehouse where captured Americans (the stories vary from eight to seventeen, either Army or Navy) who had ventured up the Mekong too far [had been held prisoner]." The men were told this by the Cambodians, and the stories varied from one telling to the next, but there was writing on the walls from the Americans who had been held there, so there was some truth to the stories.

On Sunday, 16 February 1969, the Pacific Edition of *Stars and*

Stripes printed an Associated Press article at the top of page six. The article was datelined "Saigon," and the headline read: "Plane Shot Down Over Cambodia-4 Americans Aboard."

Maybe not the Ritz, but

After their stint in the warehouse the three were moved to a Cambodian Navy bachelor officers' quarters beside the river. Two rooms had been partitioned off on one end of the small building: one room for the officer and one for the two enlisted men. Each room had two metal cots with mattresses, two chairs and a table. There was a kitchen area with a table and three chairs and a bathroom with an enclosed shower and a toilet, quite an improvement considering their recent accommodations. An area was roped off outside as a small exercise area for the Americans. "[We] even had a volleyball net," recalls Fisher, "[but] we had to crawl in and out of a window to access it." Fisher continues, "Prince Sihanouk sent his personal tailor by and he measured each of us, and we later received underwear, one pair of short sleeve and one pair of long sleeve khakis, pajamas, [and] shower shoes, [among other items]."

Soon after the three were established in the BOQ, diplomats from the Australian embassy came to see them and assure them they were in safe hands. The Aussies brought welcome food, including butter in a tin that did not require refrigeration. "I especially looked forward to getting a French baguette, with butter and some creamy hot coffee in the morning, every now and then," recalls Jack Fisher. "The Cambodians brought a roasted chicken with tomatoes one day, wrapped in leaves, but I passed on that." The Australians also brought a bottle of scotch and badly needed medical supplies for their sore feet. Other than the Australians, no one else was allowed to see the captive Americans, and for the most part, the prisoners were not allowed to leave the area where they were incarcerated. Maj. Herlik reported that on one occasion, however, they were allowed to ride bicycles that the Cambodians provided.

A fourth for cards

Some two weeks later, on 01 March 1969, Laird Osburn was released from the French hospital in Phnom Penh and moved to the BOQ with his fellow crewmembers for a great reunion. In addition to the wounds and burns he had received when their plane was shot down, he had also been wounded by shrapnel from a rocket propelled grenade during the fire-fight. He told Fisher later that after the NVA captured him, "a very tall, large oriental (Osburn was 6 feet 5) drove up in a Jeep Wagoneer. He was dressed in white shorts and a white shirt." The man, who obviously spoke with some authority, told the Vietnamese that he would take Osburn, and he took him to a hospital. Osburn was never held by the Vietnamese and never knew who the man was who rescued him, or why. Maj. Herlik was told that Osburn, who was a warrant officer, would be placed in the room with Pryor and Fisher. The Cambodians had no real understanding of the warrant officer rank. Herlik told them he wanted Osburn to room with him, but only after writing a personal request to the Cambodian Naval Commander of the Garrison, was Osburn allowed to move into the officer's room. Osburn arrived at 1230 hours that day. "We talked and compared notes the rest of the day," Herlik says, "[and it was] good to have a fourth for cards."

The Australian diplomats told the four Americans they were going to be released in early March, and on 11 March 1969, they were turned over to the Australians who threw a party for them at their Embassy. That night, the Aussies took the four men out to a local night club called "The Tavern" to celebrate their release, and they drank and danced until about 0200 hours.

Gittin' outa Dodge

Later that morning, the ex-prisoners boarded a Burma Airways DC-3 and were flown from Phnom Penh to Bangkok, Thailand. "Needless to say, we didn't feel great the next day boarding the plane," Herlik later recalled. In Bangkok, the men were queried by reporters at the airport and realized they were national (and international) news, as no P.O.W.s were being released (in early 1969). They were then turned over to U.S. authorities and flown to Bien Hoa Air Base, north of Saigon. The four were not allowed to return to their company; their belongings were inventoried and shipped directly from Vietnam back to the United States. Maj. Herlik was especially upset about not being allowed to contact the 146th, which he had commanded, and against orders, called several of his officers.

Vol. 25, No. 72   Friday, March 14, 1969

Released Airmen Say VC Gave Them to Cambodians

Pryor, Fisher, Herlik and Osburn—March 14, 1969 (Photo: U.S. Army

At Bien Hoa, they were given a rudimentary check-up, and the medics took blood samples. They then flew via a medevac plane, to Yakota, Japan, where they had more blood drawn and then boarded a C-141 hospital plane to Elmendorf A.F.B. in Anchorage, Alaska. Jack Fisher says, "I felt guilty because I had all my arms, legs, and eyes, unlike many of the guys on that plane."

When the four men deplaned at Elmendorf, they were wearing their short-sleeved tropical khakis, and there was snow plowed up in big piles all along the edge of the tarmac. "We had to walk outdoors from where the plane was moored all the way to the terminal," Fisher says, "but no one complained. I was tempted to get down and kiss that wet, salty tarmac, but I refrained."

Splitting up

The men began to separate in Alaska, with their month-long ordeal finally behind them. Pryor flew to Missouri and on to Ft. Campbell, Kentucky, which was the closest duty station to his home in Oak Ridge, Tennessee. The other three flew to Andrews Air Force Base, near Washington, D.C., and spent the night at Walter Reed Army Medical Center (where they drew more blood). "I began to think they owed me some money for all that blood," Fisher says (tongue in cheek).

Laird Osburn stayed in the hospital at Walter Reed, and Maj. Herlik and Spc.5 Fisher took a smaller hospital plane south to the U.S. Army Hospital at Hunter Army Airfield in Savannah, Georgia. They had a short debriefing and then were given eleven days leave to go home. After their leave was over, they returned to the hospital at Hunter for the remainder of their debriefings, which were very lengthy and were conducted separately. None of the men ever returned to Vietnam.

Two weeks after his return to the States, Jack Fisher came down with Hepatitis B and spent seven weeks in the hospital at Jacksonville Naval Air Station. The doctors assumed that he contracted the HB virus from the food that he was given by the NVA soldiers, the small rice cakes with the bit of fish and "spinach" leaf. He spent the last nine months of his Army duty at Homestead Air Force Base in South Florida.

Robert Pryor went home to the mountains of Tennessee for his leave, and then was subjected to the same lengthy debriefing process as his three fellow crewmates. He finished his military obligation as a Vietnamese language instructor at Goodfellow Air Force Base in San Angelo, Texas. Goodfellow was the only Air Force Security Service base in the U.S. and provided technical foreign language training for language intercept operators. He was discharged in San Antonio, Texas, in 1970.

There will always be questions as to why the four Americans wound up in Cambodian hands instead of languishing in a North Vietnamese P.O.W. camp for the remaining long years of the war. Maj. Herlik reported during one of his debriefing sessions in April 1969 that "on numerous occasions, Lt. Lim Ny, Cambodian Army interpreter (and intelligence officer), related to [him] that the Cambodian Government had pressured the representative of the National Liberation Front in Phnom Penh into releasing the American P.O.W.s to Cambodia. The rationale used by the Cambodian Government was the fact that the RU-1A and its crew had been shot down over and had landed in Cambodian territory." Since no other American flyers were ever turned over to the Cambodians, and assuming the NLF wanted to remain on good terms with the Cambodian Government in order to use their territory as a refuge from the U.S. military, that explanation is probably as close to the truth as anyone will ever know.

Sihanouk may have thought he could use the four American flyers to strike some sort of deal with the U.S. Government to help stem the spread of the war into his country. The political pressures being applied upon his government from all sides in that conflict were immense, and his overriding concern was to prevent Cambodia from being drawn into a wider regional war. So far as we know, Nixon's personal letter of friendship to Sihanouk was all that was required by the Cambodian Prince of State to bring about the release of the four ASA crewmen. There is no record that the so-called "Official U.S. Government apology for the incursion into Cambodian territory" that was reported by the press ever took place, and no ransom was paid to the Cambodian Government for their release. Some years later, however, Maj. Herlik spoke with President Nixon at a social event and revealed that he was the pilot of the plane that crashed in Cambodia in 1969. According to Herlik, Nixon said, "That little bastard (Sihanouk) tried to hold me up!"

Presidential party

Maj. Herlik and his crew were reunited some four years later in March 1973 at what *Time* magazine referred to as the "biggest, most elaborate party ever held at the White House." After most of the U.S. prisoners of war had been released by the North Vietnamese, President Nixon threw a party on the White House lawn for "680 former P.O.W.s, along with their wives and friends, and one Playboy Playmate."

"Henry Kissinger had his date, the Playboy bunny, there at the table behind where I sat," Jack Fisher recalls. "I had said I wasn't going to the White House when we got the invitation…I felt it was just a political show. But my mother and wife argued with me, and Mom convinced me when she said, 'Do you think you or Loretta will ever have another invitation to the White House?' Fisher continues, "Prior to the dinner on the South Lawn, they had all of us P.O.W.s at the State Department in a large auditorium. There was a bank of TV cameras off to the left. President Nixon began speaking to us while looking at us, but after a minute or two, he pretty much faced the TV cameras only. The White House gave us all money clips, tie clasps, matchbooks and the like with the seal of the President on them, and free booze inside before dinner. There were various organizations that offered tokens of appreciation to the returning P.O.W.s. Ford Motor Co. would let you use one of three new 1973 Ford models (LTD, Grand Torino, or Mustang) for one year, free, other than gas, oil, and maintenance; you could then buy it for wholesale plus 10%.…We went on a free dinner cruise on the Potomac.…Sears gave us a $500 gift certificate, [and there was] all kinds of other stuff to pick from.

"President Nixon had two big-top tents set up on the south lawn due to the large size [of the] crowd. [It] was the largest they had ever had, up to that time. We didn't get a lot of war stories revisited, then." Among the luminaries attending the dinner were Bob Hope, Jimmy Stewart, John Wayne, Sammy Davis, Jr., Joey Heatherton, and Irving Berlin, who joined in singing his own song, "God Bless America."

"I think John Wayne and his wife were at the same table with Kissinger," Jack says. Loretta shook hands with John Wayne, while I opted to shake hands with a real hero, Jimmy Stewart. I was literally speechless—nothing would come out of my mouth when we shook hands. Loretta approached John Wayne while he was sitting at this table and asked if she could shake his hand. As he stood up, he said, 'Why it would be my pleasure, ma'am,' and she said he just kept standing up, and up, and up, but she couldn't say anything else to him either. There were a lot of other celebrities there....I took a photo of President Nixon with Robert Pryor....We ran out of flashbulbs by the time Loretta and I met The Man,...my poor planning."

Staying in touch

The crewmen who suffered through so much together have stayed in contact with each other over the years, although each has gone his own way. Osburn and Herlik remained in the Army until they retired. Every year in July, the Osburn family would gather for a big reunion at Osburn's parents' homestead in West Virginia, with about 125 family members attending. Herlik attended their reunion three different times.

Robert Pryor, Laird Osburn, Quin Herlik and Jack Fisher–June 2000 (Photo: © Querin Herlik)

In June 2000, thirty-one years after their ill-fated mission, "the 4 U.S. fliers" (as *Stars & Stripes* had referred to them) met one last time at Quin Herlik's home in Augusta, Georgia. Laird Osburn spent four or five days with the Herliks just prior to his death. He died on May 2, 2001, and was buried in Webster Springs, West Virginia. Jack Fisher wrote: "Laird had three bouts with cancer, and it was considered 'apparent' by the Army that Agent Orange was the culprit. He was a damn good pilot and was instrumental in bringing the Otter down safely [after we were hit]. Laird was wounded during the ensuing firefight and was the only one of us that was awarded the Purple Heart."

All four of the men were awarded the Silver Star Medal. The citations were worded individually, but all were "for heroism involving voluntary risk of life while serving with the 146th Aviation Company... on a classified airborne mission over the Republic of Vietnam." It is stated that when their aircraft "came under hostile fire and was forced to land in hostile territory...knowing the potential loss to the United States effort in Vietnam if the enemy came into possession of the aircraft, took up a defensive position," and "fought valiantly" until captured, and then "resisted all interrogation efforts" concerning their highly classified mission or activities aboard the aircraft. By their "courageous action and humanitarian regard" for their fellow man, in the dedication of their service to their country they "reflected great credit" upon themselves and the United States Army.

Fisher continues, "Of the surviving crewmembers, I was the only one who attended Laird's funeral. He was buried [with full military honors] on his parent's homestead outside of that small town. I will always remember him introducing himself to folks by saying: 'Laird P. Osburn, from West-by-God Virginia!' I stood across the street from the funeral home and saluted the entire funeral procession with tears in my eyes."

B-52s for "Breakfast"

On the night of March 18th, five days after the release of Maj. Herlik and his crew by Prince Sihanouk, sixty U.S.A.F. B-52 Stratofortress bombers launched an attack along the border of Vietnam and Cambodia. The pilots had been told that their targets would be in South Vietnam, but forty-eight of the bombers were secretly diverted across the border, over the "Fishhook" area of Cambodia. They dropped 2,400 tons of bombs on suspected NVA bases in the area. The top-secret mission was designated "Operation Breakfast" after the White House morning meetings that had spawned it.

In his diary of March 17, 1969 (Washington time), H.R. Haldemann, Nixon's Chief of Staff, noted that "K's (Kissinger's) 'Operation Breakfast' finally came off at 2:00 pm our time. K really excited, as is P (The President). The next day, he wrote: "K's 'Operation Breakfast' a great success. He came beaming in with the report, very productive. A lot more secondaries than had been expected. Confirmed early intelligence. Probably no reaction for a few days, if ever."

"Breakfast" was deemed so successful that Gen. Abrams put together a list of fifteen more known NVA/VC bases along the Ho Chi Min Trail on the Cambodian side of the border. There were five more carpet-bombing missions over the next fourteen months, and all were known by gastronomic names: "Lunch," "Snack," "Dinner," "Supper," and "Dessert." The entire series of missions was known as "Operation Menu," and it is probable that the majority of the target locations were provided by ARDF missions.

By the time "Menu" ended, the B-52s would drop nearly 110,000 tons of bombs on a neutral country and keep it secret from the U.S. Congress and the American people. General Abrams had assured the White House that no Cambodian civilians lived in the areas that he wanted bombed, and the number of Cambodians who died in the bombings will never be known. Estimates vary dramatically depending on the political agenda of those doing the estimating, ranging from under 50,000 to over 750,000. In his book *Lying for Empire,* David Model wrote that Richard Nixon and Henry Kissinger had unleashed secret carpet bombing against a people we were not at war with, and resulted in the deaths of 600,000. Peter Maguire wrote: "Today, it remains difficult to estimate how many were killed by American bombs…estimates range from 5,000 to 500,000."

Nixon knew that expanding the war into Cambodia was sure to cause great debate in Congress, a lambasting by the liberal media, and a massive protest from the antiwar movement on the college campuses, so he and his top advisors went to great lengths to keep it secret for as long as possible.

Surprisingly enough, the other parties involved kept quiet, too. Although Sihanouk was not advised in advance, he chose not to complain publicly. It may have been because he wanted the North Vietnamese forces out of his country, something he was unable to do by himself. In addition, the North Vietnamese kept silent. There was no public propaganda denouncement from Hanoi and no mention of the bombings at the peace talks in Paris. Apparently they did not feel that it was in their best interests to advertise the presence of their forces in Cambodia.

Atlas wedgie

During the middle of March 1969, intelligence gained from radio-intercept, and supporting sources indicated that the NVA 7th Div. comprising 8,000 North Vietnamese regulars and its supporting units were moving into the Michelin rubber plantation. The plantation covered an area of approximately forty-eight square miles and was surrounded by dense jungle on all sides. All indications were that they were massing for an attack on Saigon, some forty miles to the south.

In response to the threat, MACV launched Operation "Atlas Wedge." The 1st Infantry Div., the 11th Armored Cavalry Reg., and the 1/4th Cavalry moved into the area on March 17th and attacked the enemy forces. The NVA division was routed using a combination punch of air strikes, air and armored cavalry, Rome plows, and infantry. The operation ended on March 24th, and U.S. Forces claimed a total of 421 NVA killed and seventeen captured. They also captured over seven tons of rice, along with small arms and a large cache of ammunition. U.S. losses were twenty killed and 100 wounded

AUTHOR'S NOTE: The Michelin rubber plantation is the same area where Lonnie Long was flying in 1965, and Dan Bonfield's U-6 Beaver crashed.

Using more of Crazy Cat's nine lives

On 21 March 1969, Aircraft 531 had another problem on their daily mission trip. From Cam Ranh, the aircraft had flown up the coast at 9,000 feet. As it turned inland toward the Ho Chi Minh Trail, the pilot, Chief Warrant Officer 4 Keith Glasgow heard a loud thump. He immediately shut down the reciprocating engines and started the jet engines. The flight was cleared for a straight-in approach to Tuy Hoa Air Base, and he brought the hefty plane down safely. After landing, the starboard engine burst into flames. Everyone was evacuated safely, and Warrant Officer Glasgow was awarded the Distinguished Flying Cross. The medal is awarded for heroism or extraordinary achievement while participating in an aerial flight.

No sooner had "lucky" #531 been repaired, when enemy gunners scored a direct hit on it on April 15th. The 37mm shell tore through the left inboard flap section and exploded above the wing. The aircraft limped safely back to Cam Ranh Bay.

Two milestones

Combat deaths for the week of 23-29 March raised the U.S. death toll in Vietnam to 33,641. That was twelve more than fell during the Korean War. There were 539,000 U.S. troops in Vietnam and allied troop strength had reached an all-time high of 1,610,500.

ASA computes

In April and May 1969, ASA began to deploy new experimental computerized systems on the battlefield. One of the systems was field tested at the 8th RRFS in May and was designed to improve target acquisition. The computers would not replace the 05H operators, but they would make their jobs easier and automate some functions that they had always done by hand.

ASA challenge looms

In May 1969, CINCPAC requested that MACV undertake an ARDF effort over an area of Cambodia where there was a suspected build-up of NVA forces. A few months later, MACV provided written authorization for overflights permitting top-secret ARDF/collection missions over Cambodian territory within thirty kms of the Vietnam border.

Vietnamization begins

In June 1969, President Nixon announced the withdrawal of 25,000 U.S. troops from South Vietnam. It was the first step in the Administration's process of "Vietnamizing" the war.

The NLF announced the organization of a Provisional Revolutionary Government of South Vietnam.

More ASA casualties

Staff Sgt. Jim Page of the 303rd RRB died of non-combat related causes on 8 July 1969. **Jim Carey Page** was thirty-one years old and from Oakridge, Oregon.

On 10 August 1969, Spc.5 John Anderson, serving with the 1st RR Co., died of natural causes. **John Keith Anderson** was twenty years old and from Southgate, Michigan.

The U.S. Navy awarded a Meritorious Unit Commendation to the 138th Aviation Co. RR for its support to the III Marine Amphibious Force - 1 May 1967 to 31 July 1969.

One small step

On Sunday, July 20, 1969, Neil Armstrong, the commander of Apollo 11, walked on the surface of the moon. In addition to Commander Armstrong, the three-man crew included Command Module Pilot Michael Collins and Lunar Module Pilot Buzz Aldrin. The lunar landing module was named *Eagle*.

Woodstock happening

The Woodstock Music and Art Fair, "An Aquarian Exposition—3 Days of Peace & Music," was held on a dairy farm near White Lake, New York, from August 15-18, 1969. Some 500,000 people showed up for the free concerts. Rain created a mire of muddy fields and roads, and poor planning left several hundred thousand people with food shortages and little in the way of sanitation. Images of hippies standing in the rain, wrapped in wet blankets and knee-deep in mud were broadcast on news programs across America.

The massive crowd reveled in the rain and mud, smoked pot, and screamed their approval of every anti-establishment and antiwar cry from the stage, but middle-America was not impressed. They were turned off by the turned-on throngs rejecting the values that they still held dear, and they were disgusted by the stories of free love and free-flowing drugs that poured from the festival. "If it feels good, do it" was the new mantra, but the solid Americans who obeyed the laws and paid the taxes wanted no part of it. They were not hip, and they had no desire to be.

In August 2009, on the fortieth anniversary of the event, Richard Kolb wrote: "While Woodstock rocked, GIs died…During the four days of Woodstock, there were 514,000 young Americans serving in Vietnam. They mirrored the U.S. population and during those four days, 109 were killed." On 12 August 1969, communist forces attacked over 150 cities, towns, and bases, including Da Nang and Hue. The heaviest attacks centered on An Loc and Viet Cong radio announced a new offensive. On the 14th and 15th, U.S. troops killed ninety-six enemy troops as they attempted to storm provincial capitals.

Meanwhile back in the States, Woodstock was described as the "defining event of a generation." *Time* magazine prated, "It may well rank as one of the significant political and sociological events of the age." There were two deaths: one individual was run over by a tractor while sleeping in a field, and one died of a heroin overdose.

No Uncle Ho

On September 2, 1969, Ho Chi Minh, founder of the communist-governed Democratic Republic of Vietnam, the People's Army of Vietnam, and the National Liberation Front died of heart failure at his home in Hanoi. Ho was seventy-nine years old.

In the U.S., there was a massive antiwar demonstration in Washington, D.C., on October 15th. Another huge antiwar demonstration took place in Washington on November 15th. And then, on November 16th, word of the My Lai massacre hit the newspapers. 2nd Lt. William Calley had been charged in September with several counts of premeditated murder in connection with the massacre, but the story had been kept quiet by both the Army and the White House for two months.

ASA's First Lady

October 1969 saw ASA's first female soldier arrive in Vietnam: Staff Sgt. Donna P. Baldwin. She was assigned to the 509th RR Group where she served in administration and personnel. Sometime after her arrival in-country, Sgt. Baldwin visited the 8th RR Field Station at Phu Bai and made a little more history.

The volunteer 81mm mortar platoon at the 8th RRFS was known as the "Trai Bac Power & Light Co." It was their primary job to light up the night skies around the secret installation if it came under enemy attack, and their routine was no different the night Staff Sgt. Baldwin became the first female to fire a mortar with the team.

Staff Sgt. Baldwin lowers a mortar round assisted by Chief Warrant Officer 2 Richard Ichinosubo (Photo: *The Hallmark*-The Army Security Agency)

When Mr. Ichinosubo yelled "fire," Sgt. Baldwin released the missile into the tube and ducked away with her fingers in her ears. Some of the regular mortar crewmen were heard to mumble, "Thank God it didn't misfire." Some twenty seconds later, the time-delay fuse ignited, and Phu Bai was bathed in brilliant light. The flare was still lighting up the sky when the sergeant received her certificate of appointment and her prized pit hat, a memento of the event from the delighted all-male crew.

Sgt. Baldwin spent approximately seventeen years of her illustrious Army career in the Army Security Agency. She was First Sergeant of Headquarters Company, 1st Battalion, U.S. Army Intelligence School at Ft. Devens, Massachusetts, and served as an ASA recruiting representative in Los Angeles from 1972-1975. She then returned to administrative duties as the senior female advisor to the commander of the ASA Field Station at Sobe, Okinawa, in 1976. She also served at Department of the Army levels at ASA Headquarters in Arlington, Virginia, working in both intelligence and personnel assignment areas.

Donna Baldwin enjoyed many "firsts" during her Army career. "Being a woman in military intelligence was so different [back then]," she said, "but I am proud I was able to do things that no one else [had] done." She continued to say that she "wasn't out to impress anyone"; she "simply had a job to do, and did it…"

Sergeant Major Donna P. Baldwin (Ret.) (Photo: © Donna Baldwin)

Baldwin attended various military and professional schools. She was an honor graduate of the Non-Commissioned Officer Academy and a graduate of the U.S. Army Sergeants Major Academy, which is the equivalent of the Army War College. She also earned a BS degree in psychology and management and retired as a Sergeant Major after twenty-six years of service.

CHAPTER 23

THE SHOOT-DOWN OF
JAGUAR YELLOW

Left Bank Huey at Phuoc Vinh–Henry Heide on right (Photo: © David Hewitt)

On 29 November 1969, a Left Bank EH-1H helicopter, *Jaguar Yellow*, was shot down by ground fire near Landing Zone Buttons in Phuoc Long Province. All four crewmen on board were killed. The Huey crew was assigned to the 1st Cav, and its mission was ARDF. The ASA team was attempting to locate the transmitters of enemy units that were directly threatening the 1st Cav's area of operations (AO). *Jaguar Yellow* was the first ASA flight crew to die in Vietnam.

After the crash, efforts were made to reach the crash site by gunships and ground forces, but enemy strength was too great, and the area remained too hot. Ultimately, it was determined that no one could have survived the *Jaguar Yellow* crash, and the decision was made to destroy the remains of the aircraft by tactical air strikes, thus preventing compromise of the classified intercept equipment and materials on board.

Hunt and kill

In a 1998 report issued by the Vietnam Helicopter Pilots Association, Larry E. North recalled: "From the 371st, Spc.4 James R. Smith and Spc.4 Henry N. Heide II died. There was significant action in this whole area as a result of the Left Bank contribution for several days afterwards. In reference to Tail Number 68-15246 and the action on 29 Nov 69: Smith and…Heide were 05Hs assigned to the 371st Radio Research Company. [The] 05Hs are [Morse] radio-intercept operators. The 371st RRC supported the 1st Cav and operated at the time out of Phouc Vinh, RVN.

"The pilots (Chief Warrant Officer 2 Jack D. Knepp and Warrant Officer Dennis D. Bogle)…were from B/229th as the aircraft belonged to the 11th (Avn. Co.) GS. The aircraft itself was configured with radio direction finding equipment and was unarmed except for personal weapons. It had a crew of four, two pilots and the two 05H operators in the back. Their mission was to track the enemy via intercepting their radio transmissions and then fixing their locations with triangulation. That called for flying slow and easy with many turning patterns and reporting back to HQ what was significant.

"Concerning the shoot-downs, Left Bank had been making many, many contacts with the enemy in the fall of '69. *Jaguar Yellow* was the callsign, and when they called for fire, all the available pink teams (pairs of hunter-killer helicopter teams) responded within minutes. In fact, in the fall of '69, pink teams would shadow Left Bank waiting to pounce. The response could have [been] anything from Arty (artillery) to Arc Lights (B-52s) diverted in flight. Left Bank found them and then moved out of the way so the guns could do the killing."

Pink teams were a combination of red teams and white teams. The mission of the white team Loaches was to fly as low as possible searching out the enemy. Those crews were a different breed. Each time they flew out on a mission, they knew that they could be shot down, and many were. If they were only shot at, they called in the red team for support. The red team Cobras were armed with rocket pods on their sides and mini-machine guns. If the white bird was shot down, the blue reconnaissance teams were called in to secure the site and aid in the extraction of the team and helicopter. In the worst case scenario, the blues were called in to recover the remains of the lost team.

**1st Cav Cobra and Loach hunter-killer Pink Team—
1969 (Photo: Spc.5 Terry Moon-U.S. Army)**

Larry North continued: "The rumor was that the enemy was getting tired of being pounded whenever this funny looking [Left Bank] helicopter would show up, and so they set a trap. Our guys got bold and went low to spot an antenna and were caught in the crossfire of a .51 cal, but it was said that an RPG round through the chin bubble was what brought them down.

"A pink team that was covering them was also caught in the hail of fire and went down…That will explain the other friendly KIAs for the day. Fast movers were scrambled and napalmed the area to keep the classified out of enemy hands. Later, blues of the 1/9th Cav [were] inserted and secured what was left [of the wreckage] while the area remained hot for several days."

The XO's report

Chief Warrant Officer 4 Phil Rohman (Ret.) was the company executive officer and flew for Project Left Bank. In November 1998, Rohman wrote: "Project Left Bank was at the time a highly classified mission... The mission Jack Knepp was flying had been scheduled for me as the AC (aircraft commander) that day; however, Jack approached me that morning and said he wanted to fly the new guy (Warrant Officer Bogle) and said that I always let the warrants stand down their last two-to-three weeks before DEROS and that I should do the same (My DEROS was 14 December 1969). I then flew a courier mission in an OH-6A down to Hotel-3 in Saigon (a milk run). During my flight back, I was notified by our flight ops that -246 had gone down to the east of An Loc, and [they] diverted me to the [crash] scene, which was under heavy [enemy] fire."

Jack Knepp in his Left Bank Huey (Photo: © Carlos Collat)

It is not likely that anyone could have survived the RPG explosion within the helicopter cabin and the ensuing fiery crash, but that was followed by the additional explosion of white phosphorous grenades. According to Rohman, phosphorous grenades, referred to as "Willie Pete," were carried on board to destroy the aircraft and its top-secret ASA equipment in the event the helicopter went down. WP grenades would burn for sixty seconds at temperatures exceeding 5,000 degrees F.

An ASA soldier's point of view

David Hewitt was a North Vietnamese linguist who flew with Project Left Bank in 1969. On the anniversary of the shoot-down of *Jaguar Yellow*, he recalled those days. "Most years, on November 29, I 'Google' around to see if anything new has been posted, and get immersed in it…I usually spend 11/29 in a way that honors and remembers and memorializes those who were lost." He paused a moment to gather his thoughts, and then began to tell the story from the point of view of an ASA Spc.4.

"I logged 300 hours flying with Left Bank in the autumn of '69," Hewitt says. "For most of the time I was the only 98G2LVN linguist for the 1st Cav. They didn't know what to do with me. I volunteered to fly with Left Bank. They didn't have a slot for me as a crew member, so I rode on the jump seat with a battery-powered transistorized radio on my lap or on the seat beside me. It was a little thing, which folded up neatly in a metal case about the size of a book. We would get a fix, and one of the pilots would talk to the pink team to describe the location of the fix. It was most often triple canopy jungle as far as the eyes could see with very few landmarks. Our pilots could see the spot and could keep their eyes on it, but it was exceedingly difficult to guide the Loach pilot to the right area. Imagine–[Left Bank pilot:] 'Head on your present course to that tall tree'–Reply from LOH pilot: 'I see a million tall trees.'

"The system worked well for a long time. At some point in early to mid-November [it was my understanding] one of the [pink-team] pilots…decided it would be a good tactic for the Left Bank pilots to go down to the deck to mark our fix by dropping a smoke grenade out the window. If this were a movie, now would be the point where the music gets dramatic, or funereal."

Hewitt continued: "I remember one day when we were cruising around at our usual altitude, and somebody on the other side of the ship saw tracers go by. That was sobering. Another member of the 371st RRC named Mike Likens, an O5H, took a .51 cal round in his thigh. [The round came] up through the bottom of the aircraft and shattered his femur.

"I clearly remember my first time with that new tactic of dropping down to the deck to drop smoke on our fix. I put away my radio, picked up my M16, locked and loaded with the switch on full-auto, like that would do any good. We didn't have door guns, and nobody else was in a position to return fire, so I figured I might be able to discourage somebody, if they conveniently happened to be on my side. That first time, we were flying through a clearing, probably along a river bed, because I was looking up at the treetops at 120 knots. We survived that one. I was on at least one more of those; after...we landed at Phuoc Vinh, our ground crew chief, Ted Hearth, pulled me aside. In a low voice, he said, 'this is nuts, somebody is going to die.'"

Heading for the hills

David Hewitt paused for a moment, and then said: "Oddly, I hadn't really thought it through. Intellectually, I understood the risk, but in my gut, I wasn't really afraid enough; probably because we [had] gotten away with it several times. But...Ted Hearth put it into words and by his tone and manner, he got through to me. The more I thought about it, the more I realized that it was sheer folly, sheer macho bravado, for that precious unarmed aircraft and crew to try to help the pink teams by marking our fixes with smoke. More like insanity, so I went to my C.O. and said I wanted to do something else. He said 'OK,' just like that. I don't remember whether or not I voiced my concern. I suspect they had weighed the risks...The testimony of an E-4 linguist wouldn't have swayed them. My last flight with them was on the 6th anniversary of the day President Kennedy died. That would have been around 22 November. I moved to LZ Thomas on the top of a mountain named Nui Ba Ra.

"I was working on the morning of the 29th when I got a call from my 2nd Lt. at Buttons on my trusty PRC-25 field radio (referred as 'prick-25s'). He told me that we had lost a ship, and all aboard were killed. I'm not sure if he told me who was flying that day. I remember that an odd numbness set in, and I could barely function for two or three days. In retrospect, I had not fully faced the prospect of death by hostile fire because it happened to our group so seldom—either nobody at the 371st had been killed, or nobody talked about it, because it just wasn't part of my thinking about what could happen. And there were all kinds of emotions about my not being part of the flight crew, which allowed me to depart on a moment's notice—while our ditty boppers, like Henry and Smitty, were absolutely stuck in a suicide mission."

Dennis Bogle (Photo: U.S. Army)

Over the past several years, Hewitt has pieced together more of the story about what happened that day. "I know more [now] than I did at the time," he says. "Two Cobra pilots were killed in the same engagement. The universal name for the Cobra gunships was 'Snake.' We often worked with what we called 'hunter-killer' teams—Snake up high and a Loach down in the bamboo. That's almost certainly what was going on that day. The guys in the Snake saw what happened and went down to look for survivors or provide cover and got hit by a .51 caliber or another B40. I learned their names by cross-referencing aircraft that were destroyed that day, and the only two other deaths in the area were two Cobra pilots—the account for one of them mentions *Jaguar Yellow*, so there is a high degree of correlation. The pilots were Warrant Officer 1 Kenneth Alan Luse [of Cedar Rapids, Iowa] and Chief Warrant Officer 2 Lawrence Joseph Babyak [of Van Nuys, California]…The [crash site] location is listed as 'Grid YU069124' for both the Left Bank aircraft and the aircraft flown by Mr. Luse and Mr. Babyak. My understanding is that the incident happened west of the village of Song Be."

AUTHOR'S NOTE: Babyak and Luse of the 1/9th Cav were killed when their Cobra gunship was shot down during the attempted rescue of the Jaguar Yellow team about ten kilometers from Song Be. Babyak was the Cobra pilot. Luse, the copilot and gunner, was firing upon the enemy positions with his mini-guns so that other helicopters could land blue-team troops. While making a rocket run, the Cobra came under heavy automatic weapons fire. Presumably Larry Babyak was either dead or wounded at that point, and Kenny Luse took over flying the chopper. Although wounded, and with total disregard for his own personal safety, Luse flew the Cobra back into the crash area in an attempt to engage the enemy position and mark it for other gunships. His effective marking and engagement of the position enabled the gunships and Air Force jets to destroy the position, but the Cobra crashed and both pilots were killed.

Larry Babyak was awarded an Air Medal and a Purple Heart. Kenny Luse was awarded the Distinguished Flying Cross, the Bronze Star with Oak Leaf Cluster, the Air Medal and the Purple Heart."

Henry Heide (Photo: © David Hewitt)

"Soon after arriving at the 371st at Phuoc Vinh," Hewitt recalls, "Henry [Heide] was one of the first people to acknowledge my presence and show me the ropes. I had a bunk in the Left Bank hootch…Henry was a good man and a friend. I wish they all could have lived out their natural lives. There, but for the grace of God, go I."

Capt. Collat

Capt. Carlos Collat served as the Left Bank platoon leader with the 1st Cav during the first half of 1969. Jack Knepp was one of his warrant officers, and for some period of time, Jack and Capt. Collat were the only two pilots assigned to the Left Bank platoon of three aircraft. Collat was flying as platoon commander of a sister helicopter unit, B Co. 229th Assault at nearby Dau Tieng with the 1st Cav and was in the air when he heard over the radio that Left Bank had suffered a shoot down and that all on board were killed, including Jack Knepp.

"What I can tell you," Collat says, "is that the mission was being conducted at treetop level, which was only done on an exception basis in better locating the bad guys and therefore the use of the scout and gunships as part of the overall mission. Unfortunately, this time the threat proved more than what the guys could handle.

"In thinking back, I do remember that Jack and I in early 1969 were the ones who developed this final 'drop down' procedure and even got an indicator instrument hardwired from the operator's equipment from the back of the helicopter to be right in front of the pilots cyclic so that we could visually track the signal and know which way to turn the aircraft at the same time that the operators in the back would know. The advantage here was that it was the pilots up front who could relate the signal/null tracking with the terrain in front of us and get a better insight as to where the signal was emanating from: woodline, paddy vegetation, caves, etc., and in turn deal and talk directly to the accompanying scouts and gunships as to the more precise location of the emitter.

"The one rule that Jack and I…absolutely insisted on as a mandate within the platoon was that we would never fly this low-level procedure two days in a row against the same target. We all knew that the odds were against us. That is why we normally flew the missions at between 1000 and 1500 feet AGL. Only by exception would we drop down to treetop level, and when we did we already had a pretty good history of the same target. It was this drop down to treetop level along with that extra indicator instrument up front that gave us the opportunity to get enough precision data for the scouts and guns to do their thing at the same altitude that we were at.

"That's about all I know, and I do not want to go any further into what might have happened surrounding that mission and if the cardinal rule was or was not adhered to. What I do know is that Jack was the most senior and experienced pilot in the Left Bank unit at the time, and I always knew Jack to be solid and cautious. If I remember correctly, he was the aircraft commander at the time, not the copilot regardless of what seat he was sitting in up front. Given this mission, I suspect he was in the left seat as the aircraft commander and pilot since that also is where the special indicator device was mounted up front."

Capt. Carlos Collat (Photo: © Carlos Collat)

Former platoon leader Collat continues: "The crews of the Left Bank missions had a special quality about them, both the pilots and the operators. Flying unarmed and in harm's way every day, both high and low, against tactical nearby threats as part of direct support to a tactical division was a challenge and a risk for all of us in the airborne recce (reconnaissance) business in Vietnam. It was our job and [the] rewards were only secondary in importance to staying alive and bringing the crews back safe and sound."

There were five Left Bank platforms in Vietnam (three with the 1st Cav and two with the 4th Infantry Division), and three of them crashed. Two of the three were shot down, killing all aboard.

"One of our first bad encounters in 1969 was on one of my early flights in country when I was low-leveling back to base at dusk," Collat says. "We apparently overflew some bad guys that we weren't even tracking, and they put holes in my Left Bank aircraft's rotor blades. Two month later, another of our Left Bank aircraft had an engine failure at 2,000 feet, and by the grace of God and aviator expertise, all survived but the aircraft was a total loss. So, as you can see, the challenges and the risks were always there and in the case of Left Bank, some real challenges and some real risks that just speak for themselves."

The crew of *Jaguar Yellow*

Chief Warrant Officer 2 Jack Dale Knepp, Aircraft Commander–Knepp was twenty-nine years old, married, and from Big Bear City, California. Jack and his wife, Catherine, had one daughter, Wendy. Jack had enlisted in the Army's warrant officer flight school program after serving six years or so in the U.S. Marines and graduated in Flight Class 68-517. He is buried at Montecito Memorial Park in Colton, California.

Jack Knepp was posthumously awarded the Bronze Star Medal for heroic achievement, the Air Medal, for meritorious achievement or heroism in aerial flight, and the Purple Heart.

Warrant Officer 1 Dennis Dean Bogle, Copilot–Bogle was twenty-two years old, and from Oklahoma City, Oklahoma. Dennis was active in his Methodist church and had been State President of the Oklahoma Methodist Youth Fellowship. He was a Boy Scout, had graduated from Southeast High School in OKC, and is remembered by all as one of the good guys.

Dennis Bogle was posthumously awarded the Silver Star for combat heroism and conspicuous gallantry in action, the Bronze Star Medal, the Air Medal and the Purple Heart.

Spc.4 Henry Nicholas Heide II, Morse intercept operator (05H)–Heide was twenty years old and from West Palm Beach, Florida. Friends recall his keen intelligence, his kindness, and his ever-present smile. Henry had been in-country for six months. Henry Heide and Dennis Bogle are buried side-by-side at Arlington National Cemetery in Arlington, Virginia.

Henry Heide was posthumously awarded the Distinguished Flying Cross for heroism in an aerial flight, the Bronze Star Medal, the Air Medal with "V" device for heroism and Oak Leaf Cluster (for subsequent awards), and the Purple Heart.

Spc.4 James Ronald Smith, Morse intercept operator (05H)–Smith was twenty-one years old, from Moore, Oklahoma, and newly married to Kathy, his high school sweetheart. Smith had been in-country for five months. James is buried next to his parents at Moore Cemetery in Moore, Oklahoma.

James Smith was posthumously awarded the Distinguished Flying Cross, the Bronze Star Medal, the Air Medal with "V" device and Oak Leaf Cluster, the Army Commendation Medal for sustained acts of heroism, and the Purple Heart.

"Tell them of us and say, for their tomorrows, we gave our today."

(The Kohima Epitaph–British Military Cemetery–Kohima, Assam, India)

Enemy ears

On 20 December 1969, a scout from 1st Brigade, 1st Inf. Div. found a long-wire antenna on the ground at the Michelin rubber plantation. Following the antenna, the scout team located a carefully camouflaged underground complex filled with radio equipment. They had stumbled across the operations center of the NVA's Technical Reconnaissance Unit A-3, a radio-intercept cell, part of the NVA's military intelligence section.

An enemy soldier threw out a hand grenade and was killed, but twelve members of the MI unit were taken prisoner. The prisoners included the unit commander, one Vietnamese voice intercept op, two English voice intercept ops, five manual Morse intercept ops, two manual Morse analysts and a female nurse. The dead soldier had been the unit's senior analyst. More significantly, all of their equipment and logbooks were captured. There was no longer any doubt that the NVA had been successfully monitoring U.S. voice traffic over an extended period of time, were able to easily decrypt it, and understood what they were hearing.

Personnel from the 509th RR Group were assigned the task of processing the NVA documents and equipment. The intercept equipment consisted mostly of captured AN/PRC-25 or AN/PRC-77 radios and other equipment bought from our South Vietnamese allies or third parties. Obviously, the equipment served their purposes. It was the same as ours. To supplement their U.S. equipment, the unit had several Chinese R-139 HF receivers, along with a number of commercial radios that they had modified to work on U.S. tactical frequencies. In addition, the Alpha-3 technicians had produced antennas that extended the operating distances of their radio-intercept receivers far beyond the normal range.

In spite of the equipment cache and the obvious expertise of Alpha-3's engineers, it was the logbooks that raised the most concerns at MACV. Those along with their training materials and obvious knowledge of our operational procedures and protocols indicated that they had been "reading our mail…knew exactly what it meant and what to do about it." They found hand-written pages of American voice conversations, transcribed verbatim in English and then analyzed with great expertise.

The logs showed that for over four years, we had been passing along artillery target information, ambush site locations, casualty reports, B-52 strike warnings, unit status reports, plans and orders, normal modes of transportation, including vehicle types and characteristics, unit message formats and radio procedures, unit weapons and capabilities, and other information, over the air in the clear, because we underestimated the NVA's COMINT capabilities.

The NVA battalion was sophisticated enough to analyze the tone and content of the unit radio traffic and use that analysis to predict unit actions. There were also indications that they had used that type of data against us during the Tet Offensive in 1968. In the four-to-five weeks prior to their capture, the team had intercepted over 2,000 U.S. unencrypted transmissions. It was reported that Gen. Abrams was "obviously shaken," but instead of blaming the tactical units who failed to follow established communications security practices, he blamed the Army Signal Corps, and NSA was directed to "produce briefings… exposing how Army combat communications were being exploited in Vietnam."

It was learned later that the North Vietnamese had as many as 5,000 radio-intercept operators listening to U.S. communications, much of which were transmitted either in the clear or easily-broken homemade codes. The full picture of Hanoi's SIGINT effort did not emerge until long after the war was over.

New Year's Eve–1969

In late November, ASA linguist David Hewitt had moved back to LZ Thomas on top of Nui Ba Ra. "I had a Sony cassette player…," Hewitt says, "[and] I adapted discarded batteries from Starlight Scopes to power it. My player and I were frequent guests at various evening get-togethers. I had the first Crosby Stills and Nash album and we had some others that we played over and over. I'm fairly sure one was Nitty Gritty Dirt Band and maybe Frank Zappa and the Mothers of Invention.

"I was there on New Year's Eve," he continues. "AFRS was counting down the hits for 1969 [and] just before midnight they reached the number-one hit song for the year: "Sugar Sugar" by the Archies. I don't know how to describe the feeling. It seemed that back home in the world, the folks who were buying records had no sense of what was going on in our world in 'Nam.

"We were inside, in our bunkers, and somebody ran in and yelled, "Come outside, quick!" From the top of Nui Ba Ra we could see Nui Ba Dinh near Tay Ninh, seventy-five miles away...The firebases were all sending up illumination rounds as a kind of fireworks display...The firebases had overlapping fields of fire, so there was a sort of grid, which was clearly visible in the pattern of the slowly-descending, parachute-supported, mortar-fired illumination rounds above each fire base. And we had the best seat in the house. Anybody who was not on similar high ground, or airborne at midnight would not have seen the whole show. It was a wondrous sight."

PART III

1970–THE FINAL STAGE BEGINS

CHAPTER 24

THE CAMBODIAN INCURSION

ARVN APCs on a road in Cambodia (Photo: U.S. Dept. of Defense)

American commanders in South Vietnam had long watched in frustration as VC and NVA units struck in South Vietnam and then retreated across the border into Cambodia, an area that was off-limits to U.S. military might. VC/NVA bases along the Ho Chi Minh Trail were kept well supplied with medicine, food, weapons and ordnance, and their troops could regroup, rest, prepare, and plan for their next offensive foray into South Vietnam with impunity. They were immune to attack because they were holed up in a neutral country.

Prince Sihanouk, the Cambodian head of state, did not like the North Vietnamese using his eastern provinces, but seemed to have little choice in the matter. He had a tacit agreement with Hanoi that they would not foment revolution against his government in exchange for him allowing the North Vietnamese use of the Ho Chi Minh Trail.

On several occasions he had been angered by the NVA and had even said in a speech that he would not object to the U.S. bombing communist military camps in Cambodia. However, in the same speech, he asserted that he knew of no such targets. Prince Sihanouk was not known for his reliability or his consistency when it came to politics.

The official peace talks remained deadlocked in Paris, but on February 20, 1970, Henry Kissinger began a series of secret meetings outside the city with the head North Vietnamese negotiator Le Duc Tho. Tho was a member of the North Vietnamese Politburo and the official representative of the communist government in Hanoi. The meetings made slow progress with both sides wanting an end to the war, but on their own terms. Nixon wanted out before the next election.

Countdown to invasion

The Angel's Wing/Parrot's Beak area of Cambodia and the Fishhook area had been selected by U.S. planners as the two areas that ARVN and U.S. forces would move into, if and when they got the word from Washington. Most of the operations in the Parrot's Beak area would be under ARVN command, and initial plans called for a thirty-day operation. On April 24th, Lt. Gen. Michael S. Davison was instructed by MACV to have his II Field Force ready to move into the Fishhook area within seventy-two hours following his orders to move out. That was later shortened to forty-eight hours.

On April 30th, President Nixon announced that American and ARVN forces had attacked communist sanctuaries in Cambodia. Spurred on by the radical left, large antiwar demonstrations broke out on campuses and in cities across the U.S.

371st RRC in Cambodia

In 2004, NSA released a "TOP-SECRET-UMBRA" document entitled: *NSA: Focus on Cambodia, Parts 1 and 2, Cryptologic History Series,*

Southeast Asia, January 1974. Part 2 discusses the ASA support units that moved with their divisions into Cambodia. The 371st RRC, which supported the 1st Air Cav, was headquartered at Phuoc Vinh, but their brigade support platoons were situated with the 1st Cav's brigade HQs at Quan Loi and Song Be. There are some indications, both from ASA soldiers who served in the unit and from NSA, that the 371st had "boots on the ground" on the Cambodian side of the border before President Nixon's April 30th announcement. The NSA report states: "By the time U.S. forces entered Cambodia, the 371st RRC had established a secure communications circuit for the exchange of SIGINT between the 1st ACD and its brigades."

Viet linguists Rick Jacobson–409th RRD and David Hewitt–371st RRC at Quan Loi (Photo: © David Hewitt)

During the incursion, the 371st provided daily SIGINT briefings for the commanding general and G-2 of the 1st Cav, and in turn, the G-2 provided non-SIGINT intelligence and information regarding planned moves and proposed firebases. That information helped the 371st plan the operations of its mobile intercept teams. According to the NSA report, the SIGINT support provided to the 1ˢᵗ Cav was "derived primarily from ARDF and LLVI...[and] some information from wiretap."

The mission success of the 371ˢᵗ primarily depended on ARDF. The unit tipped off ARDF platforms when enemy communications were active, providing a major increase in manual Morse tip-offs during the incursion. The 371st passed ARDF information to the 1ˢᵗ Cav Tactical Command Post at Quan Loi and plotted all fixes on the 1ˢᵗ ACD's situation map. The ASA unit also included all of the ARDF locations in the SIGINT portion of the daily briefing, which assisted the 1ˢᵗ Cav in planning for their own units as well as requests for B-52 missions against enemy units operating in the 1ˢᵗ Cav's AO.

Project Left Bank was of supreme importance to the success of the 371ˢᵗ's ARDF program in Cambodia. From 03 to 06 May 1970, a Left Bank position controlled by the 371ˢᵗ obtained 75% of the total ARDF fixes in the Fishhook area of Cambodia, and on 03 May, a Left Bank helicopter succeeded in locating a main base of COSVN known as "The City." The next day, a 1ˢᵗ Cav pink team working with Left Bank overflew the area identified and observed a vast complex of bunkers and military facilities adjacent to the tip of Binh Long Province, South Vietnam. Further reconnaissance revealed a vast network of interconnected trails, and there were unsubstantiated reports numerous antennas near the southern part of the complex.

Acting on the intelligence acquired through Left Bank, ARVN units struck the complex and uncovered bunkers filled with immense stores of arms and ammunition, clothing and equipment, food and medical supplies. The complex had just been evacuated and included 182 storage bunkers, eighteen mess halls, a training facility, and an animal farm. It is estimated that in that one raid, the communists lost enough rice to feed 25,000 soldiers full rations for a year, or 38,000 at reduced rations for a year. The enemy lost enough weapons to equip fifty-five full-strength VC infantry battalions and enough Mortar, rocket and recoilless rifle rounds to conduct 18,000 to 19,000 average "attacks by fire."

Maj. Gen. George W. Putnam, Jr., CG of the 1st Cavalry Division later wrote a letter to Brig. Gen. Herbert E. Wolff, CG, U.S. ASA-PAC, and stated: "Our DSU, the 371st RRC, has provided the First Team outstanding support with Project Left Bank, a heliborne RDF platform. Before and during the 1970 Cambodian cross-border operations, the terminal locations provided by the 371st and the intercepted messages were used to plan directions of our movements, and kept us reliably informed to the whereabouts of enemy elements. Project Left Bank has proved to be one of the most responsive intelligence collection assets available to this Division. It fills gaps in fixed-wing ARDF programs, actually providing the only coverage for more than three quarters of the First Teams Area of Operations. At the present time, while we are engaged in furnishing U.S. Air Cavalry support to the Vietnamese in Cambodia, Left Bank is providing us with reliable, timely information on locations of enemy elements which are being engaged by our Air Cavalry troops, often within one hour from the time of fix. I consider this to be a very effective linking of an intelligence asset with operational forces."

The 2nd Brigade, 1st Cav HQ–LZ David–Cambodia (Photo: © David Hewitt)

Linguist David Hewitt was part of the intercept team that the 371st RR deployed into Cambodia after the 1st Cav had moved in. Hewitt says, "I went to Cambodia…about a week after the first elements of the 1st Cav went in. I was on at least three different fire bases, including what I believe was the 2nd Brigade's forward headquarters at FSB David. That area had low rolling hills, much less total triple canopy jungle, more like rural SE Wisconsin where I grew up, like open pasture. We had a landing strip where fixed-wing planes could operate–not the big C-130s, but a smaller type. I don't recall the name of the operation into Cambodia. It was in the Parrot's Beak region, north and west of a Special Forces camp at Bu Dop, if memory serves me.

371st RRC operations tent and pre-fab intercept module–
LZ David–Cambodia (Photo: © David Hewitt)

"One day I was outside the firebase at the landing strip…and an NVA soldier walked out of the woods toward us. He had his rifle slung over his shoulder, hands raised, saying, 'Chieu Hoi–I surrender!' It was almost surreal. I've never been sure why, but nobody around me reacted with panic. I felt no sense of danger at all, but it could have turned into something ugly. We all just stood watching and waiting for him to approach us. He was disarmed, but not treated roughly. I wanted so badly to speak to him, but I couldn't reveal that I was a linguist."

"One sunny day in Cambodia," Hewitt recalls, "one of the mortar crews was testing their tube, or calibrating, or practicing or playing around, whatever. Somebody noticed that with a very high trajectory, the mortar round could be seen clearly as it slowed down at the top of its arc. It was fascinating to watch, and pretty soon everybody on the fire base was standing around watching and trying to catch a glimpse of each round as it topped out and began to descend. As you can imagine, they were falling not very far away, so we had to be alert in case somebody made a mistake and sent one straight up—but there were no accidents that day...I'm reminded of the saying that war is 99% boredom and 1% sheer terror. This story probably illustrates the boredom part."

Hewitt continues, "There were three of us, I think—two 05H and me. They had one of those operating positions built to sit in the back of a three-quarter-ton truck...helicoptered in, and sandbagged. I had my usual setup on boxes...with my trusty Collins R-390 receiver. I didn't like the setup, so I spent some time digging a hole under my cot. We had a tent big enough for maybe five or six people. We had a low sandbag wall around the outside of the tent, but I was accustomed to bunkers [with a] fortified roof over my head. I was not sure about the wisdom of those who set up that position. My hole in the ground was fairly narrow and deep, so that I could get my head down below grade level if necessary. It may have been like four feet deep and three feet in diameter...

"One day I wasn't feeling very well—it was...[the onset of] malaria. This was probably mid-to-late May. We arrived in Cambodia about at the end of the first week of May. The shootings at Kent State, during a protest about the invasion of Cambodia, happened on May 4. Seems to me that the Cav went in on April 30, but I'm not sure...We'd been set up for a while...and hadn't received any mail for days. I'd been in-country longer than anybody else there and knew how to get around and knew what I could get away with. At the end of the day I hitched a ride back to Phuoc Vinh to pick up the mail, get a shower, and intended to head back first thing in the morning.

"When I went back, Captain La Grey (371st C.O.) latched onto me and said he was going to ride along as well. When we arrived in the area he called my attention to a Snake firing rockets at a cluster of trees just outside the perimeter, and we could see other activity as well that made it obvious something had happened. Captain La Grey was watching my reactions...and started grilling me to find out if I had heard the VC or the NVA talking about attacking the LZ, and so I [had] decided to get out of Dodge. Naturally, I felt indignant but calmly assured him that 'no,' I had not heard anything at all and that everything I ever did hear was encrypted traffic, and, furthermore, we should not underestimate them [the enemy] by thinking that they would be so lax that they would discuss in clear speech their plan to attack the LZ that night. So he was satisfied with my response...He was a basically good sort, not the kind that inspired loathing by everyone he met. There were plenty of those, but La Grey was OK.

"Some bad guys got through the wire and managed to do some damage inside the compound. The only thing that happened at our position was an illumination round had come down on the tent and tore a hole in it. It must have been fairly heavy to tear a hole in that canvas, so it was a good thing it didn't land on somebody. We'd had a new arrival who hadn't taken the time to dig a hole for himself, so because I was gone, he climbed into the hole I'd dug under my cot... My compatriots agreed that it was a good thing I wasn't there. And I'd brought the mail with me...We didn't lose anybody, but having sappers get inside the compound was very dramatic."

David Hewitt gradually became more seriously ill and was diagnosed with malaria. "I left Cambodia in early June," he says, "and was admitted into the hospital."

The 372nd RRC and the 25th ID

From its home base at Cu Chi, the 372nd RRC, in its role as the ASA support unit for the U.S. 25th Infantry Div., had provided SIGINT to help plan the Cambodian incursion. Using ARDF, they were able to provide the locations of various enemy units, including the HQs of the VC 9th Div., the NVA 95C Regiment, and a number of other unidentified units along the western border of Tay Ninh Province. The ARDF missions and fixes were provided by the 146th Aviation Co. RR. Lt. Col. Freeze of the 25th I.D. had gone to Cu Chi to confer with Capt. Carter, the C.O. of the 372nd and Carter had presented his plans for supporting the infantry division. He planned to move the 372nd RRC's brigade support platoons along with the brigades as they moved out and would also move the least productive low-level voice intercept sites as far forward as possible. In addition, he planned to establish a radio-telephone position at Thien Ngon for secure communications between HQ 25th I.D. and its forward TOC and have a team withdrawn from FSB Gettysburg to support the 25th I.D. if needed. Capt. Carter's plans were approved and went into effect.

Maj. Gen. Edward Bautz, the commanding general of the 25th, informed Capt. Carter that he was interested in the communications of the NVA 7th Div., which was going to be a target of his division. In response, the 372nd redeployed two of its brigade support platoons to Tay Ninh Base Camp in order to support the new intelligence demand. He also sent out ARDF tip-off positions mounted in mobile vans to Thien Ngon Base Camp and to Katum in support of the 25th I.D.'s needs. During the incursion, the SIGINT support depended upon the successful ARDF program and also upon the low-level voice intercept teams which the 372nd RRC sent into the field.

ARDF information and pattern analysis assisted the 25th I.D. in planning the successful penetration into its target areas. Division G-2 praised their efforts, singling out "enemy unit identification and pinpoint locations" as having contributed significantly to the success of the division's operations. On May 15th, the HQ, NVA 95C Regiment was fixed, for example, within a 300 meter radius just below the Dog's Head inside Cambodia. The fix was in the hands of the Division G-2 within forty minutes, and shortly thereafter, four aircraft flew sorties into the area identified by the fix; several structures in the vicinity were destroyed. In the final stages of the advance into the Fishhook area, ARDF pointed to several large caches of VC weapons and supplies. The 25th ID found one of the largest caches uncovered during the incursion in an area marked by a cluster of ARDF fixes. SIGINT was considered the major factor in formulating an accurate intelligence picture throughout the Cambodia campaign.

Focusing the Arc Lights

ARDF-derived locations passed by the 372nd RRC to the 25th Inf. Div. became the basis for many of the B-52 bombing missions during the Cambodian operation. Chief among those were the B-52 strikes targeting the NVA-HQ (referred to as COSVN) and VC's intelligence apparatus. During a top-level briefing for Lt. Gen. Davison and Maj. Gen. Bautz on 19 May, a major topic of concern was the cessation of communications by COSVN two days earlier. Midway through the meeting, the commander of the 372nd interrupted the briefing to report that COSVN was attempting communication. Within fifteen minutes the DSU reported to Gen. Bautz the location of COSVN, and the command was able to plan B-52 strikes on the basis of that intelligence.

It should be pointed out that the success of ARDF location is always dependent on the ability and willingness of tactical commanders to react quickly to the timely intelligence they are given. In the early stages of the incursion, for whatever reason, from 2 to 9 May, eleven fixes on the HQ, VC 272nd Regiment and more than forty fixes on COSVN went to the 25th G-2 and failed to elicit a rapid response. By the time the air and ground attacks took place, COSVN had relocated twenty km away.

On 20 June, a 372nd RRC voice team was sent to Katum where the 25th I.D. was engaged in combat with the NVA 7th Div.'s 165th and 209th Regiments. The voice team remained in Katum until the end of June to work on any intercepted traffic found to be associated with enemy moves against the 25th during its withdrawal from Cambodia. The team's intercept from the 165th and 209th NVA revealed the disposition of the regiments and their tactics planned for that withdrawal period. The information on the planned NVA attacks and ambush sites was placed immediately in the hands of the U.S. division officials, and they were able to plan accordingly.

Binh Tay and Cuu Long

The Binh Tay or "Peace in the West" series of ARVN operations took place along the border of South Vietnam and the Cambodian provinces of Ratanakiri and Mondolkiri. The Cuu Long or "Mekong River" operations, meanwhile, took place along the border of South Vietnam and within the Cambodian provinces of Prey Veng, Kandal, and Kampot.

Binh Tay I began on 5 May 1970, with two brigades of the U.S. 4th Infantry Div. and two regiments of the ARVN 22nd Infantry Div. After B-52 Arc Light missions had pounded the area, elements of the U.S. 506th Airborne Battalion, 1st Infantry Brigade, and the ARVN 40th Regiment attacked NVA tactical and rear service units in Ratanakiri Province, west of South Vietnam's Kontum-Pleiku Province boundary. Several days later, the remainder of the 1st Brigade followed and met heavy enemy fire but managed to enter the northern and central portion of the area. U.S. elements withdrew on 16 May, and the operation was terminated on 25 May.

Binh Tay II began on 14 May 1970 and employed elements of the ARVN 40th and 41st Regiments of the 22nd Div. in operations just south of Binh Tay I. Its objective was the destruction of logistical, medical, and training facilities, and it concluded on 27 May. It overlapped by Binh Tay III which began on May 20th and was made up principally of elements of the ARVN 8th Cavalry Div. in a move overland in the southern half of Mondolkiri Province opposite northwestern Quang Duc Providence, South Vietnam. BT3 concluded on 27 June.

Binh Tay IV, which was executed by the ARVN 22nd Div. under the direction of the Commanding General of South Vietnam's II CTZ, was a humanitarian campaign. It undertook to evacuate refugees from

Bokeo and Lebansiak in Cambodia's Ratanakiri Province who had been displaced by the fighting. From 24 to 26 June 1970, the ARVN Div. moved over 8,000 Cambodian refugees to the relative security of camps in Pleiku, South Vietnam.

The 374th RRC

Working out of its base at An Khe in South Vietnam's Central Highlands, the 374th RRC was the direct support unit for the U.S. 4th Infantry Div. during Binh Tay I. The ASA unit activated two brigade support units, and each unit consisted of a brigade LNO (liaison officer), a radiotelephone position (RTO), a LLVI (low-level voice intercept) team with wiretap capability, and an ARDF monitor position. In the first week of May, the two teams moved from An Khe to New Plei Djereng, a Special Forces fighting camp in South Vietnam's northwestern Pleiku Province, an assembly point for the U.S. forces preparing to enter Cambodia.

374th RRC's home base atop Dragon Mountain
(Photo: © Clyde "Rowdy" Yates)

When the forward HQ of the 4th I.D. deployed to Pleiku, the 4th I.D.'s DSU element deployed with them. Throughout the operation, the support teams provided daily briefings for cleared staff members on all intercepted radio activity. There was a general lack of ARDF fix information and LLVI, so the SIGINT support took the form of passive intelligence because the enemy continued to pose no threat to U.S. forces. In this respect, though passive in nature, the knowledge that SIGINT was not showing a threat in the area was of positive use to the 4th I.D.

Cuu Long

Cuu Long operations took place along the Mekong River and in Cambodian territory adjacent to South Vietnam. It was a combined land and naval venture and occurred from 9 to 31 May 1970. The operation primarily involved the ARVN 9th Div. as well as forces from the South Vietnamese Navy and Marines, and the U.S. Navy. Its purpose was to conduct interdiction operations on the river from the Cambodia-South Vietnam border to Phnom Penh, contiguous waterways, and adjacent land areas in order to disrupt VC/NVA lines of communication, destroy enemy base camps and facilities, and protect friendly shipping on the Mekong River. The amphibious assault portion of the combined operation employed forces of the U.S. Navy and South Vietnamese Navy and Marine Corps, and was under the direct command of the Deputy Commander, Naval Forces Vietnam. ASA's 335th RRC provided SIGINT support.

In Cuu Long II, units of the ARVN 9th and 21st Divisions, as well as other ARVN elements, crossed the border into Cambodia north and west of South Vietnam's Chau Doc Province in order to deny the VC access to sanctuary in that area. The operation lasted from 16 to 24 May. In Cuu Long III, from 25 May to 30 June, units of the ARVN 9th Division supported Cambodian troops in constructing outposts and re-establishing local authority over the same area in which Cuu Long II had been conducted.

The 335th RRC

Located in Can Tho, the 335th RRC had the responsibility for providing SIGINT support to South Vietnam's IV CTZ units. Although it did not give direct support to U.S. ground troops, there being few or none in the area, the 335th did provide continuous SIGINT to the Delta Military Assistance Command (DMAC), a U.S. organization, and the 164th Aviation Group during the time they were involved in Cuu Long I. After sanitization, the information also went to the ARVN commanding general and his subordinate commanders for application in the tactical phase of the operation. The 335th also provided assistance to the *U.S.S. Benewah*, the command ship for the Cuu Long operations along the river. The ship, with Rear Admiral Herbert S. Mathews aboard, was to accompany the operational force from the South Vietnamese-Cambodian border to the Neak Luong Ferry landing approximately half-way to Phnom Penh.

To facilitate the use of SIGINT by the *Benewah*, the 335th prepared to place a small team on board the ship for LLVI and LLMM (low-level manual Morse) collection and ARDF monitor/tip-off. Two NSA civilians accompanied the seven-man team from ASA. The detachment would relay reports via the SPRINTCOM net aboard the *Benewah* to Binh Thuy, the site of the naval air facility north of Can Tho. From there the traffic would go via courier each hour to Can Tho where the 335th would process it for intelligence, forwarding the product through CRITICOMM channels and also back to the *Benewah*.

With men and equipment on board, the operation began on 9 May in a secure top-secret area below deck. Equipment consisted of one VHF radio telephone, one HF LLVI position, two LLMM positions, and one ARDF tip-off position. For a week, the small detachment failed to develop any intelligence from its operation on the ship. Contrary to expectations, efforts to collect low-level, low-powered communications failed, primarily due to heavy interference by the ship's radios and an inadequate antenna system.

On 16 May, the intercept team was moved off the ship and relocated to Chau Doc City. It was downgraded to one LLVI position and one

ARDF tip-off position, dropping the manual Morse collection to avoid duplicating the effort already being undertaken at Chau Doc. Later, when the LLVI position still failed to produce, the detachment functioned solely as an ARDF monitor/tip-off station, continuing this service until June 15. The later operation proved to be highly successful and made possible the passing of timely information on enemy locations to the flotilla. There were 184 ARDF fixes passed to the detachment over air-to-ground communications. Of those, 103 were significant and went to the DMAC Forward Command Post, the 164th Aviation Group, and the *U.S.S. Benewah* for application in their operation.

In January 1971, Maj. Gen. Hal D. McGowan, CG, DMAC, stated that the 335th RRC was "by far our number one intelligence source," and he was particularly pleased with the "Green Hornet" system of sanitizing ARDF fixes. He concluded by expressing his opinion that "in the continuing cross-border operations of the ARVN, SIGINT has been the most significant, timely and abundant intelligence."

On 21 July 1970, Gen. McGowan again wrote to the 335th: "Your rapid response to the requirements of this command filled a critical intelligence gap and served to stem infiltration activities and communist expansion in the Delta. It is unfortunate that the sensitive nature of your activities precludes wide dissemination of the results of a product that serves as a striking example of outstanding teamwork. The recent activities of your personnel located in Can Tho and deployed to remote sites in the Delta enabled the dissemination of early warning information that alerted friendly forces and decreased casualties. Although activities such as these cannot be freely discussed, they have won you the admiration and respect of friendly forces throughout the Delta."

For all the praise, the SIGINT effort during the Cambodian incursion was not without its problems. There seems to have been a lack of effective planning due to the secrecy surrounding the incursion. The Radio Research units were given very little if any advance notice, and the lack of information concerning the impending operation was a major problem that plagued RRU planning in the pre-invasion stage. Col. Frederick Westendorf, Deputy Commander, 509th RRG, offered the

347

opinion that had the 509th been informed of the Cambodian incursion during the planning stages, the Group could have provided a much higher level of SIGINT support. Another unidentified intelligence officer offered this opinion: "It must be assumed that this was a conscious trade-off that the command was willing to accept for security purposes. Since the bulk of operational intelligence is derived from SIGINT, I would not have opted thusly. It is interesting to note that of J-2 MACV, who operationally controlled ARDF/collection aircraft, were equally unaware of the operations, and we have been playing catch-up ever since."

The 409th RRD

ASA linguist Rick Jacobsen of the 409th RRD (Photo: © David Hewitt)

An integral part of ASA's contribution to the Cambodian incursion was the role played by the 409th RRD. On 01 May 1970, personnel from the detachment became the first DSU to enter Cambodia in support of U.S. troops. Attached to the 11th Armored Cav, the ASA detachment operated out of its own armored vehicles, traveling nearly 100 miles in 54 days.

Lt. Gen. Frederick C. Weyand, Commanding General of the II Field Force in Vietnam, was quick to acknowledge the role played by the 303rd RR Battalion and its subordinate units to include that of the 409th RR Detachment. "It is always easy for people to see the performance of an infantry battalion or brigade in fighting and winning the battle. The performance of a support unit is not so obvious, and yet in your case, you have probably contributed to the winning of more battles than any maneuver element in the country."

The 409th RRD in Cambodia with its highly mobile armored intercept site (Photo: INSCOM)

The 409th RRD was another of ASA's unique DSUs. Don Collins had been transferred to the detachment in February 1967. It was based at Long Giao, about twenty miles east of Xuan Loc. Collins said the 409th was rather unusual for an ASA unit, because they operated out of modified armored cavalry assault vehicles (ACAVs). "The ACAVs had quite a bit of firepower, and the 409th operated pretty boldly for an ASA unit," he recalled.

Collins said, "One day, one of the ACAVs was operating out of a Special Forces camp when one of the Special Forces patrols came under attack near the camp. The 409th guys saddled-up, went to their aid, and severely pounded the small Viet Cong unit, allowing the Special Forces patrol to casually stroll home. This is the only time I have ever heard of an ASA unit attacking something.

An ASA intercept op on board a 409th ACAV (Photo: INSCOM)

"Life in the armored unit was a pleasant change from being in an infantry unit," Collins continued. "For one thing, you got to ride to work and didn't have to carry anything on your back. Also, before going on an operation, we would always stop by the PX and load a three-week supply of pop and beer into the back of the track. At night we would close the track up, seal the periscopes, and play Hearts and drink beer. Now this is the way to fight a war."

ASA Spc.6 missing

On 9 March 1970, **Spc.6 Edward Robinson**, twenty-seven years old, of Kansas City, Missouri, was presumed to have died in a swimming accident off Con Son Island, Vietnam. Robinson was TDY from the 335th RRB and assigned to the 175th RRC on Con Son Island, some sixty miles off the southern coast of South Vietnam. He was off duty and had gone for a swim.

About 1400 hours, Spc.5 Leon A. Jones also went swimming and saw military clothing on the beach, later determined to be Robinson's. At the same time, Jones saw someone about a half-mile offshore. At 1605 hours a Vietnamese male reported seeing an individual on a raft indicating that he needed help. A boat was launched from the U.S. Coast Guard station on the island at about 1630, and the raft was retrieved, but there was no sign of Robinson. An extensive search was launched and continued for nine days, but his body was never found. Robinson remains MIA and presumed dead.

CHAPTER 25

THE EXPLORER SAGA

The Special Forces relay station atop Hill 950–1971
(Photo: Mike Sloniker-macvsog-U.S. Army)

Prior to 1970, airborne operations provided the most successful intercept of enemy VHF communications along the Laotian border. To augment that, a hearability test was conducted at a Special Forces communications relay station located on a mountain top in western Quang Tri Province. It was 110 km northwest of the 8th RRFS at Phu Bai. Hill 950, referred to as "Hickory Hill," was near the DMZ and overlooked Khe Sanh and the rugged jungle that served as a sanctuary for elements of the NVA who controlled the area. The intercept obtained was of equal or better quality than that copied by the airborne operators.

On 10 June 1970, the first of four remote SIGINT collection systems, code-named "Explorer," was put into operation on top of the mountain. According to a "Secret-Comint Channels Only" document released by

NSA on September 26, 2012 (FOIA Case #51546), the Explorer system consisted of four receivers at the remote site which were controlled by four ASA voice intercept operators at Phu Bai. The operators used a secure system to duplicate all of the standard functions of on-site voice intercept. The communications collected by the VHF interceptors on Hickory Hill were automatically relayed to Phu Bai by secure (encrypted) transmission where they were monitored through operator headsets and tape-recorded. The intercept and relay transmission from Hickory to Phu Bai took less than a quarter of a second, so nothing was lost by the fact that the intercept receiver was some sixty miles distant. Once installed and operational, no ASA personnel were required to operate the equipment on-site on a continuous basis.

Commo bunker (center)–buried Explorer shelter (right)–Hill 1015 is upper right (Photo: Sgt. Roger Hill–U.S. Army)

Explorer quickly became a major SIGINT contributor, and within the first month of operation, it had become the number two producer of VHF intercept in Southeast Asia. The unit was collecting communications of both tactical and logistical enemy units within fifty miles of Hill 950. Despite its initial success, the project soon began to face a number of logistical problems. The most significant was providing an adequate supply of gasoline to power the system in such a remote location.

There was also the problem of protecting the tiny foothold deep in enemy-controlled territory. The site was typically manned by a small Special Forces security platoon consisting of five to seven MACV-SOG Green Berets and approximately thirty Bru Montagnard special commandos.

To draw as little attention as possible, ASA technicians had partially buried the equipment in a special bunker, minus the antennas, and generators had been specifically designed for quiet operation. Severe environmental factors were also a problem. Humidity and dust took their toll on the equipment, and the monsoon season frequently interrupted refueling and maintenance. The SOG/Special Forces soldiers guarding the location handled the day-to-day operation and refueling of the generators, with occasional ad hoc visits by ASA technicians when the Explorer unit required maintenance or recalibration.

By March 1971, four more remote positions had been added to the Hickory Explorer when it became obvious that the volume of communications was too great to be covered by the original four. Explorer I was so successful that a month later, Explorer II was deployed on a mountain top in Laos, codenamed Golf-5 (aka "Leghorn"), and that intercept was relayed to the 330th RRC at Pleiku for processing and reporting. Unfortunately, operations at Hill 950 would come to a violent end the first week of June 1971.

Battle for Hill 950

In late May and early June, Hill 950 and neighboring Hill 1015 were surrounded by elements of an NVA battalion. MACV-SOG Operations Center was aware of the growing threat and sent Capt. John A Valersky, a Special Forces combat engineer, to Hill 950 to reinforce the outpost's fortifications. Capt. Valersky arrived at Hickory on May 31 and spent his first night sleeping on the floor in the Explorer shelter. The next day, a Cobra gunship was shot down while attempting to assault an NVA bunker on Hill 950, and both crewmen were killed. The enemy force was obviously looking for a fight.

On 03 June, an NVA artillery barrage began to pound the defensive bunkers of the SF outpost. The Americans and Montagnards remained in their bunkers, while trying to observe the NVA troop movements in the valleys below. Early the next morning, Sgt. Roger Hill was on the lower LZ when he began taking small arms fire and was wounded in the right hand. About 0630 NVA forces on the higher Hill 1015 and north of Hill 950 launched an assault against the Hickory defenders with small arms fire, RPGs, and mortars.

When the assault began, the SOG/Special Forces defenders included Security Platoon Leader Sgt. Jon Cavaiani, Sgt. Robert Jones, Sgt. Roger Hill, Sgt. Ralph Morgan, Sgt. Larry Page, and Capt. John Valersky. Also present was 2nd Lt. Skip Holland, a forward observer (FO) with (175mm) A Battery, 8/4th Field Artillery from Camp Carroll.

Sgt. Roger Hill (left) and possibly Jon Cavaiani—04 June 1971
(Photo: Sgt. Roger Hill-U.S. Army)

In addition to the ASA Explorer intercept operation, Hill 950 was also used by the 1/5ᵗʰ (Mech) to read buried movement sensors on the Ho Chi Minh trail in Laos, just west of Hickory. The two sensors readers on Hickory at the time of the assault were Spc.4 Walter Millsap and Spc.4 Robert Garrison. In addition to the eight U.S. personnel, there were approximately thirty Bru commandoes and a Vietnamese medic.

Sgt. Hill, Capt. Valersky, Spc.4 Millsap and 2ⁿᵈ Lt. Holland were all wounded on the morning of 04 June. Capt. Valersky realized that the outpost was in grave peril and told Sgt. Page, the platoon RTO (Radio Telephone Operator), to order a medical evacuation, followed by a complete evacuation of Hickory. Sgt. Page radioed the Special Forces Mobile Launch Team (MLT2) at Quang Tri and informed them of the growing number of wounded defenders.

Two medevac "dustoff" helicopters were sent to evacuate Hickory Hill: *Curious Yellow* and *My Brother's Keeper*. After Cobra gunships and F4 Phantom jets temporarily suppressed the NVA assault, *Curious Yellow* (piloted by Warrant Officer Dave Hansen) was able to land on Hill 950 at approximately noon on June 4. The wounded, including Valersky, Millsap, Holland and Hill, were quickly loaded on board the helicopter along with several wounded Bru. Capt. Valersky's last act before being lifted aboard the dustoff was to order the destruction of all classified equipment and documents. That included Explorer I.

When pilot Hansen landed his dustoff, NVA mortars and small arms fire renewed in earnest, and although on the ground for only a brief moment, *Curious Yellow* began taking hits. As Hansen lifted the Huey off the ground, he performed an evasive "falling-leaf" maneuver over the cliff at the south wall so that NVA gunners could not lead his aircraft. But in spite of his efforts, *Curious Yellow* was hit again and seriously damaged. The ship's control panel lights went red and Hansen realized he was losing his hydraulics. The dustoff was not going to make it back to the surgical hospital at Quang Tri.

The pilot of *My Brother's Keeper*, Chief Warrant Officer 2 Steve Woods, watched *Curious Yellow* venting trails of white vapor, which he knew was hydraulic fluid. Woods aborted his descent into Hickory and followed *Curious Yellow* as Hansen struggled to fly to the abandoned Marine combat base at Khe Sanh four km south of Hill 950. Dave Hansen maintained control and made an emergency landing. *My Brother's Keeper* touched down near *Curious Yellow*, rescuing its crew and wounded (approximately fourteen) and quickly lifting off the runway with some twenty individuals on board.

After the noon evacuation of the most severely wounded, four "slicks" (unarmed Huey helicopters) began arriving at Hickory later in the afternoon. Three of the four landed safely and evacuated most of the remaining U.S. defenders, including Spc.4 Garrison, Sgt. Page and Sgt. Morgan.

Ralph Morgan said later that he tried to persuade Cavaiani and Jones to come with them, but Cavaiani refused to desert the Bru Montagnards. Morgan said, "...[I] did not understand why they refused to leave because it was obvious the Hill was going to fall. There was no way it could be defended any longer as...[I] was the last defender on the east, facing Hill 1015, fighting with an M60 [machine gun]. Now there was nothing defending the saddle between Hill 1015 and 950, and the enemy could just walk across." Morgan asked to stay with them, but Cavaiani, the ranking NCO, ordered him to leave saying that he and Jones would remain with the Bru.

Other sources indicate simply that the third chopper was full and that the two Green Berets, Cavaiani and Jones volunteered to stay on Hickory when the last slick departed. In addition to Cavaiani and Jones, approximately twenty Bru Montagnards remained to defend Hickory against an NVA battalion determined to wipe out the beleaguered outpost.

Last stand

On the morning of 05 June, Hickory was fogged in, preventing a renewal of the helicopter evacuation or any kind of tactical air support. By approximately 0500, the NVA force had completely surrounded the outpost and launched their final assault. The allied team kept up a barrage of small arms fire and grenades, but it did little to slow the continuous onslaught of NVA troops. Sergeants Cavaiani and Jones and the remaining Bru abandoned the eastern half of Hickory and consolidated their fighting positions in the areas furthest from the advancing NVA troops who continued to attack from the east across the saddle.

Shortly after 0500, before the NVA troops breached the perimeter and swept over the entire outpost, Cavaiani and Jones told the Bru to try to escape. They had fought valiantly, but now in twos and threes, the small commandos silently slipped over the side of the defensive trenches to the west and disappeared into the misty darkness. Approximately thirteen are known to have survived, but the fate of the other Montagnards is unknown.

Severely wounded, Cavaiani and Jones retreated to a bunker at the NE perimeter of the outpost to make a final stand. A grenade was thrown into the bunker, and Sgt. Jones was wounded in the leg. Jones made a move to exit the bunker and was shot by an NVA soldier with a three-round burst to his chest. His forward momentum stood him in place for a split-second, and then he fell back into the bunker on top of Cavaiani. Cavaiani was bleeding profusely and pretended to be dead as the NVA searched the bunker. He was forced out when they set the bunker on fire. Though wounded and badly burned, Jon Cavaiani survived the battle and was captured on 950 a short time later.

The sun was just beginning to rise over the neighboring peaks; its pale glow visible through the mist and clouds, and all was silent. The battle for Hill 950 was over.

Jones and Cavaiani

After the weather had cleared sufficiently for rescue helicopters to land at the camp on top of Hickory Hill, the area was found to be completely deserted, and no trace was found of either Green Beret. Both Sgt. Cavaiani and Sgt. Jones were presumed dead and listed as MIA. Some months later it was determined that Jon Cavaiani was a P.O.W. He was held for nearly two years at a camp called The Plantation and then was transferred into the infamous Hanoi Hilton just prior to his release during "Operation Homecoming" in 1973. Cavaiani had weighed nearly 200 lbs. when captured; he weighed just over 90 lbs. when he was freed.

Upon his release by the North Vietnamese, Cavaiani learned that he had been recommended for the Medal of Honor for his actions as security platoon leader in the defense of Hickory Hill. President Gerald R. Ford presented him with the medal at a White House ceremony on December 12, 1974. Among his additional awards were the Legion of Merit, the Bronze Star, and the Purple Heart.

Sgt. John R. Cavaiani–1974 (Photo: U.S. Army-NARA)

Sgt. Jones remained MIA for forty years. In August 2011, former SF platoon leader Cavaiani and former platoon radioman Larry Page accompanied a JPAC team back to Hickory Hill to search for John Robert Jones, and they were successful. Using dental records and mitochondrial DNA, his identification was confirmed, and Sgt. Robert Jones came home. On December 6, 2012, at a ceremony attended by government dignitaries, Special Forces and ASA veterans, friends and family, he was laid to rest at Arlington National Cemetery.

Sgt. Robert Jones comes home–December 6, 2012 ((Used by permission. Photo by G. Duane Whitman, www.thelastsevendays.wordpress.com)

Sgt. Jones was awarded the Silver Star Medal, the Bronze Star Medal with Oak Leaf Cluster, the Purple Heart, and the RVN Gallantry Cross. Ralph Morgan was awarded the Silver Star; John Valersky was awarded the Silver Star Medal, and Walter Millsap was awarded the Distinguished Service Cross.

Explorer III

Capt. Valersky gave the order to Sgt. Cavaiani to destroy Explorer the first day of the attack, and Cavaiani delegated the destruction to radioman Page who was most familiar with Explorer. In the early afternoon, Page began the ignition of the thermite plates atop each of the intercept equipment racks inside the steel Explorer shelter. The C.O. of the 407th RRD at Quang Tri had been notified late that morning that Hickory was being assaulted and had authorized destroying the Explorer system. The attack and the destruction of the top-secret equipment were being monitored by both Quang Tri and the 8th RRFS at Phu Bai.

Although the loss of Explorer I was a serious setback, the installation on Hill 950 had proved the system's value and the wisdom of the concept. A manned operation of similar scope and locale would have required the placement of some three to four dozen SIGINT personnel at the site deep within enemy-controlled territory. Had such a plan been implemented, it would no doubt have resulted in significant losses of both those personnel and their top-secret equipment.

Replacement of the destroyed Explorer system and the resumption of its intercept effort were given the highest priority by NSA. Explorer III, consisting of two new systems with four receivers each, was immediately built and shipped to Vietnam by August 1971. Hill 950 was deemed too hot from a physical security standpoint, and an extended search was conducted to find two new sites. Fire Support Bases Sarge and Alpha-4 near the DMZ were selected, and the systems were installed by December 1971.

A side-story

Some weeks after the fall of Hickory, a United Press International news release presented an interesting hypothesis regarding the incident. The article entitled "Secret Base's Fall Laid to Negligence" referred to a "U.S. monitoring base with top-secret radio and chemical monitoring systems" that fell due to "negligence on the part of commanders who refused even to give the base barbed wire for defense."

The article reportedly was based on information coming from "U.S. officers and men" and proposed that not only had two Americans and many Montagnards been killed defending the base, but "it was virtually certain the top-secret equipment designed to detect communist troop movements in the jungles had been captured." UPI continued by speculating that the equipment was "worth hundreds of thousands or even millions of dollars."

The story, datelined "QUANG TRI, South Vietnam," stated that the base, "code-named Hickory,"…manned by "a team of Americans and guarded by Green Beret-trained Montagnards, was equipped with the latest in radio research and people-sniffer equipment." The equipment was "theoretically able to spot communist movement in the jungle and call in artillery, air strikes or even reaction forces to stop it.

"The base was so secret that the U.S. command refused to acknowledge its existence even after rumors of its fall began to circulate," the article continued. Spokesmen in Saigon had said they had "no report of any such base," but the officers and men with whom UPI was talking said that the secrecy may have been the reason the base's commanders "refused to protect it properly or pull its personnel out after communist forces first probed its defenses."

"They didn't even want to acknowledge it was there," one officer is reported to have said. "So how could they reinforce it? But Christ, these people were left out there with no defenses at all. Nothing. Not even barbed wire or big guns."

Another soldier is reported to have said, "They were just sitting there waiting to get hit, and they knew it was coming."

The story concluded by saying: "On the night of June 5, North Vietnamese forces encircled the camp and in the attack, killed the two Americans before they had a chance to destroy their equipment." The incident was said to have become known because a few surviving Montagnards had made their way back to allied camps along the DMZ.

CHAPTER 26

EDDIE VAN EVERY & "SOUP" CAMPBELL

Eddie Van Every, Jr. (Photo: U.S. Army)

Eddie Van Every, Jr., was an Iowa farm boy, and everyone called him "Junior." He was in church every Sunday and worked hard on the family farm raising corn, pigs and chickens. Surrounded by family and friends, life was simple and predictable. After a year of college, he decided to avoid the draft and joined the Army.

Like most Midwesterners, Junior Van Every had taken basic training at Ft. Leonard Wood, Missouri, and because of his poor eyesight, his career choices were limited. Having high scores on his entrance exams, he was selected for ASA language school where he excelled in the study of Arabic and Ethiopian. At that point, ASA proved that it was still part of the U.S. Army and in its infinite wisdom sent him to Vietnam.

Upon his arrival in-country on 15 October 1969, Eddie was assigned to the 335th RRC and soon made friends with several of the men he worked with, including John Campbell, John Trask, Jerry Hall, and Dennis Newbill. Some seven months later, Van Every was killed in a non-hostile related accident.

"Eddie was the only guy in my unit that we lost that whole year," John Campbell recalls. "We were not a combat unit. We were an intelligence gathering unit, and when I think of the information we had, it just boggles my mind as to why we couldn't get that war over with. We knew where…[the VC] were, we knew what they were doing, we knew where they were going, we knew what they were going to do once they got there and then…[Saigon] didn't do anything with it."

Some fifteen years later, John "Soup" Campbell wrote a letter to his fallen buddy Eddie Van Every and left it for him at the Vietnam Veterans Memorial Wall in Washington, D.C. That simple act would change the direction of Campbell's life. His letter read, in part:

"I'll never forget being awakened at three that morning by the hysterical crying of Denny Newbill and Jerry Hall. 'One of our guys is dead.' When Jerry told me it was you, I can remember demanding an answer. 'Oh God, why? Why any of us? Why Eddie?' Our whole company felt a tremendous loss. Things never did get back to normal."

All of the messages left at The Wall are cataloged and archived, and that is where author and television producer Laura Palmer found Campbell's letter. She contacted him, asking him if she could use his letter and Eddie's story in a book she was writing for Random House about letters left at the Memorial. He agreed and also volunteered to help her research some of the other letters and stories. Campbell became totally involved in the experience, sometimes sending her hand-scribbled notes, and the book, entitled *Shrapnel in the Heart*, became a best-seller.

Eight years later, after thousands of hours of his own pain-staking research and hundreds of gut-wrenching interviews, former ASA soldier Campbell published his own book entitled *They Were Ours: Gloucester County's Loss in Vietnam*. His book chronicled the lives and deaths of over forty men from Gloucester County, New Jersey, who had died in Vietnam. Four chapters of the book have since been turned into a play, and Campbell has been invited to speak at the National Constitution Center in Philadelphia and at countless other organizations since *They Were Ours* was published.

Campbell says he still thinks about the book "virtually every day," and those who were affected by it. He served in the Army from 1969-1972, including a year of combat, so the writing has been therapeutic for him. He has his own memories, many that he would like to forget. "I saw more than I wanted to, but I came back," he says. What began with a poignant note to his old buddy Eddie Van Every has changed his life forever.

On 01 June 1970 **Spc.5 Edward Van Every, Jr.**, died as the result of an accident in Phong Dinh Province, South Vietnam. He was serving as a Signals Intelligence Analyst (98C20) with the 335th RRC. Van Every was twenty-two years old and from Hampton, Iowa.

Army of one

During the summer of 1970, John Osmundsen was the commanding officer of the 407th RRD (Mechanized) and recalls the following incident: "The 407th...[was] providing intelligence information to the 1/5th (Mech) Infantry Div. along the DMZ....At one of the morning briefings with Brig. Gen. Hill, Commanding General, 1/5th, we presented some information to him, and he responded to it with shock. This information was verified and directly conflicted with the General's immediate battle plan. He was very thankful to be able to take necessary corrective action in a timely manner. He then asked for the name of the person at the 407th that was responsible for obtaining this information. We told him it was Sgt. Rory "Hack" Hakkarainen who was on ARVN's Landing Zone Sarge, a mountaintop overlooking the Khe Sanh Valley at the western end of the DMZ. Brig. Gen. Hill immediately called for his chopper and he, his adjutant, and I flew to LZ Sarge, where...[he] pinned an Army Commendation Medal on Sgt. Hakkarainen. Brig. Gen. Hill called this an 'immediate impact' award, and his adjutant would formerly write it up when we returned to Quang Tri. Sgt. Hakkarainen was certainly encouraged in his work and was one of the few soldiers to know just how much impact his work had on the top brass."

Crouching tiger

In June of 1970, it became evident that more intelligence was needed regarding the increased enemy presence in central, northern, and western portions of Cambodia. Reports submitted by the Cambodian government indicated that there had been numerous sightings of VC and NVA activity in those areas. While indicating a high level of activity, the Cambodian reports were not always the most reliable, so it made a true evaluation of enemy strength in those areas very difficult, if not impossible.

SIGINT specialists made the decision to deploy a special collection/analytical team to cover the target communications they needed to intercept. They believed that was the best way to produce the reliable intelligence required to determine enemy strength and locations. The 509th RRG made arrangements to deploy "Project Tiger Cub" under the technical control of the 175th RRC. The team consisted of a Warrant Officer traffic analyst, an NCO traffic analyst, plus two additional traffic analysts. There was also one NCO manual Morse intercept operator and seven additional manual Morse intercept operators. USM-7 at Udorn, Thailand also provided one traffic analyst and one more manual Morse operator. Tiger Cub became operational on 27 June 1970 with four manual Morse positions, three working sixteen hours, and one twenty-four hours daily. During its first day of operation, the team members conducted hearability tests of known enemy communications in the border region of the IV CTZ. They then began to search for new communications that might lead them to the intelligence they were seeking: VC and NVA units operating well inside Cambodia.

By 30 June, Tiger Cub was obtaining location data from the Southeast Asian direction finding net and began to work closely with the 175th RRC at Bien Hoa. They wanted to determine how well the 175th could hear the newly discovered communications links in Cambodia. When those communications were up, Tiger Cub alerted the 175th, and they attempted to intercept the same communications for subsequent evaluation. Since Bien Hoa could hear most of the Cambodian communications, they later undertook regular collection of the communications developed by Tiger Cub.

By the time Project Tiger Club was concluded at the end of July 1970, the team had isolated and developed ten military intelligence communications links in central Cambodia and identified forty additional links believed to be serving enemy forces in Cambodia for further development. Their most significant accomplishment was the isolation and development of the communications at Headquarters Phuoc Long Front, Cambodia, opposite South Vietnam's IV CTZ.

All honor Dew

On 30 August 1970, Spc.4 Robert Dew was killed in a rocket attack near Nha Trang. Dew served as a Morse intercept operator with the 330th RRC and was in the second month of his second tour. He was twenty-one years old and from Raeford, North Carolina.

Bobby Dew was the guy everyone in his unit liked. If anyone needed anything, and Bobby could provide it, he was always there to help. On that fateful day in August 1970, he was not on duty, but had gone into the communications van to relieve Mark, another Morse op who needed to take a break. The 330th had already suffered a rocket attack earlier in the day. No one expected another one so soon, but then the rocket struck.

Tony Lopez said: "I was with the 330th RRC in Nha Trang from June '70 through June '71. Some of the 05H gang at Nha Trang were Charlie Eads, Jim Morehead, Phil Baker, Phil Johnson, Wayne Tilbrook, Bernie Tomassetti and George Pilling. We were there when Bob Dew was killed, and five or six...were wounded...I still have a piece of the 107 shrapnel...[from the attack]."

The soldiers who knew him were devastated. Russell Suther said, "In a short time [he] greatly impacted the lives of those that knew him."

Robert Earl Dew was awarded the Bronze Star Medal and the Purple Heart. He was buried in the Raeford Cemetery in Hoke County, North Carolina.

Eyes for Laffing Eagle

Installation of the AN/ARD-23 V-Scan system on the U-21D "Laffing Eagle" platforms in October 1970 was a major coup for ASA ARDF. V-Scan was the most sophisticated HF ARDF system in the U.S. Army's inventory and placed them on a more even technological footing with the Air Force. The new system provided increased speed in recording fixes, the ability to cover larger areas, and a more accurate navigational system. The Laffing Eagle soon became ASA's primary source for ARDF intel as other platforms began to stand down.

More Left Bank

Two Left Bank helicopters were assigned to the 265th RRC (Abn) in October and November 1970 and served the 101st Airborne Div. admirably during the remainder of its tour. The units performed especially well during Operation Lam Son 719/Dewy Canyon II in western Vietnam and eastern Laos, an operation during which the 101st lost a large number of helicopters. By late summer 1971, the two Left Bank helicopters stood down as the 265th prepared to relocate to the 175th RRFS at Bien Hoa.

More ASA tragedy in November

On 02 November 1970, Sgt. 1st Class Frederick Pruden of the 101st RRC died of wounds from hostile action. Known to his friends as "Fearless Freddie," Pruden appears to have been one of those special men who are difficult to forget. He was an instructor at Ft. Richardson and Eielson Air Force Base near Fairbanks, Alaska, in 1959-60 and is remembered fondly by former students who served on the northernmost U.S. borders during those Cold War years. One former 05G referred to him as "legendary" to all 05Gs who were at Ft. Devens in the 60s. He was First Sergeant of a training company and had a ham radio installed on the top floor of the barracks.

From 1968 to 1970, Sgt. Pruden was stationed at Torii Station on Okinawa and worked at the Joint Sobe Processing Center. He still had his shortwave radio set up and his friends used it to call home. A fellow NCO said that he did not recall Fred ever having an enemy and had never met "a finer friend, soldier, mentor, or leader" during his own career in ASA. In mid-1970, Fred Pruden arrived in Vietnam, and he died there.

Frederick W. Pruden was a Signal Security Specialist (05G40). He was thirty-two years old and a resident of Summerfield, Florida.

Three weeks later

On 24 November 1970, an ARDF aircraft of the 156th Avn. Co. was on a check-ride over Phong Dinh Province, South Vietnam. Electronic maintenance work had just been completed on the aircraft, and it was being tested by pilot, Chief Warrant Officer Robert D. Perry, accompanied by Spc.5 Norman F. Evans, a DF systems repairman. Air Force Tech Sgt. Paul D. Kelly of the U.S.A.F. Special Activities Squadron was also on board. The plane was hit by an ARVN UH-1 helicopter which came straight up through the clouds and collided with the ASA plane. The helicopter was loaded with ARVN troops and their family members. Both ASA crew members and Sgt. Kelly were killed, along with thirteen passengers and crew on the ARVN helicopter.

Chief Warrant Officer Robert Dale Perry was an ASA pilot and assigned to the 156th Avn. Co. He was a native of Columbia, South Carolina, and married. He was killed the day before his thirty-second birthday.

Spc.5 Norman Francis Evans, twenty-three years old, was an ECM/DF systems repairman and assigned to the 156th Avn. Co. He was a native of Klamath Falls, Oregon, and was married. He and his wife Lana had two sons: Jeffrey Scott, two, and David Linn, fifteen months. Norman Evans' brother, David L. Evans, had been killed in Vietnam two years earlier at the age of nineteen.

Way beyond duty

"We are very sad and very proud," said James E. Evans in quiet, well-controlled tones while talking about the loss of a second son in Vietnam. "The Army has a regulation that when one member of a family is killed in war a second member is not required to fight," the elder Evans said, "but Norman wanted to go. He felt it was his duty."

Both Evans boys had been born in Great Falls, Montana, and had graduated from the same high school two years apart. A third half-brother, Robert Moholon, was also serving in the Army and was stationed in Hawaii at the time. The total time served in Vietnam for all three brothers added up to more than four years.

The senior Evans was a Navy veteran of WWII and had retired from the Air Force. "The boys believed in what they were doing and trusted the government in making the right decisions—we all do," he said quietly.

December 1970

During 1970, U.S. troop levels in Vietnam declined to around 330,000. ARVN troop strength reached 1,000,000.

The 374th RRC relocated to An Khe-Camp Radcliff.

Laffing Eagle was redesignated as "Left Jab," and three of the platforms were assigned to the 138th Avn. Co. at Phu Bai.

ASA's Green Berets

December also saw the deactivation of the 403rd RR SOD (Abn), which had supported the 5th Special Forces Group and been involved in the Battle of Duc Lap. The unit had been awarded ten Vietnam Campaign credits, one Presidential Unit Citation, one Meritorious Unit Citation, three Republic of Vietnam CGPs (Gallantry Cross with Palm), and one Republic of Vietnam CA (Civil Actions Ribbon).

Another Christmas

During Bob Hope's annual Christmas trip to entertain the troops in Vietnam, he said: "I planned to spend Christmas in the States, but I cannot stand the violence. The students are making great progress; last year they were burning their draft cards, this year they are burning their schools."

A January Left Jab

In January, the three Left Jab platforms assigned to the 138th became operational. They were JU-21A aircraft, outfitted with the most sophisticated SIGINT collecting systems fielded by ASA in Vietnam. The aircraft were outfitted with the first systems capable of 360 degree DF coverage and were the first to use a digital computer to store data. At the heart of the system was a spinning "spaced loop" antenna mounted in a radome under the plane. The antenna was extended after takeoff. The system also calculated emitter locations from the LOBs (lines of bearing) generated by the DF antenna, and aircraft position data furnished by the on-board INS. The new platforms were state-of-the-art and unlike any intelligence-gathering aircraft operating anywhere in the world.

**Two Left Jab JU21-A aircraft with lowered "spaced
loop" antennas (Photo: U.S. Army)**

CHAPTER 27

THE VVAW

Vietnam War protests at the Pentagon (Photo: NARA #530618)

In January 1971, President Nixon revealed to the American people for the first time that Henry Kissinger had been involved in secret talks with the North Vietnamese, and news reports of the meetings rallied the antiwar movement to increase their efforts. In 1967, a small group of young Vietnam veterans had founded a group called "Vietnam Veterans Against the War (VVAW). They were honest in their beliefs and felt that the war was wrong. For them, opposing the war and finding a way to end it was the only way to make sense of the months they had spent fighting it.

There were many antiwar groups springing up across the country, but VVAW garnered more attention than most. The sight of uniforms, medals and missing limbs seemed to cause a greater, more visceral stir across all dimensions of the ideological spectrum than wild-haired students or unwashed hippies. The radical left instantly saw the potential of such an organization and moved to infiltrate its ranks. By the end of the decade, their influence was in total control of the organization.

John Kerry had become familiar with the VVAW in 1969. After deciding not to run for Congress in 1970, and while still a uniformed member of the U.S. Navy Reserve, Lt. Kerry went to Paris to meet with representatives of the Viet Cong. This was in defiance of the Logan Act, a U.S. federal law that forbids unauthorized U.S. citizens from negotiating with foreign governments. Violation of the act is a felony, and punishable under federal law with imprisonment of up to three years, but Kerry was never charged.

When Lt. Kerry returned to the U.S., he began speaking at VVAW events and soon became one of their most publicly recognizable figures. As a veteran who had been awarded a Silver Star, a Bronze Star, and three Purple Hearts, Kerry received more attention and consideration than most of other ragtag antiwar protestors. He would go on to become a member of VVAW's national steering committee and use it as a springboard to his national political career.

On January 31, 1971, in order to capitalize on the publicity surrounding the court martial of U.S. Army Lieutenant William L. Calley (for the massacre of civilians at My Lai), VVAW invited veterans to conduct an investigation into the overall conduct of the Vietnam War. According to Al Hubbard, the head of VVAW, their purpose was to show that "My Lai was not an isolated incident" but "only a minor step beyond the standard official U.S. policy in Indochina." They called it the "Winter Soldier Investigation," and it took its name from Tom Paine, invoking his contempt for the "summer soldier and the sunshine patriot."

The tribunal was staged at the Howard Johnson in downtown Detroit for four days, and over one hundred individuals who claimed to be veterans spoke. They described acts they claimed to have witnessed or performed: rape and torture, brutalities and the routine killing of non-combatants, and that was just the beginning. There were four days of grisly tales of horror and endless war crimes disclosed in vivid, brutal detail. They told of using prisoners for target practice, throwing prisoners out of helicopters to their deaths and cutting off the ears of dead VC, horrendous accounts of burning villages and gang-raping women.

The U.S. military tried to investigate the atrocities that were testified about during the Winter Soldier event, but the VVAW directed its entire membership not to cooperate with the authorities. One "Winter Soldier" named Michael Schneider testified that he had shot three peasants in cold blood and was ordered by his battalion commander to kill prisoners. He said that although he had been awarded the Silver Star, the Bronze Star, and the Purple Heart, he had deserted and fled to Europe. The truth was that Schneider had deserted, but not from Vietnam, from Europe. After surrendering to authorities in New York, he deserted again and was arrested on an Oklahoma murder charge. His last recorded residence was the maximum-security ward of Eastern State Mental Hospital in Vinita, Oklahoma—hardly a credible witness. Another damning fact that the military investigation revealed was that the VVAW had used the names of real veterans during the testimonies, but those veterans were not in Detroit at the time of the hearings. The VVAW had used counterfeit witnesses to give testimony using stolen names.

It should come as no surprise that the list of organizers for the Winter Soldier hearings featured a number of known leftists from the entertainment world: Jane Fonda, Dick Gregory, Phil Ochs, Graham Nash, David Crosby, and Donald Sutherland. Another organizer was lawyer and activist Mark Lane who had published a book called *Conversations with Americans* earlier that same year. His book also featured so-called "Vietnam veterans" imparting stories of mayhem and atrocities committed by fellow soldiers. Many of the stories were obviously and physically absurd, such as a female communist sympathizer being raped by every soldier in a battalion. A U.S. battalion in Vietnam ranged from 1,000 to 1,200 men.

Critics of Lane's book repeatedly showed that many of his eye witnesses to war crimes had never served in Vietnam, or had not served as they had claimed. When asked about the many lies and misrepresentations in his book, Lane admitted that he had not checked military records and said it was not relevant. The editor of the book later admitted that the Lane book was published "as a war protest."

The New Year also saw ever-increasing efforts by the left to demonize the U.S. soldier by whatever means possible and turn the sympathies of the American people against their own sons and daughters. Thanks largely to the media who supported a pro-left agenda, the U.S. public bought it.

At the airport in Oakland, California, activists reportedly spat on returning soldiers, jeering them and throwing rocks and plastic bags filled with chicken blood. There are stories of eggs being thrown at buses loaded with returning wounded near Travis Air Force Base, and chants of "baby killers" aimed at those who dared to appear in public in uniform. For their own safety, most soldiers were told not to wear uniforms off base. Even at the Pentagon service members wore uniforms only one day a week. Otherwise, they traveled back and forth to work in civilian clothing. For their part, veterans did not (and still do not) understand why they were treated like criminals for honorably and nobly serving the country they loved.

Deadly February for ASA

On 17 February 1970, Spc.4 William Higginbotham of the 371st RRC was killed in a non-hostile vehicle crash in Binh Duong Province.

William R. Higginbotham was a clerk-typist. He was twenty years old, and a native of Greensboro, North Carolina.

Lam Son 719 into Laos

In February 1971, 21,000 ARVN troops staged a cross-border invasion into Laos. The operation was named "Lam Son 719" and was planned to cut the Ho Chi Minh Trail at one of its major hubs, the town of Tchepone, Laos. The cross-border action elicited a large reaction by NVA regular forces, indicating just how vital the trail was and how far

Hanoi would go to defend it. The ARVN campaign was successful in that it managed to disrupt supply movement for a time, but their retreat from Laos was a near-disaster.

Lam Son casualties for ASA

On 21 February 1971, ASA's 404th RRD (Airborne), attached to the 173rd Airborne Brigade, suffered four casualties while serving in support of the 173rd during its involvement in Operation Lam Son. Official records indicate that the men were killed by an "explosive device," but according to their commanding officer, they were ambushed by VC on a remote road south of the village of Bong Son. The four ASA soldiers were:

Spc.5 Carl Henry Caccia of the 404th RRD was a unit supply specialist and a native of Detroit. He was twenty-one years old.

According to friends, Caccia was scheduled to leave Vietnam on 20 February, but was delayed until 25 February. He was killed 21 February when the truck he was driving in a convoy near Landing Zone English came under enemy attack.

Spc.5 Robert James Potts was a communications center specialist. Potts was from Baltimore, Maryland, and was just a few days shy of his twenty-third birthday. He was nearing completion of his second tour in Vietnam and was engaged to be married.

Spc.5 Mitchell Bruce Smith was an EW/SIGINT Morse intercept operator and a native of Tacoma, Washington. Smith was twenty-one years old.

Spc.5 Robert Joseph Thelen was an intelligence specialist, a Green Beret, and airborne-qualified. He was twenty years old and a native of Fowler, Michigan.

ASA (Mechanized)

The 407th RRD (Mechanized) supported the 1st Brigade, 5th Inf. Div. (Mechanized) as they participated in Lam Son 719. The 407th sent an intercept team in a specially-modified APC. The vehicle, named *Silencers*, had additional armor and moved to the border of Laos near Lang Vei in support of the ARVN operation. The 407th also had ASA troops at Hill 950 (Hickory Hill) during the Laos incursion.

CHAPTER 28

YELLOW BIRD DOWN IN CAMBODIA

The 1st Cav air assaults into Cambodia–1970 (Photo: U.S. Army)

In late February 1971, units of the South Vietnamese Army were engaged in heavy combat with VC and NVA units in southeastern Cambodia. U.S. aircraft flying in support of the ARVN forces had been taking ground fire from concealed enemy emplacements of .30 caliber and .51 caliber heavy weapons, and it was suspected they had moved heavier anti-aircraft artillery into the area.

On 01 March 1971, a second Left Bank Huey helicopter, *Jaguar Yellow Bird*, was lost over Kampong Cham Province, Cambodia due to enemy ground fire. It is believed that the Left Bank bird (tail # 69-15684) was brought down by a 37mm antiaircraft gun. NVA gunners had developed considerable expertise with antiaircraft weaponry, and along the border region of Vietnam and Cambodia, the 37mm gun had proven to be quite effective against slower piston-driven aircraft and helicopters.

Other aircraft involved in the 1ˢᵗ Cav/USARV mission included Cobra gunships and Loach helicopters. The unit was flying in support of Lam Son 719, and their AO included the region along Highway 75, a major conduit along the southern tip of the Ho Chi Minh Trail.

Left Bank helicopter with trademark elephant-brander antenna (Photo: U.S. Army)

At noon, the pilot of one of the Cobras, serving as the command and control aircraft, decided to land in a clearing. As a second Cobra was providing air cover, one of its crewmen, Sgt. First Class Richard Herron, saw the Left Bank Huey pass by and fly approximately two miles south. The Huey had begun a tight turn when it suddenly tipped nose down and then straight down. As the Cobra crew watched, the pilot radioed, "Downed bird!"

Sgt. Herron said, "The main rotor blades came off intact with the main rotor head. They separated, and the aircraft just fell straight down from approximately 2,100 to 2,200 feet." Just before impact, the aircraft began to spin. "The tail rotor and the nose of the aircraft hit exactly the same place, and it looked like a knife stuck in the ground. When it impacted the ground there was an explosion. It looked like a petrol explosion; black smoke came boiling out both sides."

The Cobra crew could see only one side of the Huey, and from the time it began its nose-dive until it crashed, they did not see any of the doors open. "I saw no one jump from the aircraft," Sgt. Herron continued, "[but] the dust came up around it, and if anyone was thrown from it, I wouldn't have seen it."

Capt. Rodolfo Gutierrez, one of the Loach pilots, said, "We were flying at about 2,500 feet when I first noticed the H-model north of our area of operations. I saw a pink smoke go from the air to the ground—this is how I noticed the H-model. I warned the birds in the area that there might have been ground-to-air fire. As I began making my large circle, the H-model passed underneath and was climbing. As I was headed to the south, I looked out the left door and saw the H-model start to fall. The aircraft was at about 2,200 feet."

Gutierrez continued, "As soon as I saw the aircraft fall, I looked at the head. There were no rotor blades on the head. There was a mast. I looked up and searched for the rotor blades. I did see the blades and grips. They were intact and going up. From about 1,600 to 1,800 feet, the aircraft descended vertically to the ground, exploding in a fireball upon impact. About ten to fifteen seconds later, the blades hit the ground a little to the southwest of the aircraft. I believe they were intact when they hit."

Capt. Gutierrez stated that he saw no one jump from the aircraft and saw no doors open. "We had a good view of the aircraft…," he said. The Loach had been to the rear of the Huey, so they could see both sides of the aircraft. "Upon impacting the ground, the aircraft exploded and was engulfed in the fireball. There was an explosion inside the aircraft," Gutierrez concluded. The internal explosion may have been from ordinance designed to destroy the top-secret Left Bank equipment within the passenger compartment.

The location of the crash was approximately one mile south of Dambe, two miles northeast of Phum Chey Chetha, fourteen miles northeast of Suong, and twenty-seven miles east of Kampong Cham.

It was nineteen miles northwest of the nearest point on the South Vietnamese border. On 02 March, an ARVN unit reached the crash site and recovered fragmented remains that were transported to a U.S. military mortuary for identification.

Those remains were later identified as Warrant Officer 1 Robert Uhl, Spc.5 Gary David, and Spc.4 Frank Sablan. The remains of Warrant Officer 1 Paul Black, the aircraft commander, were not located at that time. The formal search for Paul Black was concluded on 16 March 1971, and he was listed as MIA. Some years later, after considering the testimony of those who witnessed the crash, that designation was changed to KIA/BNR (Body Not Recovered).

The Left Bank crew

Warrant Officer 1 Paul Vernon Black, 11th Avn. Co. of the 1st Cav was the pilot. He was twenty-two years old and a native of Central Valley, California. Black had been in high school R.O.T.C. and had asked for flight lessons as his graduation gift in 1966.

Warrant Officer 1 Robert Dale Uhl of the 11th Avn. Co. was the Huey copilot. He was twenty-two years old and a native of San Mateo, California.

Spc.5 Gary Charles David was a 05H EW/SIGINT Morse intercept operator (flight qualified) assigned to the 371st RRC out of Phouc Vinh. He was twenty-one years old and a native of Pottstown, Pennsylvania. David was not scheduled to go up that day but loved to fly and volunteered to go in place of another soldier.

Spc.4 Frank Aguan Sablan was a 05H EW/SIGINT Morse intercept operator (flight qualified) assigned to the 371st RRC out of Phouc Vinh. He was twenty years old and a native of Phenix City, Alabama.

Search for Mr. Black

In the fall of 1995, a team from the Joint Task Force for Full Accounting (JTF-FA) traveled from Hawaii to Kampong Cham, Cambodia, to investigate the Left Bank crash site. The team found a local resident who could show them the point of impact, surveyed the area, and began to excavate the site. Their initial test-dig resulted in bone fragments and an upper-jaw piece containing two teeth.

During the second week of November 1995, the site was thoroughly excavated recovering thousands of small pieces from the helicopter, personal items from the crew, and nearly a thousand bone fragments. The team also recovered twenty teeth or portions of teeth, some of which contained dental fillings and other identifying markers. The bone fragments and teeth were sent to a laboratory in Hawaii for DNA testing and comparison with samples from Paul Black's family. At the time, no matches were found, and none of the teeth matched Black's dental records.

Finally—farewell at Arlington

For thirty-two years, Jim and Jane Black waited, not knowing if Paul had died in the crash or taken prisoner. Finally, in April 2003, they received an unexpected call. JTF-FA had found a match. Using a new laboratory technique that tested mitochondrial DNA, the experts had retested the materials from the crash site and had positively identified some of the remains as belonging to Paul Black. Paul was coming home.

Paul Black in his Huey (Photo: U.S. Army)

On November 6, 2003, Paul Black was buried at Arlington National Cemetery along with his three comrades: Robert Uhl, Gary David, and Frank Sablan. In the presence of some seventy-five family members and mourners, the remains of the four young soldiers were borne on a horse-drawn caisson to their joint grave-site through a cold November drizzle. During the funeral service, Chaplain Douglas Fenton told mourners he hoped that Arlington would serve as "a place of profound peace" after so many years of uncertainty. Warrant Officer Black's parents, both in their eighties, attended the service. The families of the four soldiers heard the volleys of rifle fire, the bugler playing "Taps," and prayed for closure. As the service concluded, Jane Black said, "Let this be the end."

The four ASA crewmen were buried together at Arlington (Photo: U.S. Army)

Some gave all

At the time of his death, Paul Black was serving his second tour in Vietnam. During his initial months in the Army, he had gone through ASA training and then served thirteen months in Vietnam. When the Army offered him the chance to fly helicopters, he had signed up for another tour. He told his mother Jane: "I don't have a 50% chance of coming home with what I'm doing." His brother Darryl said, "[Paul] wasn't afraid to take on a challenge, right up to the end."

Don Garner, a cousin, had grown up with Paul and also served in Vietnam. Black had arranged a meeting and flown to see Garner shortly before his death. The two had shared a meal, talked about family, and enjoyed the visit. Garner did not like the Army, but felt it was his duty, and asked Paul why he had re-enlisted. Paul replied that he wanted to "do more for the country."

"Paul accepted the whole philosophy of what he was doing," Garner said, "and 100% believed it." After the service at Arlington, Garner mentioned his long-standing doubts about the war, and concluded by saying, "Today proved to me that it was worth it—the war in Vietnam, the whole thing."

CHAPTER 29

THE DISAPPEARANCE OF *VANGUARD 216*

Left Jab JU21-A aircraft (Photo: U.S. Army)

On 04 March 1971, *Vanguard 216,* one of the premier Left Jab aircraft (#18065), departed the airport at Phu Bai. The unarmed JU-21A plane and crew were assigned to the 138th Avn. Co. and left on an early morning intelligence gathering mission in the vicinity of the DMZ. Although the missions were extremely dangerous, Project Left Jab had been operating for three months without serious incident.

Two hours into the mission, at 0840 hours, radio and radar communications were lost. When the aircraft with its highly trained crew and top-secret equipment failed to return at the appointed time, a massive search effort was initiated. The search continued for two days over a 300 square mile area, but proved negative. Intelligence sources indicated that an aerial detonation had occurred in the vicinity of the DMZ on 04 March at the same flight altitude and route flown by *Vanguard 216*, but the hostile threat in the area precluded any possible ground search of the suspected crash site. No conclusive evidence has ever been found of the aircraft or the remains of its five-man crew.

Hush-hush

The missing crewmen were initially listed as MIA, but within ninety days of the incident that designation was changed to Killed-in-Action/Body-not-Recovered (KIA/BNR). The soldiers' families were told by the Army that all information pertinent to the incident was classified and would remain so for ten years. Additional information would not be released before 1981.

When the families were eventually provided with information, they were told the aircraft was "involved in electronic surveillance and the mission was top-secret." They were also informed the aircraft had been hit by "enemy artillery and was downed over North Vietnam." The revelations, from a "classified source," stated officially that the crew had died in the incident, and all other information remained classified.

Numerous inquiries were made, including a Congressional inquiry in 1982, asking the Army to reveal what other information was contained in the "classified source." Those inquiries proved fruitless, and Congress was advised all additional information regarding the loss of *Vanguard 216* would be classified until the year 2010.

The Crew of *Vanguard 216*

Capt. Michael Wayne Marker was a fixed-wing unit commander with the 138th Avn. Co. Marker was twenty-six years old and married. He and his wife Kay had a son, Jeff. He was from Wichita Falls, Texas, and had been an R.O.T.C. company commander at Midwestern State University in Wichita Falls.

Warrant Officer 1 Harold Lowell Algaard was a fixed-wing pilot with the 138th Avn. Co. Algaard was twenty-two years old and married. He and his wife Judy had a six-month-old baby. He was from Fosston, Minnesota.

Spc.6 John Thomas Strawn was a 98C/SIGINT analyst with the 138th Avn. Co. Strawn was twenty-eight years old, single, and from Salem, Oregon. He was awarded a Bronze Star Medal, the Air Medal with twenty-one OLC, and the Purple Heart.

Spc.5 Richard Jay Hentz was a 98G/voice interceptor (North Vietnamese linguist) with the 138th Avn. Co. Hentz was twenty-three years old and married with one son. He was from Oshkosh, Wisconsin.

Spc.5 Rodney Dee Osborne was a 05D/EW/SIGINT identifier with the 138th Avn. Co. Osborne was twenty-one years old, single, and from Kent, Washington.

Vanguard 216 remembered

Retired Chief Warrant Officer 2 Joseph Hayes recalls: "I was scheduled to fly on that aircraft. I had previous Morse and DF experience. That morning, I was just climbing in when someone came running up to the plane and told me that I had been bumped. Spc.6 John T. Strawn jumped on in my place. My duty assignment as briefing team chief just took priority over this mission. The commanding general of ASA-Pacific, General Wolfe, was coming in and a briefing was required. I was put on the next C-130 out of Phu Bai for Tan Son Nhut. Spc.6 Strawn and the rest of the crew took off shortly thereafter, and they never landed."

Jim Methvin was a Vietnamese linguist assigned to Project Left Jab from May 1970 until October 1971. He was a member of the original Left Jab crew and went through training at Monmouth, New Jersey, and Ft. Huachuca, Arizona. He returned to Vietnam for his second tour and was assigned to the 138th Avn. Co. from October 1970 until October 1971.

Methvin recalls the day *Vanguard 216* disappeared: "Around noon,

4 March 1971, Manny Bringas came into my hootch and woke me up. He said that '65 (tail # 10865) had not returned from its mission. But let's go back to earlier in the day. There were several E-5s and E-6s in the 138th Avn. Co. RR that were designated as briefers. We looked at all the incoming messages from around RVN (South Vietnam) and the world, decided which ones were pertinent, and prepared an informal briefing of the activity in the mission zone, notably Arc Lights, SAM sites, and any other activity that would affect the mission.

"A couple of days earlier we had gotten notification that a SAM site had been located in the southwestern portion of NVN (North Vietnam). The stand-off range for the SAM site was fifty k or twenty-seven NM. I got out the trusty grease pencil and string and drew an arc from the site the recommended distance. I don't remember if 18065's crew was the only one I briefed that morning or not. Briefing completed, the crew and I went to breakfast at the "O" Club. I think I had my normal bacon, egg and cheese sandwich. Then off we went to the flight line. Ironically, one of the last things you see before you turned on the flight line was the Graves Registration Point. I…brought back the three-quarter-ton truck to wherever and went to the hootch and sleep.

"Fast-forward to Manny Bringas waking me up; got up, dressed and headed for ops. There was a lot of commotion, to say the least. I hitched a ride with an older Warrant Officer who had commandeered a U-8 and flew into and along the southern half of the DMZ on a search for the aircraft. The DMZ part I found out later when I asked him where we were, and [he] just pointed along the DMZ.

"Later on, and I don't remember how long, a couple days maybe, the 8th got some message traffic. Steve Radisch and I went into the 8th's ops area and looked at the message. It stated in part: 'Vinh Linh Special Zone shot down an American aircraft, killing all five American air pirates.' Later the 8th got a back-up copy from the Chi Nats (Chinese Nationalists) in Hue which cleared up a couple of garbles.

"There had been some manual Morse activity in the VHF band, and that's why Tom was on the flight. There had been a manual Morse transmission that was coming from the vicinity of YD0174." [Tom

Strawn was a 95C/SIGINT analyst, but obviously had Morse intercept experience.]

"The Left Jab aircraft flew either a racetrack or figure-8 search pattern in the mission area. This is my theory: That manual Morse target came up, and Tom and Rod started working it. I think Capt. Marker turned NW to get closer, and between 0830 and 0845 the NVA launched a SAM from the site in southwest NVN and either hit or exploded near 18065. There were two lights on the center console: a yellow and red, I think. One was to alert the pilots that they were being interrogated by acquisition radar, and the red that guidance radar was activated. I found out from a reliable source that the lights were not hooked up. But, after '65 was shot down, they were finally activated."

This is the original Left Jab crew, taken at Monmouth County Airport, N. J. - May 1970. Jim Methvin is kneeling in the center, just right of the Left Jab sign. Mike Marker is standing, #5 from the left; Rod Osborne and Ricky Hentz are standing, #4 and #3 from the right. (Photo: U.S. Army)

The Senate Select Committee

In August 1991, during the George H. W. Bush administration, the U. S. Senate convened the Senate Select Committee on POW/MIA Affairs. Its mission was to investigate the fate of U.S. service personnel listed as MIA during the Vietnam War. Senator John Kerry was chairman of the committee, and Senator Bob Smith of New Hampshire was vice-chairman. Both were Vietnam veterans. Other Vietnam vets on the committee included Senators John McCain, Bob Kerrey, Chuck Robb, and Hank Brown. The remaining members were Senators Chuck Grassley, Nancy Landon Kassebaum, Herb Kohl, Tom Daschle, Harry Reid, and Jesse Helms.

From November 1991 until November 1992, the committee held five hearings, with committee members making several trips to Vietnam in an effort to follow the most positive leads. Ultimately, the committee concluded that while there was "some evidence suggesting the possibility a P.O.W. may have survived to the present, and while some information remains yet to be investigated, there is, at this time, no compelling evidence that proves that any American remains alive in captivity in Southeast Asia."

One of the MIA cases that the Senate Select Committee investigated was *Vanguard 216*, and their report reveals more details about what probably happened on 04 March 1971 than NSA has been willing to provide. In late June and early July 1992, a joint team of U.S. and Vietnamese investigators visited the area where the Left Jab aircraft is believed to have crashed. The site is in the Gio Linh District of northern Quang Tri Province and is located along what was the southeastern section of the DMZ.

Revisiting 04 March 1971

According to the investigative report, "On March 4, 1971, a People's Army of Vietnam (NVA) unit in the area of the Demilitarized Zone radioed it had launched one of its surface-to-air missiles and had shot down an unidentified aircraft it had been tracking. It also reported that the aircraft had crashed and the five crewmen on board were dead. U.S. analysis of the NVA reports about the aircraft's flight path and crash location indicated the aircraft crashed approximately two miles inside the DMZ in Quang Tri Province. Further analysis indicated the aircraft was shot down after the JU-21A's last radio transmission. Based on the flight path and circumstances of the North Vietnamese report, it was correlated to the loss of this aircrew and its aircraft. Following the loss, the Vietnam News Agency [had] reported that a U.S. aircraft had been downed in

Quang Binh Province killing many of the men on board [Quang Binh lies just north of Quang Tri]. This report was believed also associated with this air loss…After the [1971] Vietnamese reports of their shoot-down of an aircraft and the death of its crew, the U.S. Army declared the [JU21-A] crew had been killed-in-action, body-not-recovered…"

In addition to the testimony from the witnesses in the area of the crash, U.S. intelligence obtained a wire photo from the Vietnam News Agency showing aircraft wreckage in Quang Tri Province on 04 March 1971. Analysis by U.S. military experts, working with technicians from Beechcraft, the aircraft's manufacturer, determined the wreckage was of a U-21 and probably related to the wreckage of the missing flight. There were no other known crashes of U-21-type aircraft in that area. From all indications, the photograph was probably not provided to the crewmen's next-of-kin because "it was not asked for and because of indecision about how to declassify a twenty-one-year-old wire photo." Presumably the photograph is still classified top-secret, although, since it is a Vietnamese photo, it is not clear who or what is being protected by the secrecy.

The investigators at the crash site interviewed several witnesses who claimed to have been at the crash scene shortly after the crash and to have seen four or five human remains at the site. The witnesses reported the bodies had been moved to a nearby bomb crater and buried. Investigators stated there was aircraft wreckage located at the site in 1992, as well as pieces of personal equipment. There was some variation in the accounts from the different individuals, however the consistent information they provided was that the crew of the plane had died in the crash and been buried nearby. It was recommended by the team that the JTF-FA (now JPAC) excavate the site, but the Senate Committee recommendation was never pursued.

Still waiting

A second Congressional inquiry was made on behalf of the families by Congressman Bill Young of Florida in May 2010, but any additional information regarding the shoot-down of *Vanguard 216* had still not been declassified. The "classified source" that has provided such limited information to the families over the years has to be NSA and the U.S. Army knows only as much or as little as NSA is willing to tell them.

NSA says officially that *Vanguard 216* was collecting intelligence regarding surface-to-air missile sites, either in the DMZ or just north of it, and was "lost to hostile fire." Apparently *Vanguard 216* was successful in finding what it was looking for. The aircraft was almost certainly brought down by an NVA SA-2 surface-to-air missile.

The Senatorial report indicates that the wreckage in the wire photo was still identifiable as a U-21-type aircraft. If the North Vietnamese, or more importantly their Soviet allies, realized the significance of the aircraft and the top-secret equipment within their grasp, most of the wreckage was probably shipped to Moscow for inspection, regardless of its condition. The Left Jab platform was so highly classified and so scientifically advanced in 1971, that the remaining two aircraft were employed virtually unchanged into the mid-1980s when an updated version was introduced to the 138th Avn Co. then headquartered at McCoy A.F.B. in Orlando, Florida.

The families of the *Vanguard 216* crewmen have little hope that their loved ones are alive, but they deserve to know what happened that day. After waiting for so many years, there is no logical reason why NSA should continue to keep the details of the incident a secret.

Vanguard 216 was the last ASA aircraft lost to hostile fire in Vietnam.

More deactivations

On 6 March 1971, the 372nd RR Co. was deactivated. The 372nd had been at zero strength since November 1970. The unit had been awarded five MUCs, three RVN CGP, and one RVN CA. The 372nd was relocated to Hawaii and continued to support the 25th Inf. Div.

The 409th RR Det. was deactivated.

The 856th RR Det. was deactivated. The 856th actually stood-down in December 1970. The unit had been awarded one VUA, four MUCs, three RVN CGPs, and two RVN CAs.

On 11 March 1971, Spc.5 Ronald Northrop, a Vietnamese linguist with HHC, 509th RR Group, died of non-hostile causes in Gia Dinh Province.

Ronald Robert Northrop was twenty-three years old and a native of Kansas City, Missouri.

Calley convicted

On March 29, 1971, a six-officer court martial convicted Lt. William L. Calley of the premeditated murder of twenty-two South Vietnamese civilians at My Lai. Two days later, he was sentenced to life imprisonment and hard labor at Ft. Leavenworth, Kansas. Of the twenty-six officers and soldiers initially charged for their part in the massacre or subsequent cover-up, Calley was the only one convicted, and many were outraged by Calley's sentence. The White House received over 5,000 telegrams, and they were 100 to one in favor of leniency. In a survey of the American public, 79% disagreed with the verdict, 81% believed the life sentence was too severe, and 69% believed Calley had been a scapegoat.

On April 1, only a day after Calley's sentencing, President Nixon ordered him transferred from Leavenworth to house arrest at Ft. Benning, Georgia, pending appeal. On August 20, 1971, the convening authority, the Commanding General of Fort Benning, reduced Calley's sentence to twenty years, and the Army Court of Military Review affirmed both the conviction and the sentence. The Secretary of the Army later reduced Calley's confinement to ten years. During 1974, there was a series of legal maneuvers involving petitions, releases, reversals, and appeals, and ultimately, President Nixon issued Calley a limited Presidential Pardon. His court martial conviction and dismissal from the Army were upheld; however, the prison sentence and parole obligations were commuted to time served. Calley was a free man.

April 1971

During the month of April 1971, ASA continued to reorganize and realign its assets in South Vietnam. On 05 April, the 335th RR Co. was reorganized in support of the Delta Regional Assistance Command and located in Can Tho.

The 303rd and 313th RR Battalions were redeployed back to the U.S., along with the 371st RR Co. The 371st was awarded two Presidential Citations, one Valorous Unit Award (for Det. 2, 371st ASA Bn.) four MUCs, 3 RVN CGPs and 1 RVN CA.

The 144th Avn. Co. RR stood down with its mission transferred to the 146th Avn. Co. RR. During their tour in Vietnam, they received five MUCs, three RVN CGPs, and one RVN CA.

The 335th RR Co. was deactivated, and during their tour they had received five MUCs, three RVN CGPs, and one RVN CA.

More ASA realignment

On June 15th, with its mission transferred to the ASA Field Station, Bien Hoa, the 303rd RR Co. was redeployed to Ft. Hood, Texas. The unit had served with distinction, earning five Meritorious Unit Citations, one RVN Cross of Gallantry with Palm, and one RVN Civil Action Honor Medal.

On June 18th, the 313th RR Bn. was deactivated and its mission transferred to Pleiku. The unit had received five MUCs and 1 RVN CGP.

On June 30th, the 328th RR Co. was reassigned command from the 313th to ASA Field Station, Pleiku, and the Brigade RR Det. (Provisional) was reassigned under command of the ASA Operations Co. at Bien Hoa. The unit was deactivated at the end of September.

More accolades

On 20 July 1971, the 1st Brigade, 4th Inf. Div. was awarded the Presidential Unit Citation for "heroism in action against a hostile force in Dak To

District" for the period October-November 1967. The citation also cited their support units including the 374th RR Co., Det. 1. Of special note in the citation was the following: "Reacting prudently to intelligence indicating a major enemy offensive against Dak To and the Central Highlands..."

In August 1971, the Australian prime minister announced the bulk of Australian forces in Vietnam would be withdrawn, leaving only a modified training team.

The 1st Brigade, 5th Inf Div (Mechanized) stood down; however, the 407th RR Det. (Mech.) remained at the fire support bases just south of the DMZ. The area had recently experienced a severe rocket attack.

On 30 September, the ASA Field Station, Pleiku, was established under the cover designation 330th RRFS to support MACV and SRAC. The unit was based in Nha Trang. There was a plan to relocate to Pleiku, but it was never implemented.

The ASA Co., Bien Hoa is redesignated the ASA Field Station, Bien Hoa, under the cover designation 175th RRFS and reassigned under the command of the U.S. Army Security Group.

The 405th RR Det is reactivated under the command of the ASAFS, Bien Hoa in support of the 3rd Brigade, 1st Cav Div and is located at Phuoc Vin-Bien Hoa. The unit had earned three MUCs and 1 RVN CA.

On 24 October, the 328th RRC was relocated to Da Nang and assigned as a DSU to the 196th Inf. Brigade. Seven months later, they were deactivated. The unit had received three MUCs and three RVN CGPs. Det. 2 had received the VUA.

Aussies depart Nui Dat

In October, the 3rd Royal Australian Regiment was airlifted onto *HMS Sydney*, leaving only one battalion at Nui Dat.

In November, the 4th Australian Regiment moved out of Nui Dat to Vung Tau, ending Australian combat operations in Phuoc Tuy Province.

On 13 December, the 547 Signal Troop closed operations at Vung Tau. The flying team ceased operations at 1200 hours and the communications center at 1800 hours. On 23 December 1971, the 547 Signal Troop boarded their plane and departed Vietnam for Australia.

South Vietnamese Presidential election

The Presidential election was held in South Vietnam on October 2, 1971. There were originally three candidates, but incumbent President Nguyen Van Thieu ran unopposed after the two opposition candidates boycotted the election. Turnout was reported to have been near 88%.

Waiting for *Debra*

John R. Cutler was a RU-21D crew chief in Vietnam from 1971 to 1972 and recalls that time: "During most of my time at the 146th, our birds largely flew day missions. But, as December 1971 approached, we began to fly night missions. As I reflect back and now know some of the history of the war at that time, I would suspect those night missions were used to prepare for an upcoming B-52 bombing campaign during that December.

"I will never forget one specific night mission when my bird (Tail #67-18127 *Debra*) departed at approximately 2000 hours. As our missions were for the most part four hours in duration (with one hour of fuel to spare), I left the flight line for refreshments at the EM club while the flight crew did their thing. I planned to return to the flight line prior to their return at 2400 hours. Getting back at the flight line in plenty of time, I climbed the revetment and lit up a cigarette to enjoy the night sky and watch for the mission to return. Midnight came and went. As I knew the bird had an ample supply of fuel, I became fidgety, but not concerned. [When]…I again looked at my watch, five hours were up. No *Debra*!

"Now I became very concerned. As the only crew chief on the flight line at that time of night, I decided to call the Long Thanh North control tower ([It] was not your typical flight control tower at

Chicago-O'Hare—it was a shade bigger than a guard tower around a perimeter). I asked the controller on duty if he had heard any news… Negative. At that time, I began to think the worst. Had they been shot down by a SAM? [Had they] run out of fuel and crashed somewhere without making radio contact?

"Although it seemed like hours and countless stares into the sky looking for—praying for navigation lights of an RU-21D, 0100 hours came, and there they were. Landing lights on, making an approach for the strip. My heart began to beat again as I habitually lit up another cigarette, waiting for them to taxi to the 4th Platoon flight line and home to the Super Snoopers.

"As the bird's props slowly spun to a stop, I could hear the crew talking about 'one great mission'…They stepped down from the air-stair door and saw a very pissed-off and concerned crew chief, [so] they began to explain why the bird could fly six hours on five hours of fuel… They had picked up some very valuable signals during the last part of their mission, and as the pilot realized they would need more fuel, had flown into Tan Son Nhut and made a deal to get refueled there. It is a shame that I cannot remember any of the crew's names. I can still see their faces, [but I do not]…recall their names.

"Toward the end of my tour with the 146th, our birds were being outfitted with SAM detection equipment. One aircraft at a time was flown to Thailand to be retro-fitted with that much-needed device. Although the retro-fit came rather late (about nine months after the Left Jab shoot-down in March), it was still welcomed by the crew members flying those aircraft. Prior to those…modifications, I do recall one incident sometime late summer 1971 concerning a near-miss. One of our very experienced pilots had managed to shake a SAM by flying the aircraft as though it had terrain-following radar. The only unfortunate result was a very airsick radio operator. Though I can't remember his name, I will always remember his expression when the mission landed. The poor guy had upchucked into his flight helmet, only because we crew chiefs had warned that anyone making a mess in the aircraft had to clean it up. I really felt sorry for him."

CHAPTER 30

THE NVA EASTER OFFENSIVE

Bob Slater, 8th/4th Arty, watches as fog fills the Khe Sanh Valley below FSB Sarge—Peaks to the right of Slater's head are Hills 1015 and 950 [Hickory Hill] (Photo: © Dave Ward)

In early 1972, across the remote fringes of northern South Vietnam, a handful of ASA intercept operators began to see and hear the signs of an enemy build-up. From small underground bunkers in some of the most isolated and hazardous locations, they intercepted NVA communications that reflected increased infiltration by enemy troops, artillery units moving south toward the DMZ, and increased activity by surface-to-air missile crews. The Americans had also seen an increase in the number of refugees moving toward Hue, indicating that the local Vietnamese knew something was going to happen, and soon. Further south, a secret U.S. installation monitored vehicle traffic crossing the DMZ, and by the end of the month the monitors were recording heavy traffic twenty-four-hours-a-day. That had never happened before, but the generals at MACV did not find it reason for concern. They were more focused on the continuing U.S. troop drawdown and the "Vietnamization" of their ongoing operations.

The 407th RRD (Det A-8th RRFS) was located just north of Quang Tri City on the MACV Three Star Compound. It was a DSU for the 1st Brigade, 5th Mechanized Infantry Division and consisted of their headquarters at Quang Tri and intercept sites at various remote "vacation spots" across the northern rim of South Vietnam: FSB Fuller atop Dong Ha Mountain, FSB Charlie-2 (north of Dong Ha on Hwy 1), FSB Barbara south of Quang Tri City, FSB Sarge and FSB Con Thien. Con Thien, also called Alpha-4, was located on the eastern edge of the DMZ and Sarge was located farther west, on Dong Toan Mountain (Hill 550) in the Cam Lo District.

Fire Support Base Sarge—"The top of nowhere" (Photo: INSCOM)

No time for Sarge

In 1970, Spc.4 David Ward was an ASA Viet Linguist (98G). "I arrived in-country in April...," Ward recalls. "I was initially assigned to the

8th RRFS, with my time spent translating, [but] after a month, I was transferred to the 407th RRD. I was immediately sent to FSB Sarge.

ASA's "Tough Dudes" at Sarge: Brian Leon (Poss. 05H); ARVN soldier Lam; Kim "Easy" Rider (05H); Larry Hoffman (05H)–1970 (Photo: © Dave Ward)

"At the time I arrived, we had six people…[on Sarge]: three 05Hs, one 05K (SIGINT non-Morse interceptor), and two lingies. Within a month or so, we staffed down to three 05Hs and one lingie, and we kept pretty much at that level until I rotated off the hill sometime after Thanksgiving.

Ward pauses, remembering the months he spent in the bunkers on top the mountain, and then he continues: "Our bunker had a small ops area, about five by seven feet…When I first arrived on Sarge, it contained three portable battery powered receivers—two FM and one AM. By the time I left, we were using just the two FM receivers, one for me (the lingie) and one for the 05Hs. The bunker contained six bunks, [and] we had our electricity provided by a pair of 3KW generators. The electricity provided power for our lights. All of our commo gear, intercept gear, etc. was powered by batteries.

"The intercept operators would scan for traffic and copy it using pencil and paper. One of the guys would then hop onto the secure radio and read the transcriptions to the guys back in Quang Tri, who would type it up for processing. All of our intercepts were low-level NVA tactical comms."

The top of FSB Sarge in 1970 (Photo: © Dave Ward)

There were also other U.S. personnel on FSB Sarge when Ward was there. "[We had] a quad-50 crew of four men (quad-mounted .50 cal. machine gun), and the advisors to the ARVNs on the firebase. (At least one of the advisors was Australian.) There was also an artillery FO [forward observer], Jim Slater, for example, who had his gear set up on top of our bunker, which had the best view to the west."

Ward concludes by saying, "We usually received resupply from the 407th once a week or so. [That included]…fresh batteries, gas for the generators, our mail, C-rats, etc." Ward was a Spc.5 when he rotated off Sarge around the first of December 1970.

In the thick of it

In the spring of 1971, David Ward was reassigned to FSB Con Thien. To paraphrase an April 1971 issue of *The Hallmark* magazine, the fourteen men of the 407th Radio Research Detachment's team in Con Thien, Vietnam, did not have to wonder what the war was like, because they were in the middle of it. ASA's three bunkers at Alpha-4 were one-point-five miles from the DMZ. On a clear day they could see the star on the huge North Vietnamese flag flying on the other side and watch NVA troops drill at a base camp inside no man's land.

Life at A-4 has been described as austere. It could certainly be harsh and forbidding. The ASA soldiers who served there were mostly volunteers. They lived on C-rats, endured surprisingly cold weather and a sea of mud during the monsoon season (October to February) and slept and worked in sandbagged, half-buried bunkers which were infested with centipedes and rats. Hot showers were a thing of the past, and at night intermittent serenades from mortars, machine guns, quad-50s and occasional artillery fire lulled the men to sleep.

For many of the soldiers, however, life on the firebases had its advantages. To say the life-style there was unmilitary might be a bit euphemistic. There was a freedom and informality that was not found in more traditional settings, even within the ASA. Morale was good; the men enjoyed working together to accomplish their mission, and they spent their free time reading, writing letters, talking and listening to Radio Peking rail about "the U.S aggressors." In the evenings, the team had Alice's Restaurant, a mud and sandbag retreat that promised cold beer and a real black and white TV that could pull in snowy programming from the armed forces station in Quang Tri. Alice's also had a pet rat named "Leonardo" who was the resident mascot.

If they grew bored, they could always go topside and check out the war. The men would climb to the top of one of their bunkers and watch as Cobra gunships, B-52s, and jet fighters pounded enemy positions along the DMZ, cheering like fans at a Sunday football game. That was fine as long as the war didn't come to them, which it did on more than one occasion when they began to receive incoming mortar rounds and rockets, and had to beat a hasty retreat inside their bunkers.

The soldiers kept touch with civilization by making weekly trips to Quang Tri to resupply, pick up mail, and get paid. Armored personnel carriers were the only vehicles that could reliably make it through the terrible roads and high-risk tactical situations. The two-mile stretch of road from A-4 to the next firebase at Charlie-2 was the most dangerous and was subject to VC ambushes. The rutted dirt track was closed at night, and U.S. forces cleared it of mines each morning before anyone was allowed to use it. Then, the passengers donned steel helmets and kept their weapons close at hand until they reached C-2. The men rotated making the trip so that each one got a hot meal and a shower at least once every two or three weeks.

Ray Ridlon was an analyst (98C) assigned to the 407th HQ at Quang Tri. "When I arrived at Quang Tri the unit was short on qualified APC drivers," Ridlon says, "[so] I volunteered to be trained…That gave me an opportunity to periodically get off the main base and take personnel or supplies out to the satellite bases."

In September 1971, Ridlon spent a two-week period on A-4. "The site was short a man," Ridlon recalls. "I filled in for those two weeks, primarily as a radio operator, and to file 'sit-reps' (situation reports), which were required anytime one of the sites came under fire. A-4 would receive mortar or rocket fire almost every day, usually around 1100… One day, we received an unusually large number of rounds. I was teased afterwards, because every time a round landed, I would radio in, 'there's another one' or 'number eleven–twelve–etc.' [I] sounded calm, but I remember thinking, 'Get me out of this one, God, and I'll be a good boy for the rest of my life.'"

Ray Ridlon (L) and the "Libertines" of Alpha-4: Greg Andrews (05H), Kelvin "Kool Breeze" Hunt (05H), Michael Carroll (98G), NCOIC Sgt. "Rocket" Ron Messinger, Richard Petry (05H) and Felix Rodriguez (05H) (Photo: © Ray Ridlon)

Ray Ridlon continues: "Our unit on A-4 used to utilize two bunkers at the site; one for operations and one for sleeping...The sleeping bunker was hit [by a delayed-fuse rocket], wounding Floyd Youngblood." Felix Rodriguez was also in the bunker and slightly wounded.

Jim "Woodstock" Arrowood said, "The 1st of the 5th Infantry stood down in August 1971. Around that time A-4 was severely attacked by rockets. Staff Sgt. Messinger was the NCOIC...Spc. [Youngblood] was wounded during the attack. Bob Whitenack...after being on shift all night decided not to go to bed, but to have a beer. A 122mm rocket came through the bunker and went right through his bed."

"Equipment was brought in to reinforce the bunkers with additional feet of dirt," Ridlon concludes. "However, the sleeping bunker was determined to still not be safe. The operations bunker had a shell of concrete over it. They added a number of feet of dirt on top of the concrete, so the cots were moved into the operations bunker. The sleeping bunker was abandoned."

According to *The Hallmark*, the men from Alpha-4 "enjoyed something of a celebrity status given them by detachment personnel" when they made the trip down to Quang Tri. David Ward says, "My heroes while I was there were the guys who had spent time on FSB Fuller; they were constantly under fire."

"Hot spot"

Capt. John Osmundsen was C.O. of the 407th from July to December 1970. "Firebase Fuller was the only site where the 407th had personnel that I was never able to visit. It was always too hot," Osmundsen says. "Exchanging personnel on Fuller was quite risky since helicopters approaching Fuller usually drew fire. At one time a Chinook re-supply chopper was shot out of the air by a mortar round, while hovering above and crashing on LZ Snoopy." LZ Snoopy was the "postage-stamp-sized" landing area on Fuller. In April 1970, Bill Coverstone and John Cardano of the 407th were wounded on FSB Fuller and had to be medevaced off the mountain. Both men survived their wounds.

The U.S. Marines cryptological unit was on Fuller, too. The 1st Radio Battalion (formerly 1st Composite Radio Co.) had an HFDF team on top of the mountain. In September 1969, Cpl. Chuck Truitt volunteered to "work DF" and caught a "bird" to Dong Ha Mountain. He met the other Marines he would be working with, and then surveyed the area of the installation's defenses that they were responsible for defending. "The side of the mountain fell away at about a 45 degree angle," Truitt says, "and we had maybe sixty or seventy yards cleared out for a clean field of fire. A ravine was on past our cleared area. There were, if I recall properly, about three strands of coiled French concertina, 'razor wire.'

[There were also]…several other strands of just plain old barbed wire. The whole area was booby trapped with numerous cans in the wire to detect movement, plus…illumination flares, 'foo gas' barrels, and claymore mines. Foo gas was nasty stuff, a mixture of napalm, diesel fuel, and some kind of detergent to help it stick to whatever it landed on, rather than just running off like a liquid. The foo gas was mixed and poured into some kind of container (usually a drum or artillery round tube container) and…half-buried. [The container was then]… sandbagged behind it, so that when it was detonated, it would blow out toward the bad guys. Most of the time, the foo gas was blown with a charge of C4, using a blasting cap and a squeeze detonator."

John Osmundsen says: "During 1968-69, when the 407th arrived in the AO with the 1/5th Inf. to relieve the Marines, and before the Marines departure, the 1st Marine Radio Bn and the 407th established a joint processing facility at Dong Ha, a small base halfway between Quang Tri City and Con Thien (A-4). The OPCON was through the 8th RRFS."

Bernie Murphy with the 407th said, "I was on Fuller for forty days in…[the spring of] 1970. A couple of weeks before I arrived, the 5th Mech abandoned the base after fighting a serious siege attempt by the NVA for about forty days. They had been taking hundreds of rounds daily, but managed to successfully hold them off. After the siege was broken, they humped down the mountainside, still under fire,…to waiting choppers at the Rockpile. The base was turned over to the 1st ARVN Div.

"When I was there, there were only about a dozen Americans, the rest being ARVN soldiers and an Australian captain as base commander. It remained relatively quiet for several months but always under sporadic fire. [During the fall of 1970,] a round hit the mortar pit outside the 407th bunker door and set off the ammo killing thirty-three ARVNs… [The 407th personnel were uninjured, even though most of our bunker was blown away in the explosion."

John Osmundsen concluded, "To my knowledge, no personnel from the 407th were on FB Fuller after July 1971…The 1/5th Mech Inf.

redeployed to CONUS in September 1971. The 407th was redesignated as Det A, 8th RRFS and reduced to about half its original size, which was eighty enlisted and three officers. Warrant Officer Wilson was put in charge of the downsized unit, now receiving its security from ARVN."

FSB Fuller as viewed from Con Thien—the "Malt Shoppe" was a "two-seater" latrine (Photo: © Dave Ward)

Springtime 1972

In late March 1972, there were only two ASA personnel on duty at FSB Sarge: Spc.4 Bruce Crosby, Jr., and Spc.5 Gary Westcott. Crosby was a terminal receiving system repairman and was charged with maintaining the Explorer III system that was housed in a reinforced bunker. He had helped build the specially-designed bunker and had been stationed at Sarge since November. The newly-built Explorer III systems had been deployed to Sarge and A-4 five months after Explorer I was destroyed on Hill 950.

Gary Westcott was a North Vietnamese linguist and Explorer technician who had helped set up the Explorer III equipment when it first arrived in South Vietnam. Terry Stanfill worked on the Explorer Project at Phu Bai from January until June 1972, when he was transferred to the 7th RRFS in Udorn, Thailand. In 2002, Stanfill recalled working with Westcott. "A small group of us, all North Viet linguists, had trained at NSA for this project when we deployed to the 8th RRFS (407th RRD) at Phu Bai shortly before Christmas 1971," he said. "It took a few weeks for the sophisticated radio equipment to arrive at Phu Bai, but [it] was eventually operational sometime during late January of 1972. We pulled various intercept assignments waiting for the project to start, and it was at that time that I met…Gary."

Stanfill continued, "He [Westcott] was one of a couple of fellas setting up the equipment in a special area of the ops compound at Phu Bai. The main receiving equipment was located at Phu Bai, but the antennas for the project were located on a series of advance firebases up next to the DMZ. The antennas picked up the signals and were transmitted fifty km back to Phu Bai via [a] live, encrypted link. The equipment was new advanced technology at that time and required a lot of tweaking and TLC, especially from Gary, to keep it working and on line.

Westcott, Brown and Crosby fixing a generator—Camp Carroll—January 1972 (Photo: © John Mastro)

"I had gone through training for over two years with my fellow linguists," Terry Stanfill said, "but didn't meet Gary until we worked together on Explorer as his training background was much different than mine. Maybe some other tech guys might have spent more time with him during his training. I always remember Gary having a calm patience with the equipment when we wanted to take a baseball bat and beat it into working properly. He would have something cheerful to say when we were just cussing the equipment. The dedicated work…[he] did allowed our mission to be successful and resulted in intercepts that undoubtedly saved some American lives. On at least two occasions that I know of, the information was critical and was communicated to the highest level of the chain of command."

"Every day, Gary changed the encryption codes on the equipment, and sometimes it continued to work and sometimes not. He was highly committed to fixing any problems, and if he couldn't fix it on our end (at Phu Bai), then it would require him taking a chopper out to the antennas to fix whatever problem right at the antenna location. Over the course of the several weeks we worked together, he was out at the antennas one or two days every week, sometimes requiring an overnight stay if the chopper couldn't get back to pick him up before nightfall or bad weather.

"There were just four or five of us linguists," Stanfill said, "Roger Shea, Bill Hueblein, Freddie Lee, and a couple of ARVN intercept operators, and Gary and another tech I didn't know very well that mostly worked at the forward antenna bases…on Explorer. Whenever Gary needed to go out to the antennas, he would almost always invite us along, and occasionally one of us would go just for grins if we could get away.

"It was during this period of time that the NVA decided to mount a large offensive push into South Vietnam, and they started by attacking some of the northern firebases along the DMZ. As luck would have it, Gary was out there at FB Sarge on the day it was attacked, doing his regular routine of fine tuning our equipment just so we could get a good signal. It wasn't uncommon to frequently take incoming rounds at Phu Bai or on the firebases, but up to this point it had only been a few rounds at a time meant mostly as harassment," Stanfill said. This time, however, it was different.

Black Thursday

In addition to Westcott and Crosby, the only other American at Firebase Sarge was Maj. Walter Boomer, a U.S. Marine advisor to the 4th Bn, South Vietnamese Marines. The SVMC unit was assigned to protect the firebase. Earlier in the month, Maj. Boomer had warned Gen. Giai, the C.O. of the ARVN 3rd Div. that he was concerned about the increase in enemy activity in the area, but the general said there was little he could do.

Rocket attacks had been occurring more regularly but not of sufficient force to warrant concern until 29 March. On that afternoon, the firebases were being hit at least hourly, and the 407th C.O., Warrant Officer 2 Larry Wilson (and his superiors) began to consider evacuating Sarge and A-4. Throughout the following morning the proposed evacuation was discussed, but no decision was reached.

Just before noon on Thursday, 30 March 1972, an intense artillery barrage began at Firebase Sarge, and this time it did not let up. The shelling continued to build in intensity, convincing Maj. Boomer that the offensive he had predicted had begun. What he did not know was that the small remote outposts along the DMZ were under attack by two NVA Divisions, the 304th and the 308th, with some 30,000 regular infantry troops, five artillery regiments, and two tank regiments with over 400 tanks and APCs.

Hunkered down in his dust-filled command bunker, Maj. Boomer contacted his headquarters and advised them that Sarge was being shelled. "The NVA's fire is as accurate and as heavy as we have ever experienced up here," Boomer said. "We're all okay now, but there is probably a big battle coming our way…It looks like this could be their big push." With artillery rounds slamming into his underground post, Boomer contacted Crosby and Westcott and ordered them to remain in the Explorer bunker where they would be better protected and to keep in radio contact with him and with the other ASA outpost at Alpha-4.

The Explorer system was housed in a custom-designed precast shelter along with several other pieces of NSA/ASA crypto equipment. The shelter was partially buried and surrounded by a reinforced bunker made of several rows of sandbags and a steel roof that was covered with another five feet of sand bags. For ventilation, there was one small opening set high in the side of the bunker wall.

Below Sarge, the NVA were firing Soviet 130mm guns the size of telephone poles, along with automatic and small arms fire and 122mm rockets. With sweat stinging his eyes and soaking through his dust-covered uniform, Maj. Boomer again contacted headquarters and demanded to know why there seemed to be no response from friendly forces to stem the incoming enemy barrage. The NVA shells continued to bombard his bunker and the other fortifications at Firebase Sarge.

Walter E. Boomer, later General Boomer, Assistant Commandant of the Marine Corps—Marine Commander during Operations Desert Shield and Desert Storm (Photo: U.S.M.C.)

About thirty minutes after the attack began, Boomer and the radioman at A-4 lost all contact with Crosby and Westcott. Boomer continued his efforts to contact the two men over the roar of the artillery and rocket barrage, but there was no response. He heard only dead silence on the other end. Disregarding his own safety, the Major left the battalion command bunker and made his way toward the Explorer bunker.

Shortly after noon, a 122mm rocket with a delayed fuse had scored a direct hit on the tiny vent in the Explorer fortification. The rocket exploded inside the bunker, partially collapsing the steel roof laden with tons of sandbags, and setting off the built-in thermite destruction panels that were attached to each piece of top-secret equipment. The result was a fire of solar intensity that would burn for two days.

Upon discovering that the bunker which the two young soldiers were occupying had been hit, Boomer courageously made several attempts to enter the inferno and rescue them but was repulsed by the extreme heat. Maj. Walter Boomer would later receive a second award of the Silver Star for "conspicuous gallantry" from 30 March to 03 April 1972 as the senior advisor to the 4th Infantry Bn, SVMC.

Gary and Bruce

Firebase Sarge was abandoned on 01 April, and the devastated Explorer bunker was still smoldering. Both Crosby and Westcott were initially listed as MIA, but on 27 June 1972, their status was changed to KIA/BNR. The 407th RRD had manned its dangerous outposts along the DMZ for four years, and Gary Westcott and Bruce Crosby were the unit's first and only combat fatalities. More than ten years after Spc.4 James T. Davis became the first ASA soldier to die in combat, Westcott and Crosby were the last.

Spc.5 Gary P. Westcott
(Photo: U.S. Army)

Spc.4 Bruce A. Crosby, Jr.
(Photo: U.S. Army)

Spc.5 Gary Patrick Westcott was from Pomona, California, and one month shy of his twenty-first birthday.

Spc.4 Bruce Allen Crosby, Jr., was from Springville, New York. He was twenty years old.

Good Friday

The 407th headquarters staff in Quang Tri could do nothing to help those lost at Sarge, but now they were becoming extremely concerned about their men at A-4. Nightfall was approaching, and no decision had been made to extract the Explorer techs and intercept team who were holed up in their bunker and being subjected to a relentless barrage. Headquarters contacted Alpha-4 by radio every fifteen minutes to check their status. They were being pounded by 122mm rockets, 81mm mortars, 240mm rockets, and 130mm artillery.

Alpha-4's concrete bunker was buried ten feet underground and could hold six to eight personnel during an artillery or rocket attack. Their Explorer III system was housed nearby in a precast shelter that was partially buried in the ground and covered over with several feet of sandbags. The 407th had eight men working on the hill at the time of the attack: Chuck Billingsly, Chuck Glaubitz, Randy Kruger, Chuck Martin, Rex Millspaugh, John Parks, Rick Stauter, and John Stone.

On Friday morning, the radioman at A-4 reported that the eight ASA ops and techs working there were the only ones still on the hill. The ARVN infantry company charged with their security had quietly pulled out and left the area during the night. About midday, headquarters was advised that A-4 was going to be evacuated, and a UH-1 Huey slick escorted by two Cobra gunships was headed for Con Thien. The ASA team was ordered to destroy the Explorer III, along with the other crypto equipment and classified documents—everything but their portable radio.

Like all of the Explorer sites, the installation had thermite panels mounted on top of its receiver racks for quick and total destruction. The plates were wired together and could be electrically activated from outside their protective shelter. After the thermite was ignited, the housing shed would burn for two days, consuming all of the equipment within it. By Easter Sunday, there would be no evidence that NSA or ASA had ever had an installation at A-4 or Fire Support Base Sarge.

The rutted dirt road at Alpha-4 (Photo: © John Mastro)

The last words headquarters heard from A-4 before they destroyed their main communications equipment was an urgent call for the choppers to hurry—NVA infantry units were at the camp's perimeter, and they were closing in fast. The rescue plan called for the two helicopter gunships to go in first and clear out as many of the enemy troops around the approaches to the ASA bunkers and helipad as possible. The Huey would then move in and touch down just long enough for the men to pile on board.

The ASA team would have to run from their bunker, about 500 feet down a rutted dirt road to the helipad while both they and the chopper were fully exposed to enemy mortars and small arms fire. The headquarters crew at Quang Tri huddled around the radio and waited for the next transmission.

Finally, they heard the chopper pilot say, "Grab your radio and run!"

And after several agonizing minutes of total silence, they received another transmission. "Got eight aboard and am coming home."

April fool's day

Soon after the Friday rescue of the men at Alpha-4, the NVA launched its attack on Quang Tri Combat Base, and the 407th RRD HQ began to prepare for its own evacuation. The weather was bad, so there was no tactical air support, and the artillery attacks became more intense. The HQ team began destroying everything that was not absolutely necessary, and that continued most of the night along with the shelling.

The 407th RRD compound at Quang Tri prior to the NVA attack–April 1972 (Photo: © John Mastro)

Saturday morning finally arrived with no improvement in the weather, but the artillery and rocket attacks eased a bit. The men stayed busy as they continued destroying equipment and materials that must not fall into enemy hands. During the afternoon, evacuation plans were discussed, but there was still some hope they could avoid leaving. The artillery barrage had eased again, but promptly at 1700 hours the base was hit with the worst bombardment they had experienced. Over 500 shells hit the compound in about thirty minutes. That barrage knocked out the generator and all of their electrical power.

The heaviest artillery fire let up about 1730 hours, and the men resumed destroying documents and everything not essential to their survival. The work was completed by 2200 hours, and the ASA soldiers stretched out on the concrete floor of their fortified headquarters building. With each explosion outside, the concrete floor jolted and vibrated, making sleep extremely difficult to come by. Each near-miss artillery shell threw a deluge of rocks and shrapnel against the metal roof of their refuge, and the men could only think of Gary and Bruce on Sarge, wondering if the same fate awaited them.

Sunday morning comin' down

Sunrise on Easter Sunday saw a continuation of the artillery and rocket barrage, with a few new twists. The main force of the NVA infantry was moving ever closer and introducing more accurate short-range weapons into the attack. Mortars and 90mm recoilless rifles were targeting anything that moved within the ARVN compound.

Sunday dragged by with nothing for the men to do but wait for their evacuation. By noon they were beginning to wonder if it was going to happen. There seemed to be no end to the NVA supply of munitions; the barrage was continuous and nerve-wracking.

At 1400 hours, their C.O. gave orders to implement the final destruction of the 407th RRD's equipment and facilities and head for the perimeter of the compound. Thermite grenades were attached to each piece of classified equipment, and diesel fuel was poured around the interior of the building. A thermite grenade was tossed inside to ignite the inferno, and the men headed for the pick-up area to await their chopper. Their only helipad had been destroyed by the constant shelling, so they would have the board the chopper outside the perimeter.

A Chinook helicopter came in, and following a MACV directive, the eight-man ASA team was boarded first, followed by as many of the MACV personnel as they could get aboard. The chopper lifted off, but had been airborne only a few minutes when it landed at a small helipad, and everyone was told to get off. The team assumed they were at a safe LZ, but soon found out they were only a few miles from Quang Tri City at a village called La Vang, and the area was crawling with NVA troops. The chopper departed and the men began to hear the now-familiar sounds of mortars being fired and then exploding just south of their position.

Warrant Officer 2 Wilson took charge of the situation and moved the group of about thirty-five GIs to a row of bunkers manned by ARVN troops along the edge of the field. Making sure that all were under cover, he then tried to contact Phu Bai for another chopper. Some twenty minutes later, the group was told to run for the LZ as a second chopper landed. That chopper did not have room for everyone, so Mr. Wilson was told that five would have to remain on site to await a third helicopter.

Wilson and four of the RRD members had just turned to run back to the bunker when a firefight broke out with the men still in the middle of the helipad. AK-47 fire was coming from both sides of the small compound. The group threw themselves into the grass alongside the pad, but soon realized that they were not the targets of the gunfire. They were about forty meters from the nearest bunker, so they lay quietly until the gunfire began to subside and then sprinted for the bunkers. Mr. Wilson got on the radio again, and contacted Phu Bai for a third helicopter, but received bad news. The men might have to spend the night in the ARVN bunker. No one wanted to spend the night in La Vang. Based on past experience, the Americans expected the ARVN troops to be gone by morning. They would be left alone, and the mortars and small arms fire had resumed all around them.

A short time later, Wilson announced that he had found a chopper to take the four soldiers, but there would not be room for him. He would follow later. During the next twenty-four hours, the four 407th teammates and Warrant Officer 2 Wilson would take various short chopper hops, wade waist-deep through muddy rice paddies, ride on jeeps, separately and together from camp to camp, trying to rejoin the rest of their team at Phu Bai.

At one point the four teammates (without Mr. Wilson) were dropped off at the MACV compound in Hue, and the event was recorded this way by Duane Whitman of the 407th: "Apparently we weren't expected, or they weren't expecting what they saw. Into the compound we tramped, in clothes that we had been wearing for at least a week, soaking wet, covered with mud, decked out with gear that we had acquired throughout the day, ammunition threatening to fall out of our crammed full pockets…and there they were in their freshly starched fatigues, khakis or clean civilian clothes, wide-eyed and mouths gaping! What a sight we must have presented." The next morning, the men took one more chopper ride; this time they were able to rejoin their teammates at Phu Bai.

Terry Stanfill said, "A short time after the attack at FB Sarge, Explorer was abandoned in Vietnam as the forward antenna bases could no longer be maintained…" The 407th RRD, which had destroyed its top-secret documents, equipment and facilities at the MACV Compound in Quang Tri, would not return when the area was retaken from the North Vietnamese some weeks later. The unit's outposts could no longer be secured and it was deactivated. Its personnel were rotated to other ASA units or back to the U.S.

Searching for Westcott and Crosby

Chuck Martin, one of the eight men rescued from Alpha-4 on Good Friday, was also one of the soldiers who helped build the Explorer bunker on FSB Sarge. Martin remembered one of the guys from the engineer battalion called "Okie" and recalled running into him after he was evacuated from the DMZ. "He looked at me like I was a ghost," Martin said. "I was one of the guys who stayed on Sarge after the bunker was built. The other guy's name was Crosby. I was moved on to Con Thien (A-4) in the beginning of '72, and Crosby stayed on at Sarge. Of course…Crosby and Westcott were killed on Sarge, 30 March 72. Okie didn't know that I had moved to A-4, [thus]…his reaction to me there at Phu Bai that day. [I will] always have good memories of the engineers. They helped us build up other areas that proved to save our lives from heavy artillery (130mm) on A-4. We all survived on A-4…"

Kirchner photo of FSB Sarge–December 1971–Explorer shelter is on upper left (Photo: © Richard Kirchner)

For years, most people assumed there was little chance of recovering the remains of Westcott and Crosby due to the devastation of the rocket explosion, the extreme heat of the thermite fire, and the erosion that had taken place over the decades; however, in 1999, JTF-FA (now JPAC) launched a mission to Dong Toan Mountain and attempted their recovery. Unfortunately, the team was unsuccessful, but there has been a continuing effort to gather additional information that could spur a second attempt and improve the chances for success.

In late November 1971, the 27th Combat Engineer Battalion based at Camp Eagle was assigned to build the Explorer III bunker on Firebase Sarge. Richard Kirchner was one of the engineers, who helped build the bunker, and he had taken photographs of the firebase and the bunker after it was completed in December. In 2009, Kirchner wrote:

"Around mid-2000, [my] locational data and the photos were shared with the then JTF-FA in Hawaii to aid their search for Westcott and Crosby…"

Aerial view of FSB Sarge (Photo: © Richard Kirchner)

There was also a story emerging that has created renewed interest in Westcott and Crosby's case (DOD/JPAC Case 1808). In 1997, some thirty Nung families were being held by authorities in Hong Kong and applying for resettlement in the U.S. During the INS interview, one of the Nung males claimed to be a veteran who had fought with U.S. Special Forces and later joined the South Vietnamese Marines. The man said that as a member of the 4th Bn, SVMC, he had fought against the NVA at FSB Sarge and was a survivor of the final battle on the night of 30 March 1972. That information had been turned over to the Joint Casualty Resolution Center (JCRC) liaison office in Bangkok. That organization's sole mission was to resolve the fate of U.S. servicemen still missing and unaccounted for in Indochina, and a representative had traveled to Hong Kong to interview the man.

JTF-FA search at Dong Toan Mountain–1999 (Photo: John Mastro)

The Nung veteran told the interviewer that by the time the defenders were preparing to withdraw from FSB Sarge, the fire in the Explorer bunker had subsided to the point that he and one or two other RVN Marines, acting on their own initiative, had removed the bodies of two Americans from the bunker. The Marines had then placed the remains in a trench or foxhole near the Explorer bunker and covered them with sandbags just before being ordered to withdraw. The JCRC interview had been included as an item of evidence which INS officials considered to support the man's eligibility for resettlement in the United States.

Some forty-plus years after that tragic Thursday in March '72, Case 1808 seems to be very active. With the information provided by the JCRC report and the location provided by Richard Kirchner and his remarkable photography, perhaps there is still a chance of bringing Westcott and Crosby down from the top of Dong Toan Mountain.

Tet with tanks

The NVA had launched their biggest offensive in four years, and in spite of all the indications and warnings from the ASA outposts along the DMZ, the U.S. and ARVN commanders were just as surprised as they had been during Tet in 1968. MACV in Saigon, some 350 miles to the south, refused to believe a major offensive was taking place, even after it had begun. In spite of all ASA's success over the previous ten years, the generals at the top had learned absolutely nothing. Over 30,000 well-armed NVA regular infantry, supported by hundreds of tanks, armored vehicles, missile launchers and long-range artillery had poured across the DMZ into South Vietnam, and the generals and politicians were shocked.

Those in charge had chosen to ignore the intelligence they had been presented and were caught flat-footed again. But, as usual, they were not the ones paying the price for their failures. The outlying fire support bases, sparsely protected by South Vietnamese troops and Montagnards, and the remote ASA listening posts manned by Viet linguists and Morse intercept ops had become shooting galleries for the invading NVA forces.

Crazy Cats out of lives

The advancement of aeronautical technology finally caught up with the Neptunes (again), and they were replaced with smaller, better equipped aircraft. Their SIGINT equipment was more compact and required fewer operators, so the old reliables were moth-balled again. The last Crazy Cat mission was flown on 31 March 1972. The unit had amassed nearly 46,000 hours of mission time during their years of service and had surpassed a mission flight time of seventeen hours without refueling.

In early April, the 101st RRC was deactivated, effectively ending the 509th RRG's COMSEC mission. The unit had been awarded two meritorious Unit Commendations and a RVN Cross of Gallantry with Palm.

On 30 June 1972, the 328th RRC and the 405th RRD were the last of the Direct Support Units to be deactivated. The 335th RRC in Can Tho was also deactivated.

Late summer 1972

In August, Hq. Co., 224th AB relocated from Long Thanh North to Saigon, and the 146th Avn. Co. (RR) was moved from Long Thanh North to Can Tho.

In September, the ARVN retook Quang Tri City. The 330th RRFS was deactivated, and the 175th RRFS was relocated from Bien Hoa to Saigon.

In October the 138th Avn. Co. moved from Phu Bai to Da Nang for the second time.

October surprise

On October 26, 1972, Secretary of State Kissinger announced in Paris: "We believe that peace is at hand." Kissinger stated that a breakthrough had been reached in the talks with North Vietnamese representative Le Duc Tho. South Vietnamese President Thieu was adamantly opposed to the agreement with the North Vietnamese.

Kissinger's announcement was just a few weeks before the 1972 Presidential election, and the timing may have been somewhat suspect. George McGovern would go on to suffer one of the worst defeats in U.S. political history, winning just one state, Massachusetts, and the District of Columbia.

Nixon landslide

On November 7, 1972, President Richard M. Nixon was re-elected and pledged to continue his efforts to end the war. Kissinger resumed his talks with Le Duc Tho and presented him with sixty-nine amendments to their agreement demanded by President Thieu.

More talks and bombs

A new round of talks between Kissinger and Le Duc Tho began in December, but soon broke down. Not only was peace not "at hand," it seemed more elusive than ever. Nixon responded by launching a new campaign of heavy bombing against Hanoi and Haiphong. Operation Linebacker II began on 18 December and the U.S. media immediately denounced the "Christmas bombing campaign," accusing Nixon of lying, again, just to win re-election.

Whether or not the bombing was effective can be argued, but on 26 December, Hanoi announced that the Paris talks would resume in early January on the basis of the October agreement. The bombing campaign was ended on 30 December. A total of 36,000 tons of bombs had been dropped on the northern capital and surrounding areas, during the twelve-day campaign. The talks resumed on 03 January 1973.

SIGINT support for the "Christmas bombing" was extensive. Six ground intercept sites and four airborne units provided coverage of the NV air defense network. Most of the intelligence came from Air Force Security Service operations at Ramasun, Thailand, and Clark Air Base, Philippines.

By the end of the year, U.S. troop levels in South Vietnam had declined to 24,000, the lowest number in almost eight years.

New Year 1973 dawns

On 22 January 1973, the 138th Avn. Co. ceased operation of its Left Jab ARDF flights. The South Vietnamese ARDF mission, left to its own devices, quickly declined in effectiveness.

Beginning of the end

President Nixon announced that Henry Kissinger and Le Duc Tho had initialed an agreement in Paris "to end the war and bring peace with honor in Vietnam and Southeast Asia." The cease fire took place at 0800 hours, Vietnam time, on 28 January 1973. At that point in time, the

Saigon government controlled 75% of South Vietnam's territory and 85% of its population.

Four Americans were killed in the last week, and the last U.S. serviceman to die in combat in Vietnam was Lt. Col. William B. Nolde, who was killed by an artillery shell at An Loc, at 2100 hours on 27 January, eleven hours before the truce took effect. Secretary of State Melvin Laird announced an end to the U.S. draft.

Last "lingie" out

On 31 January, the last ASA Vietnamese linguist left the Da Nang Processing Center and their cryptanalytic/linguistic section was closed. They could no longer process low-level communist tactical voice intercept or issue reports based on the intercept. The material was transmitted directly to Saigon for processing.

Two weeks later, all reporting on communist communications from the northern part of the country was transferred from Da Nang to Saigon, leaving the ARVN command in I Corps without any local SIGINT support.

No peace, no honor, just a whimper

The terms and conditions of the final peace agreement were quite similar to those agreed upon in October 1972. The document was theoretically intended to outline the steps toward to meaningful and enforceable peace, but it would soon become the vehicle by which the communists and the U.S. media could limit American response and doom the South Vietnamese government.

The U.S. agreed to cease all military activities, acts of force, and acts of terror or reprisal, and begin removal of all mines from the northern ports and rivers. They would withdraw the remainder of U.S. forces, except for a small number of security and logistics personnel, within sixty days, and begin the expeditious return of P.O.W.s.

To police and enforce the cease-fire agreement, several commissions were formed with representatives from the communist and non-communist world. Canada, Indonesia, Hungry, and Poland would be the initial four parties to police the truce, and with that in place, President Nixon could proclaim to the world "Peace with Honor" on January 23, 1973, in a nationwide television address. It would soon become apparent that there would be neither peace nor honor in South Vietnam.

Fitting conclusion

Early on the morning of 28 January 1973, the 509th RR Group's staff gathered atop the Newport Hotel to welcome the cease-fire by watching an enemy rocket attack on Tan Son Nhut Air Base. On the following day, an NVA contingent arrived at the same base to occupy the former Davis Station compound as members of the joint military commission set up under the truce agreement. No sooner had the unit moved in and posted guards, than antennas began to sprout from the building. To the ASA personnel watching the developments, it was obvious that the NVA were setting up a SIGINT installation right on Tan Son Nhut Air Base. It seemed the height of irony and a fitting conclusion to the strange war that they had fought so hard to win.

The NVA delegation is reported to have complained about the living conditions at Davis Station, calling it a "concentration camp." Davis Station had been occupied by ASA for nearly twelve years and had served as home for untold thousands of ASA enlisted personnel throughout the conflict. It has been suggested that the NVA might have been more comfortable with accommodations in the Hanoi Hilton.

Last USAFSS crew down

On 05 February, a USAFSS EC-47Q intelligence-gathering aircraft (*Baron 52*) was shot down by 37mm antiaircraft fire thirty-five miles southeast of Saravan in southern Laos. It was the largest hostile loss of 1973 with eight airmen KIA—four from the 361st TEWS and four from Det. 3, 6994th SS. The flight crew included George Spitz, Robert Bernhardt, Arthur Bolling and Severo Primm III. The Security Service intercept team consisted of Dale Brandenburg, Joseph Matejov, Peter Cressman and Todd Melton.

ASA, over and out

Early in 1973, ASA closed its last two SIGINT sites in Vietnam, the venerable missions at Phu Bai and Bien Hoa. In reality they had been inactive since 1972.

In February, the 8th and 175th Field Stations were closed. The 175th had been awarded five MUCs, one RVN CGP, and one RVN CA.

The last ARDF flight was flown in Vietnam on 16 February 1973. One of two Left Jab JU-21As left in Vietnam flew the mission. Both were then assigned to the 7th RR Field Station at Udorn R.T.A.F.B. in Thailand. The 7th RR was set to become the center of the U.S. SIGINT effort in Southeast Asia. It was based at Ramasun, just south of the provincial capital of Udorn, and was the last major American signal intelligence site in Southeast Asia.

The 146th Aviation Co. RR was deactivated on 17 February. The unit had received three MUCs and one RVN CGP.

"Operation Homecoming"

On 12 February 1973, three U.S. Air Force C-141 transports flew to Hanoi and one C-9A to Saigon to pick up released American P.O.W.s. From that day to 04 April, fifty-four C-141 missions flew out of Hanoi bringing the former P.O.W.s home. The men were released based on the length of time they had been imprisoned, and the first group to leave had spent six to eight years as prisoners of war.

In March, the 224th Aviation Bn. and the 138th Aviation Co. RR were deactivated. One of their RU8-Ds flown in Vietnam is now on display at the National Cryptologic Museum at NSA Headquarters, Ft. Meade, Md.

On 07 March, the 509th RR Group was deactivated, ending ASA's twelve-year presence in South Vietnam. ASA would continue to provide the South Vietnamese government sanitized SIGINT on a limited basis, but its in-country mission was over. NSA continued to play a limited role, but due to the ever-present problem of security leaks within the South Vietnamese government, the amount and quality of both intercept and ARDF information provided was also very limited. The 509th RR Group had received three MUCs and two ARVN CGPs for their service in South Vietnam.

Last man out

On 29 March 1973, the last U.S. combat troops left South Vietnam, with flags flying and bands playing. Two months later, Ambassador Ellsworth Bunker sent a secret cable to President Nixon in which he said, "It is true that communist violations have enabled them to strengthen and resupply their forces and to consolidate their position in the areas they control...What we may be seeing, I believe, is the slow working out of a balance of forces which, once achieved, could lead to a stable ceasefire." After thirteen years of war in Southeast Asia, and the loss of over 58,000 young Americans, the naiveté of the American leadership is astounding.

PART IV

1973-1975—AN INGLORIOUS END

CHAPTER 31

BLOOD IN THE WATER

ARVN troops defending Saigon (Photo: U.S. Army)

French Colonel Roger Trinquier was an expert in counter-insurgency theory and wrote a book in 1961 entitled *La Guerre Moderne* (*Modern Warfare*). His controversial book dismissed the traditional military and espoused a new kind of warfare using small, mobile commando teams, locally recruited self-defense forces and psychological operations. The U.S. Army considered his theories when it created U.S. Special Forces. Trinquier fought with the French army in Vietnam and then served in Algeria. After years of experience, he maintained that "revolutionaries prevail not because they win their wars, but because the politicians sell out the military at precisely the moment when it is winning the war."

July 01, 1973: With a majority vote in the Democrat-controlled Congress, the Fulbright-Aiken Amendment became law, and made certain that battlefield achievement would no longer determine the freedom or the fate of tens of millions of South Vietnamese; American politicians would. And the death knell began to toll in Saigon.

The amendment cut off all funding for ongoing U.S. military operations in support of our longtime Vietnamese allies, and outlined a dramatic change in policy. In brief, it said: "Notwithstanding any other provision of the law, on or after August 15, 1973, no funds herein or heretofore appropriated may be obligated or expended to finance directly or indirectly combat activities by United States military forces in or over or from off the shores of North Vietnam, South Vietnam, Laos, or Cambodia."

In President John F. Kennedy's 1961 inaugural address, he told the world that "we shall pay any price, bear any burden, meet any hardship, support any friend, oppose any foe, in order to assure the survival and the success of liberty." Twelve years later, however, the Democratic Party of JFK had moved decidedly to the left.

The saddest part of the decision by Congress not to "pay any price, bear any burden...support any friend," was that by 1972, the Army of the Republic of Vietnam was beginning to stand on its own feet. After the NVA's big Easter Offensive in March 1972, the ARVN had successfully pushed the enemy forces back across the DMZ without the help of U.S. ground forces. Most American advisors concluded that with continued logistical support and the promise to U.S. retaliation if the enemy violated a peace treaty signed later in 1973, the South Vietnamese stood a good chance of being able to maintain their sovereignty.

The NVA is believed to have lost more than 100,000 troops during their various incursions into the South during 1972, two-and-a-half times ARVN losses. And those unpopular Christmas bombings had taken a terrible toll, driving Hanoi back to the peace talks, but U.S. politicians did not take advantage of the situation. They were too busy with Watergate, and feeling little loyalty or obligation to a President who was on his way out, the Democratic majority quietly passed Fulbright-Aiken.

With one stroke of the pen, Congress accomplished for the communists what all of their fighting and dying had been unable to accomplish for over a decade. Concurrently, it betrayed the trust, not only of the South Vietnamese, but of all those in Southeast Asia who had fought alongside the U.S. military to stop the communist takeover of that part of the world. And last, but certainly not least, it betrayed the trust of every soldier, sailor, and airman who had fought so valiantly for so long. They were the "JFK generation" who still believed that liberty was worth fighting and dying for. United States military forces were never defeated on the field of battle in Vietnam. They were sold out in the halls of the U.S. Capitol in Washington, D.C., just as Colonel Trinquier had predicted some twelve years before.

For the communist brain trust in Hanoi, Beijing and Moscow, the backroom treachery of Fulbright-Aiken was an astonishing gift. Moscow and Beijing had no restrictions on the amount of aid they supplied to North Vietnam, and did not face public scrutiny, so it was just a matter of time. The North Vietnamese were free to move forward toward their final guaranteed victory without fear of reprisal. Their greatest foe had been hogtied by its own politicians and lay helpless on the floor.

No one will ever know whether or not the South Vietnamese could have survived on their own. Certainly the North was not going to stop its continuing effort to overthrow the government in Saigon and impose communist rule over the southern nation. What we do know is that the South never had the chance to try. Their million-man army stood alone in 1975, out of fuel and out of ammunition as the North made its final drive south, and the fault for that lies at the feet of the Congress of the United States.

On October 16, 1973, the Nobel Committee of the Norwegian Storting (Parliament) announced the awarding of the 1973 Nobel Peace Prize jointly to Mr. Henry Kissinger and Mr. Le Duc Tho for their successful efforts in arranging the ceasefire in Vietnam. Mr. Kissinger accepted his half of the prize. Le Duc Tho declined the award until such time as "peace is truly established."

More Congressional business

On November 7, 1973, Congress passed the War Powers Act over the veto of President Nixon. The act was designed to restrain the ability of the President to commit American forces overseas by requiring the executive branch to consult with and report to Congress before involving U.S. military forces in foreign hostilities. It was championed by the left, but Nixon regarded it as an unconstitutional usurpation of Presidential authority. Congress also passed a resolution banning all use of funds for U.S. military action anywhere in Indochina without Congressional approval.

On April 1974, the U.S. House rejected the administration's request for increased military aid to South Vietnam.

May 1974: The House Judiciary Committee began impeachment hearings against President Richard M. Nixon.

At noon on August 9, 1974, President Nixon became the first U.S. President to resign his office, and Vice President Gerald R. Ford was sworn in as the 37th President of the United States. President Ford was viewed as a decent individual who could heal the nation, but after pardoning former President Nixon, his popularity plummeted. The Democrats quickly took advantage of the situation, and in the off-year elections in November made gains in both the House and the Senate, becoming veto-proof.

1975—year of infamy

January 1975: Communist forces captured Phuoc Long Province in South Vietnam, and Khmer Rouge forces besieged Phnom Penh in Cambodia.

On 10 March 1975, Ban Me Thuot fell to NVA forces and the ARVN retreated from the Central Highlands of the South.

On 26 March 1975, Hue fell to communist forces as they pushed ever closer to Saigon, and the last NSA personnel departed Da Nang on the last commercial flight out of the city.

On 30 March 1975, Da Nang was captured by the NVA.

On 28 April 1975, the last NSA message was sent from Saigon. It read: "1. Have just received word to evacuate—Am now destroying remaining classified material—Will cease transmissions immediately after this message. 2. We're tired but otherwise all right, looks like the battle for Saigon is on for real. 3. From Glenn: I commend to you my people who deserve the best NSA can give them for what they have been through. But especially for what they have achieved. XGDS-2"

The last NSA representative in Saigon left with two cryptologists on a rescue helicopter on 29 April 1975.

On 30 April 1975, South Vietnam surrendered. South Vietnamese President Duong Van Minh ordered the remaining ARVN troops to cease fire and retired to the presidential palace to await the arrival of communist troops. The U. S. military airlifted the remaining personnel from the roof of the U.S. Embassy, thus ending one of the most disgraceful and tragic periods in American political history. As a nation, the U.S. had paid a heavy price for its involvement in Vietnam. It had cost hundreds of millions of dollars in military and financial aid, caused terrible rents in the social fabric of our nation, and most importantly, cost the lives of tens of thousands of young American dead and wounded. However, as someone once wrote: "We must pay the price for freedom, but whatever the price, it is only half the cost of doing nothing."

Winston Churchill said: "Socialism is the philosophy of failure, the creed of ignorance, the gospel of envy. Its inherent virtue is the equal sharing of misery." The same can be said of communism, and Southeast Asia was about to enter a period of shared misery and death without equal.

Fitting epitaph

The bias of the major U.S. media sources, which had gone on throughout much of the war, continued, and as usual, CBS News led the charge. A few hours after the last Americans left South Vietnam, the network telecast a two-and-a-half-hour special entitled *Vietnam: A War That is Finished*. The program traced U.S. involvement through five presidential administrations: Eisenhower through Ford (for some reason they left out Kennedy).

As per their regular pro-North Vietnam agenda, the CBS producers were selective in the video films that were shown during the course of the program. They did not include film of returned U.S. P.O.W.s, nor were there interviews of those prisoners detailing the tortures they had undergone at the hands of their VC and North Vietnamese jailers. They did, however, rerun a North Vietnamese propaganda film showing how well-treated the P.O.W.s were.

Moderator Charles Collingwood explained to his audience that after the 1954 Geneva Accords were signed, establishing the 17th parallel as the temporary dividing line between North and South Vietnam, neither side had supported the agreements. What he did not mention was that during the twenty-one years since the Accords were signed, no South Vietnamese forces had ever crossed the line into the North. That fact was conveniently left out.

The special then turned its focus on two young girls who had lost limbs during the war, and illustrating the plight of 80,000 South Vietnamese amputees as a result of the war. Of course, the two girls selected had not been injured as a result of VC or NVA action; they had been mistakenly shot by ARVN soldiers.

In another segment of the show, reporter John Lawrence said: "The beginning of American involvement became evident in the spring of 1970 as the gears of the Vietnam death machine were grinding more slowly. Four thousand Americans were to die that year, many more Vietnamese, and for the first time, Cambodians. Then days after promising to withdraw another 150,000 American troops from Vietnam, President Nixon, on his own authority and without advice and consent of Congress, decided to widen the war. It was time, he said, to take action and to clean out the communist sanctuaries in Cambodia. He gave his generals the authority to do what they wanted, to send some 31,000 American soldiers across the border in a final and fateful assault in Cambodia. Huge quantities of arms and ammunition, mostly outdated or obsolete, were captured, but the retreating North Vietnamese and Viet Cong carried the war deep into Cambodia and laid the foundations for the successful struggle of the Khmer Rouge."

Walter Cronkite, in his gravest monotone, said: "We, the American people, the world's most admired democracy, cannot ever again allow ourselves to be misinformed, manipulated, and misled into disastrous foreign adventures…"

Dinh Ba Thi, the North Vietnamese representative in Paris, expressed his "warm thanks to all socialist countries of national independence and all peace and justice-loving peoples, including the American people who have supported and helped our people in its just struggle. The victory gained today is also theirs."

Peter Kalisher of CBS then summed up the entire program for his American television audience: "For better or worse, the war is over, and how could it be for worse."

And the spew continued

After the fall of Saigon, Newsweek published an eight-page photographic history of the Vietnam War for the enlightenment of the American people. There were no photographs of the discovered mass graves after the Hue massacre, during which 2,750 South Vietnamese were slaughtered by the VC and NVA. As a matter of fact, here was not a single photo of any victim from communist aggression during the entire decade-long conflict. But, the pictures had obviously been selected by *Newsweek's* editors with great care in order to present the image of the war they wanted to promulgate.

Their choices and their political leanings can be easily understood by reading their captions: "Police Chief Loan executes Viet Cong, 1968;" "Marine burns hut, 1965;" "Victims of My Lai massacre, 1968;" "GIs with Saigon whore, 1969;" "National Guardsmen fire into crowd of students at Kent State;" "Outside Pentagon, antiwar demonstrators spike the guns of military police with flowers, 1967;" "ARVN soldier retreats from Laos, 1971;" "South Vietnamese prisoner in 'tiger cage,' 1970;" "North Vietnamese capture U.S. pilot, 1972;" "American deserter in Sweden, 1968;" "B-52 Stratofortress rains bombs on North Vietnam during renewed U.S. air strikes at Christmas, 1972;" "North

Vietnamese hospital, 1968;" and "Screaming with pain, children flee misdirected napalm attack, 1972."

Dominoes fall

Contrary to what Vietnam War critics and leftists had maintained, after the U.S. pullout, the "domino theory" in Southeast Asia soon became a "domino fact," at least in the two nations that had long been plagued by the North Vietnamese army. White flags flew in Cambodia as the Khmer Rouge captured Phnom Penh and brought to power Pol Pot, one of the most radical and brutal leaders in the history of mankind. Under Pol Pot's leadership, the Khmer Rouge carried out a program to isolate "Democratic Kampuchea" from all outside influences. They closed hospitals, factories and schools, abolished banking, finance and currency, outlawed all religions, confiscated all private property and relocated all people living in urban areas to collective farms and forced labor camps. Thousands of sick, elderly and children died in the forced evacuations of the cities.

All books were burned; teachers, merchants, and almost all of the intellectual elite of the country were executed in an effort to bring about Pol Pot's twisted vision of agricultural communism. During the four agonizing years that the Khmer Rouge held power, the United Nations estimates between two and three million Cambodians died.

U.S. Senator Eugene McCarthy (D-Minn.), who had been the anti-Vietnam War candidate in the 1968 Democratic Presidential primaries, said in reference to prospective killings by the communists in Southeast Asia, should they win the war: "I don't think there is any evidence or any real reason to believe that that kind of mass execution will take place."

When it was apparent that the U.S. was not going to intervene to save Saigon, Hanoi gave the go-ahead to the communist Pathet Lao in Laos. With the support of 30,000 NVA and the Soviet Union, Pathet Lao troops advanced on Vientiane and within a few months toppled its legal government. On December 2, 1975, King Savang Vatthana submitted his letter of abdication to the Pathet Lao and the Lao People's

Democratic Republic was established with Prince Souphaqnnavong as president.

All non-communist news media were closed or taken over. There were large-scale purges of the civil service, army and police, and tens of thousands were shipped off to re-education camps in remote areas of the country. Most were never heard from again. Many of the professional and intellectual class fled, and it is estimated that within two years, ten percent of the population had left the country. The Hmong people, an ethnic group from the mountains, had fought the Pathet Lao and were singled out for special retribution. More than 100,000 Hmong tribesmen fled the country, many immigrating to the U.S.

Governor Ronald Reagan of California said: "The very fact that practically two million North Vietnamese fled to South Vietnam to escape the communist regime is an indication that this government did not represent the will of the people."

The South Vietnamese price

The cost of the war on South Vietnam is nearly unfathomable: 9,000 of 15,000 villages and hamlets destroyed; twenty-five million acres of farmland laid waste; twelve million acres of forestland leveled; the social structure destroyed; one million widows; 879,000 orphans; 181,000 disabled victims. In their long struggle to remain free, the South Vietnamese military lost 275,000 KIA, along with 465,000 civilians, many slaughtered by the Viet Cong or by the NVA's indiscriminate shelling of cities and towns in the South. And that was before the communists took full control of the nation.

With Hanoi's takeover of the South came additional untold misery. Over a million South Vietnamese were sent to re-education camps and "new economic zones," and it is estimated that over 250,000 innocent people died in the process; as many as 65,000 were simply executed by their liberators.

In 1979, hundreds of thousands attempted to flee the country by boat and became known as the "Vietnamese boat people." Unknown thousands died of hunger and thirst in the open boats, and were simply never heard from again. The refugees included many ethnic Chinese (Nungs) and even some North Vietnamese. Camps were eventually set up in Hong Kong, Malaysia, the Philippines and Thailand to assist in the Vietnamese diaspora, but the humanitarian effort came too late for too many.

U.S.S. *Ranger* rescues 138 Vietnamese boat people in South China Sea (Photo: U.S. Dept. of Defense)

Later that year, the communists finally established a program called the "Orderly Departure Program," for Vietnamese who had worked for the Americans and wanted to leave the country. The U.S. accepted over 800,000, along with Australia and Canada with over 100,000 each, followed by France with 90,000, Germany with 40,000, and the U.K. with 20,000.

The Montagnards

Thousands of Montagnards fled Vietnam after the war, fearing reprisals from the communist forces because of their support for the U.S. war effort. It has been estimated that 50% of adult Montagnard males were killed fighting alongside American soldiers during the war. Thousands of U.S. Vietnam veterans still consider the hill tribesmen to have been "America's most loyal allies." The Montagnards disliked the Vietnamese, both North and South, and the dislike was mutual. The Vietnamese referred to the Montagnards as "moi"–savages.

In April 2002, Human Rights Watch released a 200-page report detailing an ongoing program of repressive activities against the Montagnard people by the government of Vietnam. The official campaign has included arbitrary arrest, torture, imprisonment, and religious persecution since the communist takeover of the South. Unofficially, there were reports of NVA soldiers hunting down Montagnards and shooting them on sight in the late 1970s, and even later.

Attorney Scott Johnson, a human rights advocate for the Montagnard Foundation in South Carolina, has helped document more than 1,000 cases of Montagnard women who were forcibly sterilized as part of the Vietnamese government's ongoing program of repression, and the Vietnamese government admits that it implemented such a policy.

Before the French-Indochina War, Montagnard populations in Vietnam were estimated to be approximately 2.5 million people. According to the 2000 Vietnam census, Hanoi estimates the current Montagnard population in Vietnam to be 750,000 people. It is not surprising that Montagnard human rights organizations use the term "ethnic cleansing" when referring to the plight of the hill tribesmen who still reside in their native region. The decades-long campaign against the Montagnards continues with little apparent notice or concern from either U.S. media or U.S. politicians.

Thousands of Montagnards now reside in the U.S., Canada, Australia, and Europe. Over 3,000 live in North Carolina, with a large community of 2,000 Christian Degar Montagnards established in Greensboro. There are also several hundred Nung tribesmen living in North Carolina.

Dominoes revisited

It was General Maxwell Taylor who said in October 1961: "If Vietnam goes, it will be exceedingly difficult to hold Southeast Asia." The left had contemptuously referred to that remark as the "domino theory." McGeorge Bundy, the National Security Advisor to both President Kennedy and President Johnson pointed out later that the Vietnam War had provided the rest of Southeast Asia twelve years of breathing room during which they could develop their societies peacefully. Neighboring nations such as Laos and Cambodia were impacted, but because the U.S. and its allies tied up the communist surge, countries such as Thailand, Malaysia, Singapore and the rest of Southeast Asia did not fall to communist aggression. The incredible economic success of South Korea might be some indication of what could have happened in South Vietnam had they not been betrayed by politicians in Washington.

EPILOGUE

WELCOME HOME!

Reflected Glory–Vietnam Veterans Memorial (Photo: © G. Blackburn)

"If you are able, save for them a place inside of you…and save one backward glance when you are leaving for the places they can no longer go…

Be not ashamed to say you loved them…Take what they have left and what they have taught you with their dying and keep it with your own…

And in that time when men decide and feel safe to call the war insane, take one moment to embrace those gentle heroes you left behind…"[*]

Spc.4 James T. Davis	3rd RRU	22 Dec 1961
Pvt. 1st Class Donald R. Taylor	3rd RRU	09 Feb 1964
Spc.4 Arthur W. Glover	3rd RRU	09 Feb 1964

---

[*] From a letter by Maj. Michael D. O'Donnell–Shot down over Dak To, Vietnam, while attempting to rescue eight soldiers trapped by attacking enemy forces–New Year's Day 1970–Listed as KIA–07 February 1978.

Staff Sgt. Robert F. Townsend	10th RRU	04 Nov 1965
2nd Lt. William E. Leatherwood, Jr.	8th RRFS	17 Feb 1966
Staff Sgt. Donald D. Daugherty	3rd RRU	13 Apr 1966
Capt. James D. Stallings	337th RRC	25 Sep 1966
1st Lt. John F. Cochrane	409th RRD	24 Oct 1966
Sgt. 1st Class John F. Stirling	335th RRC	08 Mar 1967
Spc.4 Thomas M. Huntley	8th RRFS	23 Jul 1967
Spc.5 William L. Stewart, Jr.	8th RRFS	08 Oct 1967
Spc.4 Richard G. Feruggia	8th RRFS	08 Oct 1967
Spc.4 Terrance H. Larson	8th RRFS	08 Oct 1967
Spc.4 Robert D. Nelson	8th RRFS	08 Oct 1967
Spc.4 Joseph P. Rowley	8th RRFS	08 Oct 1967
Spc.4 John D. Saville, Jr.	8th RRFS	08 Oct 1967
Spc.4 Ronald A. Villardo	8th RRFS	08 Oct 1967
Sgt. 1st Class Robert D. Taylor	335th RRC	26 Nov 1967
Sgt. Diego Ramirez, Jr.	335th RRC	26 Nov 1967
Spc.5 Michael P. Brown	335th RRC	26 Nov 1967
Staff Sgt. Jose L. Miranda-Ortiz	330th RRC	30 Nov 1967
Staff Sgt. Robert J. Wiggin	335th RRC	13 Feb 1968
Capt. John M. Casey	371st RRC	25 Mar 1968
Spc.4 Kendall A. Stake	8th RRFS	05 Apr 1968
Spc.4 Christopher J. Schramm	371st RRC	13 May 1968
Spc.4 Jeffrey W. Haerle	372nd RRC	13 May 1968
Spc.5 Samuel C. Martin	01st RRC	17 May 1968
Sgt. Thomas J. Tomczak	403rd SOD	23 Jul 1968
Sgt. Richard L. Jernigan	415th RRD	10 Sep 1968
Spc.5 Harold D. Biller	175th RRC	25 Feb 1969
Spc.5 Harold J. Colon	409th RRD	21 Jun 1969
Staff Sgt. Jim C. Page	303rd RRB	08 Jul 1969
Spc.5 John K. Anderson	335th RRC	10 Aug 1969
Chief Warrant Officer 2 Jack Knepp	11th Avn. Co.	29 Nov 1969
Warrant Officer 1 Dennis D. Bogle	11th Avn. Co.	29 Nov 1969
Spc.4 Henry N. Heide II	371st RRC	29 Nov 1969
Spc.4 James R. Smith	371st RRC	29 Nov 1969

Spc.5 Edward Van Every	335th RRC	01 Jun 1970
Spc.4 Robert E. Dew	330th RRC	30 Aug 1970
Spc.4 William R. Higginbotham	371st RRC	17 Feb 1971
Spc.5 Carl H. Caccia	404th RRD	21 Feb 1971
Spc.5 Robert J. Potts	404th RRD	21 Feb 1971
Spc.5 Mitchell B. Smith	404th RRD	21 Feb 1971
Spc.5 Robert J. Thelen	404th RRD	21 Feb 1971
Warrant Officer 1 Paul V. Black	11th Avn. Co.	01 Mar 1971
Warrant Officer 1 Robert D. Uhl	11th Avn. Co.	01 Mar 1971
Spc.5 Gary C. David	371st RRC	01 Mar 1971
Spc.4 Frank A. Sablan	371st RRC	01 Mar 1971
Capt. Michael W. Marker	138th RRC	04 Mar 1971
Warrant Officer 1 Harold L. Algaard	138th RRC	04 Mar 1971
Spc.6 John T. Strawn	138th RRC	04 Mar 1971
Spc.5 Richard J. Hentz	138th RRC	04 Mar 1971
Spc.5 Rodney D. Osborne	138th RRC	04 Mar 1971
Spc.5 Bruce A. Crosby, Jr.	8th RRFS	30 Mar 1972
Spc.5 Larry P. Westcott	8th RRFS	30 Mar 1972

"Here dead we lie because we did not choose to live and shame the land from which we sprung. Life to be sure, is nothing much to lose; but young men think it is, and we were young."

–A.E. Housman–Honoring the men of the USMA Class of 1950

"We remember them, frozen in time, as they were on the day they died; lives ended at an age too early, hopes remaining no longer and growing no older as we have. They shared our burdens, our hopes, aspirations, letters from home, pictures, C-rations, water and fears. We shared their joys, sense of humor, shade on a hot day, honesty, courage, guidance and their last can of warm beer. They are known as "buddies," a word that is difficult to describe to a layman until they have shared a life."

–30th Field Artillery Regiment Association–Hardchargers.com

NOTES AND ACKNOWLEDGEMENTS

Unlikely Warriors was written after twelve-plus years of research and is intended to be a factual and historical portrayal of the soldiers of the U.S. Army Security Agency who served during the Vietnam War. ASA was an elite intelligence unit whose members served with honor. Every effort has been made to accurately portray their mission and service.

This book could not have been written without the input and support of hundreds of individuals. Our wives, Randie Long and Myra Blackburn, must top our thank-you list for their support and assistance on so many levels. Myra, a career English teacher, spent dozens of hours proofing and advising on the finer points of the language and Randie secured our new web domains. Most importantly, they were both behind our literary effort every step of the way. Thanks too, to Mark Long (brother) who helped set up our websites and Connie Blackburn Robinson (sister) for proofing early copies of the chapters.

Thank you to the historians at INSCOM, Karen Kovach (now retired), Michael Bigelow and Thomas Hauser, who provided ongoing support and advice and offered their photographic and art collection for our use. Thanks also, to Amy Davis and the family of Tom Davis, Sharon, Rose and Ed Minnock, Sr., and to the many other family members and "buddies" of soldiers whose stories we have tried to tell.

There are many veterans with immense knowledge on various aspects of the Vietnam War. They do not consider themselves experts, but they lived it. Thanks to Jim Alward, Robert Destatte, Col. Querin Herlik, Jack Fisher, Robert Pryor, Richard McCarthy, Roger Trussell, Col. Charlie Dexter, David Hewitt, Col. Carlos Collat, Duane Whitman, Gary Spivey, Bob Flanagan, John Osmundsen, Dave Ward, Rich Kirchner, Ray Ridlon, John Mastro, Darwin Bruce, Robert Noe, and our "silent partners" who asked to remain anonymous.

Thanks to the guys who took those great photographs as nineteen and twenty-year-olds in 'Nam, and allowed us to publish them in our book. And last but certainly not least, there are our friends from Down

Under, who have always seemed to have our backs. This list could go on, and we will undoubtedly leave out some who should be here. "Thank you" seems inadequate to express our appreciation.

Lonnie M. Long
Gary B. Blackburn

SOURCES

Dedication

Chapter 32-*War Story*-Jim Morris, Paladin Enterprises, Inc., 1979

Prologue: Setting the Stage

Chinese Colonization (200BC – 938AD)-asia.isp.msu.edu/wbwoa/
southeast_asia/vietnam.

The Tran Dynasty and the Defeat of the Mogols-countrystudies.us/
vietnam.

Colonialism-Melvin Eugene Page and Penny M. Sonnenberg, Google
Books.

French Counterrevolutionary Struggles: Indochina and Algeria, U. S.
Military Academy.

Vietnamese Communism, 1925-1945-Kim Khahn Huynh, Cornell
University Press, 1982.

Vietnam: A History-Stanley Karnow.

From Colonialism to Communism-Hoang Van Chi, 1964.

Interview with OSS officer Carleton Swift, 1981-openvault.wgbh.org/
catalog/vietnam.

Giap: The Volcano Under the Snow-John Colvin, Soho Press, 1996.

*Knowing Your Friends: Intelligence Inside Alliances and Coalitions
from 1914 to the Cold War*-Martin S. Alexander, Frank Cass,
Routledge, 1998.

*Nihil mirare, nihil contemptare, Omnia intelligere: Franco-Vietnamese
Intelligence in Indochina*-Alexander Zervoudakis.

The Indochinese Experience of the French and the Americans-Arthur J.
Dommen, Indiana University Press, 2001.

Vietnamese Communism: Its Origins and Development-Robert F.
Turner, Hoover Institution Press, 1975.

Last Reflections on a War-Bernard Fall, Doubleday, 1967.

The Blood Red Hands of Ho Chi Minh-Reader's Digest-November 1968.

The Origins of the National Security Agency 1940-1952-Thomas L. Burns, Released by NSA, 03-02-2007, FOIA Case #51510.

Body of Secrets: Anatomy of the Ultra-Secret National Security Agency-James Bamford, Anchor, 2002.

Valley of Death: The Tragedy at Dien Bien Phu that Led America into the Vietnam War-Ted Morgan, 2010.

Vietnam at War: The History 1946-1975-Paul B. Davidson, Jr., 1988.

The Shootdown of "Earthquake McGoon"-Check-Six.com-2012.

Embassy of France in the USA, February 25, 2005: U.S. Pilots Honored for Indochina Service.

Harry G. Cramer, Jr.-Westpoint.org.

Part I The Listening Game

Chapter 1 The '60s—Decade of Defiance and Death

Spartans in Darkness: American SIGINT and the Indochina War, 1945-1975-Robert J. Hanyok, Center for Cryptologic History, National Security Agency, 2002.

The Hidden History of the Vietnam War-John Prados, Ivan R. Dee, Inc., 1998.

The Most Secret War: Army Signals Intelligence in Vietnam-James L. Gilbert, Dane Publishing Co., 2003.

Where the Dominoes Fell: America and Vietnam 1945-1995-James S. Olson and Randy W. Roberts, Blackwell Publishing, 2008.

The puzzle palace: a report on America's most secret agency-James Bamford, Houghton Mifflin, 1982.

A History of the English-Speaking Peoples since 1900-Andrew Roberts, Orion, 2010.

Chapter 2 Tennessee Hero

They Served in Silence: The Story of a Cryptologic Hero Specialist Four James T. Davis, USA–nsa.gov.

Old Spooks & Spies.org.

Official INSCOM (ASA) Incident Report.

The Eyewitness History of the Vietnam War 1961-1975-George Esper and The Associated Press, Ballantine Books, 1983.

The 50th Anniversary of Tom's Death-Amy Davis, *The Herald-Citizen*, Livingston, Tennessee.

Josephine's Journal-Josephine Bundaberry, *Overton County News*, Livingston, Tennessee.

The Most Secret War: Army Signals Intelligence in Vietnam-James L. Gilbert, Dane Publishing Co., 2003.

A History of the English-Speaking Peoples since 1900-Andrew Roberts, Orion, 2010.

Spartans in Darkness: American SIGINT and the Indochina War, 1945-1975-Robert J. Hanyok, Center for Cryptologic History, National Security Agency, 2002.

The enemy's jungle cover was no match for the finding capabilities of the Army's Radio Research Unit–William E. LeGro, *Vietnam Magazine/Arsenal*, June 1990.

U.S. Army Transportation Museum-Aviation Section, Ft. Eustis, Virginia.

The Spy Who Loved Us: The Vietnam War and Pham Xuan An's Dangerous Game–Thomas A. Bass, Public Affairs, 2009.

Chapter 3 Phu Bai

Spartans in Darkness: American SIGINT and the Indochina War, 1945-1975- Robert J. Hanyok, Center for Cryptologic History, National Security Agency, 2002.

The Vietnam War Almanac-James H. Willbanks, Infobase Publishing, 2009.

Department of the Army General Order #22.

Department of the Army General Order #28.

Chapter 4 Changing Horses

JFK and the Diem Coup-John Prados, National Security Archive, 2003.

Newsweek-December 2, 1963.

Spartans in Darkness: American SIGINT and the Indochina War, 1945-1975- Robert J. Hanyok, Center for Cryptologic History, National Security Agency, 2002.

Westmoreland: The General Who Lost Vietnam-Lewis Sorley, Houghton Mifflin Harcourt, 2011.

Chapter 5 Truth, Lies, and Consequences

Tonkin Gulf and the Escalation of the Vietnam War, 1996-Edwin E. Moise, The University of North Carolina Press, 1996.

Vietnam War Almanac-John S. Bowman, Barnes & Noble, 2005.

The White House Tapes: Eavesdropping on the President-John Prados, Perseus Distribution Service, 2003.

Spartans in Darkness: American SIGINT and the Indochina War, 1945-1975-Robert J. Hanyok, Center for Cryptologic History, National Security Agency, 2002.

The New York Times-Scott Shane, October 31, 2005.

Essay: 40th Anniversary of the Gulf of Tonkin Incident-John Prados, National Security Archive, 2004.

nsa.gov.

1st-radio-company-usmc.org.

Roger Trussell letters.

Department of the Army General Order 6, 1966.

America: The Last Best Hope-William J. Bennett, Thomas Nelson, 2006.

Our Vietnam: The War 1954-1975-A. J. Langguth, Simon & Schuster, 2000.

PART II 1965– The Year of Total Commitment

Chapter 6 First Bird Down

Old Spooks & Spies.org-Bill Snyder.

Enotes.com.

Chapter 7 The Marines Have Landed

This Time We Win, Revisiting the Tet Offensive-James S. Robbins,
    Encounter Books, 2010.

Kintner.com- Per Barry Kintner: Notes were provided by Col.
    Donald E. Gordon, Ret., State College, Pennsylvania.

Triumph Forsaken: The Vietnam War 1954-1965-Mark Moyar,
    Cambridge University Press, 1971.

Time-August 6, 1965.

Saigon Daily News-August 6, 1965.

Thechickenworks.com-Dr. J. P. Santiago.

Chapter 8 The 3rd RRU-Aviation Section at War

The Secret Sentry: The Untold History of the National Security Agency-
    Matthew M. Aid, Bloomsbury Publishing, 2009.

In Country: The Illustrated Encyclopedia of the Vietnam War-James
    Stuart Olson, Metro Books, 2008.

Operation Starlight: A SIGINT Success Story-National Security
    Agency, FOIA Case # 7319, 09/18/2007.

Rollingstone.com.

The Evolution of American Military Intelligence-U.S. Army Intelligence
    Center and School, Ft. Huachuca, Arizona, 1973.

This Time We Win, Revisiting the Tet Offensive-James S. Robbins,
    Encounter Books, 2010.

History.com.

American Soldier: General Tommy Franks-Tommy Franks and
    Malcolm McConnell, Harper Collins, 2004.

The Hidden History of the Vietnam War-John Prados, Ivan R. Dee, Publisher, 1998.

Annual History Report-3rd RRU-Page 23, 1965.

Special Electronic Mission Aircraft (SEMA)-Dennis Buley, Carlos Collat and Richard Mitchell, webring.org, 22 October 1996.

Col. Charlie Dexter letters.

Vignettes-Richard McCarthy, Lulu, 2012.

Chapter 9 Spring Raid on Tan Son Nhut

From the Delta to the DMZ: The Army Security Agency in Vietnam-Tino "Chui" Banuelos, chui101.com.

This Time We Win, Revisiting the Tet Offensive-James S. Robbins, Encounter Books, 2010.

Chapter 10 Wild Blue Yonder

6994th.com.

Enlisted History Research Project-Master Sgt. Bruce F. Nelson, ec-47.com.

Nsa.com.

Asalives.com-Dennis Buley.

Chapter 11 Harry Locklear's Story

Vignettes-Richard McCarthy, Lulu, 2012.

Chapter 12 The Diggers of Nui Dat

547 Signal Troop-Pronto in South Vietnam 1962-1972, Ch.5, Royal Australian Corps of Signals.

Diggers: From 6 June 1944 to 1994-George Odgers, Lansdowne Publishing Pty, Limited, 1994.

Abc.net.au.

Mike Conaghan letters.

Bob Harland letters.

Chapter 13 The 330th RRC Sails In

James "Sakk" Frankenfield's Home Page, Verne Greunke, Webmaster, Verizon.net.

South Vietnam: After the Nests-Time-January 1967.

In Country: The Illustrated Encyclopedia of the Vietnam War-James Stuart Olson, Metro Books, 2008.

Who the Hell are we Fighting? The story of Sam Adams and the Vietnam Intelligence Wars-C. Michael Hiam, Steerforth Press, 2006.

New York Times-M. A. Farber, January 25, 1985.

Spartans in Darkness: American SIGINT and the Indochina War, 1945-1975-Robert J. Hanyok, Center for Cryptologic History, National Security Agency, 2002.

Chapter 14 Crazy Cats & Left Bank

Callsign: "Cats-Paw"-Documentary produced in Thailand, democraticunderground.com.

U.S. Army Aviation in Vietnam-Wayne Mutza, Squadron Signal Publications, 2009.

Radiovietnam.net.

This Time We Win, Revisiting the Tet Offensive-James S. Robbins, Encounter Books, 2010.

In Country: The Illustrated Encyclopedia of the Vietnam War-James Stuart Olson, Metro Books, 2008.

Kintner.com-Per Barry Kintner: Notes were provided by Col. Donald E. Gordon, Ret., State College, Pennsylvania.

The Tet Offensive: Intelligence Failure in War-James J. Wirtz, Cornell University Press, 1991.

The Denver Republic-December 4, 1967.

The Chronicle-Camden, South Carolina, January 1968, Quoted in *This Time We Win*-James S. Robbins.

Chapter 15 The *Pueblo* Incident

*The Capture of the USS Pueblo and Its Effect on SIGINT Operations-*U.S. Cryptologic History, Special Series, Crisis Collection, Vol. 7, National Security Agency-Robert E. Newton, 1992.

*Attacked by North Koreans-*Usspueblo.org.

*The Tet Offensive: Intelligence Failure in War-*James J. Wirtz, Cornell University Press, 1991.

*Coordinated Vietnamese Communist Offensive Evidenced in South Vietnam-*National Security Agency, 25 January 1968, FOIA Case #63653.

Chapter 16 Holiday in Da Lat

*Eyewitness Accounts of the 1968 Tet Offensive in Vietnam-"TDY at Dalat"-*Warren "Skip" Galinski, 2nd Platoon, 101st RRC.-chui101.com/tet68.

James "Sakk" Frankenfield's Home Page, Verne Greunke, Webmaster, Verizon.net.

*The Spy Who Loved Us: The Vietnam War and Pham Xuan An's Dangerous Game-*Thomas A. Bass, Public Affairs, 2009.

*None So Blind: The Personal Account of the Intelligence Failure in Vietnam-*George W. Allen, Ivan R. Dee, Inc., 2001.

*TET!: The Turning Point in Vietnam-*Don Oberdorfer, Doubleday & Co., 1971.

*A Viet Cong Memoir-*Truong Nhu Tang, Indiana University Press, (1985) 2000.

Radio Hanoi Broadcast, April 27, 1969.

*Viet Cong Repression and its Implications for the Future-*Stephen T. Hosmer, Rand Corp., 1970.

*America: The Last Best Hope-*William J. Bennett, Thomas Nelson, 2006.

*Readings in Current Military History-*David Richard Palmer, U.S. Military Academy, 1969.

*The Vietnam War Almanac-*James H. Willbanks, Infobase Publishing, 2009.

Kintner.com-Per Barry Kintner: Notes were provided by Col. Donald E. Gordon, Ret., State College, Pennsylvania.

Chapter 17 The Wizard of Tuy Hoa

Private Minnock's Private War–Don E. Gordon, International Journal of Intelligence and Counterintelligence, Summer 1990.
Sharon Minnock letters-2013.
Philadelphia Inquirer-May 18, 1968.

Chapter 18 Death on the Black Virgin

The Nui Ba Den Massacres–Katzenmeier's Weblog, Ivan Kazenmeier.
Story of the Black Virgin Mountain-25th Aviation Battalion, 25thaviation.org.
Nui Ba Dinh: Black Virgin Mountain-Hugh R. Taylor, oneshotonekill.org.
Attack on Nui Ba Den-May 13, 1963-Ed Tatarnik, Manchu.org.
After Action Report-Attack on Nui Ba Den-5th Special Forces Group, A-324.
S3's Report-Attack on Nui Ba Den-Capt. Harold R. Winton, S3, Det. B32, 5th SFGP, Tay Ninh, RVN.
Buck Buchanan, ASAlives.org.
Rootsweb.com.
A Life On The Way To Death-Time, June 16, 1968.

Chapter 19 A Different Kind of ASA Soldier

ASA SODs-ASAlives.org.
Top Secret Missions-John E. Malone, Trafford Publishing, 2003.
MSG Travis C. Bunn-sotazone.50megs.com/Bunn.
MI Corps Hall of Fame-Master Sergeant Travis C. Bunn-Military Intelligence Professional Bulletin.

Chapter 20 The Battle of Duc Lap

403rd SOD: The Battle of Duc Lap-The Hallmark, Official magazine of the Army Security Agency, 1968.

Airforce-magazine.com.

Combat After Action Interview Report, Battle of Duc Lap Special Forces Camp, 23-28 August 1968–Capt. Joseph Meisner, Staff Historian, 5th Special Forces Group.

Account of Battle from Interviews-Capt. Joseph Meisner, Staff Historian, 5th Special Forces Group.

Duc Lap Withstands Enemy Siege-The Green Beret, September 1968.

Mike Dooley cartoon-*The Green Beret,* August 1968.

James Alward letters and interviews-2012-1013

Chapter 21 The Siege of A-239

Combat After Action Interview Report, Battle of Duc Lap Special Forces Camp, 23-28 August 1968-Capt. Joseph Meisner, Staff Historian, 5th Special Forces Group.

Account of Battle from Interviews-Capt. Joseph Meisner, Staff Historian, 5th Special Forces Group.

Duc Lap Withstands Enemy Siege-The Green Beret, September 1968.

James Alward letters and interviews-2012-1013

Mike Force-Lt. Col. L. H. "Bucky" Burruss, USA (Ret.), iUniverse, 2001.

America: The Last Best Hope-William J. Bennett, Thomas Nelson, 2006.

Nixon and Kissinger: Partners in Power-Robert Dallek. Harper Collins Publishers, 2007.

Chapter 22 The Long Way Home

Major Querin Herlik's Journal.

Querin Herlik Interview.

Jack Fisher Interview.

Robert Pryor Interview.
Querin Herlik U.S. Army Debriefing Notes.
Jack Fisher U.S. Army Debriefing Notes.
Robert Pryor U.S. Army Debriefing Notes.
Stars and Stripes, Pacific Edition-February 16, 1969.
Time-June 4, 1973.
The Irawaddy.org-Dominic Faulder, October 2001.
Lying for Empire-David Model, Common Courage Press, 2005.
Facing Death in Cambodia-Peter H. Maguire, Columbia University
   Press, 2005.
Vietnam War Almanac-John S. Bowman, Barnes & Noble, 2005.
*The Encyclopedia of the Vietnam War: A Political, Social, and Military
   History*-Spencer C. Tucker, Editor, ABC-CLIO, LLC, 2011.
The Most Secret War: Army Signals Intelligence in Vietnam-James L.
   Gilbert, Dane Publishing Co., 2003.
*Focus on Cambodia-Parts 1 and 2, Cryptologic History Series, Southeast
   Asia, January 1974*-The National Security Agency, FOIA Case
   #3058.
America: The Last Best Hope-William J. Bennett, Thomas Nelson, 2006.
While Woodstock Rocked, GIs Died-Richard Kolb, VFW Magazine,
   August 2009.
The Hallmark-Fall Issue 1969.
*Missouri State Society Daughters of the American Revolution Proudly
   "Spotlights" our June 2012 Patriot of the Month: Donna Baldwin*-
   Rhoda Fairchild Chapter, Carthage, Missouri.

Chapter 23 The Shoot-down of *Jaguar Yellow*

Vietnam Helicopter Pilots Association Report-Larry E. North, 1998,
   vhpa.org.
David Hewitt letters.
Col. Carlos Collat letters.
The Most Secret War: Army Signals Intelligence in Vietnam-James L.
   Gilbert, Dane Publishing Co., 2003.

Army Communicator-David Fielder, Spring 2003.

Intelligence Wars: American Secret History from Hitler to Al-Qaeda-
Thomas Powers, The New York Review of Books, 2004.

PART III 1970–The Final Stage Begins

Chapter 24 The Cambodian Incursion

Focus on Cambodia-Parts 1 and 2, Cryptologic History Series, Southeast Asia, January 1974-The National Security Agency, FOIA Case #3058.

USS Benewah (APB-35)-navsource.org/archives.

Rinaldol.tripod.com.

Asalives.org/ASAONLINE/409thdc.htm

Pownetwork.org.

Chapter 25 The Explorer Saga

Explorer Project-Document ID 4001127-"Secret-COMINT Channels Only"-National Security Agency, FOIA Case #51546, 9/26/2012.

Macvsog.cc.

The Last Seven Days-G. Duane Whitman, thelastsevendays.com.

The Final Flight of Curious Yellow-Dave Hansen, vhpa.org/stories/ yellow.

Hall of Heroes: Jon R. Cavaiani-freerepublic.com.

In Memory of John R. Jones-George "Sonny" Hoffman, sflistteamhouse.com.

Project Explorer 1971-72 (Hill 950)-yahoo.com/group/vetsof407thrrd.

Jon Cavaiani and Hickory Radio Relay Site-macvsog.cc/jon_cavaiani.

The Most Secret War: Army Signals Intelligence in Vietnam-James L. Gilbert, Dane Publishing Co., 2003.

Chapter 26 Eddie Van Every & "Soup" Campbell

A Soldier's Story-Letter to war buddy results in visit to Nevada-Becky R. Hamar, *Nevada Daily Mail*-Nevada, Missouri, May 19, 1987.

War book opens doors for vet John "Soup" Campbell-South Jersey Times-Bob Shyrock, November 07, 2011.

Shrapnel in the Heart-Laura Palmer, First Vintage Books, 1988.

Military Magazine-Osmundsen.

Focus on Cambodia-Parts 1 and 2, Cryptologic History Series, Southeast Asia, January 1974-The National Security Agency, FOIA Case #3058.

Robert Earl Dew-asalives.com.

The Most Secret War: Army Signals Intelligence in Vietnam-James L. Gilbert, Dane Publishing Co., 2003.

Herald & News-Klamath Falls, Oregon, February 12, 1970.

Nsa.gov.

Chapter 27 The VVAW

Paperlessarchives.com.

Vietnam Wars 1945-1990-Marilyn Young, Harper Collins, 1991.

Stolen Valor: How the Vietnam Generation was Robbed of its Heroes and History-B. Bernard Gary Burkett, Verity Press Incorporated, 1998.

Chapter 28 *Yellow Bird* Down in Cambodia

Task Force Omega, Inc.-usvetdsp.com.

Armyaircrews.com.

Paul Vernon Black-taskforceomegainc.org/b392.

Paul Vernon Black-arlingtoncemetery.net/pvblack.

Robert Dale Uhl-arlingtoncemetery.net/Robert-uhl.

Gary Charles David-arlington.net/gary-david.

Frank Aguan Sablan-arlingtoncemetery.net/frank-sablan.

Chapter 29 The Disappearance of *Vanguard 216*

Nsa.gov.

ASAlives.org/ASAONLINE.

Osborne-*Tri-City Herald*.

Senate Select Committee on POW/MIA Affairs: Smith 324 Compelling Cases- South Vietnam-Case #1715.

MIA Facts Site: Report of the Senate Select Committee on POW/MIA Affairs Appendix: 2i.

Yahoo Groups: 138th Aviation Co. (RR).

Korea Veterans on the Web-Mike Marker-Vanguard 216.

The Encyclopedia of the Vietnam War: A Political, Social, and Military History-Spencer C. Tucker, Editor, ABC-CLIO, LLC, 2011.

Coming to Terms with the Past: My Lai-Oliver Kendrick, *History Today.com*.

Elections in Asia: A data handbook, Volume II-Dieter Nohlen, OUP Oxford, 2001.

Chapter 30 The NVA Easter Offensive

The Last Seven Days-G. Duane Whitman, thelastsevendays.com.

David Ward letters.

John Osmundsen letters.

Ray Ridlon letters.

407thrrd.proudlyserved.us.

Alice's Restaurant-The Halmark, April 1971.

8th RRFS Guestbook-cswayne.com.

Body of Secrets: Anatomy of the Ultra-Secret National Security Agency-James Bamford, Anchor, 2002.

Robert Destatte letters.

U.S. Army Aviation in Vietnam-Wayne Mutza, Squadron Signal Publications, 2009.

America: The Last Best Hope-William J. Bennett, Thomas Nelson, 2006.

Spartans in Darkness: American SIGINT and the Indochina War, 1945-1975-Robert J. Hanyok, Center for Cryptologic History, National Security Agency, 2002.

PART IV 1973-1975—An Inglorious End

Chapter 31 Blood in the Water

La Guerre Moderne (Modern Warfare)-Col. Roger Trinquier, La Table Ronde, 1961.

The Spy Who Loved Us: The Vietnam War and Pham Xuan An's Dangerous Game-Thomas A. Bass, Public Affairs, 2009.

Washington Times-Richard Botkin, August 19, 2009.

Vietnam: A War That is Finished-CBS News, April 30, 1975.

An American Amnesia: How the U.S. Congress Forced the Surrender of South Vietnam and Cambodia-Bruce Herschensohn, Beaufort Books, Incorporated, 2010.

Newsweek-May 1975.

The Montagnards-Washington Times Editorial, September, 19, 2002.

Montagnards Human Rights Organization.

Historyplace.com.

ABOUT THE AUTHORS

Lonnie M. Long was born in North Carolina and served with the Army Security Agency from August 1962 to November 1965. After completing ASA training at Ft. Devens, Massachusetts, Lonnie served with the 76th Special Operations Unit, Shu Lin Kou Air Station, Taiwan. In 1964, he volunteered for duty in Vietnam and began a fifteen-month tour with the 3rd Radio Research Unit, Aviation Section, Tan Son Nhut Air Base, Saigon.

Lonnie is a graduate of the University of Miami and the Wharton Executive Education program, University of Pennsylvania. He and his wife, Randie, live in Davidson, North Carolina, and have two sons, Graham and Greg.

Gary B. Blackburn is a native Iowan and served with the U.S. Air Force Security Service from April 1961 to November 1964. Gary studied Mandarin Chinese at the Institute of Far Eastern Languages, Yale University, followed by assignments to the Joint Sobe Processing Center, Torii Station, Okinawa, working for NSA, and the 6987th Security Group, Shu Lin Kou Air Station, Taiwan.

Gary is a graduate of Laurel University and is a published writer and photographer. He and his wife, Myra, have two sons, Aaron and Brendan, and reside in Oak Ridge, North Carolina.

INDEX

470

G

H

I

J

K

L

M